CONVERSATIONS WITH LANDSCAPE

Anthropological Studies of Creativity and Perception

Series Editor: Tim Ingold, University of Aberdeen, UK

The books in this series explore the relations, in human social and cultural life, between perception, creativity and skill. Their common aim is to move beyond established approaches in anthropology and material culture studies that treat the inhabited world as a repository of complete objects, already present and available for analysis. Instead these works focus on the creative processes that continually bring these objects into being, along with the persons in whose lives they are entangled.

All creative activities entail movement or gesture, and the books in this series are particularly concerned to understand the relations between these creative movements and the inscriptions they yield. Likewise in considering the histories of artefacts, these studies foreground the skills of their makers-cum-users, and the transformations that ensue, rather than tracking their incorporation as finished objects within networks of interpersonal relations.

The books in this series will be interdisciplinary in orientation, their concern being always with the practice of interdisciplinarity: on ways of doing anthropology *with* other disciplines, rather than doing an anthropology *of* these subjects. Through this anthropology *with*, they aim to achieve an understanding that is at once holistic and processual, dedicated not so much to the achievement of a final synthesis as to opening up lines of inquiry.

Conversations With Landscape

Edited by

KARL BENEDIKTSSON and KATRÍN ANNA LUND
University of Iceland, Iceland

ASHGATE

© Karl Benediktsson and Katrín Anna Lund 2010

All rights reserved. No part of this publication may be reproduced, stored in a retrieval system or transmitted in any form or by any means, electronic, mechanical, photocopying, recording or otherwise without the prior permission of the publisher.

Karl Benediktsson and Katrín Anna Lund have asserted their right under the Copyright, Designs and Patents Act, 1988, to be identified as the editors of this work.

Published by
Ashgate Publishing Limited
Wey Court East
Union Road
Farnham
Surrey, GU9 7PT
England

Ashgate Publishing Company
Suite 420
101 Cherry Street
Burlington
VT 05401-4405
USA

www.ashgate.com

British Library Cataloguing in Publication Data
Conversations with landscape. -- (Anthropological studies
 of creativity and perception)
 1. Human beings--Effect of environment on. 2. Nature--
 Effect of human beings on. 3. Landscape assessment.
 I. Series II. Benediktsson, Karl. III. Lund, Katrín Anna.
 304.2-dc22

Library of Congress Cataloging-in-Publication Data
Conversations with landscape / [edited] by Karl Benediktsson and Katrín Anna Lund.
 p. cm. -- (Anthropological studies of creativity and perception)
 Includes index.
 ISBN 978-1-4094-0186-5 (hardback) -- ISBN 978-1-4094-0187-2
(ebook) 1. Environmental psychology. I. Benediktsson, Karl. II. Lund, Katrín Anna.
 BF353.C668 2010
 304.2--dc22
                                                                                            2010033523

ISBN 9781409401865 (hbk)
ISBN 9781409401872 (ebk)

Reprinted 2012

 Printed and bound in Great Britain by
the MPG Books Group, UK

Contents

List of Figures vii
List of Contributors ix
Preface and Acknowledgements xiii

1 Introduction: Starting a Conversation with Landscape 1
 Katrín Anna Lund and Karl Benediktsson

2 Conversations with Ourselves in Metaphysical Experiences of Nature 13
 Sigridur Thorgeirsdottir

3 The Limits of our "Conversations with Nature" 27
 Gabriel Malenfant

4 Landscape as Conversation 45
 Edda R.H. Waage

5 Time for Fluent Landscapes 59
 Oscar Aldred

6 Grief Paves the Way 79
 Arnar Árnason

7 Slipping into Landscape 97
 Katrín Anna Lund and Margaret Willson

8 Landscape and Aesthetic Values:
 Not Only in the Eye of the Beholder 109
 Guðbjörg R. Jóhannesdóttir

9 The Sublime, Ugliness and "Terrible Beauty" in Icelandic
 Landscapes 125
 Emily Brady

10 Transporting Nature: Landscape in Icelandic Urban Culture 137
 Anna Jóhannsdóttir and Ástráður Eysteinsson

11	Ways of Addressing Nature in a Northern Context: Romantic Poet and Natural Scientist Jónas Hallgrímsson *Sveinn Yngvi Egilsson*	157
12	A Stroll through Landscapes of Sheep and Humans *Karl Benediktsson*	173
13	Sentience *Anne Brydon*	193
14	The Empty Wilderness: Seals and Animal Representation *Bryndís Snæbjörnsdóttir and Mark Wilson*	211
15	Aurora Landscapes: Affective Atmospheres of Light and Dark *Tim Edensor*	227
16	Epilogue *Tim Ingold*	241

Index — 253

List of Figures

6.1	The cairn in Kúagerði (*Photograph*: Sigurjón Baldur Hafsteinsson)	86
6.2	Advertisement for road safety (*Source*: Umferðarstofa)	89
6.3	Crosses at Suðurlandsvegur (*Photograph*: Tinna Grétarsdóttir)	92
8.1	On the glacier (*Photograph*: Þorvarður Árnason)	120
9.1	Eruption on Heimaey 1973 (*Photograph*: Ævar Jóhannesson)	128
10.1	Magnús Jónsson: Dalbær í Hrunamannahreppi, Miðfell (*Photograph*: Anna Jóa)	142
10.2	Ásgrímur Jónsson: Húsafellsskógur, Strútur (*Photograph*: Anna Jóa)	147
10.3	Kjarval: Frá Þingvöllum (*Photograph*: Anna Jóa)	149
10.4	Guðbergur Auðunsson: Landnáma (*Photograph*: Anna Jóa)	154
11.1	A drawing of Skjaldbreiður by Jónas Hallgrímsson (*Source*: Þjóðminjasafn Íslands)	161
12.1	Sheep in rofabarð (*Photograph*: Andrés Arnalds)	181
12.2	Sheep licking salt on the road (*Photograph*: Guðjón Magnússon)	185
14.1	Film still from interview with Knútur Óskarsson	215
14.2	Film still from the video work *the naming of things*	220
14.3	Film still from the video work *Three Attempts*	224

List of Contributors

Oscar Aldred is an archaeologist interested in landscape, movement and materiality, as well as the theory and practice of archaeology. He is currently studying for a PhD at the University of Iceland, as well as working for Institute of Archaeology, Iceland. He has carried out fieldwork and research projects in England and Iceland, and has published several articles.

Arnar Árnason is a senior lecturer in social anthropology at the University of Aberdeen. His research topics centre on death and the politics of grief. He is also interested in how landscape is implicated in processes of memorialisation and forgetting.

Karl Benediktsson is professor of geography at the Department of Geography and Tourism, University of Iceland. His research fields include rural and regional development, as well as cultural geographies of landscape. He is the author of *Harvesting Development* (2002) and has published a number of journal articles and contributed to edited volumes.

Emily Brady is a philosopher and senior lecturer in human geography at the University of Edinburgh. She has written extensively on environmental aesthetics and ethics, including the book *Aesthetics of of the Natural Environment* (2003), in which she integrates subjective and objective approaches to aesthetic experience. She is also co-editor of *Humans in the Land: The Ethics and Aesthetics of the Cultural Landscape* (2008) and *Aesthetic Concepts: Essays After Sibley* (2001).

Anne Brydon is associate professor and chair of anthropology at Wilfrid Laurier University, Canada. She focuses on the anthropology of modernity and modernism, particularly the dynamics of culture and power, and the aesthetics of knowledge. Her research has concerned nationalism and the cultural politics of environmentalism in Iceland as well as the study of visual arts and material culture. Her current research investigates how visual artists working in Iceland are re-imagining changing social relations with nature, science, and technology.

Tim Edensor is a reader in cultural geography at Manchester Metropolitan University. He is the author of *Tourists at the Taj* (1998), *National Identity, Popular Culture and Everyday Life* (2002) and *Industrial Ruins: Space, Aesthetics and Materiality* (2005). He has written widely on tourism, urban and rural geographies, mobilities, working-class identities, football and materiality. He is currently researching landscapes of illumination, geographies of rhythm and urban materialities.

Sveinn Yngvi Egilsson is professor of Icelandic literature at the Faculty of Icelandic and Comparative Cultural Studies, University of Iceland. He is the author of the monograph *Arfur og umbylting. Rannsókn á íslenskri rómantík* (Tradition and Revolution. A study of Icelandic Romanticism, 1999) and has contributed to and edited a number of scholarly publications, including a critical edition of the collected works of Jónas Hallgrímsson (in 4 volumes, 1989). He is presently working on a book on Icelandic poetry and the environment.

Ástráður Eysteinsson is professor of comparative literature and dean of the School of Humanities, University of Iceland. His publications include several articles in the general areas of literary, cultural and translation studies, and co-translations of a number of works by Franz Kafka into Icelandic. His books include *The Concept of Modernism* (1990), *Translation – Theory and Practice: A Historical Reader* (co-edited with Daniel Weissbort, 2006) and *Modernism* (co-edited with Vivian Liska, 2007).

Tim Ingold is professor of social anthropology at the University of Aberdeen. He has conducted research in northern Finland and has published a extensively on temporality and movement in landscape. His most recent books include *The Perception of the Environment* (2000) and *Lines: A Brief History* (2007).

Guðbjörg R. Jóhannesdóttir is a PhD student in philosophy at the Faculty of History and Philosophy at the University of Iceland and a researcher at EDDA Center of Excellence. Her research interests include the aesthetics and ethics of landscape evaluation.

Anna Jóhannsdóttir is a visual artist and art critic. She studied art at the Icelandic School of Arts and Crafts, Reykjavík, and at École Nationale Supérieure des Arts Décoratifs, Paris, as well as art history and theory at the University of Iceland. She has exhibited her artwork (as Anna Jóa) in a number of solo and group shows in various countries.

Katrín Anna Lund is an anthropologist and senior lecturer at the Department of Geography and Tourism, University of Iceland. She has carried out fieldwork on landscape, mobility, place and perception in Spain and Scotland and has published in several journals and edited volumes.

Gabriel Malenfant is a PhD student in philosophy at the University of Iceland. He has translated a monograph by French philosopher Jean-Luc Nancy (with Bettina Bergo and Michael B. Smith) as well as essays by Canadian ethicist Daniel Weinstock and philosopher Georges Leroux. Author of essays both in

Jewish and environmental philosophy, he is currently working on a contribution to environmental ethics influenced by Emmanuel Levinas' phenomenology.

Bryndís Snæbjörnsdóttir is a visual artist, with a practice-based PhD from the Valand School of Art, Gothenburg. She is the author of *Spaces of Encounter: Art and Revision in Human-Animal Relations.* Her artworks (in collaboration with Mark Wilson) include *Big Mouth* (2004), *(a)fly* (2006), *nanoq: flat out and bluesome* (2004–6), and *Uncertainty in the City* (2010).

Sigridur Thorgeirsdottir is professor of philosophy, chair of the academic board of EDDA Center of Excellence, and chair of the board of the Gender Equality Training Programme at the University of Iceland. She has published articles on environmental philosophy, books on German philosophy and feminist philosophy, such as *Vis creativa. Kunst und Wahrheit in der Philosophie Nietzsches* (Königshausen and Neumann 1996), and she is co-author of *Birth, Death and Femininity. Philosophies of Embodiment* (Indiana University Press 2010).

Edda R.H. Waage is a PhD student in geography at the Department of Geography and Tourism at the University of Iceland. Her research interests are focused on nature conservation, governmentality and landscape aesthetics.

Margaret Willson is Affiliate Assistant Professor in Anthropology at the University of Washington and International Director of Bahia Street/Institute for Social Change. Her current research areas are equality, gender and race in Brazil and notions of gender and risk in Iceland. Her latest book is *Dance Lest We All Fall Down: Breaking Cycles of Poverty in Brazil and Beyond.*

Mark Wilson is a visual artist. His collaborative projects with Bryndís Snæbjörnsdóttir explore issues of history, culture and environment in relation to the interaction between humans and non-human animals. Their artworks and publications include *Big Mouth* (2004), *(a)fly* (2006), and *nanoq: flat out and bluesome* (2004–6), and *Uncertainty in the City* (2010). He is a senior lecturer in fine art at the University of Cumbria in England.

Preface and Acknowledgements

As this is being written, Europe is in the midst of a strange and unexpected "crisis" that is more than human. Ash particles from the volcano Eyjafjallajökull, in South Iceland, are upsetting the patterns of mobility that have become the norm in the contemporary world. The volcano – with a name which many non-Icelanders find unpronounceable – has spoken, and suddenly everybody is forced to listen. It refuses to take part in negotiations of any sort and pretends not to hear the exasperated calls from airline owners and passengers, let alone from politicians who fiddle with regulations in order to minimise the disruption. Millions of people are affected by this fiery landscape, which extends itself way beyond national boundaries.

For us, this in a way encapsulates the themes of this volume. We present a collection of writings that investigate whether conversations occur between humans and landscape and if so, which forms such conversations could take. The idea for the volume came out of our own experience in teaching a course on landscape at the University of Iceland. When asking students about their understandings of landscape and its significance, we were struck by the strong sense of emotional contact with landscape and nature that was evident in many of their responses. At the same time, we were somewhat concerned about the apparent lack of attention in many traditional approaches to landscape to the importance of personal affect. Landscapes do not need to erupt in order to affect people.

Copious quantities of coffee imbibed at Reykjavík's venerable institution, *Mokka*, helped to sharpen our ideas into a book proposal. We contacted a number of scholars from various disciplines, all of whom were willing to take part in this exploratory venture. It should be said that our contributors were simply drawn from our own personal networks who, although coming from quite different disciplinary backgrounds, shared the same passion for understanding landscapes and human relations with them.

We want to thank all the authors for their enthusiasm about the project and their diverse and creative takes on the basic theme we had introduced. We hope that the conversations we have had during the birth of the volume will continue and perhaps trigger further investigations that may further broaden the scope of landscape studies. Special thanks are due to Tim Ingold for his endorsement of our idea and support throughout the process. Neil Jordan and the staff at Ashgate are thanked for their patience and professionalism.

Karl Benediktsson and Katrín Anna Lund

Chapter 1
Introduction:
Starting a Conversation with Landscape

Katrín Anna Lund and Karl Benediktsson

> We say that we "conduct" a conversation, but the more genuine a conversation is, the less its conduct lies within the will of either partner. Thus a genuine conversation is never the one we wanted to conduct. Rather, it is more correct to say that we fall into conversation, or even that we become involved in it. [...] No one knows in advance what will "come out" of a conversation (Gadamer 2004 [1960]: 385).

This volume seeks to explore issues of landscape through the metaphor of *conversation*. Landscape is at once a fascinating subject for research and forbiddingly difficult to define once and for all. A concept with the ring of the familiar and everyday, it has often been understood in a taken-for-granted manner as purely objective and material reality, exterior to the subjective self. On the other hand, its hidden ideological complexities and diverse meanings have given rise to a large corpus of cultural critique that sometimes almost seems to ignore its materiality; the grounded solidity of landscape melts into the air of social and cultural construction. For us, landscape implies a more-than-human materiality; a constellation of natural forms that are independent of humans, yet part and parcel of the processes by which human beings make their living and understand their own placing in the world. By exploring the possibilities afforded by the conversation metaphor, we hope to find different ways to engage with the landscape concept.

We were drawn to the conversation metaphor for several reasons. One is a general interest in approaches that seek to avoid the dualism between the human and the non-human. We see conversation as enabling recognition of the more-than-human character of all meaningful exchanges involving humans and landscape. Moreover, we see such exchanges as involving much more than the visual sense on the part of humans. An oft-repeated critique of conventional landscape approaches – indeed of the very concept of landscape – is that they are irredeemably centred on the sense of sight. At the very least conversation mobilises other human senses, most notably of course that of hearing, but more importantly it points towards a two-way communicative process, as Hans-Georg Gadamer draws attention to in the opening quote of this chapter. A successful conversation – that is, one which results in increased understanding (albeit not necessarily agreement) – involves a "fusion of horizons" (Gadamer 2004 [1960]: 304). On the human side, such communication involves both attention and action: landscape encapsulates "embodied practices of being in the world, including ways of seeing but extending beyond sight to both a sense of being that includes all senses and an openness to being affected" (Dewsbury and Cloke 2009: 696).

As Solnit (2003: 9–10) has observed, speaking of artistic engagements with landscape, "conversation provokes response, not silence". Artists converse with landscape in the practice of their work. It is in the conversational responses that meaning appears. But meaning does not emerge out of the blue. Rather it is entwined in the process by which the conversation takes place. A conversation will "meander from subject to subject, so that public life spills into personal anecdote, emotion evolves into analysis" (Solnit 2003: 10). Thus a good conversation travels in different directions, touches on various topics and brings in different points of view. In this opening chapter, we will make a start by briefly discussing the two central concepts – "conversation" and "landscape" – calling attention to some important aspects of their use in the past and present. It is not our intention to force any kind of theoretical closure upon the reader, but rather to open up a space for a variety of strategies by which human-landscape interactions can be addressed.

Conversations – With Landscape?

All conversations are suffused with metaphors (Lakoff and Johnson 1980), and "conversation with landscape" is indeed itself a metaphor. Metaphors are often understood in a narrow sense, as simply a matter of rhetorical or poetic embellishment. As such, they may direct attention to certain aspects of phenomena that may be otherwise overlooked, or communicate meanings to which the speaker wants his or her listeners to pay particular attention. But philosophers such as Ricoeur (1986 [1975]) and Gadamer (2004 [1960]) have argued that metaphors are more elemental than that: they do fundamentally important work in that they reveal possible worlds and possible modes of being. Thus, metaphor "is not a matter of adornment, but installs a new order; in effect it is the discovery of meaning" (Vedder 2002: 198).

The metaphoric idea that landscapes can "speak" is not particularly novel. Indeed, in those most ancient of cultures, the Aboriginal Australian ones, the land itself is imbued with an ability to transfer meaning to humans, who interpret its will through stories of the Dreaming. Animistic beliefs, which presuppose that animals, trees, stones, and the very forms of nature do possess a soul, are found in numerous other cultures. They often involve an intricate consultation with these entities by humans, or "conversation". As Ingold has observed, it would be misleading to suggest that animism is "a way of believing *about* the world" – it is rather

> a condition of being *in* it. This could be described as a condition of being alive to the world, characterised by a heightened sensitivity and responsiveness, in perception and action, to an environment that is always in flux, never the same from one moment to the next (Ingold 2006: 10, original emphasis).

In Western cultures, while Judaeo-Christian religious doctrines have long been held responsible for the alienation of humans from the natural world, it is noticeable that strong and recurrent themes of a more reciprocal relationship are also found within this tradition (Glacken 1967). Even with the arrival of Enlightenment and industrial modernity, the "disenchantment from the world" was never complete: as Latour (1993) has suggested, perhaps we have never been modern. As an antidote to Enlightenment rationalist strictures, the possibilities of direct communication with nature on an emotional basis were stressed by movements such as Romanticism and American Transcendentalism in the nineteenth century, where aesthetic sensibilities were considered particularly important (cf. Chapter 11 by Egilsson). Certain types of landscapes and landscape representations rose to prominence as a result.

The idea that a conversation of some sort can be had with landscape thus has a long and complex history. It has been taken up by various social and environmental theorists, surfacing in various guises. Sometimes it seems to be interpreted fairly literally, but at other times it serves as a metaphor for more ethically sound relations with the non-human world (cf. Chapter 3 by Malenfant). In a famous essay, the central figure of American environmentalism, Aldo Leopold (1949), suggested the possibility – indeed the necessity – of "thinking like a mountain" in order to achieve a new ecological consciousness attuned to not only human but also non-human needs and goals.

The author who has in recent times perhaps argued most cogently for more-than-human conversations is David Abram. He speaks for a radical reconsideration of subjectivity and agency: "To define another being as an inert or passive object is to deny its ability to actively engage us and provoke our senses; *we thus block our perceptual reciprocity with that being*" (Abram 1996: 56, original emphasis). Taking his cue from Merleau-Ponty, Abram makes the point that both sensory perception and language are inexorably *embodied* (see Chapter 2 by Thorgeirsdottir, Chapter 7 by Lund and Willson, and Chapter 8 by Jóhannesdóttir). The voice that speaks is a voice that is of the body: "a profoundly carnal phenomenon" (Abram 1996: 74). This allows him to argue that in effect the *human* language is not fundamentally different from myriad other forms of expression, not only by animate (and vocal) non-human nature (cf. Chapter 12 by Benediktsson), but also inanimate features of the landscape – the tree, the rock, and the mountain. Abram even surmises that while the ability to communicate with non-human nature is found in most pre-modern societies, it has been lost with the advent of written (and thus disembodied) language, most notably through the invention of alphabetic script. This has made abstraction possible and thus contributed to the alienation from nature.

Abram's eco-phenomenological *oeuvre* has been criticised for not paying due attention to the content of what is being said: "in conversation we speak *with* each other, *about* the world" (Vogel 2006: 151, original emphasis). According to this critique, as non-human entities are unable to formulate claims to truth, they should not be thought of as partners to a conversation, however much we would like to instigate such exchange in the name of ethical concerns (cf. Malenfant,

Chapter 3). Others disagree, arguing that this implies a too narrow consideration of language and subjectivity, as exclusively human (Klenk 2008). The metaphor has indeed been used for other kinds of encounters between humans and things. Gadamer, writing about aesthetic experiences when encountering art, says that "[a]n encounter with a great work of art has always been ... like a fruitful conversation, a question and answer or being asked and replying obligingly, a true dialogue whereby something has emerged and remains" (Gadamer 1985: 250). This can be extended to encounters with landscape, many of which are precisely of an aesthetic kind (see Chapter 8 by Jóhannesdóttir, Chapter 9 by Brady, Chapter 10 by Jóhannsdóttir and Eysteinsson and Chapter 13 by Brydon).

An intriguing effort to widen the consideration of communication beyond humans is provided by the recently-established discipline of biosemiotics (Emmeche and Hoffmeyer 1991, Sebeok 2001). Drawing on the semiotics of American pragmatist philosopher Peirce as well as biological and ethological research, biosemioticians suggest that all life be recognised as an exchange of signs. Peircean semiotics allow for a much more encompassing definition of "conversation" than that of an intentional linguistic exchange between human subjects (see Benediktsson, Chapter 12). In biosemiotics, the boundary of subjectivity is moved to encompass non-humans, although most biosemioticians stop short of including inanimate nature in their analyses.

Suggestions for a thorough reconsideration of the relations between humans and non-humans have in fact proliferated in recent years. One is provided by actor-network theory, which has had great impact in human geography and related disciplines. Its proponents argue for nothing less than a radical redistribution of the capacities for agency (Latour 1993, 2005, Law and Hassard 1999). Instead of attributing agency solely to intentional human subjects, they suggest that it be understood as a product of relational engagements of non-human and human entities (Jóhannesson and Bærenholdt 2009). The crucial point, in other words, is not whether "the actor" is able to articulate its intentions through human linguistic conventions, but how he/she/it is created in the very process whereby the network is established, involving translations of interests. This fits with a widened conceptualisation of conversation, which goes beyond a narrowly human linguistic approach (cf. Chapter 4 by Waage), and has generated much interest by those concerned with understandings of nature and the politics of landscape. To mention just two examples, rivers have been analysed as actor-networks (Kortelainen 1999), and Cloke and Jones (2001, 2004) show how the (nonhuman) agency of trees is manifested in the co-constructed landscape of the orchard or the cemetery; a landscape which must be understood as "a complex performative achievement of different human and nonhuman actors, interrelated in time and space" (Cloke and Jones 2004: 314). Importantly however, they do point out that the trees have to be simultaneously understood as "actors" and "dwellers": the landscape cannot be adequately accounted for by reference to actor-networks alone. This chimes with the suggestion by Rose and Wylie (2006) that the "topographical" sensibilities of the landscape concept may sit uneasily with the "topological" concerns of the network.

We do not want to pass a final judgement on the divergent ideas presented so far, some of which diverge fairly radically from the ontological and epistemological norms of much science – certainly natural science. What we want to stress, however, is that there seem to be numerous tracks of theory that are commensurable with the metaphor of "conversation with landscape", counterintuitive as it might seem at first glance. Our own preferred path is through the somewhat complex and fractured terrain of phenomenology.

Landscape – Extending the Horizon

As Bender (2002: S106) has pointed out, landscapes by their very existence "refuse to be disciplined". Attempts by academics to define the landscape concept have certainly revealed how it is capable of resisting discipline. Perhaps historically speaking closest to the heart of the subject of geography, landscape was up until the 1980s usually understood in fairly straightforward objectivist terms as a silent and passive surface of forms sculpted by the historical efforts of nature and humans (Sauer 1996 [1925]). While the so-called "new" cultural geographies that gained ground during the 1980s and 90s approached the concept from a more critical standpoint, they also cast landscape in rather passive terms. The symbolic meaning and iconic significance of landscape was to be analysed (Cosgrove 1984, Cosgrove and Daniels 1988), and landscapes were to be "read" as a text (Duncan and Duncan 1988) in order to uncover the (often elitist and unjust) politics of culture. However, Bender pointed out that people always and everywhere – in the past and the present – relate to landscapes in different ways, and thus understand them differently also: "the experience of landscape is too important and too interesting to be confined to particular time, place and class" (Bender 1993: 1). This observation resonates again in her later remark, referred to above, that landscapes "refuse to be disciplined".

In 1993, Ingold published an article which spoke to wide audience of scholars, emphasising the need for a phenomenologically-based landscape analysis. Here he weaves together a sense for landscape through the notion of "dwelling", where landscapes continuously unfold through how people move in and through them, going about their daily tasks. He suggests that forms in the landscape are best understood as "the embodiment of a developmental or historical process … rooted in the context of human dwelling in the world" (Ingold 1993: 170). This process could be apprehended through a phenomenological method, emphasising a qualitative description of the world that the observer encounters through his or her senses and bodily involvement (cf. Chapter 5 by Aldred). Perception is central to this encounter. Merleau-Ponty (2002 [1945]: 253) spoke about a "tactile perception of space". Through such perception he claims that "the way is paved to true vision" (2002 [1945]: 259); vision that happens through bodily immersion rather than detached observation.

The dwelling concept thus usefully emphasises the intertwining of landscape and humans through everyday life and mundane practices, although many critiques (e.g. by Massey 2006, Tilley 1994, Urry 2000, Wylie 2003) have pointed out that its ideological overtones (from Heidegger's original formulation) of harmony and authenticity can downplay the sense of tension and disharmony. The concept of dwelling therefore connects people to landscape in a way in which naturalises the sense for landscape, providing a sense of rootedness (Wylie 2003), assuming "an essential harmony of rhythms and resonances – a *coherence* of landscape" (Massey 2006: 41). In this, Ingold's conception of landscape comes very close to that of *place* in the academic literature.[1]

While landscape may still "refuse to be disciplined" once and for all, a phenomenological approach can indeed be broadened to include a consideration of fluidity, transition and motion. It not only prompts awareness of how people are forever moving in and through landscapes, but also of how the landscape itself is simultaneously on the move. Ingold writes:

> Imagine a film of the landscape, shot over years, centuries, even millennia. Slightly speeded up, plants appear to engage in very animal-like movements, trees flex their limbs without any prompting from the winds. Speeded up rather more, glaciers flow like rivers and even the earth begins to move. At yet greater speeds solid rock bends, buckles and flows like molten metal. The world itself begins to breathe (Ingold 1993: 164).

Landscapes are thus in constant motion, taking on new shapes and forms. The lives of human beings are tangled up with the temporalities of constantly unfolding landscapes, in a never-ending journey (cf. Chapter 6 by Árnason). This recalls Jackson's argument against the Heideggerian notion that "being is primordially a mode of dwelling"; rather it can be understood as a "mode of journeying" (Jackson 2002: 31). This allows us to comprehend a world of fluid landscapes that are never bound nor framed (cf. Aldred, Chapter 5). As Bender (2001) has pointed out, although the phenomenological approach may be able to account for "familiar" places – the places we inhabit and know – the unfamiliar and unknown always exists. Awareness of the unfamiliar is, however, generated through encounters with the familiar.

The concept of the *horizon* may be helpful here, in that it allows for an appreciation of the differences between place and landscape. As Husserl put

---

[1] In fact, Cresswell (2003, 2004) has suggested that awareness of this lived-in and meaningful quality is much better ensured by using the concept of *place* rather than *landscape*, the latter carrying in his view irredeemably strong notions of a distant visual gaze. See Setten (2006) for a critical review.

it, "every experience has its own horizon" (quoted in Casey 1996: 17). From a phenomenological perspective, the horizon characterises

> the way one's range of vision is gradually expanded. A person who has no horizon does not see far enough and hence over-values what is nearest to him. On the other hand, "to have a horizon" means not being limited to what is nearby but being able to see beyond it (Gadamer 2004 [1960]: 301).

The concept of the horizon thus denotes not a fixed limit to perception, but an invitation to go further. Horizons are inherent in any consideration of perception, as they "make it possible to perceive more than what is directly sensed" (Vessey 2009: 535–6). Casey (2001: 417) has suggested that the horizon is the "primary feature of landscape" that "opens it up for further exploration, that is, for bodily ingression".

The idea of horizons thus also grants a depth to the concept of landscape beyond vision: the landscapes that humans perceive and converse with are certainly visual, but not merely "seen". In discussing Merleau-Ponty's phenomenology, Abram (1996: 68), talks about "the reciprocity of the sensuous": to see is also to be seen; to touch is also to be touched. In this way it is possible to speak of the "touching eye" (Lund 2005a, see also Tilley 2008): visual perception of landscape happens through a more general bodily engagement that involves all senses. Conversations resulting from such an engagement are based on mutuality and direct affect. By making use of the conversation metaphor, we want to explore how studies of landscape can be enriched through attention to such embodied processes.

However, conversations do not always flow smoothly and the perceptual touching between humans and landscape is not necessarily comfortable (cf. Chapter 14 by Snæbjörnsdóttir and Wilson). As Gadamer (2004 [1960]) emphasises, how one is situated in the conversation has a bearing on what points of view are brought in and what kind of understanding is brought about by the process. In a similar way, the result of the perceptual encounter between humans and landscape depends upon where and how the human is positioned in the landscape and what intentions he/she may have for acting upon it. This brings attention to political issues and contests of power. Solnit points out that the situation involves not only varying emotions, but also complex interests:

> [Landscapes] have political as well as aesthetic dimensions; on the small scale they involve real estate and sense for place, on the large scale they involve nationalism, war, and the grounds for ethnic identity ... [Landscape is] not just where we picnic but also where we live and die. It is where our food, water, fuel, and minerals come from, where our nuclear waste and shit and garbage go to, it is the territory of dreams, somebody's homeland, somebody's gold mine (Solnit 2003: 10–11).

In other words, conversations between humans and landscapes are almost never conducted from a neutral position (cf. Chapter 13 by Brydon). They are often very much tied to the interests at stake, excluding or ignoring messages and understandings that are not deemed to be advantageous for the individual or social group to which he or she belongs.

In sum, we argue that the metaphor of conversation can assist in finding a variety of new directions in the complex terrain of landscape studies by bringing attention to the mutuality of human-landscape encounters. Landscape is not comprehended as a predetermined, culturally contrived and passive "text", but as a conversational partner that is certainly more than human. The concept of the horizon, with its implication of movement and constantly shifting positions, takes landscape away from the often romantic and rather static association with place. It brings forth the importance of the visual as a part of a more encompassing sensuous engagement of humans with landscape. And lastly, by thinking of human-landscape relations as conversations we can also appreciate the diverse interests and challenges of power which are inherent in these relations in many cases.

The Book

For some years, the editors of this volume – a geographer and an anthropologist – have been studying landscape issues, broadly speaking, from their own differing disciplinary standpoints, on their own and with others (Benediktsson 2000, 2007, Benediktsson and Waage 2005, Huijbens and Benediktsson 2007, Lorimer and Lund 2003, 2008, Lund 2005a,b, 2006, Waage and Benediktsson 2010). The idea for this book came out of a certain feeling we both had, that recent theorising was not really satisfactory when it came to analysing those landscapes we are most familiar with. These are the landscapes of Iceland.

While Icelandic society and culture is unmistakably Nordic in origin, Icelandic landscapes are somewhat unusual in many respects, as visitors are often quick to recognise (cf. Brady 2007); not least as they are so obviously "in the making" by the forces of nature. The relations between humans and landscapes in Iceland also have their specific characteristics. Nordic landscape scholars, heirs to a long and remarkable tradition in landscape studies, have emphasised that there exists a "Nordic" cultural understanding of landscape as lived/worked/practiced (cf. Mels and Setten 2007, Olwig 1996, 2002), which is quite removed from the visually-centred and pictorial understanding prevailing in Britain and much of the English-speaking world (Setten 2006). While a useful antidote to the pictorial emphasis, an analysis of landscape that proposes another essential conceptualisation in its stead is not the road we want to follow. If nothing else it would, we argue, be unable to do justice to the diversity and dynamism of Icelandic landscapes. This book can be seen as a search for alternative understandings and metaphors, which take visual sensibilities as well as other aspects of perception seriously, and hopefully open up for a more diverse set of enquiries into human-landscape relations. It should be kept in mind that "[t]he hermeneutic power of metaphor comes from the creative ability of the imagination" (Vedder 2002: 202). The metaphor of conversation is only one of many possible options for enlarging the imagination about landscape: we hope there will never be one officially sanctioned way to undertake landscape studies. We fully expect the concept of landscape to remain "undisciplined".

The contributors to this book come from widely varying backgrounds, but all share a curiosity about where this metaphor can take scholars of landscape. Their disciplinary home provinces include anthropology, geography, environmental studies, philosophy, archaeology, literary studies and visual arts. Apart from making use of the metaphor of conversation (in quite different ways), a common thread which is found in many chapters is in fact a connection with the landscapes of Iceland. The authors include Icelandic, British, American and Canadian scholars.

Following this introduction, three chapters (2, 3 and 4) explore the meanings, opportunities and limitations of the metaphor itself. The next four chapters all depart from a phenomenological standpoint. Movement and temporality is the subject of three of these, tackling such divergent themes as the production of archaeological knowledge (Chapter 5), narratives of speed and death in the contemporary roadscape (Chapter 6), and walking in mountain landscapes (Chapter 7). The eighth chapter shifts the focus to the aesthetics of landscape, making use of the concepts of *flesh* and *atmosphere*. Aesthetics are also the subject of Chapter 9, but this time with an emphasis on what the author terms "difficult aesthetic appreciation". The two chapters that follow (10, 11) give examples of the entanglement of landscapes within the worlds of art and literature. Landscape paintings, poetry and prose are all forms of conversations that reflect the *Zeitgeist*. Then four chapters address conversations with non-human nature beyond landscape per se: animals, rocks and waterfalls, and the perpetual motion in the sky at night. The book concludes with an Epilogue by anthropologist Tim Ingold, whose ideas have informed recent landscape studies considerably and whose influence is actually felt in many of the chapters. Thus the book is itself a meandering conversation of various disciplinary approaches. We hope that the reader will enjoy the different vistas presented here across the complex theoretical landscapes of landscape.

References

Abram, D. 1996. *The Spell of the Sensuous: Perception and Language in a More-Than-Human World*. New York: Vintage Books.

Bender, B. 1993. Introduction: Landscape – Meaning and Action, in *Landscape: Politics and Perspectives*, edited by B. Bender. Oxford: Berg, 1–17.

Bender, B. 2001. Introduction, in *Contested Landscapes: Movement, Exile and Place*, edited by B. Bender and M. Winer. Oxford: Berg, 1–18.

Bender, B. 2002. Time and Landscape. *Current Anthropology*, 43, S103–S112.

Benediktsson, K. 2000. „Ósnortin víðerni" og ferðamennska á miðhálendi Íslands ["Wilderness" and tourism in the Icelandic central highlands]. *Landabréfið*, 16/17(1), 14–23.

Benediktsson, K. 2007. "Scenophobia" and the Aesthetic Politics of Landscape. *Geografiska Annaler*, 89B(3), 203–17.

Benediktsson, K. and Waage, E.R.H. 2005. Producing Scenery: Tourism and the Establishment of Protected Areas in Iceland, in *Land Use and Rural Sustainability*, edited by A.S. Mather. Aberdeen: International Geographical Union, 175–81.

Brady, E. 2007. Sense and Sensibility. *Environmental Values*, 16(3), 283–85.

Casey, E. 1996. How to Get from Space to Place in a Fairly Short Stretch of Time: Phenomenological Prolegomena, in *Senses of Place*, edited by S. Feld and K.H. Basso. Santa Fe: School of American Research Press, 13–52.

Casey, E. 2001. Body, Self and Landscape: A Geophilosophical Inquiry into the Place-World, in *Textures of Place: Exploring Humanist Geographies*, edited by P.C. Adams, S. Hoelscher and K.E. Till. Minneapolis: University of Minnesota Press, 403–25.

Cloke, P. and Jones, O. 2001. Dwelling, Place, and Landscape: An Orchard in Somerset. *Environment and Planning A*, 33, 649–66.

Cloke, P. and Jones, O. 2004. Turning in the Graveyard: Trees and the Hybrid Geographies of Dwelling, Monitoring and Resistance in a Bristol Cemetery. *Cultural Geographies*, 11(3), 313–41.

Cosgrove, D.E. 1984. *Social Formation and Symbolic Landscape*. London: Croom Helm.

Cosgrove, D.E. and Daniels, S., eds. 1988. *The Iconography of Landscape*. Cambridge: Cambridge University Press.

Cresswell, T. 2003. Landscape and the Obliteration of Practice, in *Handbook of Cultural Geography*, edited by K. Anderson, M. Domosh, S. Pile and N. Thrift. London: Sage, 269–81.

Cresswell, T. 2004. *Place: A Short Introduction*. Oxford: Blackwell Publishing.

Dewsbury, J.-D. and Cloke, P. 2009. Spiritual Landscapes: Existence, Performance and Immanence. *Social & Cultural Geography*, 10(6), 695–711.

Duncan, J. and Duncan, N. 1988. (Re)Reading the Landscape. *Environment and Planning D: Society and Space*, 6(2), 117–26.

Emmeche, C. and Hoffmeyer, J. 1991. From Language to Nature: the Semiotic Metaphor in Biology. *Semiotica*, 84(1/2), 1–42.

Gadamer, H.-G. 1985. Philosophy and Literature. *Man and World*, 18(3), 241–59.

Gadamer, H.-G. 2004 [1960]. *Truth and Method*, translated by J. Weinsheimer and D.G. Marshall. London: Continuum Books.

Glacken, C.J. 1967: *Traces on the Rhodian Shore: Nature and Culture in Western Thought from Ancient Times to the End of the Eighteenth Century*. Berkeley: University of California Press.

Huijbens, E. and Benediktsson K. 2007. Practising Highland Heterotopias: Automobility in the Interior of Iceland. *Mobilities*, 2(1), 143–65.

Ingold, T. 1993. The Temporality of the Landscape. *World Archaeology*, 25(2), 152–74.

Ingold, T. 2006. Rethinking the Animate, Re-Animating Thought. *Ethnos*, 71(1), 9–20.

Jackson, M. 2002. *The Politics of Storytelling: Violence, Transgression and Intersubjectivity.* Copenhagen: Museum Tusculanum Press.

Jóhannesson, G.Þ. and Bærenholdt, J.O. 2009. Actor-Network Theory/Network Geographies, in *International Encyclopedia of Human Geography* (Volume 1), edited by R. Kitchin and N. Thrift. Oxford: Elsevier, 15–19.

Klenk, N. 2008. Listening to the Birds: A Pragmatic Proposal for Forestry. *Environmental Values*, 17(3), 331–51.

Kortelainen, J. 1999. The River as an Actor-Network: The Finnish Forest Industry Utilization of Lake and River Systems. *Geoforum*, 30(3), 235–47.

Lakoff, G. and Johnson, M. 1980. *Metaphors We Live By*. Chicago: University of Chicago Press.

Latour, B. 1993. *We Have Never Been Modern*, translated by C. Porter. Cambridge, Massachusetts: Harvard University Press.

Latour, B. 2005. *Reassembling the Social: An Introduction to Actor-Network-Theory*. Oxford: Oxford University Press.

Law, J. and Hassard, J., eds. 1999. *Actor Network Theory and After*. Oxford: Blackwell.

Leopold, A. 1949. *A Sand County Almanac and Sketches Here and There*. Oxford: Oxford University Press.

Lorimer, H. and Lund, K. 2003. Performing Facts: Finding a Way Over Scotland's Mountains, in *Nature Performed: Environment, Culture and Performance*, edited by B. Szerszynski, W. Heim and C. Waterton. London: Blackwells, 130–44.

Lorimer, H. and Lund, K. 2008. A Collectable Topography: Recording and Remembering the Act of Walking, in *Culture from the Ground: Walking, Movement and Placemaking*, edited by T. Ingold and J. Lee. Aldershot: Ashgate, 185–200.

Lund, K. 2005a. Seeing in Motion and the Touching Eye: Walking over Scotland's Mountains. *Etnofoor*, 18(1), 27–42.

Lund, K. 2005b. Finding Place in Nature: "Intellectual" and Local Knowledge in a Spanish Natural Park. *Conservation and Society*, 3(2), 371–87.

Lund, K. 2006. Making Mountains, Producing Narratives, or: "One Day Some Poor Sod Will Write their Ph.D. on this". *Anthropology Matters* [Online], 8(2), 1–12. Available at: http://www.anthropologymatters.com/ [accessed: 9 March 2010].

Massey, D. 2006. Landscape as a Provocation – Reflections on Moving Mountains. *Journal of Material Culture*, 11(1–2), 33–48.

Mels, T., and Setten, G. 2007. Romance, Practice and Substantiveness: What do Landscapes do? *Geografiska Annaler*, 89B(3), 197–202.

Merleau-Ponty, M. 2002 [1945]. *Phenomenology of Perception*, translated by C. Smith. London: Routledge.

Olwig, K.R. 1996. Recovering the Substantive Nature of Landscape. *Annals of the Association of American Geographers* 86, 630–53.

Olwig, K.R. 2002. *Landscape Nature, and the Body Politic*. Madison: The University of Wisconsin Press.

Ricoeur, P. 1986 [1975]. *The Rule of Metaphor*. London: Routledge & Kegan Paul.

Rose, M. and Wylie, J. 2006. Animating Landscape. *Environment and Planning D: Society and Space*, 24(4), 475–79.

Sauer, C.O. 1996 [1925]. The Morphology of Landscape, in *Human Geography: An Essential Anthology*, edited by J. Agnew, D.N. Livingstone and A. Rogers. Oxford: Blackwell, 296–315.

Sebeok, T.A. 2001. Biosemiotics: Its Roots, Proliferation, and Prospects. *Semiotica*, 134(1), 61–78.

Setten, G. 2006. Fusion or Exclusion? Reflections on Conceptual Practices of Landscape and Place in Human Geography. *Norsk Geografisk Tidsskrift – Norwegian Journal of Geography*, 60(1), 32–45.

Solnit, R. 2003. A*s Eve Said to the Serpent: On Landscape, Gender, and Art*. Athens: University of Georgia Press.

Tilley, C. 1994. *A Phenomenology of Landscape: Places, Paths and Monuments*. Oxford: Berg.

Tilley, C. 2008. *Body and Image*. Walnut Creek: Left Coast Press.

Urry, J. 2000. *Sociology beyond Societies: Mobilities for the Twenty-First Century*. London: Routledge.

Vedder, B. 2002. On the Meaning of Metaphor in Gadamer's Hermeneutics. *Research in Phenomenology*, 32, 196–209.

Vessey, D. 2009. Gadamer and the Fusion of Horizons. *International Journal of Philosophical Studies*, 17(4): 525–36.

Vogel, S. 2006. The Silence of Nature. *Environmental Values*, 15(2), 145–71.

Waage, E.R.H. and Benediktsson, K. 2010. Performing Expertise: Landscape, Governmentality and Conservation Planning in Iceland. *Journal of Environmental Policy and Planning*, 12(1), 1–22.

Wylie, J. 2003. Landscape, Pperformance and Dwelling: a Glastonbury Case Study, in *Country Visions*, edited by P. Cloke. Harlow: Pearson Education, 136–57.

Chapter 2
Conversations with Ourselves in Metaphysical Experiences of Nature

Sigridur Thorgeirsdottir

Introduction

Pristine natural environments and wild landscapes are for many places of "metaphysical experiences" (Abram 1996, Ritter 1989, Skúlason 2006). One of the reasons that modern people seek refuge in nature is precisely the fact that one can have experiences in nature that, almost for a lack of better word, are termed as metaphysical. I say for a lack of a better word because the term "metaphysics" has for many a dubious ring to it. Metaphysics is associated with an outdated idea that metaphysics offers knowledge about the true nature of reality. In post-metaphysical times when we do not believe in the possibility of having knowledge about the essence of reality, what sense, if one at all, can it make to talk about metaphysical experiences? To be more precise, how can one philosophically articulate a metaphysical experience if one does neither explain it in terms of religion nor natural sciences? Ronald W. Hepburn, one of the pioneers of environmental aesthetics, defines a metaphysical experience of landscape as having a cognitive and reflective element, in addition to sensory appreciation. The metaphysical experience is cognitive because it enables to "see in a landscape some indication, some disclosure of how the world ultimately is. We may experience a landscape as "revealing something fundamental ... about how things really, or ultimately are" (Hepburn 1996: 191). Hepburn distinguishes such a metaphysical experience that he claims is "on secular lines" from experiences that are theistic (Hepburn 1996: 202). He also distinguishes the cognitive content of metaphysical experiences from that of the natural sciences because metaphysics is about knowledge that transcends the grasp of natural sciences. The type of metaphysical experiences Hepburn discusses are experiences of nature, and therefore these experiences must disclose some knowledge about nature, our relation with it and our place in it. Such experiences can be subsumed under aesthetic appreciation of nature because they are not confined to a strictly instrumental or utilitarian disposition towards nature. Basing metaphysics on experience also entails a widening of this discipline since it means going beyond an analysis of the being of things to analysis of metaphysical experiences. This entails a kind of a paradigm shift that can be traced to the naturalizing of metaphysics in Schopenhauer's and Nietzsche's philosophies and Heidegger's criticism of traditional metaphysics as occupied with non-empirical content. With this shift the human body of the experiencing subject comes into play.

As opposed to instrumental or utilitarian values of nature, aesthetic values are often not taken seriously in environmental debates about land use. That was at least the case in the controversy surrounding the building of the huge Kárahnjúkar dam in the northeastern highlands of Iceland that was completed in 2007. At best, aesthetic arguments were considered a luxury that one can admit as part of deliberations when all other arguments have to be taken into consideration. Such arguments were not seen as having a place in strong and effective preservation arguments (Carlson 2008). At worst, aesthetic arguments were, especially by the spokespeople of the construction of the dam, considered to be sentimental and worthless as "emotional" or mere subjective judgments (Thorgeirsdottir 2007). Instrumental values and economic values thus trump aesthetic values that are either understood to be insignificant or too subjective in order to be taken seriously in debates over the use of land. This type of belittlement of aesthetic arguments is based on an outdated and untenable idea about the duality of subjective and objective, of reason and emotions. Hepburn's idea about the cognitive content of metaphysical experiences of nature undermines the idea that emotional responses to nature cannot be taken seriously as arguments. The cognitive content of the emotion is derived from an idea, opinion or belief about the worth of what is experienced or felt as being beautiful, precious, intense or grim. The cognitive content can therefore be made explicit (if not fully, at least up to an extent) and articulated. Other proponents of environmental aesthetics, such as Muelder Eaton (2008), Brady (2003) and Carlson (2008), agree with Hepburn about the necessity of giving aesthetic arguments due consideration in environmental debates.

In this paper I will argue that the cognitive content of metaphysical experiences should be taken seriously as part of aesthetic arguments about the value of land. Metaphysics is often being misunderstood as offering some totalizing grasp on the nature of reality or some mystical or diffuse kind of feeling, or what Carlson calls "blooming, buzzing confusion" (Carlson 2008: 126). The term metaphysics, if one takes it as literally meaning beyond or after (meta) the natural/physical (physics) can give reason to such an understanding. The traditional understanding of metaphysics, as based on Platonic distinction of the world of the senses and the world of ideas, is however the main reason for the idea that metaphysics is about principles of life that transcend natural life. It was not until in the nineteenth century that metaphysics of life became properly (re)grounded in the natural world, as manifested in the naturalized metaphysics of Schelling, Schopenhauer and Nietzsche (Thorgeirsdottir 2004). The conception of metaphysical experiences I venture here is based on such naturalized metaphysics. In the philosophies of Schopenhauer and Nietzsche it is human, embodied life that is seen as the venue for experiences that offer a metaphysical insight into the fact that human life as embodied life is part of nature. In the following, I will discuss certain kinds of metaphysical experiences of wild landscapes as embodied experiences, and how they can make us aware of some important dimensions of our relation to nature and our place in it. The reflection on such experiences is a conversation with nature as a conversation with ourselves as nature, as part of nature, and yet taking a reflective stance towards it. I take Hepburn's portrayal of the "metaphysical imagination" that landscape can evoke as a point of departure for my deliberations. What I find missing in his analysis is an elaboration of the sense of being part of the land. Hepburn acknowledges how the sense of "oneness with nature" that can characterize the metaphysical imagination entails being "in the scene and bodily continuous with it" (Hepburn 1996: 198). He does however not elaborate this thought further. The goal here is to extend this notion of being bodily continuous with the landscape. I argue that it is precisely the body, our embodied existence that provides an important link between nature and our capacity to reflect metaphysically about it. It is the body, as a sensory apparatus and as embodied consciousness that allows us to enter into conversation with ourselves as nature. It is also our body as the locus for the socio-historical context in which we are situated that makes us experience nature differently in different times and different places.

It is especially important to reflect on the body in this context of experiences of wild nature because these kind of metaphysical experiences are often experiences that have been characterized as experiences of the sublime. In the Kantian tradition of the sublime, experiences of sublime nature such as such as magnificent mountains, sea-storms and chasms are often characterized by detachment. The subject is at a safe distance from a powerful, overwhelming nature that allows the spectator to reflect on its dynamics, vastness and sublimity. Such notions of the perceiving subject represent independent, sovereign subjects in control of themselves (Mann 2006). This idea of the subject goes hand in hand with the traditional idea about the human relation to nature as one of control and domination. By reflecting on these kinds of experiences as embodied experiences, as I propose, a different notion of the subject emerges, a subject that is part of nature. This also, as I argue, entails a different notion of subjectivity from the traditional idea of the spectator of sublime natural phenomena. The notion of embodiment necessarily entails a relational subject, a subject which stands in relation to nature and to other living beings. The subject is thus not only seen as sovereign and independent, but as subject to nature (to its internal as well as to external nature) and to other beings and people. The landscape is not merely an object, but being part of it, we are in important respects subject to it. The goal of this "naturalizing" of the notion of the subject of metaphysical experience is twofold (Schroeder 2006). In the first place, I argue that such a notion of the subject is a precondition of countering the traditional notion of the sovereign subject that implies that man's disposition towards nature is one of domination. Secondly, I argue that the values that can be derived from this type of metaphysical experience have important implications for environmental discourses in terms of extending our understanding of our relation to nature. The conception of embodied metaphysical experience yields in the first place a notion of the subject that is embedded in nature and interrelated with other people and other living beings. Secondly, a metaphysical experience of nature at times makes nature appear as foreign and awesome, and such an experience undermines the idea of domination of nature. The metaphysical experience of nature is thus a source for values that are of relevance for environmental debates.

Metaphysical Experience of Landscape

I argue against the idea that it is senseless to talk about metaphysical experiences of nature in secular times, and I argue that one can discuss such experiences without refuting to spiritual and pantheistic arguments. Both Hepburn and Berleant with his aesthetics of engagement with nature discuss the imagination that is evoked by experiences of nature (Berleant 1992, 2005). Phenomenological descriptions of such experiences yield knowledge about their cognitive content. I will argue that such descriptions show how metaphysical experiences are one way of "getting real" about our place in nature, and our condition as natural beings. As I take Hepburn's idea of the metaphysical imagination of nature as a point of departure, it is fitting to begin with his description:

> We may experience a polar scene of ice and snow as revealing something fundamental (and no doubt grim) about how things really, or ultimately are; something concealed from us in more familiar, temperate, framed countryside. Or, in sharpest contrast, we may experience a nature whose poignant beauty on some occasion seems to speak of a transcendent source for which we lack words and clear concepts (Hepburn 1996: 191–2).

Hepburn terms this as "metaphysical imagination". I prefer calling this kind of a perception of nature as a metaphysical experience. The term imagination has in some respects something to do with fancy and figments of imagination. That understanding is not Hepburn's intention with the term since he emphasizes the cognitive content of the kind of imagination pristine or sublime landscapes can evoke. I however want to use the term "experience" rather than the concept of the metaphysical imagination for several reasons. For one, experience is a broader concept and it entails more than imagination insofar it is in a more concrete way tied to perceiving or having a specific sense of reality that evokes metaphysical thoughts. Secondly, I want to accentuate that these kinds of experiences need to be described in a phenomenological manner because by doing that the experiences present themselves in a multitude of ways.

Hepburn's description of the landscape that evokes metaphysical imagination centers on its scenic qualities. The landscape is primarily perceived as an object of vision, but that has been rather typical for aesthetics of landscape. The picturesque and scenic qualities are thus emphasized as they present themselves to a spectator. One of the main reasons for this is that environmental aesthetics has been modeled on the basis of aesthetics of art, primarily visual arts (Muelder Eaton 2008: 339). There is a longstanding tradition of viewing landscape as a visual scene or as a frame around a picture with some objects. Landscape is therefore aesthetically grasped similarly to an artistic object, but that results in a detachment of the landscape from nature or the ecosystem, as well as a separation from the object and the aesthetically appreciating subject. This very fact has also been one hindrance in forging a link between aesthetics of nature and environmental ethics. The emphasis on scenery has inevitably led to a focus on beauty and the aesthetically pleasing, often without giving due regard to the soundness of the ecosystem or the preservation value of a particular landscape in terms of biodiversity.

From the perspective of the idea of a metaphysical experience, the focus on beautiful landscapes has at least two shortcomings. Beauty can be an important aspect, but it does not suffice to appreciate a landscape metaphysically as a source of value. Therefore, the idea of the sublime has been central to a metaphysical idea of nature, as becomes evident in the tradition from Kant to Hepburn. Secondly, the idea of aesthetic appreciation of a landscape as scenic is embedded in the above mentioned notion of the aesthetic subject that is detached from the perceived object of a nature that evokes a feeling of the sublime. The experience of the sublime does not only entail being moved by the beauty of something, but so to speak to be shaken to the core.

The Self of Metaphysical Experiences

Metaphysical experiences of wild or non-anthropogenic landscapes can be of many sorts, but I will only underscore a few aspects. When confronted with a sublime landscape, one of the things it triggers is how small one is compared to the enormity of landscape and the natural forces in it. This experience modifies the notion of the sovereign, independent subject. A phenomenological understanding of the metaphysical experience of landscape shows how this experience involves a decentering of the subject, compared to the traditional Enlightenment understanding of a dichotomy of the subject and the natural world. Like Hay has argued, phenomenology teams up with ecological thought with its de-individualized idea of the human being, and its understanding of the unity between person and world (Hay 2002: 145). The metaphysical experience of landscape is a certain type of immersion in the world, but the prime focus of phenomenological investigations is to illuminate different modes of being-in-the-world. Phenomenology's intention, ever since it beginning in Husserl's phenomenology, is to elaborate an alternative investigative method from that of the sciences and other ruling discourses that are each in their own way schematic and reductionist. The scientific view can, like Hepburn argues, not grasp the metaphysical experience of being-in-the-world because science necessarily eliminates "most or all the features of the world that are of human concern" (Hepburn 1996: 194). For science, the phenomena of the natural world are objects of investigation for the investigating subject. Heidegger, a disciple of Husserl and proponent of existential phenomenology, put forth a notion of a metaphysical experience that counters this dichotomy of subject and object. In his lecture on metaphysics, he formulates metaphysics as a questioning about the world where the inquiring subject is part of the question (Heidegger 1929). The metaphysical questioning, as opposed to questions about the basic principles of the being of objects, is based on a certain experience of being self in the world. Out of wonder over what life is all about the questioning subject raises metaphysical questions about the meaning of being. There are certain emotions (that Heidegger called *Stimmungen*) that trigger metaphysical questioning. These can be emotions like dread, boredom, joy or delight.

Heidegger's understanding of metaphysical experiences point to the cognitive content the emotions have that trigger metaphysical reflection. With this approach Heidegger puts forth an epistemological alternative that counters the dualisms of body and mind, reason and emotion, subjective and objective.

The Embodied Self of Metaphysical Experiences

Apart from discussing the affective component of metaphysical experiences, Heidegger does not address the embodied aspects further. These aspects come especially to the fore, like I argue, in metaphysical experiences of nature. When experiencing a landscape, one can experience oneself as part of this nature. The body as a natural and material entity is an intermediary between oneself and nature. It is at once an object that one can experience as object in the material world of things, and it is at the same time a site of the self, the point from which all one's experiences and reflections originate. When appreciating a landscape aesthetically, the landscape can open itself to one in a metaphysical experience that one gives meaning to by articulating or communicating it. The landscape, the body, perception and cognition unite in the experience and in making it explicit. Nature and the body interact in this experience, even though one is merely looking at something and wondering about it. Contrary to the romantic notion according to which nature is the prime source of the values, it is the interaction of nature that presents itself, the event itself and the meanings we give to it that results in the cognitive content of the metaphysical experience of landscape (Böhme 1992: 99).

The bodily perception of landscape can be of many sorts. It can be sensing the breeze, being blinded by the reflection of the sun in the snow, sensing the violent force of a waterfall in a glacial river or being immersed in the element as when swimming in the ocean. What is important is the form of identification with the natural element that one senses. The intensity can also vary, from being a very light acknowledgement of sounds to feeling nothing but being a body when swimming in the ocean and struggling in the ice-cold water. The metaphysical meaning also depends on the kind of landscape one experiences. Let us dwell with the example of the ocean. The ocean can not only be a metaphor of eternity, of circulation and eternal becoming. It can also feel like throwing oneself into the cycle of eternal becoming, that is at once beginning and end. As opposed to being on solid ground of the earth, one is thrown into fluidity, and one has to go with the flow. This form of experience therefore requires giving into the element in order to be able to go with the element and master being in it. One's control is therefore not one of one-sided domination but rather an interaction with the natural force, by giving into it in order to have it carry one. By giving into the element, one often experiences fear of the uncontrollable and unpredictable force one is encountered with. Such metaphysical experiences are therefore not characterized by pure awe, wonder or delight. On the contrary, they are highly ambivalent. One is at the mercy of a force of nature that can endanger and even destroy one. In other words, one subjects oneself to an element, and this experience offers an intensified and exaggerated idea of how human beings are subject to nature. Not only in the very general sense of being mortal beings that will unite with non-human nature in the end, but also in the sense that the destiny of the human race is intertwined with the condition of nature. Let me give another example of a similar sort. When wandering on one of the constantly moving glacier tongues at the margins of Vatnajökull, the largest glacier in Iceland (and Europe), one is highly aware of the risk of being there. There are cracks and holes in the glacier that could literally swallow the traveler. The glacier and the rivers emerging out of it also pose a danger for the surroundings. One can for example see how the farming communities in the vicinity of the glacier have throughout the years tried to protect themselves by constructing levees to shield grazing land against the destructive and unpredictable force of the glacial rivers.[1] In addition to this, the glacier itself is a kind of measure for how the condition of the earth is changing, and most likely in ways that are endangering the foundations of human life. Glaciers in most parts of the world are melting and shrinking, and one can see how the glacial line is receding. Glaciers are therefore perhaps one of the most visible markers of global warming. In many parts of the world, this will lead to water shortage. One can for example only imagine the catastrophic effects of diminished water supply in the rivers of India and China that have their origins in glaciers of the Himalaya mountain range.

This kind of an experience of interaction with nature is an experience of the intertwining of culture and nature. Like Bruno Latour argues, the world is one gigantic laboratory in which nature and culture are in constant interaction (Latour 2003). There can be no experience of a pure and original nature since there is no such thing. Even the wilderness is affected by climatic changes and other man-made changes that affect nature on a large scale. There are all kinds of imbalances in the interplay of nature and culture, and the closest one can get to "purity" is a natural environment that is ecologically healthy and sound. This does not imply that the meaning given to nature (for example with the help of ecological research) is only dependent on what kind of knowledge man imposes on nature in attempts to grasp and understand it, like a one-sided social constructivist approach would have it (Gandy 1997). There is an interaction between mind and world, and the sensing and perceiving body is an intermediary between nature and culture.

---

1   I thank Þorvarður Árnason for a guided trip to this area with students in our seminar on environmental aesthetics at the University of Iceland in the spring of 2008.

My understanding of embodied metaphysical experiences means a change of emphasis in the conception of metaphysics from the *meta* to the *physical*. To be more precise, one could say that the meta is taken down from the sphere of transcendence and relocated in the physical (Thorgeirsdottir 2000). I build on the theories of Merleau-Ponty, who argued against traditional metaphysics by claiming that it is impossible to understand the world without the mediation of embodied cognition (Merleau-Ponty 2002 [1945]). Our embodied point of view cannot be transcended because the body is the site of our perception and perception makes something appear to us. The body is related to the world in a profound way, and an analysis of the body is of utmost importance for our understanding of the relation between mind and world and mind and body (Gallagher and Zahavi 2008: 135). The body is already in the world and the world is given to us through the body (Gallagher and Zahavi 2008: 137). We perceive and do things with the living body that is in a constant relation with the world. The sphere of perception is determined by embodied intentionalities. The living body intends towards the sphere of perception and the sphere of perception embodies its intentionalities. We therefore form our world and the world forms us at the same time. Intentionality flows in a circle that goes from the world into us and from us into the world, over and over again.

Merleau-Ponty (1969) ties the body to nature by elaborating the conception of "flesh" (fr. *chair*). The flesh of the world is everything, world, society, nature, body and so on. The body is one of the instantiations of the flesh. With the conception of the flesh he articulates how body and mind, and nature and culture are interwoven. The sensate and the sensible are thus intertwined. Merleau-Ponty relates the body and being-in-the-world by talking about how the body is a situation. Embodied intentionalities are historically and culturally determined. At the same time nature is at work in the body, and therefore the body is the prime example of the meeting of nature and culture.

These ideas of the intertwining of body and culture prefigure all experiences. The phenomenological approach allows to understand scientific approaches and the metaphysical experience I discuss as different ways of understanding nature, i.e. as different forms and differently validated forms of knowledge of nature. The metaphysical experience discussed here can not lay claim to scientific validation. It nevertheless yields important knowledge that has ethical relevance for our relation to the natural world and our place in it. It is one important experience in the number of experiences and dispositions that determine ideas about the value of a natural environment. I do not claim that certain wilderness experiences should be given preference to other experiences as means of disclosing metaphysical ideas about the human place in the natural world. I mainly argue that these kinds of experiences can generate philosophical ideas about our place in and relation to nature. Insofar such ideas emerge out of certain experiences that natural sciences cannot grasp they are important for our understanding. These kinds of experiences can be multifarious, but insofar I link them to the tradition of philosophies of the sublime, I underscore two features of them. In the first place, when experiencing wild nature one can at once be overcome by joy over one's own life and sense the insignificance of individual human life on the large scale of things. In face of the unpredictability of the forces of nature one becomes aware of the vulnerability of human life as natural. Such sentiments correspond in many ways to features of human embodiment. Nature's force and fertility as well as its destructive powers correspond to natality and mortality, sickness and health, fragility and robustness. These are the forces of nature human life is subject to. One is reminded of the temporality and finality of human existence, as well as the never ending cycle of life of which human life is part of. Due to the wonder that life exists on this earth and that it is a riddle how it came to be and how it will evolve one can also be filled with awe. The second point to be underscored is that the clandestine character of life one can experience in wild landscapes gives one a sense of the otherness of nature. Nature is and will remain other insofar it will never completely disclose itself. Metaphysical reflection seeks the other, according to Levinas. The desire for alterity is a driving force of metaphysical reflection (Levinas 1991 [1961]: 33). From this point of view, nature as alterity is a source for metaphysical reflection. Levinas spoke of such experiences in terms of interpersonal relations, but nature, in my view, also offers a prime possibility of such metaphysical experiences.

In Heidegger's lecture on metaphysics, mentioned above, philosophy is described with the metaphor of the tree. The branches are the various subdidsciplines of philosophy but the roots are metaphysics. Heidegger did not tie his understanding of metaphysics as the questioning of the basic features of human existence to one's place in the natural world, even though he argued that the idea of temporality of human existence is the most basic knowledge a metaphysical expierence offers. The metaphysical cognition disclosed in metaphysical experiences of nature is about our relation to nature and our relation to ourselves as part of nature. Heidegger objected to the tradition of metaphysics that consisted in an enquiry of the non-empirical character of existence. By situating the search for metaphysical knowledge in the experience of basic features of human existence, he however paved the way for relating this experience to the dimension of nature in human life.

Ethical Implications of Metaphysical Experiences of Wild Landscapes

The idea of the cognitive content of metaphysical experiences of nature may sound like high-flown speculation. It is however merely an articulation of some of the thoughts that come up for many people when confronted with wild landscapes. Such thoughts can undoubtedly come up in other experiences. I have however articulated them with reference to this type of natural environments. The fact that this is a "natural" and "wild" environment does not entail that the experience of it discloses some primordial features of nature. Like I have suggested, the experience of nature is always an experience of a historically and culturally situated subject. The very fact that we are bodies contextualizes us in a certain time and place, and in a certain bodily condition like age, sex or capability. Our embodied intentionalities, i.e. what we look for, what we see and what we are blind or insensitive to, is culturally determined, just as the landscapes we experience are affected by human operations on the planet, and therefore undergo changes. This may not seem the case when discussing the central highlands of Iceland that apparently seem to be rather unaffected. Their status and the meanings they are given are however heavily affected by such external forces. Let us give an example. There is a photograph, taken at night from a satellite perspective, that shows Iceland and other countries in Northern and parts of Western and Central Europe. What is striking about this picture is that almost everywhere the land is illuminated because most parts of Europe are densely populated. There are lights almost everywhere except in one place, where there is a large area of darkness, and this area is the central highlands of Iceland.[2] This area is therefore the last remaining dark place in most of Europe. Not only because it is a large uninhabited area, but also because there are no street lights there. This fact alone gives this area a higher rarity-status. The diversity of natural landscapes in a condensed area like this (glaciers, geothermal areas, sands and vegetated land) has for a long time given this area a status of rarity. It is however in recent times in which there is talk about "light pollution" that a feature like darkness becomes a fact that contributes to the special value of this place.

Darkness and silence are features that are important in this context of metaphysical experiences. Being in a vast area that is silent and unlit when darkness sets in takes one out of the normal conditions of urban and inhabited environments. These features are also constitutive of the ambiguity that characterizes sublime places. One can sense peacefulness under these conditions, but one can also sense the foreignness of the environment that can imbue a feeling of insecurity. This sense of insecurity rarely has to do with danger, but rather with a heightened sense of the fact that nature is not predictable, and that men are like visitors in these areas that primarily belong to other living beings, like wild animals. Folkloristic beliefs, myths and tales of hidden people and natural beings, are also still quite common in Iceland, and that can heighten the awareness of subjecting oneself to forces that are ungraspable. Such sentiments are part of the idea that metaphysical experiences of wild landscapes undermine a disposition of control and domination over nature. Even though such beliefs are meanings that are imposed on nature they do underscore the othersidedness of nature, i.e. the fact that nature is always something more than a reflection of human beliefs and knowledge.

Limits of knowledge set limits to domination, and that fact shows the ethical relevance of metaphysical experiences. The ethical relevance of aesthetical arguments in environmental debates is often contested, as has been mentioned. One of the reasons are the difficulties involved in deferring ethical claims from claims of beauty (Carlson and Lintott 2008). Even if aesthetical categories are extended beyond beauty, and other experiences of nature are included in a list of aesthetical values of nature, it is difficult to delineate their meaning. Berleant has been

---

2   I thank Þóra Ellen Þórhallsdóttir for pointing out this photograph to me.

instrumental in widening the scope of aesthetical disposition towards nature. He goes beyond aesthetical appreciation of beauty towards aesthetics of engagement with nature (Berleant 2005). Berleant's conception of engagement means that the natural world not only surrounds, but assimilates us when we immerse with it in aesthetic perception (Berleant 1992: 169–70). Hepburn's and my conceptions of metaphysical experiences when dwelling in a landscape correspond to this idea of engagement with nature. Carlson however criticizes Berleant's notion for not being able to adequately answer "what [in nature] and how to aesthetically appreciate" nature (Carlson 2008: 124). It seems like everything can be appreciated. Carlson makes this claim about Berleant's theory of aesthetic appreciation from his own stand of cognitive aesthetics of nature, according to which human appreciation of nature is limited to the "common sense and scientific" knowledge that we can have of natural environments. The knowledge provided by naturalists, ecologists, geologists and natural historians is in his view central to an aesthetic appreciation of nature (Carlson 2008: 126–7).

If Berleant's position of aesthetics of engagement is too wide and too undifferentiated, Carlson's position is too narrow. With my conception of metaphysical experiences of nature, I have attempted to delineate a specific notion of aesthetic experience of nature. It is the kind of experience that reveals "something fundamental ... about how things really, or ultimately are" (Hepburn 1996: 191). I have tried to show that the kind of knowledge such a metaphysical experience of wild landscapes generates does not have to be any ultimate or essentializing form of knowledge. The metaphysical experience is dependent on the condition and the socio-historical context of the person experiencing a particular landscape. Such experiences therefore generate different knowledge in different times and different places, in accord with changing needs, interests and outlooks. In my analysis of metaphysical experiences I have furthermore illuminated two features. On the one hand, I have discussed how metaphysical experiences of wild landscapes undermine a dominant disposition towards nature. Secondly, I have shown how the fact that metaphysical experiences are embodied experiences is the basis for a disposition towards nature that makes us aware of how we not only control natural life on the planet, but are also subject to forces in nature that we cannot control. I thus extend Hepburn's conception of the metaphysical imagination by showing how it needs to be anchored in bodily experience. By doing that metaphysical experiences can disclose knowledge about us as part of nature. That is how such experiences powerfully expose our relations to the natural world and ourselves as part of this world. By becoming aware of how we are dependent on changes in the natural environment we also become better aware of our responsibility for maintaining an intact and sustainable natural environment. The fact of relationality, i.e. the fact that our existence depends on nature, is the core of the ethical obligation that a metaphysical experience of the sort I have ventured here can evoke. (Not only is this fact more ethically motivating than ethical theories about how nature depends on us. It is also more convincing. Nature does not really depend on us because in the long run nature will outlive the human species, unless the human species manages to annihilate the planet.) Our conversation with ourselves as nature that a metaphysical experience of this sort offers, shows us how the considerations that can emerge out of it are not abstract speculations. They are, like Saito claims about aesthetical experiences of the environment in general, "often thoroughly entrenched in and integral to our profound, yet everyday concerns, such as moral virtues" (Saito 2007: 239). I therefore argue that the model of metaphysical experience I propose here is not only about aesthetical imagination of nature. It has strong ethical implications because this kind of an experience makes us aware of aspects about our condition as beings that are part of nature. Scientific knowledge can tell us much about the condition of nature and our place in it. Aesthetic, speculative perceptions about the beauty of a landscape or the desolate condition of a damaged landscape can inform us about our condition as natural beings. Metaphysical experiences of the sort that have been discussed here can be instrumental in making knowledge about our condition as natural beings "hit home" or become real to us, especially with regard to the ethical values that can be derived from them. Needless to say, the confrontation with a natural environment that is sensed as threatened or damaged calls for a scientific confirmation. A receding glacier can be a natural occurrence that is no concern of worry about the ecosystem, but it can also be a sign of climate change due to global warming that threatens human life. By seeing and experiencing it with our own senses does however make us wonder and ask about the condition of the natural environment of the glacier. But first and foremost, it makes us aware of ourselves as part of this nature. By being in nature, we somehow sense something that seems essential about it (although it does not have to be essential in any totalizing sense). Our destiny, and the destiny of coming generations, is therefore perceived as somehow interrelating. The knowledge gained from metaphysical experiences of wild landscapes is therefore relevant aesthetical knowledge. It deepens aesthetical knowledge insofar it pertains to more than the scenic and beauty. It can also generate an insight that science cannot do. Science can offer knowledge about something that is imperceivable about the natural environment, and as such it can either confirm or refute some of cognitive content of a metaphysical experience of the condition of nature (Muelder Eaton 2008: 346). Even though the type of metaphysical experience discussed here cannot necessarily inform us in such a scientific way, it is a perception of nature that can tell us in a profound way something about our place in the natural environment. It can make us "get real" about ourselves as beings whose destiny as living beings is intertwined with the larger scale of nature. According to etymology one of the meanings of conversation is the act of living with and keeping company with. Metaphysical experiences of nature can make us aware of how we live with nature due to the fact that we are part of it.

References

Abram, D. 1996. *The Spell of the Sensuous*. New York: Vintage.
Berleant, A. 1992. *The Aesthetics of Environment*. Philadelphia: Temple University Press.
Berleant, A. 2005. *Aesthetics and Environment: Variations on a Theme*. Aldershot: Ashgate.
Böhme, G. 1992. An Aesthetic Theory of Nature: an interim report. *Thesis Eleven*, 32, 90–102.
Brady, E. 2003. *Aesthetics of the Natural Environment*. Edinburgh: Edinburgh University Press.
Carlson, A. 2008. Aesthetic Appreciation of the Natural Environment, in *Nature, Aesthetics, and Environmentalism: From Beauty to Duty,* edited by A. Carlson and S. Lintott. New York: Columbia University Press, 119–32.
Carlson, A. and Lintott, S. (eds.) 2008. *Nature, Aesthetics, and Environmentalism: From Beauty to Duty*. New York: Columbia University Press.
Gallagher, S. and Zahavi, D. 2008. *The Phenomenological Mind: An Introduction to Philosophy of Mind and Cognitive Science*. London: Routledge.
Gandy, M. 1997. Contradictory Modernities: Conceptions of Nature in the Art of Joseph Beuys and Gerhard Richter. *Annals of the Association of American Geographers*, 87(4), 636–59.
Hay, P. 2002. *A Companion to Environmental Thought*. Edinburgh: Edinburgh University Press.
Heidegger, M. 1929. *Was ist Metaphysik?* Frankfurt am Main: Vittorio Klostermann.
Hepburn, R.W. 1996. Landscape and the Metaphysical Imagination. *Environmental Values*, 5, 191–204.
Latour, B. 2003. Atmosphère, Atmosphère, in *Ólafur Elíasson. The Weather Project*. London: New Tate Gallery, 29–41.
Levinas, E. 1991 [1961]. *Totality and Infinity*. Dordrecht: Kluwer.
Mann, B. 2006. *Women's Liberation and the Sublime*. Oxford: Oxford University Press.
Merleau-Ponty, M. 1969. *The Visible and the Invisible*, edited by C. Lefort, translated by A. Lingis. Evanston: Northwestern University Press.
Merleau-Ponty, M. 2002 [1945]. *Phenomenology of Perception*, translated by C. Smith. London: Routledge.
Muelder Eaton, M. 2008. The Beauty that Requires Health, in *Nature, Aesthetics, and Environmentalism: From Beauty to Duty,* edited by A. Carlson and S. Lintott. New York: Columbia University Press, 339–62.
Ritter, J. 1989 [1963]. Landschaft. Zur Funktion des Ästhetischen in der modernen Gesellschaft, in *Subjektivität*. Frankfurt am Main: Suhrkamp, 141–63.
Saito, Y. 2007. *Everyday Aesthetics*. Oxford: Oxford University Press.
Schroeder, B. 2006. Naturalizing Continental Philosophy: Breaking Ground in Environmental Thinking. *Human Studies*, 29(4), 509–15.

Skúlason, P. 2006. *Meditations at the Edge of Askja*. Reykjavík: University of Iceland Press.

Thorgeirsdottir, S. 2000. Metaphysik, in *Nietzsche Handbuch,* edited by H. Ottmann. Stuttgart: Metzler Verlag, 281–3.

Thorgeirsdottir, S. 2004. Nietzsche's Feminization of Metaphysics and its Significance for Theories of Gender Difference, in *Feminist Reflections on the History of Philosophy*, edited by L. Alanen and C. Witt. Dordrecht: Kluwer, 51–68.

Thorgeirsdottir, S. 2007. Nature's Wholeness and Nature's Otherness. Aesthetical Aspects of Sustainability, in *Sustainable Development and Global Ethics*, edited by C.H. Grenholm and N. Kamergrauzis, 51–64.

Chapter 3
The Limits of our "Conversations with Nature"

Gabriel Malenfant

Introduction: A Generative Metaphor

> Metaphors, it might be said, do not *entail* impreciseness, but they invite it. It would, of course, be wrong to say that metaphorical expressions are by nature imprecise; on the contrary, a metaphorical expression may be far more precise than a "literal" one. This is again a matter of context (Naess 1966: 69).

As Arne Naess points out in the quote above, a metaphor can be many things: useful, banal or even terribly wrong. It can become a catchphrase causing harm, enabling labelling and reductionism. But it also allows for literary beauty and even, sometimes, for deeper understanding of certain experiences. To be sure, in studying the particularities of this linguistic process, one can find a variety of characterisations of the way metaphors are used – a variety of which I do not pretend to do an exhaustive study in this chapter. Yet, the use of metaphors in environmental philosophy is unsurprisingly very common, even endemic. In colloquial language, trivial metaphors such as "man is a wolf", or other expressions used by newspapers and marketing companies like "the president is under fire because of his position on the environment" and "this veggie-burger is an explosion of flavour" are "significant only as symptoms of a particular kind of *seeing-as*, the "meta-pherein" or "carrying over" of frames or perspectives from one domain of experience to another" (Schön 1981: 254). This type of metaphors can be seen as simply descriptive. It has a hyperbolic role in a specific context, but remains the mere description of a reality.

By contrast, according to philosopher Donald A. Schön, who wrote extensively on the role of metaphors in fields as various as policy implementation and pedagogy, the same linguistic process can also evince the existence of another kind of metaphoric expression. This second instantiation of metaphors can best account for the "conversation with nature" saying often found in environmental philosophy, since the latter does not only propose to emphasise the selected feature of a pre-existing reality, but rather helps creating a new domain of interpretation concerning a mundane experience. Schön calls them *generative* metaphors because of the purpose that is attributed to such expressions, which is of giving new perspectives on an experience rather than simply enhancing one of its already enclosed characteristics:

> Once we have constructed a generative metaphor, once we have concluded that in this story we are seeing *A* as *B*, then we can explore and reflect upon similarities and differences between *A* and *B*. In doing so, we draw upon a repertoire of additional ways of perceiving and understanding both *A* and *B* (Schön 1981: 267).

So if "conversation with nature" can be called a generative metaphor, it would be because of its ability to create new horizons for thinking, according to environmental specialists who think of nature in these terms. But for thinking what exactly? Not nature *per se*. Rather, the generative content of the metaphor touches on the particular relationship taking place between man and nature – *perception of* and *conversation with* are here the comparable *A* and *B* from which a new understanding of our relationship with nature is said to arise. Schön's generative metaphors are related, tentatively at least, to what Lakoff and Johnson (1999: 45–73) call *complex* metaphors, which are contrasted with the basic *primary* metaphors that link together subjective judgments and sensorimotor experiences.[1] As they explain, complex metaphors are like molecules formed of simpler atoms (i.e. the primary metaphors), and these molecules can in turn entail both metaphorical and non-metaphorical statements about the world. As a result, "not all of [a complex or generative metaphor's] entailments may be literally true", since "a metaphorical mapping may be apt in some respects, but not in others" (Lakoff and Johnson 1999: 73). Correlatively, one of the goals of this essay will be to show how a literal interpretation of the "conversation with nature" metaphor led some environmental philosophers to move from "a non-literal ontology" – which has a generative content, and can be considered as "crucial to reasoning" at least in their field – towards thorny propositions in environmental ethics.

Now, to understand better the "conversation with nature" metaphor as generative and show its importance in environmental thought, I propose to analyse it as a sort of *maieutics*. As it is generally recognised in philosophy, maieutics is one of the conversation methods used by Socrates in the Platonic dialogues – a method that has the following characteristics:

1. It is a relationship or process that entails the participation of a knowledge-seeker that is both passive and active, as well as a second party playing

---

[1] I share a great deal of the common scepticism that concerns Lakoff and Johnson's work, especially as regards some of their seemingly dubious inferences touching on morality and politics. The materialistic claims they make are also subject to controversies which I do not have time to get into. However, their account of metaphoric expressions is widely known, and useful to some extent.

the role of a "midwife" that allows for knowledge to arise within its interlocutor;
2. It is a relationship or process that puts into question the very conditions allowing for the acquisition of knowledge through a dialogue;
3. It is a relationship or process that implies the acquisition of a practical kind of knowledge through humility, i.e. a change in attitude and behaviour.[2]

In this chapter, I will venture that non-anthropocentrist environmental philosophers – as well as other scholars who deal with nature[3] – are using metaphors such as "conversation with nature" (whether they speak of animals or landscapes) to portray the human relationship with nature as evincing most of the aforementioned characteristics hitherto attributed to Socratic maieutics. For instance, Cheney (1989) and Haraway (1988) argue that, in order to start from a proper epistemological ground for understanding nature, it would be necessary to conceive of nature as a "conversational partner" and of our inquiry concerning nature as a conversation (Preston 2000: 230). According to them, only then could an ethical relationship with nature truly emerge. Moreover, Abram (1996, 2004) and Plumwood (2005) recently developed narratives that remain very close to this same idea. To discuss these, I will first take account of what environmental philosophers gain by the use of this metaphor in examining how the characteristics of traditional Socratic maieutics apply to their views. Secondly, I will point out what I believe to be important limitations to these views, that is to say, limitations that are made clearer by this very metaphor they use. From there, I will finally propose a reframing of the prominent anthropocentric/non-anthropocentric clash in environmental ethics.

---

2 Undoubtedly, Socratic maieutics is the object of various theories and could be presented in different ways. Many other characteristics could be added to the three I mention, but most theorists seem to agree at least on these. I am aware of the debates surrounding the Socratic method as regards the use of irony (which consists in showing an interlocutor that he does not know what he thought he knew) *and* maieutics (which consists in allowing for a knowledge held by an interlocutor to arise in himself even though he was unaware he had this knowledge). The two are indeed interwoven in the Platonic dialogues. Nevertheless, I hope the features I mention are representative enough of the "maieutics" concept to avoid such controversies, which belong to fascinating debates in Greek philosophy rather than to the topic I undertake in these pages.

3 This metaphor is used in very different ways and in many fields of research – not only in environmental philosophy – for example, by David L. Hull (philosophy of biology, Northwestern University) who describes one of the dimensions of the scientific relationship with nature, and by Reinhold Brinkmann (musicology, Harvard University) who stresses the parallels existing between Schönberg's music and Romantic paintings (Munch and Friedrich, namely). Cf. Hull (1988) and Brinkmann (1997).

What do Environmental Philosophers Gain in Using Such Metaphors?

An Ontological "Decentering"

> The language of *sunousia*, "being together", runs throughout Socrates' account of maieutics....*Sunousia* spans a range of meanings including conversation, association, community, and even sexual intercourse (Grazzini 2007: 138).[4]

The first feature put forth by the "conversation with nature" metaphor as it is used by many environmental philosophers is a shift in ontology. Through it, the question of Being is no longer asked from a subjective or objective perspective since the question rather becomes that of "being-together", of *sunousia*.

Since the mid-twentieth century, most environmental philosophers have aimed at "decentering the human subject from the commanding position it imagined it occupied in the operation of the world" (Andermatt Conley 1996: 5). For these thinkers, human subjects do not create meaning by way of their rationality in a world that would be devoid of such a dignified attribute if it were not for them. On the contrary, the point of this new way of thinking nature is "the very liquidation of a subject/object division ... [because] no full subject can exist where all is said to be nature" (Andermatt Conley 1996: 24). As such, the human relationship with nature has to be redefined, i.e. "decentered". These philosophers do not criticise the anthropomorphisation of nature, but rather, the anthropo*centrisation* of it.[5] The difference is important: anthropomorphism attributes human characteristics to nature or sees the latter under human traits, whereas anthropocentrism – in its most extreme form at least – thinks of humanity as the only phenomenon, the only being able to bring meaning and value into the world. Because of our philosophically and religiously based anthropocentrism, our relation to the non-human world has always been orientated one-sidedly: only humans were seen as playing an active part in their understanding of the world, a world which cannot but remain a passive reality, a variable that does not "operate" or "signify" but is rather acted upon in order to be thematised rationally. In science, for instance, one isolates a natural phenomenon in a laboratory to ensure all other natural inputs to

---

    4 Grazzini, B.J. 2007. Of psychic maieutics and dialogical bondage in Plato's Theaetetus, in *Philosophy in Dialogue: Plato's Many Devices*, edited by G.A. Scott. Evanston, IL: Northwestern University Press, 130–51. Reproduced with permission.

    5 Criticism of anthropocentrism does not strictly pertain to the twentieth century. Arthur Schopenhauer, for instance, was already outraged before the duties of Kantian ethics, since Kant excluded animals from its moral sphere and overlooked the "metaphysical fact" that the world is unified, instead of divided by way of a "kingdom of ends". One could also find other thinkers who advocated for such dissolution of radical anthropocentrism throughout our philosophical history (Lucretius, for instance), but non-anthropocentrism nonetheless became an actual trend of thought in the twentieth century, with environmental philosophy and ecology. Cf. Schopenhauer (1995 [1839]).

the phenomenon are inactive, which in turn allows for a proper objectification of the analysed phenomenon. However, reflecting on "Being" qua "togetherness" (or again, on what "is-together" instead of on what merely "is") implies the rejection of this kind of simplified objectification processes.

As such, many non-anthropocentrist environmental philosophers want to avoid seeing humans as being "above" or even "in the middle" of nature: for them, nature is neither something outside of us, reified, isolated, nor is it something *in* which we are. Their goal is roughly to understand our relationship with nature without the use of the concepts of inside and outside. A "conversation with nature", in that sense, should be defined as a perceptual relationship "of association, of community". Therefore the experience of a landscape, for example, should not be understood as happening from a human positioning in which a man becomes nature's distant spectator. Non-anthropocentrism aims at reminding us that in having such an embodied experience of nature, we are "becoming-with" the landscape, since we *are* nature. Hence, the modalities and consequences of this different ontology are to become the proper object of philosophical reflections in environmental thought. This different ontology is thus seen as a condition of possibility for our conversations with nature which, as we will see, include ethics as well.

To achieve this goal of "community" and "association" with nature however means that, like in the case of the landscape, we must let nature act on us in order to grasp the active part nature plays in our lives, with us, through our bodies. This partly explains the fascination of these philosophers for Heidegger's and Merleau-Ponty's phenomenological narratives concerning Being or nature. Haraway (1988), Abram (2004), and Plumwood (2005) argue for example that in avoiding the imposition of our rational categories on nature, another layer of meaning is brought forth: that of the perceptible, of the sensuous, of the fact that I do not differ from the rest of the world, that I am born *through* and live *with* it.

Therefore, users of the "conversation" metaphor often see non-anthropogenic nature, and landscapes in particular, as playing the role of a "midwife" that allows for such a deeper meaning to emerge in humans: a human being attentive to nature's aesthetic impact (from *aesthesis*, perception; cf. Brady 2003: 8) is, according to this view, like an interlocutor questioned by the Socratic maieute. I am neither saying here that non-anthropocentrist philosophers make use of the "maieutics" terminology nor that this analogy with maieutics is actually appropriate to describe our embodied relationship with nature. Clearly, the dialogical component of the Socratic relationship is not present. However, I want to point out that some environmental philosophers (especially in the ecofeminism and Deep Ecology trends) *do* depict nature as a Socratic midwife: "Haraway and Cheney both suggest that what is required is a conception of nature actively engaging the inquirer" (Preston 2000: 230). They, in short, entreat us to "acknowledge the agency of nature" (Preston 2000: 230), a formulation which also recalls Karen Warren's recent work.[6] Cheney (1989, 1998) even mentions that

---

6 In a conference entitled "The Earth as Our Home: An Ecofeminist Perspective" which was presented at the thirteenth annual meeting of the International Association

rocks can "teach us things", Preston remarks. We will later provide a critique of this view. But what Cheney means by this is that via his conversation with nature, the inquirer is endlessly reminded of both his ontological kinship with the world and his own condition as member of a species living among other species. He is most of all reminded that some kind of knowledge can arise in him only through the acceptance of his own passivity, of his own participation in a relationship that puts into question the theoretical knowledge he took for granted.

An Epistemological Shift

> Perhaps more significantly, [the maieute] shifts the terms of the discussion from what seems to be a statement of method to a description of the relations binding those who seek knowledge together. Crucially, this is not the substitution of one method or account of method for another; it is the articulation of the conditions in virtue of which philosophical inquiry can be pursued in conversation (Grazzini 2007: 138–9).

From this ontological repositioning comes an epistemological shift as well. As we saw, a "conversation with nature" institutes a particular kind of knowledge that comes out of an active/passive relationship with nature. But what Grazzini notes here with regard to maieutics as transforming the conditions of possibility of philosophical inquiry also applies to the "conversation with nature" paradigm. As in the Socratic dialogues, a non-anthropocentric relationship with nature does not pretend to provide us with an actual objective truth concerning the world. While Socratic maieutics aimed at a rebirth of the subject, non-anthropocentric conversations with the natural midwife should here be understood as the processes through which our individuality would become devoid of its pretensions to dominate or grasp nature one-sidedly. The particular kind of deeper knowledge said to be conveyed by non-anthropocentrism as well as by maieutics can be regarded as a form of *praxis*, a knowledge bound to be put in practice. Before we discuss this aspect further, let us remark that it is the very way in which we use rationality that is said to be modified by non-anthropocentrism: "human inquirers should adopt what [Cheney (1998: 265)] calls an "epistemological-ethical framework" that "understand[s] the known as "earth others" who are active moral and epistemic agents, co-participants in the construction ... of knowledge" (Preston 2000: 229).

According to this view, which is symptomatic of a whole trend of thought in environmental philosophy, the fact that rationality is a specific attribute (i.e. available only to humans) does not entail an ontological or moral privilege in nature. This faculty should help us understand the world better, but not separate us

---

of Environmental Philosophy (2009; Arlington, VA), Karen Warren provided a personal account of the eye-opening experience she had with dolphins – a meaningful experience that could only happen once she acknowledged their agency, according to her.

from it by way of an objectifying Cartesian *cogito* that could cut our human world from the natural one. In refusing anthropocentrism, philosophers subscribing to the non-anthropocentric paradigm argue that philosophy cannot return to *any form* of monadic idealism or rationalism. Like in aporetic maieutics, the point here is not so much to find an answer to a question posed rationally about nature, but to discover with the help of reason that one "does not know" all about nature and should then not act as if one did. That does not mean that rationality is impotent or that knowledge is impossible for non-anthropocentrist philosophers. But like in maieutics, the "midwife" – here, nature – should make us realise the limits of our rational powers.

A Shift in Attitudes – Against Hubris

According to most environmental thinkers advocating for a non-anthropocentric view of nature, these two aforementioned features – the ontological and epistemological shifts – lead to a third one, this time touching on our attitudes towards nature. And here again, the maieutics analogy is relevant to make it clearer.

Plato is famous for a particular epistemological stance that, I believe, many non-anthropocentrist environmental ethicists take on as an implicit premise of their argumentations: that of considering, like in *Theaetetus*, "wisdom (*sophia*) and knowledge (*epistêmê*) [as] the same thing" (Plato 1979: 145d–e). In *Protagoras*, the same idea is formulated anew in Socrates' famous tirade: "No one," he says, "who either knows or believes that there is another possible course of action, better than the one he is following, will ever continue on his present course" (Plato 1979: 358b–c). The point is for Socrates (or Plato, perhaps) that one cannot truly *know* the Good and refuse to act accordingly. If one does not act in accordance with something one knows to be good, it is because this person saw a greater good in doing something else, the ultimate point being that evil can only be caused by ignorance. In Plato's account of Socrates' philosophy, proper knowledge, attitudes and ethical behaviours are thus tied together. Likewise, a shift from ontological and epistemological claims towards moral and ethical ones is often effectuated in non-anthropocentric environmental theories. As an illustration of this, Val Plumwood's account of the properly described human relationship with nature can be seen as paradigmatic of non-anthropocentric environmental ethics:

> Humans *are* part of nature, in the sense that they are subject to ecological principles and have the same requirements for a healthy biosphere as other animals, but they, like other species, also have their own distinctive species identity and relationship to nature ... [Hence,] to define nature as a lack of human qualities, for example, is not only to deny continuity and overlap but to define it both as inferior and always in relation to the human as center (Plumwood 2005: 33, 48).

And the same is true of David Abram's assessment:

> Indeed, as soon as we acknowledge the active influence of other beings and elements, we find ourselves negotiating relationships with every aspect of the sensuous terrain that surrounds us. And reciprocity – the simple practice of mutual respect – becomes an imperative (Abram, 2004: 84).

Their accounts of the relationship humans as a species have with nature start with an ontological position. As mentioned in the first section of this essay, they first attempt to describe the true way in which human beings *are* in the world, that is, as *entities among others*. Most non-anthropocentrists do not want to refute that our relationship with nature evinces features that are peculiar to our species, but rather point out that other species also evince specific features they use in their relationship with the environment. Therefore, to see language and rationality as a necessary ground for the inclusion of an entity into our ethical reflection is, for them, simply wrong: it refers to an ill-defined analytic segregation of humans from nature. In a stance that is characteristic of non-anthropocentrism as a paradigm, both Plumwood (2005) and Abram (2004) claim above that acknowledging this ontological reality immediately *entails* not only an epistemological shift, but also and especially, *a moral repositioning*. Cheney (1998: 265) affirms this even more strongly when he speaks of the establishment of an "epistemological-ethical framework".

The fact that *all* species evince specific features in their relationship with their environment implies that none of these species or features should be seen as especially morally relevant – just in the way different human nations have different cultural mores that should not impede them from being seen as equally valuable from a universal ethical viewpoint. Plumwood (2005: 33) describes negatively the position contrary to hers – anthropocentrism, whatever its form – as manifesting a will to dominate the "more-than-human". In a similar move Abram (2004) asserts, positively this time, that knowing the active role nature plays on us through a sort of conversation implies that our relationship with it is a "reciprocal negotiation", which in turn brings forth a moral imperative to act respectfully towards nature. Thus, for both of them, the knowledge of our true place in nature sheds light on the type of behaviours one ought to adopt towards nature. In other words, understanding *being* as *being-together* directly entails an ethical proposition. Knowledge and wisdom are indeed, according to them, the same thing.

As I mentioned earlier, in Socratic maieutics, something similar is usually acknowledged: acquiring a true knowledge ought to bring a modification in attitudes and behaviours. However, such wisdom was not considered by Plato to come from the mere acquisition of a particular knowledge, but also from a feeling of humility before the recognition of a lack of knowledge. That is to say, one must first be humbled before one's own ignorance if one is to change one's own ways. In the *First Alcibiades*, for example, Socrates' interlocutor is bound to admit he does not know what "justice" is (Plato 1967: 117a–c), only to accept afterwards to become Socrates' disciple (Plato 1967: 135c–e) instead of aspiring at ruling the Athenians. Accordingly, non-anthropocentrist thinkers seem to share this early Platonic view that *humility*[7] is paramount if men are to modify their ways, but this time, towards nature.

What is gained for non-anthropocentrist environmental thinkers through the "conversation" metaphor is hence not only an analogy accounting for an epistemological or ontological theory concerned with a different positioning of humanity in the world. According to their view, having a "conversation with nature" means above all assenting to a mindset embedded in a particular view of morality, a mindset entailing that our species ought to be "drinking a full glass of humility … an act that would stand in stark contrast to other contemporary activities glaring with unexamined hubris" (Abram 2004: 90).

Theoretical and Practical Limitations of the Non-Anthropocentric Approach

The limitations of the "conversation" metaphor I wish to point out are theoretical and practical and they address what I believe to be a confused interpretation of our relationship with nature often presented in non-anthropocentric environmental philosophy. This confusion is however made clearer by the "maieutics" interpretation of "conversation" since through it, we can better distinguish between what specifically belongs to the inter-human domain of signification and what does not.

As I mentioned earlier, Platonic maieutics implied a *dialogical* relationship between two agents whereas our relationship with nature does not. Obviously, it is the major point separating the traditional use of maieutics from this peculiar one. This distinction applies to our relationship with nature: to understand the generative sense of the "conversation" metaphor, we must not go one step too far and trespass its interpretation as *sunousia*, "being-together", towards the more literal (and not generative) interpretation of "conversation" as "dialogue". This is, I believe, the mistake made by Cheney, Warren, Haraway, Abram and Plumwood as well as by other philosophers supporting non-anthropocentric versions of an environmental ethic: their will to depict nature as a kind of midwife that would allow for ontological-epistemological knowledge to arise in us should not orient

---

7 "Once the embarrassment is resolved about not having a real grasp of the concepts being discussed – once humility is established – then the serious task is undertaken to philosophically construct an adequate and acceptable rational foundation for the concept… until better knowledge is reached" (Angeles 1992: 283). In addition, it should be noted that the moral imperative of true knowledge is already imbedded in that claim, since "the Socratic assumption is that if that conclusion were completely rational it would conform to the good, beautiful, and true, since the good, beautiful, and true are truly rational" (Angeles 1992: 283).

us towards an understanding of nature qua *moral agent* even if they are right in reminding us that nature *is* active.

Contrarily to what has been said by Plumwood (2005) and Abram (1996, 2004), for instance, human language is not just a feature comparable to any other feature that can be found in nature. Communicative acts are indeed found elsewhere in nature, but no other communicative act allows for the moral reciprocity found in morally-coded societies, or even for mythical tale telling (cf. Heyd 2001). Language and rationality played and still play important roles in the foundations of what morality and ethics are. To speak of a "language of nature" that we could learn to hear and appreciate, like Cheney does[8] – and thanks to which we could dialogue *with* nature – is thus either to overlook the importance and complexity of a particularly inter-human modality of existence in the world or to dubiously overvalue the communicative abilities of certain natural entities. The consequence of this literal interpretation of "conversation with nature" brings confusion, in David Abram's work for example, between ecological reciprocity and moral reciprocity, as if one undoubtedly implied the other. We must hence avoid seeing this metaphor as proposing a dialogue with nature: it is not because we are natural beings like all the other animals that the moral and intentional dimensions of our specific way of signifying and understanding the world can immediately be superimposed on that of animals or landscapes.

One could reply that the act of "speaking to nature", however, has existed in animist societies, and the amount of publications in the environmental ethics field referring to animism or aboriginal spiritualism is impressive. But again, we must avoid falling into the trap which consists in arguing either that nature in general or some landscapes in particular respond *to us* through their transformations and cyclic events (catastrophes, seasons, etc.), or even that once upon a time, human beings were at peace with their natural environment because they were considering animals, trees and rivers as agents. If there is no answer coming to us from nature, it is because there is no intentionality coming from it (i.e. in Husserl's phenomenological sense) – not even in potentiality. One could again reply that global climate change and soil erosion are, for instance, natural responses to human activity. However these responses are not *answers* addressed to *me*, they are not value-laden in the ethical sense: the dog or the landscape cannot "ask why" nor apologise and ask for forgiveness – these are just some of the features that make the phenomenological complexity of the ethical phenomenon. The occurrence of signification (through our interpretations of the communicative abilities of animals, for example) is one thing, but the presence of a will to freely signify, ask or answer a question about what is just is another. And the distinction is crucial for ethics. Responsibility and justice – concepts lying at the core of the ethical relationship – do not simply and directly come out of reciprocal relationships and meaningful

---

8 Preston (2000) notes Cheney's depiction of rocks found beside a hiking trail as "companions, partners, some of them quite active, youthful, with funny stories to tell, perhaps, if we had listened with more care" (Cheney 1998: 276).

significations (Blais and Filion 2001). Our deepest non-instrumental relationships with non-human nature always were characterized mainly by *perception* and *sentience*, not by dialogue. This does not mean that animal or landscape ethics are impossible. It however means that signification and reciprocity do not imply morality by themselves. It moreover means that if nature can be addressed as a moral patient, it cannot be thought of as a moral agent (Jeangène Vilmer 2008).

More importantly and complementarily however, this common movement from a generative to a literal interpretation of the "conversation with nature" metaphor is one that explains some of the pitfalls of non-anthropocentric theories in general as they move away from ontological and epistemological claims towards *ethical* ones:

> The serious problem [with the many forms of non-anthropocentrism] is that even if the facts [concerning our relationship with nature] are clear, the values that accompany them remain ambiguous and subject to dispute ... Facts and values are difficult – if not impossible – to separate in human experience, and ... the relationship between them may be something subtler than the kind of logical deduction forbidden by Hume. On the other hand, ... Hume is basically right in his belief that facts and obligations are at least relatively independent of one another, so that the validity of a normative claim must be established, if at all, on grounds that are essentially different than those of the facts with which they are associated (Kirkman 2002: 130).

The "conversation" metaphor may help us understand anew many features of the human-nature relationship, and even of philosophical reflections at large; notably, the perceptual reciprocity with nature, the transformations in the methods of inquiry of true knowledge concerning nature and even some changes in our attitudes concerning it. There *is* a moral dimension to attitudes like hubris or humility which can be induced by a shift in our understanding of nature. But to speak, like Abram (2004) does, of a moral reciprocity existing between us and nature (he writes explicitly about salmons, rivers and trees) because of a "conversation with nature" is to confuse "being-together" with "dialogue": it is to confuse *the ecological fact* that human beings are part of a larger natural perceptual community with *the ethical obligation* according to which the members of this community ought to be responsible for each other. Statements about what is true of our place in nature or about the intrinsic "goodness" of a natural entity do not entail normative statements about how one should or ought to act towards nature (cf. Nolt 2006). A change in our personal attitudes towards nature (like humility, which can arise in us by way of new ecological facts or experiences of nature) does not *eo ipso* imply new duties, or even new responsibilities. There can be no substantive moral content to an ecological fact unless there is an underlying value theory that supports the derivation of an "ought" (i.e. a moral obligation) from that particular "is" (i.e. the ecological fact of our being-together with non-human nature). For instance, to know that the given state of an ecosystem is ecologically "good" (in a factual sense referring to the ecosystem's health, efficiency or sustainability) does not directly entail that the ecosystem has a moral value or that we have a moral obligation to protect it. In other words: even if *ontological* non-anthropocentrism was universally accepted, it does not follow that *moral* and *ethical* non-anthropocentrisms would or even should be.

Hence I want to suggest a theoretical reframing that I have not encountered explicitly in environmental ethics (even if it is implicit in many theories, I believe): that of distinguishing between ontological and moral non-anthropocentrism, as well as between ontological and moral anthropocentrism. Many meta-ethical descriptions of the non-anthropocentric paradigm do not attempt at distinguishing between the ontological and ethical or moral claims made by different theoretical propositions, a situation which sometimes brings about confusion and/or unnecessary discordance between thinkers. Yet, it is clear that for non-anthropocentrist philosophers, the different forms of moral anthropocentrism are to be avoided in environmental ethics precisely because they do not reflect the ontological reality in which they reside, i.e. a reality evinced mostly through phenomenological accounts of nature or, some would argue, of certain sciences like ecology. I want to suggest, however, that non-anthropocentrist environmental philosophers should take Kirkman's (2002) Humean critique more seriously and recognise the importance of deliberation and language for ethics. I do not wish to "define nature as a lack of human qualities", as Plumwood (2005: 48) says, but rather point out that it is *these* qualities, specific to human beings, that allow for ethics to happen in the first place (even if our perceptual relationship with nature has, of course, an important role to play in that story). To illustrate my point, here is an excerpt from a dialogue Singer had with his daughter taken from a discussion on J.M. Coetzee's (1999) work *The Lives of Animals*:

> [Naomi] – When you kill a bat, you take away everything that the bat has, its entire existence. Killing a human being can't do more than that.
>
> [Peter] – Yes it can. If I pour the rest of this soymilk down the sink, I've emptied the container; and if I do the same to that bottle of Kahlúa you and your friends are fond of drinking when we are out, I'd empty it too. But you'd care more about the loss of the Kahlúa. The value that is lost when something is emptied depends on what was there when it was full, and there is more to human existence than there is to bat existence (Singer 1999: 90).

Of course, it is well-known Singer would never mean that bats, dogs, primates or landscapes have no place in our ethical reflections. He rather means that differences in qualities or capabilities *do* matter when we think of the ethical values of the beings we encounter: often, the value of a loss does not depend on the essence of what is lost, but rather on the qualities that made the lost entity valuable for us. For example, a landscape x has hardly any value *qua* landscape, yet x should be assigned a value because of its important aesthetic, perceptual features, or because of its heritage or bequest value. As a matter of fact, if a genuine "conversation with nature" is possible for human beings, it is precisely because linguistic and deliberative abilities that exist in us allow us to acknowledge and reflect on the prominence of such perceptual encounters for the creation of value[9] – an argument which mirrors what Bryan G. Norton has put forth with his concept of "transformative value" (cf. Norton 1990). Even though a "conversation with nature" cannot happen literally and directly at a rational or dialogical level on account of the perceptual modality of our relationship with nature, a sublime, awesome or wonderful landscape certainly has the ability to provoke a change in one's own worldview, or at least in one's conception of what is valuable.

Thus, in distinguishing between ontological and moral discursive features of the anthropocentric/non-anthropocentric clash, one can reject anthropocentric ontology to accept the relevance of non-anthropocentric ontology while recognising the outstanding human capabilities for metaphysical and ethical reflections, *which should of course include nature nonetheless*. Non-anthropocentrist thinkers are indeed right in criticising idealism and rationalism when it comes to the divide they bring about between us as a species and the rest of nature. However, the fact that humans are the only full-blown moral agents in nature has to mean something for our ethical deliberations, even when thinking about the value of nature. For this reason, I would like to propose that moral non-anthropocentrism should be understood *as a genre* of moral anthropocentrism because *it unavoidably stems from the discussions happening within the scope of human perspectives*.

It does not mean that non-anthropocentric theories are unsound in terms of *content*: the inclusion of the non-anthropocentric discourse within the wider scope of a meta-ethical anthropocentrism does not make an attempt at portraying non-anthropocentrism as an inconsistent position. As it was shown with the landscape example, one should be aware of the significance of non-anthropocentric ontological discourses, and of the active part played by nature as regards *perception*, notably for the creation and support of human values (and preferences) both in terms of aesthetic appreciation *and* in terms of cultural, generational, and natural belongings. This brings back the ontological theme of *sunousia*, as it was argued earlier. However, no normative claims can be inferred directly from this shift in ontology and epistemology. By subsuming moral non-anthropocentrism to moral anthropocentrism, I mean that environmental philosophy cannot do away with the fact that ethics, as a deliberative process, is first an inter-human reality at

---

9 This argument recalls Katie McShane's neosentimentalism, for which "it is only by identifying the particular way in which something is valuable (i.e., the particular kind of value that it has [e.g. awesomeness, respectworthiness, admirability, etc.]) that we can know how we ought to behave toward and feel about it" (McShane 2007: 7). She then goes further on this topic than what I intend to do within these pages, but she is nonetheless probably right in suggesting that "the most promising type of evaluative standard [for sentiments] is a procedural one, i.e., one on which a sentiment is deemed merited so long as the claim that it is survives a specified procedure for subjecting it to critical scrutiny" (McShane 2007: 8).

least on a *formal* level even when it wants to understand humans solely as natural beings (or, perhaps, as beings that have a spiritual bond with nature qua creation, or *natura naturans*). However one conceives of humans or nature, one cannot omit the uncanny fact that being human is not the same as being another natural entity precisely because of the moral dimension of our discourses and actions. In sum, linguistic and deliberative capacities are both natural *and* human features – that is ontologically, since non-anthropocentrists are undeniably right in saying that humans are beings that belong to the natural realm. But moral and ethical reflections are mostly based on these capacities, which can only be found within us *specifically* – literally, within us as a species. Therefore, all moral and ethical reflections are *de facto* anthropocentric at a formal and meta-ethical level – especially since, furthermore, they are also part of a larger philosophical human tradition.[10] Theories such as Norton's (2003; cf. Afeissa 2008) already acknowledged this meta-ethical anthropocentric necessity for policy implementation without presenting it as such, and the same is true of Andrew Light's (2002, 2003, 2005) environmental pragmatism. I thus believe that the necessary reliance of non-anthropocentrism on forms of discourses that are by nature anthropocentric explains why it has to go through some sort of pragmatism (such as Light's methodological theory) to have a motivational impact[11] on a larger scale than what has been seen as of now.[12]

---

10   Without discussing it extensively, this claim could be supported even by theories in controversial "evolutionary ethics". These argue that morality and ethical systems are nothing but the results of an evolutionary adaptation. However, even if this is the case, the fact that we are subjected to evolution like any other species does not mean that all species should equally enter the scope of ethics, especially not if we are the only species that developed this particular deliberative process. Neither does it mean we have to leave some species out of it. Evolutionary theories in ethics as well as anthropology can, perhaps, help us understand where this ethical "capability" comes from, but not so much what it means from a normative perspective. In any case, even if evolutionary ethics is sometimes mentioned in environmental ethics to accentuate the fact the ethics could be nothing but a natural process (which could again bring us closer to nature), it is noteworthy that evolutionary ethics also brought about some of the worst ethical propositions to date, like that of Herbert Spencer's social Darwinism.

11   As McShane (2007: 14) writes: "If value just turns out to be some property that inheres in parts of the natural world, much like carbon or magnesium, independently of whether we're around or happen to notice it, then it doesn't automatically follow from this that the presence of value is something that we ought to care about, desire, or seek to promote. That is to say, even if we can show that this property is in fact part of the fabric of the universe, we still need an independent argument to show that it is something we have any reason to care about."

12   "Because most environmental ethicists are not interested in elucidating reasons for protection of the environment which stem from anthropocentric considerations, the field as a whole has unfortunately found itself unable to make a substantial impact on the actual debates over environmental policy commensurate with the contributions that have been made by other environmental advocates in the academy" (Light 2005: 344).

The will to know what is morally good and bad, even if this will remains frustrated or unfulfilled; the will to know what is valuable or not from a moral point of view: this will is exclusively human. Our deep-seated interest in "the Good" is, indeed, a human trait. Assigning a moral value to oneself, to a fellow human being, or to a non-anthropogenic environment it is thus, in itself, both an anthropogenic and an anthropocentric gesture. Therefore, even if the content of one's ethical valuations is non-anthropocentric (i.e. when one assigns an intrinsic value to a landscape, or adopts a form of eco-, bio-, or zoo-centrism as a viable ethical framework, for example), these valuations remain formally anthropocentric nonetheless – this has to be taken into consideration by environmental ethics as a field. Ethical responsibilities are felt in part because of one's perceptive abilities, but also because of the rational and linguistic meanings one shares with other human beings. Ethics does not arise solely from the aesthetic or empirical relationship one has with a natural entity. Because it relies on values, ethics is *also* a matter of discourse and metaphysics; it is first and foremost an inter-human realm.

Conclusion

Because the linguistic and dialogical components of ethics are tantamount to the possibility of ethics itself (just as perception and sensibility are), there is a lack of *de facto ethical* intertwining between human beings and nature despite the profound aesthetic intertwining that is indeed present. This is not the case because nature is described as "lacking human qualities", but because ethics needs a complex web of shared meanings to arise as a *social* reality. Now, this social reality asks for a potential moral reciprocity (at a political level), which is found in inter-human relationships only. Ethical relationships with landscapes or ecosystems fortunately and obviously exist, but they do so because they rely on perceptual *and* rational grounds that are mediated by considerations derived from concerns *of* human communities *for* these non-human entities. It does not mean that environmental concerns are less important in ethics, but rather that ethics is in itself a human process with a human purpose, from which follows that there is always, through ethical reflections, a "humanisation" process of whatever is considered as entering the scope of ethics. As Preston argues, the fact that we are embodied natural entities "ensures that the metaphor of nature speaking *through us* is much more readily supportable than the metaphor of nature speaking *to us*" (Preston 2000: 239). Therefore, we should not understand the "conversation with nature" metaphor literally, in spite of what has been argued by several non-anthropocentrist philosophers. For that reason, I proposed a reframing of theories in environmental ethics which, in dividing between a fourfold ontological/moral anthropocentrism/non-anthropocentrism, could help us interpret the "conversation with nature" metaphor in a generative way; i.e. in a way that allows for phenomenological accounts of our relationships with nature without purporting the literal sense of "dialogue with nature", which is effectively problematic because of the normative layer of meaning it adds to its phenomenological description. Moreover, acknowledging the part of anthropocentrism present in all environmental ethics theories has the advantage of giving us certain argumentative tools that are less likely to be used by hardcore non-anthropocentrist philosophers, like that of inquiring into the cultural/heritage value of non-anthropogenic environments for example (cf. Thompson 2000).

That being said, non-anthropocentric theories in environmental ethics are very important, albeit in a different manner than what has been often considered: even though we cannot avoid considering the world from a human point of view, non-anthropocentric theories still have to remind us that we "are-together" with nature. Moreover, they are very efficacious in reminding us that we should remain humble before what surrounds and transcends us. Other points of view than ours, as humans, *do* exist in nature and to be conscious of this fact is primordial for an accurate understanding of the world we share with other species and ecosystems.

Sadly, however, it takes more than a change in knowledge and general attitude to change the interactions humans have with nature. Ethics is still, and will remain, an inter-human concern.

References

Abram, D. 1996. *The Spell of the Sensuous: Perception and Language in a More-Than-Human World.* New York: Pantheon Books.

Abram, D. 2004. Reciprocity, in *Rethinking Nature: Essays in Environmental Philosophy*, edited by B.V. Foltz and R. Frodeman. Bloomington: Indiana University Press, 77–94.

Afeissa, H.-S. 2008. The Transformative Value of Ecological Pragmatism: An Introduction to the Work of Bryan G. Norton. *S.A.P.I.E.N.S.*, 1(1), 73–9.

Andermatt Conley, V. 1996. *Ecopolitics: The Environment in Poststructuralist Thought.* London: Routledge.

Angeles, P.A. 1992. Socratic Method, in *The HarperCollins Dictionary of Philosophy*. 2nd Edition. New York: HarperPerennial, 281–2.

Blais, F. and Filion, M. 2001. De l'éthique environnementale à l'écologie politique. *Philosophiques*, 28 (2), 255–80.

Brady, E. 2003. *Aesthetic of the Natural Environment.* Tuscaloosa: University of Alabama Press.

Brinkmann, R. 1997. Schoenberg the Contemporary: A View from Behind, in *Arnold Schoenberg and the Transformations of the Twentieth Century-Culture*, edited by J. Brand and C. Hailey. Berkeley: University of California Press, 196–215.

Cheney, J. 1989. Postmodern Environmental Ethics: Ethics as Bioregional Narratives. *Environmental Ethics*, 11, 117–34.

Cheney, J. 1998. Universal Consideration: An Epistemological Map of the Terrain. *Environmental Ethics*, 20, 265–77.

Coetzee, J.M. 1999. *The Lives of Animals*, edited by A. Gutmann. New Jersey: Princeton University Press.

Grazzini, B.J. 2007. Of Psychic Maieutics and Dialogical Bondage in Plato's Theaetetus, in *Philosophy in Dialogue: Plato's many Devices*, edited by G.A. Scott. Evanston, IL: Northwestern University Press, 130–51.

Haraway, D. 1988. Situated Knowledges: The Science Question in Feminism and the Privilege of Partial Perspective. *Feminist Studies*, 14 (3), 575–99.

Heyd, T. 2001. Aesthetic Appreciation and the Many Stories about Nature. *The British Journal of Aesthetics*, 41(2), 125–37.

Hull, D.L. 1988. *Science as Progress: An Evolutionary Account of the Social and Conceptual Development of Science.* Chicago: University of Chicago Press.

Jeangène Vilmer, J.-B. 2008. *Éthique animale.* Paris: Presses Universitaires de France.

Kirkman, R. 2002. *Skeptical Environmentalism: The Limits of Philosophy and Science.* Bloomington: University of Indiana Press.

Lakoff, G. and Johnson, M. 1999. *Philosophy in the Flesh: The Embodied Mind and its Challenge to Western Thought.* New York: Basic Books.

Light, A. 2002. Taking Environmental Ethics Public, in *Environmental Ethics: What Really Matters, What Really Works*, edited by D. Schmidtz and E. Willott. Oxford: Oxford University Press, 556–66.

Light, A. 2003. The Case for Practical Pluralism, in *Environmental Ethics: An Anthology*, edited by A. Light and H. Rolston III. Oxford: Blackwell, 229–45.

Light, A. 2005. What is a Pragmatic Philosophy? *Journal of Philosophical Research*, 30 (Special supplement), 341–56.

McShane, K. 2007. *Neosentimentalism and Environmental Ethics.* [Online]. Available at: http://www.environmentalphilosophy.org/ISEEIAEPpapers/2007/McShane.pdf [accessed: 18 November 2009].

Naess, A. 1966. *Communication and Argument: Elements of Applied Semantics*, translated by A. Hannay. Oslo and London: Universitetsforlaget and Allen & Unwin.

Nolt, J. 2006. The Move from *Good* to *Ought* in Environmental Ethics. *Environmental Ethics*, 28(4), 255–75.

Norton, B.G. 2003. Environmental Ethics and Weak Anthropocentrism, in *Environmental Ethics: An Anthology*, edited by A. Light and H. Rolston III. Oxford: Blackwell Publishers, 163–74.

Norton, B.G. 1990. *Why Preserve Natural Diversity?* New Jersey: Princeton University Press.

Plato. 1967. *Premiers dialogues*, translated by É. Chambry. Paris: Garnier–Flammarion.

Plato. 1979. *Plato's Theory of Knowledge: the* Theaetetus *and the* Sophist *of Plato*, edited by C.K. Ogden, translated with commentary by F.M. Cornford. London: Routledge & Kegan Paul.

Plumwood, V. 2005. Toward a Progressive Naturalism, in *Recognizing the Autonomy of Nature: Theory and Practice*, edited by T. Heyd. New York: Columbia University Press, 25–53.

Preston, C. 2000. Conversing with Nature in a Postmodern Epistemological Framework. *Environmental Ethics*, 22(3), 227–40.

Schön, D.A. 1981. Generative Metaphor: a Perspective on Problem-Setting in Social Policy, in *Metaphor and Thought*, edited by A. Ortony. Cambridge: Cambridge University Press, 254–83.

Schopenhauer, A. 1995 [1839]. *On the Basis of Morality*, translated by E.F.J. Payne. Cambridge: Hackett Publishing Company.

Singer, P. 1993. *Practical Ethics*. Cambridge: Cambridge University Press.

Singer, P. 1999. Reflections, in J. M. Coetzee's *The Lives of Animals*, edited by A. Gutmann. New Jersey: Princeton University Press, 85–91.

Thompson, J. 2000. Environment as Cultural Heritage. *Environmental Ethics*, 22(3), 241–58.

Chapter 4
Landscape as Conversation

Edda R.H. Waage

Introduction

> The earth in all of its natural glory is an independent reality into which we are born and with which we engage in a complex relationship (Skúlason 2005: 27).

In examining the relationship between humans and nature, "landscape" has been a key concept for numerous scholars and has prompted a variety of theorisations. The concept however does not belong to any single discipline, nor to academia for that matter, for landscape is a culturally embedded concept, used by ordinary people in their everyday life. As culturally embedded, the conceptualisation of landscape can vary between linguistic communities (see Coeterier 1996, Gehring and Kohsaka 2007, Shaw and Oldfield 2007). Various disciplines may also define landscape in different ways, whether within linguistic communities or across them. Landscape in this sense amounts to theory; theory however, while offering an explanation of the world we live in, inevitably connotes a reduction of the world, purposefully constructed. Furthermore, a demarcation between disciplines does not guarantee a univocal conceptualisation of landscape. In geography alone different conceptualisations of landscape have been produced that for example depict landscape either as objective reality (e.g. Sauer 1996 [1925]), perceptional reality (e.g. Granö 1997 [1929]), political arena (e.g. Mitchell 1996), culturally defined territory (e.g. Olwig 2002), or a social construction (e.g. Cosgrove 1984), to mention only a few. Indeed there is a wide variety.

The aim of this chapter is to delve into some ontological aspects of the Icelandic landscape concept. For this purpose landscape is theorised as a relational space, constituted by humans and nature, and brought to existence by way of human perception. Lately the idea of "conversation with landscape" has emerged as a way of portraying human relations to the world, both in landscape architecture (see Spirn 1998), and art (see Solnit 2003). Conversation in these terms represents communication between people and landscape, and emphasises somewhat the need to learn, listen to, and respond to the "language of landscape". Arguably however, conversing "with" landscape may suggest landscape to be an independent reality apart from humans. The idea of conversation therefore seems not to facilitate an ontological examination of landscape as a concept. Furthermore, the way landscape is theorised here – as a relation between humans and nature – a conversation "with" landscape may be regarded as a contradiction in terms. Still, the idea of "conversation" with relevance to "landscape" is a challenging thought, which may shed a new and different light on the human-nature relation that is inherent in the landscape concept.

Generally, the word conversation refers to talk between two or more people who express and share their thoughts, feelings and ideas; ask and answer questions; and/or exchange information. For obvious reasons the term can hardly be adopted literally to describe a human-nature relationship, for nature is not a being as such in possession of mind and body that unmistakably are required for such utterly human interaction. Metaphorically however, it offers some delightful and democratic ways for contemplation of the human-nature relationship: it is possible to picture conversation as a performative relation (cf. Thrift and Dewsbury 2000) between two participants; a relation that exists only by means of the two, and only as long as they are both committed to forming the relation. The conversation does thus not exist materially but relationally, and it ceases to exist with the absence of one of the participants. However, the actual conversation can be recorded and replayed, or transcribed, and thus a representation of the conversation is feasible. Additionally, the conversation may be considered as a creative process, as the interchange of thoughts, feelings, and ideas, brought to the conversation by the two participants, can generate a new perspective; a new meaning of the topic under discussion. In these terms then, landscape can be conceived of "as" a conversation, rather than an independent reality that is conversed "with". This perspective implies that whoever speaks of landscape is essentially a constituent of the topic. This would include the author of this chapter. Let me therefore to start at the beginning.

I am Icelandic; I was born and raised in downtown Reykjavík. In my childhood I used to travel with my family around Iceland during the summertime, until the age of eight that is. From then on till I was thirteen I spent the summers on a farm in the countryside where I participated in the everyday life of the family who lived there. My mother tongue is Icelandic and that was the only language I knew until the age of ten. I am not sure when I first learned the word *landslag*, which is the Icelandic word for "landscape". But I am convinced it must have been early in my childhood, as I have no recollections at all of learning the word. In fact it feels as if it has always been a part of my vocabulary, clear and perspicuous. And I do remember myself as a child admiring the *landslag* of Hjaltadalur,[1] thinking that surely there was no other place in the world where the shape of the mountains had reached such perfection and beauty. Thus, for as long as I remember I have used the word *landslag* as an expression to describe some of my experiences of the world. And in this regard I believe I am no exception; in retrospect I can honestly say that never did the use of the word raise any questions of what was being referred to. Only as a PhD student did I first problematise the meaning of *landslag* as a concept.

The beginning of my problematisation started with my reading of those authors who have been most influential within geography. Although inspired by

---

1   Hjaltadalur is a valley in the region of Skagafjörður in North-Iceland.

their texts and eager to make use of them in my research, none of the various landscape ideas, presented by these authors, resonated with my understanding of *landslag* (painfully undefined though at the time). To begin with I was unaware of this inconsistency, although it proved to be a hindrance at first in my research, of which I was very much aware. My project focused on nature conservation in Iceland with reference to landscape, and this entailed interviews conducted in Icelandic with Icelanders. It took me some time to realise that probably I was taking for granted that the two words: "landscape" and "*landslag*", could be used interchangeably, failing to note the conceptual differences that may be present in the idea of landscape between linguistic communities, as mentioned above. The interviews yielded some interesting results however, which has prompted me to explore the Icelandic landscape concept in more detail.

The analysis here presented is partly based on two case studies that deal with the conceptualisation of landscape in Icelandic context. The first of these is the case study mentioned above, the focal point of which was the introduction of landscape as a premise for selecting conservation areas in Iceland's first Nature Conservation Strategy. This study revealed a very clear connection between landscape and experience of beauty (see Waage and Benediktsson 2010). The second is a case study on the Icelandic landscape concept as it appears in the "Sagas of Icelanders", in which the aesthetic component of the concept was traced back to the fourteenth century and discussed in comparison with the English landscape concept. From these studies I argue that *landslag* is the name given to an aesthetic relation between humans and the inanimate natural world.

Much of literature on the landscape concept, within geography and related fields, mentions its ambiguity and complexity: dissimilar discourses are provoked by its application to the extent that sometimes it may be more relevant to speak of different landscape concepts (Jones 2006). As mentioned in the beginning of this introduction the diverse conceptualisations of landscape may be divided into culturally embedded concepts on one hand, and theoretically defined concepts on the other. Perhaps it may be helpful to understand the diverse landscape concepts as different sets, each defined by its characteristics. But despite the variety, many of the sets intersect with each other to a greater or lesser extent where the same characteristics are shared; some may even be regarded as subsets within others. What seem to be two connecting themes are that landscape connotes: a) relation between humans and nature, and b) a holistic point of view. For example, landscape is frequently described as the total sum of characteristics, both natural and cultural, in a given area. What differs is the nature of the relation, how and where it is manifested, and what is included in the whole. For instance, according to some conceptualisations, landscape is perceptional, thus turning the onlooker into an inseparable part of the landscape. Some even go so far as to argue that landscape is first and foremost a construct of the mind. Then there are other conceptualisations that represent landscape as a place where human-nature interactions in the past can be witnessed, thus ignoring the onlooker of the landscape in the present. Landscape is thus not homogeneous as a concept, but varies between cultures in more than one way, and this must be acknowledged and kept in mind when it comes to implementing the concept in concrete projects, such as planning and conservation. For despite the clarity of landscape theories and definitions that might be expected within any given discipline, landscape conservation does not occur in a cultural void: the culturally embedded meaning of landscape may necessarily co-constitute the scientific performance in landscape conservation, despite efforts being made to the contrary (Waage and Benediktsson 2010), and may therefore always be present, even when theoretical conceptualisations of landscape are being employed. The focus of this chapter then is on the culturally embedded meaning of the Icelandic landscape concept.

Landscape as a Relational Space in the World of Perception

For the purpose of the argumentation I partly rely on some strands of actor-network theory (ANT), which Bruno Latour, one of its originators, has described as a "theory of the space or fluids circulating in a non-modern situation" (Latour 1999a: 22). The first strand to mention relates to the "non-modern" situation, which implies a rejection of dualism between nature and society. In regard to this, Latour (1993) has described how modernity saw a complete separation between the natural world and the social world, and how this separation paradoxically made possible the creation of "hybrids" of nature and culture that however fitted neither of the categories. Paradoxically, because conceiving of nature and society as two different ontological zones with no middle ground forbids us to conceive of hybrids, and yet it is the very separation that allows for their creation and proliferation. The separation thus both denies and permits at once the existence of hybrids. Acknowledging the hybrids is therefore to call modernity into question, because it undermines the very belief that nature and society are necessarily separated. In a non-modern world this dualism is therefore rejected. Nature and society still exist of course and are present in their common productions, but they are not separable.

The second strand of ANT that is of importance for my argumentation concerns the conception of networks, which correspond to the hybrids of nature and culture mentioned above. As the name suggests the network is one of the primary tenets of ANT. An important notion of the theory is that it sees the entities enrolled in the network both to be: social and natural, human and non-human, subjects and objects. As a result of interrelations within the network the entities take their form and acquire their attributes. It is thus in, by, and through the relations between these entities that they achieve their form; the relations between the entities are performative (Law 1999). The co-construction of heterogeneous entities, and their performative relations, suggests uncertainty and reversibility, for "when a phenomenon "definitely" exists that does not mean that it exists forever, or independently of all practice and discipline, but that it has been entrenched" in a network (Latour 1999b: 155–6).

Finally, the third strand from ANT that is significant for the context presented here concerns its spatial conception. The conventional conceptualisation describes space as three-dimensional, through which objects can be transported. ANT on the other hand proposes space to be relational, as emerging from within the hybrid networks. Its shape and form is thus determined by the networks. In other words: networks make space (Law 1999, Murdoch 2006).

Back to the topic of this chapter then: One of the most common characteristics of the landscape concept is that it represents a relation between humans and nature. By means of ANT it is possible to conceive of this relation as a hybrid network of heterogeneous entities, which humans and nature certainly are. The relation between humans and nature is performative in the sense that it exists only by means of the two, and at the same time through their relation the two acquire the form they have within the network. And thus from within this hybrid network of humans and nature emerges a relational space; a space called landscape. Humans and nature can therefore not be separated in terms of landscape, but neither do they remain the same once they co-constitute the network. For example, a mountain and a landscape is not one and the same thing, but when gazed at by a human, the mountain becomes part of a landscape. It can thus be argued that the mountain and the human co-constitute the landscape. Consequently there is no landscape without humans, as there is no landscape without nature. To sum this up: landscape can be conceived of as a relational space; a space that is determined by the performative relations of humans and nature in a hybrid network.

According to John Law (1999: 4), ANT "may be understood as a semiotics of materiality. It takes the semiotic insight, that of the relationality of entities, the notion that they are produced in relation, and applies this ruthlessly to all materials – and not simply those that are linguistic". Taking this step and applying the semiotic insight of the human-nature relationship to a network that is manifested in its materiality might therefore be useful to seek understanding of the emergence and progression of landscapes conceived of differently than done here. This chapter however aims at examining the aesthetic relationship humans have with nature in terms of landscape, and is based on the assumption that beauty is neither inherent in the objects" qualities nor in the mind of the subjects, but that it is integrated with their relation (see Brady 2003). I will therefore suffice with ANT's semiotic insight, for the landscape under discussion is not to be found in the material world, but in the "world of perception".

This last notion brings me to the final part of my argumentation, which is meant to deepen its relational aspect, drawing upon the philosophy of Maurice Merleau-Ponty. The world of perception is "the world which is revealed to us by our senses and in everyday life" (Merleau-Ponty 2004 [1948]: 31) and yet this world is hidden to us beneath sediments of knowledge and social living. Critical of the Cartesian dualism, which entails a separation between mind and body, Merleau-Ponty called attention to how rationalism and scientific thought imposed on us the idea that we are deceived by our senses, that the real world lies behind our sensory illusions, and that it can only be revealed to us by our intellect. Opposing this, he argued that scientific explanations and theories constitute knowledge by approximation, and that scientific research is always determined by the observer and his perception of the world. Thus Merleau-Ponty highlighted and opposed to at the same time what rationalism had implied, although such reasoning never was explicated, that humans were first and foremost thinking subjects; disembodied and without spatial position. And so he argued on the contrary, that the observer can not be abstracted from a given situation: a pure intellect does not exist, for "rather than a mind *and* a body, man is a mind *with* a body, a being who can only get to the truth of things because its body is, as it were, embedded in those things" (Merleau-Ponty 2004 [1948]: 43, italics original). The space in which we humans are situated is only accessible to us through our sense organs, thus the body becomes essential for relating to the world, and consequently our perspective is always limited to our bodily position. As embodied subjects we inhabit the world together with other subjects, and things inanimated. What distinguishes us as subjects from things "in the world" (Merleau-Ponty 2002 [1945]) is that we are actively involved with other subjects and objects of the world, by means of our senses. Their qualities as we perceive them are human definitions, limited by our sense organs, and thus the things of the world are also combinations of mind and body (Merleau-Ponty 2004 [1948]). In the world of perception it is therefore impossible to separate things from their way of appearing; the subject and the world are inseparable. To explore the world of perception is to explore how we relate to the things and subjects that surround us in the world. To do so we need to focus on the lived and immediate experience.

Let us now turn back to landscape again. While ANT enables a conception of landscape as a relational space that is determined by the performative relation of humans and nature in a hybrid network, Merleau-Ponty's philosophy offers a deeper understanding of the emergence of this relation. It explains how the human-nature relation is brought into existence by means of the human's sense organs, and how the space that is thus created is at the same time limited by the bodily position of humans in the world. Landscape thus connotes a delimited and relative perspective, for each and every human is bound up with its bodily position in the world. And yet it is universal for each and every human, in theory at least, has equal possibility of the same bodily position (cf. Kant's (2000 [1790]) idea on "subjectively universal validity", see also Brady's (2003) idea of "intersubjective validity"). Landscape, in this line of reasoning, also connotes a lived experience of the world in the present; it is therefore transitory. And yet it is eternal as long as this kind of human-nature relation emerges in the world.

This last notion begs the question of what is the kind of this relation I have depicted so far, for not all relation humans have with nature by means of their sense organs, can be conceived of as this relational space called landscape. Evidently there is something about the nature of these relations that defines whether we call it landscape or not. And presumably this "something" cannot be reduced to a single theory, for this is where cultural differences enter the stage. In different societies there are different relations to nature that depend of course on nature as it were, but also on the culture; the environmental circumstances people cope with in their everyday life and their cultural values. Regarding the Icelandic landscape concept a reference to aesthetic appreciation has already been made which hints at the conclusion; this however needs to be discussed more clearly. In the next section I will introduce the Icelandic landscape concept and highlight some of its arguably important aspects. In the subsequent section I draw some conclusions in terms of the theoretical perspective presented above in order to provide an understanding of the human-nature relation that is inherent in *landslag* and its embedded meaning.

The Icelandic Landscape Concept

The lexical entry for *landslag* is "total appearance of an area of land, the form of nature in a particular place"[2] (Árnason 2007: landslag, my translation). What is noticeable first is the emphasis on its visual quality through "appearance", and morphological quality through "the form of nature". A lexical definition however only portrays part of the picture. How the word is being put to use can also help to illuminate its meaning. According to a dictionary of the use of Icelandic, *landslag* is most often accompanied by qualifying adjectives such as: "beautiful, scenic, impressive, magnificent, effective, spectacular, majestic, expressive, grand, tremendous, unimpressive, monotonous, bland, insignificant"[3] (Jónsson 1994: landslag, my translation). *Landslag* is thus most often associated with an aesthetic expression or experience. An aesthetic quality may therefore arguably also be regarded as an integral element of the concept, just as its visual and morphological qualities.

A discourse analysis of interviews conducted with experts in nature conservation in Iceland provides a comparable outcome, which also contributes to a deeper understanding, but in their conceptualisation of landscape a tension of the same qualities emerged (see Waage and Benediktsson 2010). Physical qualities of land, i.e. different combinations of natural features, such as geological formations, vegetation, and hydrology, featured in the interviews when referring to landscape. At times these corresponded to a physical world from which humans were excluded. Many of the interviewees however, while recognising such reasoning, disagreed with it, as landscape in these terms merely involves objects that are already covered by the natural sciences. In their mind, landscape was something much more than that. Hence, visual qualities of land were prominent as well. Then the same physical qualities were involved, not their materiality however, but their interplay seen from an actual viewpoint. Their forms, outlines, textures, and colours were thus at the forefront. It may be argued that conceiving of landscape

---

2   In Icelandic: Heildarútlit landsvæðis, form náttúru á tilteknum stað.

3   In Icelandic: Fallegt, fagurt, tilkomumikið, mikilfenglegt, áhrifamikið, stórbrotið, tignarlegt, svipmikið, stórgert, hrikalegt, tilkomulítið, tilbreytingarlaust, sviplítið, lítilfjörlegt.

in these terms implies that landscape is brought into existence through the human gaze. The analysis furthermore revealed that aesthetic judgment was strongly embedded in the landscape concept, in fact it seemed that in the experts' mind landscape and the experience of beauty were so tightly connected that they could not be taken apart; landscape was thus repeatedly equated with beauty. At times these aesthetic judgments were explained by affects and emotions resulting from previous landscape experiences, but the interviewees identified as well aesthetic judgments that seemed neither to result from personal experience nor knowledge, but yet were general. This subjective character of the landscape concept had provoked deep contemplation among some of the interviewees: For one thing, they recognised that the Icelandic landscape concept could not be treated by objective methods alone, and for another, they were puzzled by the fact that a non-cognitive aesthetic judgement, that supposedly is subjective could yet be general (for further discussion see Waage and Benediktsson 2010). The analysis thus demonstrated that among the interviewees, the morphological, visual, and aesthetic qualities of land, despite being conflicting, arguably were all interwoven in their conceptualisation of *landslag*.

The visual and aesthetic qualities of *landslag* bring to mind its English counterpart "landscape", which shares the same characteristics. These mutual qualities however do not necessarily indicate a shared meaning, as a brief historical comparison of the two concepts will elucidate. Indeed they have different connotations.

Whatever the meaning "landscape" may have in all the different landscape theories that have been developed within the English language, the concept most commonly refers to scenery; either an area of land seen from a particular point of view and often considered in terms of its aesthetic appeal, or a pictorial representation thereof – a landscape painting (Wylie 2007). This scenic notion of landscape inherent in its popular use has been of interest to some geographers in the last thirty years. Denis Cosgrove (1984, 1985) has accounted for this understanding of landscape, tracing it back to Florence in Italy in the fifteenth and sixteenth century, as a dimension of European elite consciousness. At this particular time and place in history emerged an artistic technique for representing the world in a supposedly realistic and truthful way, namely the linear perspective. In Britain, this artistic perspective of landscape was somewhat superimposed on natural vista, not least by the educated classes, and nature was in that way turned into a scenic resource (cf. Olwig 2002). The emergence of landscape as a term, or an idea, is thus associated with arts. Cosgrove's argument is that the landscape idea in European context, rather than representing the visible land as such, represents a "way of seeing", a socially constructed behaviour that is informed by arts. Cosgrove's intention was to clarify certain assumptions that he believed to be embedded in the landscape concept, which had to do with the relationship between humans and their environment. His claim was that representing a three-dimensional space on a two-dimensional surface, directs the external world towards the onlooker, which is situated outside that space. It thus gives the eye a mastery over space. Landscape becomes appropriated by a distanced observer and offers the illusion of order and control, where evidence of conflicts between social classes is suppressed. Landscape as a "way of seeing" thus arguably increases the gap between humans and nature.

Turning back to the Icelandic landscape concept, the word *landslag* is deeply rooted in the Icelandic language. The archaic spelling *landsleg* is found in a few parchment manuscripts of Icelandic literature, some of which were written in the early fourteenth century. Apparently the meaning of the word has not changed discernibly since medieval times, although its lexical entries have become more specific. In a dictionary of Old Icelandic, *landslag* has been defined as: "the nature, "lie" of a country" (Cleasby and Vigfusson 1975 [1874]: *landslag*); a rather wide definition as "lie" indicates features or characteristics of an area. Arguably it refers to spatial arrangement and thus connotes a holistic point of view. A discourse analysis focusing on *landslag* as a concept in the "Sagas of Icelanders" has helped to illuminate its conception in medieval times and revealed that the visual, morphological and aesthetic were already intertwined and embedded in the concept at the turn of the fourteenth century.

The "Saga of Erik the Red" holds a good example of the interrelations between these qualities. The saga narrates the settlement of Erik the Red in Greenland and the discovery of new lands in the west. It thus describes Norse settlement on the east coast of North America at some time around the year 1000. Two parchment manuscripts of this particular saga have been preserved, one that dates back to the first decade of the fourteenth century, and another that dates back to the early fifteenth century. Both are copies of an older manuscript that has perished (Jansson 1945). What makes this example intriguing is that the two manuscripts differ strikingly in their wording. While the fifteenth century manuscript is believed to be closer to the original text, the fourteenth century manuscript contains text that presumably is a paraphrase of the original. Thus coincidentally a comparison of the two manuscripts helps to elucidate the conceptual meaning of some words that are used in the text. At one point in the narrative the fifteenth century manuscript says (in my literal translation):

> They headed up the fjord and called it Straumsfjördr and carried the cargo from the ships and prepared for staying. They had with them all kinds of livestock and searched for resources from the land. *There were mountains and beautiful to look around.* They paid no attention to things other than exploring the land. There the grass grew tall (Eiríks saga rauða 1985, 424-425, italics added).[4]

The fourteenth century manuscript on the other hand says:

---

4 "Þeir heldu inn með firðinum ok kölluðu hann Straumsfjörð ok báru farminn af skipunum ok bjöggusk þar um. Þeir höfðu með sér alls konar fénað ok leituðu sér þar landsnytja. Fjöll voru þar, ok fagrt var þar um at litask. Þeir gáðu einskis nema at kanna landit. Þar váru grös mikil."

They called it Straumfjördr. They carried the cargo from their ships and prepared for staying. They had with them all kinds of livestock. There was beautiful *landsleg*. They paid attention to nothing other than exploring the land (Eiríks saga rauða 1935, 224, italics added).[5]

If only the fourteenth century manuscript had been preserved, we would not know what was being referred to explicitly with the word *landsleg*. We could assume that it referred to some natural features in this particular fjord and that they provoked an aesthetic response. The fifteenth century manuscript thus illuminates the meaning of the word. Comparing these two sentences it becomes obvious that shortly after 1300 the scriber of the Saga of Erik the Red regarded the word *landsleg* to be a concise explanation when referring to mountains that were beautiful to look at.

From the above it becomes evident that there are cultural differences between the two concepts. They have different origins, so while the popular usage of the English "landscape" is associated with the emergence of artistic techniques in the fifteenth and sixteenth century, and was later superimposed on natural scenery, the Icelandic *landsleg* can, in its current meaning with reference to natural features, be traced back to the early fourteenth century. It is also relevant for the discussion that landscape painting was unknown in Iceland until the turn of the twentieth century. The cultural differences of the two concepts may also be explained by differences in social order. While the English concept "landscape" emerged amongst members of the European elite, who lived in a developed society on land that had been populated for centuries, the Icelandic *landslag* appears in a society of subsistence farmers and seafarers, living in a country that had only recently been settled.

They way Cosgrove describes the English landscape concept, it is marked by modernity and the gap that was created between humans and nature by the Cartesian move. The Icelandic landscape concept on the other hand can be traced in its current meaning back to pre-modern times when humans and nature were not yet performed as opposites. It is too early to state whether *landslag* can indeed be regarded as a pre-modern concept that has survived modernity and thus connotes a human-nature relation that supposedly is not embedded in its English counterpart. Landscape research in Iceland is in its infancy and hopefully arguments for such reasoning may be developed later. But from the historical comparison above, it may yet be argued that the aesthetic quality of *landslag* on the one hand, and "landscape" on the other have different origins.

---

5 "Þeir kölluðu þar Straumfjörð. Þeir báru þar farm af skipum sínum ok bjuggusk þar um. Þeir höfðu með sér alls konar fénað. Þar var fagrt landsleg; þeir gáðu einskis, útan at kanna landit."

The Culturally Embedded Meaning of *Landslag*

I have argued here that landscape can be conceived of as a relational space that is determined by the performative relation of humans and nature in a hybrid network. A space that is brought to existence by means of the human sense organs and is consequently always bound up with the bodily position of humans in the world. This entails that landscape is delimited, relative and transitory, and can yet be universal and eternal. However, not all relations humans have with nature are referred to as landscape, what defines a relation as landscape is culturally dependent. Having examined some essential features of the Icelandic landscape concept, it is time to derive a conclusion regarding the character of this human-nature relation and the meaning that is embedded in the concept.

Whether looking up entries in dictionaries, analysing the discourse of experts in nature conservation, or examining the old texts of the Sagas of Icelanders, it becomes obvious that *landslag* is essentially visual. Arguably therefore, of all the human sense organs, it is the eye that is most significant for giving birth to this relational space. This is not to say that other sensory perceptions do not enhance the *landslag* experience, e.g. hearing the noise of a tumbling waterfall; or the sound of silence in the highlands; smelling freshly mown grass; and so on. Although these perceptions may be integral to our experiences they are not necessary constituents for defining *landslag*. Regarding nature's role in this hybrid relation, its morphological quality is clearly of great significance; indeed mountains are most often central to *landslag*. Other visual qualities of nature, such as texture or colour, do enhance the *landslag* experience; needless to say all forms come in different colours and textures, which may produce different sentiments, and affects, that are integral to our experience. And yet, despite being important for describing a particular *landslag*, colours and textures are not necessary constituents for defining the concept.

The weight of mountains in the conceptualisation of *landslag* may be explained by the fact that Iceland is a volcanic island, and natural scenery with no mountain is indeed hard to come by. It is not unlikely that this natural setting may have influenced the being-in-the-world of Icelanders. This emotional and symbolic expression of Salka Valka, one of Halldór Laxness great protagonists, may be regarded a case in point: "The shadow of some mountain always falls on our village" (Laxness 1932: 149). The quasi-omnipresence of mountains in Iceland also explains why in the Icelandic language it is possible to state that in some places "there is no *landslag*". Such a statement would refer to areas where land is relatively flat, e.g. Denmark.[6] An Icelander might also claim to "see no *landslag*" where the view is blocked, for example by forest, as in Finland. From the above, one might jump to the conclusion that whenever an Icelander looks at a mountain

---

6 Once, while staying in Denmark the artist Pétur Gautur was asked why he painted still lifes. His reply was: "Well, I can't paint landscape for there is no landscape here in Denmark. Therefore I have to make use of things that are near to me" (Svavarsson 1997).

s/he would call it *landslag*. This however is not the case, even though s/he would probably find it difficult to argue on the contrary when confronted with such a statement. It is when this relation, between the human (through his/her sight) and nature (its morphological quality in particular), produces an aesthetic response that is felt within the human, that s/he refers to it as *landslag*. And just as the visual and morphological qualities are necessary constituents for defining this experience as *landslag*, so is the aesthetic aspect. I therefore argue that *landslag* is the name given to an aesthetic relation between humans and the inanimate nature; a relation that is brought to existence by way of ocular perception of the world, and that centres upon nature's morphological quality.

Now, how can the metaphor of landscape as conversation, as delineated in the introduction of this chapter, enhance our understanding of this relational space called landscape? Well, to begin with it underpins what ANT already suggests, which is the collective contribution of humans and nature to landscape. The advantage of conversation over ANT in this regard, however, is the sense of democracy embedded in the concept of conversation; a sense of respect that so very much is needed in our conduct towards nature. The conversation metaphor also emphasises that landscape is always in the making; landscape is an ongoing conversation between humans and nature, but not a conversation that was had at some time in the past and has come to an end. That would rather refer to a representation of landscape. The creative factor of the conversation metaphor suggests that a new meaning is created through the interaction of humans and nature. In the case of *landslag* it is its aesthetic quality, but the conversational metaphor furthermore emphasises the impermanence and fragility of this aesthetic quality (and hence of *landslag*). It therefore implies that *landslag* is something that is very precious. In short, what the conversation metaphor brings to landscape is a moral aspect of this human-nature relation.

Acknowledgements

During the writing of this chapter I received comments and support from a few individuals to whom I am most grateful: Karl Benediktsson, Katrín Anna Lund, Gunhild Setten, Gunnþóra Ólafsdóttir and Heiðdís Jónsdóttir. The Icelandic Research Fund for Graduate Students (Rannís), the University of Iceland, and the Margrét Björgólfsdóttir Memorial Fund, provided financial support for the research.

References

Árnason, M. (ed.). 2007. *Íslensk orðabók* [Icelandic Dictionary]. 4th Edition. Reykjavík: Edda.

Brady, E. 2003. *Aesthetics of the Natural Environment*. Edinburgh: Edinburgh University Press.
Cleasby, R. and Vigfusson, G. 1975 [1874]. *An Icelandic–English Dictionary*. 2nd Edition. Oxford: Clarendon Press.
Coeterier, J.F. 1996. Dominant Attributes in the Perception and Evaluation of the Dutch Landscape. *Landscape and Urban Planning*, 34, 27–44.
Cosgrove, D.E. 1984. *Social Formation and Symbolic Landscape*. Wisconsin: University of Wisconsin Press.
Cosgrove, D.E. 1985. Prospect, Perspective and the Evolution of the Landscape Idea. *Transactions of the Institute of British Geographers*, 10(1), 45–62.
Eiríks saga rauða – Texti Skálholtsbókar AM 557 4to [The Saga of Eric the Red, text from Skálholtsbók manuscript AM 557 4to] 1985. In Viðauki við íslenzk fornrit, IV bindi (pp. 401–434), edited by Ó. Halldórsson. Reykjavík: Hið íslenska fornritafélag.
Eiríks saga rauða [The Saga of Eric the Red] 1935, in Íslenzk fornrit (Vol. IV, pp. 193–237), edited by M. Þórðarson. Reykjavík: Hið íslenzka fornritafélag.
Gehring, K. and Kohsaka, R. 2007. "Landscape" in the Japanese Language: Conceptual Differences and Implications for Landscape Research. *Landscape Research*, 32(2), 273–83.
Granö, J.G. 1997 [1929]. *Pure Geography*, translated by M. Hicks. Baltimore and London: Johns Hopkins University Press.
Jansson, S.B.F. 1945. *Sagorna om Vinland*. Stockholm: Wahlström & Widstrand.
Jones, M. 2006. Landscape, Law and Justice – Concepts and Issues. *Norwegian Journal of Geography*, 60(1), 1–14.
Jónsson, J.H. 1994. *Orðastaður: Orðabók umÍslenska Málnotkun* [Dictionary of the Usage of Icelandic]. Reykjavík: Mál og menning.
Kant, I. 2000 [1790]. *Critique of the Power of Judgment*, edited by P. Guyer, translated by P. Guyer and E. Matthews. Cambridge: Cambridge University Press.
Latour, B. 1993. *We Have Never Been Modern*, translated by C. Porter. Cambridge, Massachusetts: Harvard University Press.
Latour, B. 1999a. On recalling ANT, in *Actor-Network Theory and After*, edited by J. Hassard. Oxford and Malden: Blackwell, 15–25.
Latour, B. 1999b. *Pandora's Hope: Essays on the Reality of Science Studies*. Cambridge, MA: Harvard University Press.
Law, J. 1999. After ANT: Complexity, Naming and Topology, in *Actor-Network Theory and After*, edited by J. Law and J. Hassard. Oxford and Malden: Blackwell Publishing, 1–14.
Laxness, H. 1932. *Fuglinn í Fjörunni: Pólitísk Ástarsaga* [The Bird on the Beach: A Political Love Story]. Reykjavík: Bókadeild Menningarsjóðs.
Merleau-Ponty, M. 2002 [1945]. *Phenomenology of Perception*, translated by C. Smith. London: Routledge.
Merleau-Ponty, M. 2004 [1948]. *The World of Perception*, translated by O. Davis. London and New York: Routledge.

Mitchell, D. 1996. *The Lie of the Land: Migrant Workers and the California Landscape*. Minneapolis: University of Minnesota Press.

Murdoch, J. 2006. *Post-Structuralist Geography*. London, Thousand Oaks and New Delhi: Sage Publications.

Olwig, K.R. 2002. *Landscape Nature, and the Body Politic*. Madison: The University of Wisconsin Press.

Sauer, C.O. 1996 [1925]. The Morphology of Landscape, in *Human Geography: An Essential Anthology*, edited by J. Agnew, D.N. Livingstone and A. Rogers. Oxford: Blackwell, 296–315.

Shaw, D.J.B. and Oldfield, J.D. 2007. Landscape Science: a Russian Geographical Tradition. *Annals of the Association of American Geographers*, 97(1), 111–26.

Skúlason, P. 2005. *Meditation at the Edge of Askja: On Man's Relation to Nature*, translated by M.M. Karlsson. Reykjavík: The University of Iceland Press.

Solnit, R. 2003. *As Eve Said to the Serpent: On Landscape, Gender, and Art*. Athens: The University of Georgia Press.

Spirn, A.W. 1998. *The Language of Landscape*. New Haven and London: Yale University Press.

Svavarsson, J. 1997. Leikur að Uppstillingu [Playing with Still Lifes]. *Lesbók Morgunblaðsins*, 15 November, 16.

Thrift, N. and Dewsbury, J.-D. 2000. Dead Geographies – And How to Make them Live. *Environment and Planning D: Society and Space*, 18, 411–32.

Waage, E.R.H. and Benediktsson, K. 2010. Performing Expertise: Landscape, Governmentality and Conservation Planning in Iceland. *Journal of Environmental Policy and Planning*, 12(1), 1–22.

Wylie, J. 2007. *Landscape*. London: Routledge.

Chapter 5
Time for Fluent Landscapes
Oscar Aldred

Introduction

Brian Massumi opens his book *Parables for the Virtual* by asking why his body deserves to be called "body". His answer is that two things stand out: it moves and it feels (Massumi 2002: 1). In this chapter I ask a similar but different question: why does landscape deserve to be called landscape? A short answer can be given. It depends on how we understand our relationship to landscape, which to all extents and purposes is subjective and dependable on the fluidity of our own interactions; like Massumi's body we move and feel the relationship with landscape. It is hard to deny that we are *not* part of landscape because we are intimately involved in the entanglement of its production in several different ways. However, with an analytical gaze, does this necessarily mean that our relationalities, and specifically the variations and displacements associated with how we are moving and feeling, should structure our discourse; our "conversations with landscape"? And why should this matter?

Landscapes today are produced through discourses of one kind or another, in all kinds of interactions and arrangements of physical space but also the space that is cogent to the way we feel and understand the world around us. Furthermore, these interactions are also temporal. In this chapter I want to present a longer answer, and explore this issue of human-landscape relationship with a little more depth. In the first and second parts of this chapter, I want to explore the types of relationships that take place between the archaeologists and landscape by examining three specific approaches to landscape that archaeologists use. The third part, explores some of the issues arising from this critique. And the fourth part, brings it all together in a project on an archaeology of movement located around Vatnsfjörður in the north west of Iceland.

Archaeologies of Landscape

As an archaeologist the landscapes and cultures that I want to communicate with are situated in the past which adds a further complication to the issue of the relationship to landscape because in one sense I am not part of the landscapes that I want to study because they have *already* happened; they are past. In a conventional way I cannot reverse time's directionality by moving backwards through it. However, in another sense, I can bring the past forwards because in its naturally perceived state time advances, and therefore past landscapes are always going to be part of the landscape because I study them in the present as a result of the nature of accumulation. This temporality however, adds a further complication, because there is a temporal paradox at work. Time simultaneously follows two opposite directions: one forwards towards the future by transforming *and* moves backwards towards the past through a process of ageing (Olivier 2001: 65–6). Time in this sense is not only transformation and ageing, it is also duration. This perhaps expresses what Ingold and Vergunst (2008) remind us, though slightly out of context, that time is always of the moment. Collections of entities in a landscape all have life both before *and* after but also during, and in many ways they have constantly a contemporary configuration; they have no tense other than the present, but can at the same time become worn or alter into something else. Landscapes in this way are a nexus or a convergence of multiple temporalities.

And in many ways this is how the temporality of landscape works: it is the product of past temporal events, and as such the present-day landscape is a product of *all* contingent processes. And that these contingent processes have a material presence but are susceptible to fragmentation and ageing. This is perhaps why landscapes are particularly interesting in unravelling the human relations that cogently exist with the world that emplaces us in relation to it both in the past, in the present and in the possibilities that might happen in the future; as Bender suggests, landscapes are "time materializing" and "like time never stand still" (Bender 2002: S103). As a result I can mediate past landscapes by moving and feeling with them through my body in the present-day landscape and theoretically connect to what has happened while foregrounding the situation of the past in the present.

All archaeologists mediate the past through the present in this way, but how this human-landscape communication is represented after the point of contact often involves a different type of index. Archaeologists tend to reverse their temporal relation to the object of their study by making it an image of the past that is disconnected from the present. The present is metaphorically pushed to the background and becomes a material frame which envelopes the past. This is not only to reduce the experience of landscape as a representation, such as a map, as argued by Thomas (1993), but this process of decontextualising time from its temporal context and fixing it in a representational "space" also reduces landscape to a series of abstractions. So on the one hand there are field practices which are situated in the present-day landscape, and on the other hand a tendency to establish a temporal distance in the way that these are represented; reversing as it were the positioning of present and past. As such the landscapes that archaeologists engage with are the present *past* which is understood as the temporality of landscape (Ingold 1993) but also the *present* past which is essentially the practice of archaeology and the gathering of material. In this way, a tension resides and often remains unresolved in the temporality of landscape between a representation of the past and its setting mediated through the present.

As I have indicated an important arena for discourse by archaeologists, as well as anthropologists, is material culture.[1] Recently, the materiality of things has been the focus of debate (Ingold 2007). This debate has focused on different definitions of materiality, and whether or not this is a useful term to use. In this chapter, rather than think about materiality as a physical property of something material, or materiality as an ether-like quality (in terms of the reciprocal relationship of the subject making the object, but also the object making the subject), I want to consider materiality as a process of *materialisation*, not a description. This is a process that is attentive to the conditions of landscape in that it considers landscapes as both ideological *and* substantive. The translation of the landscape out-there, to the landscape on the page, is a materialisation process along which the "paths" are made. In attempting to understand processes of materialisation in both the discourse and production of landscape, I question the need to employ one approach, or use one conceptual toolkit, over another? Instead, the approach should be kept undisciplined in the sense of allowing it to flow and be fluid by attending to the conditions of archaeology and landscape.

Communicating with landscape brings to our attention to all kinds of issues, from thinking about our involvement in the production of knowledge, to the contribution of the past to the present by considering temporality, and to the issues associated with the relationality between the material world and ourselves and processes of materialisation. Communication forms a centre-piece for most investigations into landscape. In archaeological terms, the form of communication tends to use two types of approaches. On the one hand, approaches that use a vulgar empiricism, which is to say that the collected data speaks for itself without the need for intervening theory. Landscapes, in this sense, are already past and have little or no relevance for the now, and stop materialising as soon as they removed out of their situational contexts. On the other, there are more situated approaches, which retain the experiences of landscape and its embedded qualities. And in this sense landscape is a field of engagement, in which lived-in and varied conditions of how we interpret the past are heavily influenced by the way in which our bodies move.

Archaeological Approaches to Landscape

How the archaeologist relates to the material world has consequences for the task of understanding the processes involved in the formation of landscape. There are essentially three approaches to landscape that fall under the rubric of vulgar materialism and embeddedness. They are: *reconstructions*, which is a world seen

---

[1] Although the term material culture tends to exclude what is material and natural. One though has to question whether the distinctions culture and nature are useful here in reinforcing the artificial division between different components of landscape in terms of Culture and Nature.

from above or at a distance; *embodiment*, which is a world sensed from within; and a third-way, *relational*, which views in multiple ways, material-centred, sensed and experienced, from above, within and every which way it can so long as these ways of following can be connected and sustained.

The first type of approach, landscape reconstructions, are by far the largest type but have had relatively little critique (though cf. Ingold 1993, Thomas 1993). A reconstruction is comprised of two distinct landscapes. One which is a past landscape, divided from the other called the present. The division is marked by an absence of time between the past and present. Not only is this viewed from above, as in a bird's eye view, but it is also a distancing of the human. Archaeology repeatedly attempts to straddle the temporal void by building "bridges" of various kinds, through abstractions and glass-houses (e.g. middle-range-theory, analogy, "scientific" techniques). Part of the problem though is connected to the removal of material from its context by making data; a transformation from the real to the virtual. This often involves a mediator such as a physical process like recovering buried material from an excavation, or in a non-destructive way, by the removal of attributes associated with real things in the field context through survey. The information is used to create a *resemblance* of the past, by replacing the contextual meanings together with representational ones. These contextual meanings come in packages, such as a material category, like a settlement, a field system, or a date, whether associated with an absolute date such as 871 AD ±2, or a generalised one, the Viking age.

The second approach is less used, but has a growing currency in archaeological practice, and relates to a proposition: the construction of the world whereby the landscape is wrapped by a synaesthesis (of an irrational mind) in a blending of experiences through the body. This places more emphasis on spatial and temporal continuities by positioning the body within the landscape being studied so as to mediate this experience by establishing a series of dialectical relationships: between the body and the landscape (e.g. Thomas 1993, Tilley 1994, 2004, 2008).[2] The emphasis here is on a phenomenology in which a framework of perception is grounded through an embodied experience, and a temporal continuity is established because the experience of the world is happening in the present, rather than being cordoned off and separated between the past and the present. This temporal experience is a starting point for a discourse about the past through the present (Bender et al. 2007: 77, 237). The relations between past and present are in this way mediated through the body in its embodiment.

I would like to make some comments about these two approaches before moving on to a third. In the first approach, an abstract sense of belonging is created because these are things given terms and values that us "Moderns" can relate to. However, trying to put something back in the same way and in the same place once it has been removed, is like trying to complete a jigsaw with

---

2 Although particular types of sites and landscape are chosen to be studied; ones that address specific temporal settings such as the Neolithic, though not exclusively.

most of the pieces missing. While entropy and decay are effects in the way things age, other processes have already begun the dispersal and fragmentation of things. For instance, the temporal origins of a thing determines how naturally dispersed and fragmented a thing becomes; producing a different entity in which original meanings may only be subtly evident. Furthermore, disassembling and re-assembling a pre-existing configuration is a destructive process, and therefore places a heavy burden on techniques of documentation and reconstruction: on the relation forming processes between our experiences and knowledge, and on our epistemology that we use to assign meaning. Excavation is largely better equipped to cope with these transformations because it is already to a large extent been deconstructed through a forensic and physical removal of one sort or another along which a chain of reference can be followed: removing topsoil, revealing what is hidden, documenting material things like soil or artefacts displaced, putting into spoil heaps, buckets, bags, and then further removing from the "scene of the crime", and analysing in the lab. However, the archaeological material of landscape remains largely where it has always been and essentially there is no need to be so destructive in the way it is disassembled and put back together.

In the second approach the body perceives the world, but it does so through a series of asymmetrical opposites by centring perception entirely in the body (perception being of course a human-centred production): up – down, left – right, front – back (Tilley 1994, 2004, 2008). And while the temporal distinctiveness of the past and present are brought together by foregrounding of synaesthetic experiences of the senses while moving (cf. Tilley 1994: 170), the world remains split into the raw elemental and the social world of things (cf. Tilley 2007: 17). Underlying therefore this the embodied approach, in terms of phenomenology, is a structural ordering of the world, but rather than finding its way in semiotic understanding, it is instead embodied as a specific rendering of the structure of the human – landscape relationship.

So long as landscape reconstructions are treated as inadequate representations or mediations of past landscapes, then there are no particular problems in either of these approaches. However, as soon as it is argued that this *is* the past, then this is an altogether different proposition. Unfortunately, archaeology has a tendency to make all kinds of assumptions that legitimise the interpretation of landscapes in such a way, for example in the use of historical context or ethnographic analogy to create a bridge between the past and the present. Or in a more archaeological way, to rely on the methods and techniques of enforcing a "chronometric hygiene and spatial integrity of the data we use" (David and Thomas 2008: 345). Embodiment does not go so far as to say that this is the past, but it defers its authenticity to subjectivity and in particular the reflexivity and multivocalities that go hand in hand with this type of approach. The world and the material things in it are disclosed and mediated through a body that feels and moves in a particular way, which opens it up towards criticisms relating to the immediacy and relevance of the experience and subjectivity and its reflection of the material world. Regardless of how the relationship is exposed and experienced it creates a separation between the object of perception and the subject or perceiver; which in many ways is one of the things that is being attempted to be dissolved.

The third approach is a relational view of the landscape, and offers a more coherent way to deal with the objectives-subjectivities that take place during a landscape archaeology. In particular, it is the way that it establishes a series of relationships between things no matter where one is situated; whether from a distance or within a landscape. As such, the approach partly resolves the continued splits between past and present by establishing a trace-presence along which people and things are linked to one other through various types of transformations; in spatial, temporal, material terms, as well as the agency resulting from these sets of relations (Latour 1999, see also e.g. Jones 2002, Olsen 2003, Witmore 2007a,). The call is for nothing less than a suspension of the epistemology of bifurcation by building on the strengths of archaeology as the "discipline of things" and its attendance to hybrid configurations (Callon and Law 1997, Olsen 2007, Witmore 2007b). The relational approach emphasises the material relations that form assemblages or gatherings as the outcomes of relations; for example a boundary is not an enclosure until the relations between the boundary and the space are understood. As such, it is concerned with not only one moment to the next, or one coherent period (however one defines that), but the chain along which continuous transformations take place. Everything is in process, in becoming; landscapes are decidedly on-the-move; not a record but a recording that is continuous (Bender 2001, 2002).

As landscape entities accumulate but also undergo transformation which alter and reconfigure landscape along its trace, there is considerable mobility. For example, a boundary is built, but over time parts are truncated, or partly removed, which alters the boundary in such a way that its original function and meaning have changed. The processes and its results in transformation also set in motion other changes for a whole series of activities; such as creating a new entrance and path, altering the flow of water and creating a further set of boundaries to manage the flow of water. In this way, the context to which one entity belongs to is also undergoing transformation, not only in relation to a particular feature, such as a boundary, but also other aspects related to it, such as the movement of water. However, through these transformations the entity and the context may have altered entirely, and are perhaps not the same as they were before. The phases of transformation are then characterised by mobility in the relations between things: the point at which we call something one thing and not another depends on our ability to recognise these transformations or points of change. Part of being able to adequately interpret these transformations is to keep things together on the same level, or within the same ontology, rather than bifurcate distinct entities such as space and time into two distinct realms. In terms of landscape archaeology, this is contending with the notion of situating the interpretation of archaeology within the same ontology of its evidence. What this is arguing for is a shift in the practice of archaeology from a process where the material traces are *recovered* or are evidence of past social processes to one in which the "interpretative experience is produced" through the relations that are made with things (Tilley 1989: 278, Lucas 2001: 2).

Approaches that reconstruct landscape, in taking one moment out of time, and repositioning by using a technique and an epistemology that carries many assumptions, is to reduce landscape to a static image; to literally remove its motion to recover meaning. And while the approaches that rely on the body and on the relations between people and things retain more motion and level-ness, there is something arguably lost archaeologically. So in order to give landscape back its life there is a need to think more about the evolutionary nature of landscape, and archaeologically place the objects and events as part of the same ontology. Doing this, arguably, holds on to the indivisible movements that constitute *movement* and an *affective* image (Bergson 2004 [1912], Deleuze 1995: 47, Massumi 2002).

Addressing the problem of retaining the qualities of landscape from an archaeological perspective, I argue, largely relies on precisely *how* we understand the formation of the landscape. Which, in other words, is to trace archaeology's material practices, evidence and interpretations as part of the same experience of the material; i.e. not to separate them. The connection therefore between time, space and motion operates through a mutual relationality; to conceive of one makes an immediate connection to the others through their shared boundaries. For example, if an object moves it has a spatial extension and a temporal duration; which is to say that if an object transforms (for example it becomes worn and ages), it moves spatially and temporally through its transformation and change. To work on this problem as archaeologists we need to retain the archaeological in both the experiential nature of archaeology as a material practice and in the material organisation of landscape as mutually constitutive of one another. Organisation and practice here are based on the events and the processes that flow through these projects. Therefore, what is materially traced in the objects that are formed and the contact that takes place with archaeologists is explored through two processes that I want to consider here: residuality and *bricolage*.

Material Events: Residuality and Bricolage

Ingold suggests that "landscape is constituted as an enduring record of – and testimony to – the lives and works of past generations who have dwelt within it, and in doing so, have left there something of themselves" (Ingold 1993: 152). Ingold's "enduring record" is something that is present in landscape through the residuality of material things. Residuality in a landscape archaeology context are landscape entities and their material resilience to alteration while other aspects of the landscape change; which is to say that residuality is a relational quality borne out of the things that are moving around an entity, while it stays still. Material resilience refers to landscape entities' ability to endure during and after its formation and initial use. In landscape, like most other contexts, material residuality depends on the relations within its networked assemblage and the way in which the residual elements work when gathered with other entities. The bonds between entities are in themselves residual, and an assemblage, as a gathering of entities, has its own autonomy (its own agency), but is also part of a larger entity through the connections that are made with other assemblages. Inevitably, these connections constrain autonomy because of the limits of its constitutive parts and what is available around it to be used. For instance, geology underpins the landscape in such a way that its character has a profound effect on the way in which the surface of landscape develops. And although something may have a residual potential, this does not mean it remains constant. For example, geology changes according to the forces that act upon it. Therefore, the material hardness or size of an entity is no guarantee of residuality. The added pressure derived from the material hardness of geology produces volatility, particularly when associated with volcanic activity, although its hardness is also a quality that allows it to be eroded slowly. We might then consider that geology is residual both in terms of its presence but also what is left after subtraction.

Based on Lucas' (2008) examination, when we think about landscape in terms of residuality, with all the time-depth involved in landscape's formation, what we can see is a landscape composed of multiple types of assemblages, varying in their residual qualities. Rather, than taking a fragmented and separate view of residuality, by isolating distinct entities and analysing them individually, the issue of residuality is perhaps best used when expanded upon to include a more general view of material organisation in which the concept of reversibility is foregrounded (Lucas 2008: 59). This is to examine closely the concept of the archaeological event, and in doing so suggest that there are not several distinct ontologies on which historical phenomena exist (such as long-term structure or small-scale events) but rather a flattened temporal plane that allows links between different historical phenomena to be maintained (Lucas 2008: 59–60). The upshot of using a temporal concept such as this one is that it literally keeps ones feet on the ground, situated in the concreteness of the data by examining the patterns of material organisation that archaeologists deal with on a day-to-day basis. Instead of thinking only about the material in terms of spatial organisation we can also examine the organisation in terms of time: as material events (Lucas 2008).

By bringing the spatial and temporal together, and giving places and paths more historicism, I am suggesting an alternative way of thinking about archaeological landscapes. However, there remain several problems. Time-geography brought attention to the idea of *stations* (Hägerstrand 1970, 1976, Lenntorp 1976, Pred 1977, 1985),[3] which are, on the one hand, like the material events that Lucas

---

3   Time-geography offers some possible avenues to pursue for thinking about landscape (Hägerstrand 1970, 1976, Pred 1977, 1985). In Hägerstrand's own words time-geography is "a physical approach involving the study of how events occur in time-space framework" (Hägerstrand 1970: 20). It provides a framework for both spatial and temporal coordinates and the "paths" that are made (Pred 1977: 208). These paths or trajectories connect events

discusses because they potentially have residuality through their presence and inclusion in a way that Casey expresses in terms of an *occurrence as event:*[4] " ... a given place takes on the qualities of its occupants, reflecting these qualities in its own constitution and description and expressing them in its occurrence as event: places not only are, they happen" (Casey 1996: 27). However, on the other hand, they are unlike the temporality that I am pursuing because the residuality of time-geography is predetermined and fixed in a way that is devoid of the accumulated histories that flow through place. Although residuality offers us a ready-made template with which to work with, it needs to be balanced by the processes of accretion and innovations that come hand in hand with alteration and change. In a way, this focuses our attention on the need to retain the durability not between the events in terms of their concreteness, but a durability in terms of their fluidity and their ability to transform but hold enough of their originality so as not to become redundant. As Bergson suggests change is the "most substantial and durable thing possible. Its solidity is infinitely superior to that of fixity which is only *an ephemeral arrangement between mobilities*" (Bergson 2007 [1946]: 125; my italics). How things change and transform then, in the context of landscape, is determined in part by their usefulness and ability to become something else, in short a paradoxical *fluid* residuality, by extending the idea of Bergson's fixity as an ephemeral arrangement.

One of the important things that Lucas (2008) develops in connection with residuality are the problems in identifying material and immaterial processes amongst the residual features that characterise the archaeological record. To assist in this discussion in understanding residuality Lucas turns to another issue; that of reversibility.[5]

---

which occur at spatially fixed units of observation, such as buildings or territories, called stations or domains (Lenntorp 1976).

4   But here I am not drawing on Casey's emphasis on phenomenology in which self has to do with the agency of the geographical subjects and body in linking this self to the lived place in its sensible and perceptible features. Nor his articulation of landscape as a presented layout of a set of places which are a series of recollections which draw the body into place (Casey 2001). Rather I am retaining the material nature of place and its involvement with landscape, by focusing on entanglement and multi-scalar linkages. The aim is to retain the tangle but look at the individual strands or processes behind their entanglements.

5   In Lucas' paper two examples are used to explore the issue of residuality and reversibility (Lucas 2008: 62–3). The first is a book collection, which is as a good example of an immaterial and reversible residuality because an arrangement of books in a library can be rearranged without leaving a material trace; in short the ability to re-order in multiple ways is not tied to a particular system because subsequent events of re-ordering have erased antecedent ones. The second is a traffic system, which is a good example of an irreversible residuality because the material system of traffic lights and the side on which the steering-wheel is put in a car cannot be reversed easily without large-scale changes (and energy) to all of the components in the system. Change is therefore difficult to acheive with objects

Reversibility in the context of this chapter is a quality associated with the ability for an entity to become something else, denoting how easily it can be changed: along a sliding-scale of reversibility. In another paper, the issue of residuality in the development of the landscape was explored; in connection with Þegjandadalur in north-east Iceland (Aldred and Lucas forthcoming). In it the boundaries (which can be dated to before the twelfth century but remain visible in the present-day) not only disrupted the material organisation of the landscape, but also influenced the formation of other parts of the valley and its settlement. But while these influences occurred most radically when the boundaries were constructed, they nonetheless influenced subsequent events; the most recent being the archaeological interest in them. The ability to change while retaining a recognisable material form in terms of their residuality is perhaps a key issue that needs to be explored in landscape. What I want to examine here is another quality of residuality, not only its reversibility or the ability to continue to structure and influence, but the way in which material entanglements that have a durational presence, beyond the intended and original use.

A *bricoleur* is someone who makes do with what is to hand in a devious way compared to craftsworkers who use skill; the *bricoleur* employs a process which Lévi-Strauss calls *bricolage* (Lévi-Strauss 1966: 16ff.). Although the context of *bricolage* used by Lévi-Strauss is connected to drawing distinctions between the tamed and savage (i.e. untamed) mind between those who could perform diverse tasks, over those that did only specific ones, it nonetheless has currency in thinking about residuality. The implications I am drawing out here though do not maintain the separation between making do and reliance on skill, but in the propensity for something to exist beyond the use for which it was originally intended for.

A *bricolage* in this respect is both a retrospective and forward looking project, in which one considers the signification of the things gathered in performing the project at hand. This is a combination of a thing's design for an original use and its ability to be used in a different way for a new project, which results in some elements of its associative properties being lost while others are gained (Lévi-Strauss 1966: 18–19). For example, a road that is built for transportation also establishes house-plots; while the road is still used for transportation it is also a boundary from which other boundaries have been off-set and around which new dwellings have been placed. This ability to reuse and gather things and apply them in different ways is precisely the types of processes that occur during the formation of the landscape. In terms of the temporality of landscape, *bricolage* is a process

---

with low reversible, but is the commonest form of material trace left in the archaeological record. And while the fragmentary nature of the archaeological record might be seen as a problem for some, it can be seen as an important facet in itself. The important point being what survives archaeologically has survived precisely because it has resilience and it has continued to contribute to the organisation and formation of other entities in the landscape.

which is "the act of using and adapting existing elements in a *fresh* way" (Tilley 1991: 96), and, although a *bricoleur* may never finish a project, she will always leave something of herself in it (Lévi-Strauss 1966). *Bricolage* in this way allows us to establish concrete connections between what we might call residual things in a landscape that continue to have a material presence, with those things that are possible subjects for *fresh* transformation and alteration in their use through their transition from one assemblage to another.

If the archaeological project of landscape is to understand past material conditions in which people and things were mixed together by giving them order, then by all means we should continue to decontextualise and create distinct but separate entities in order to understand the past; understood in this chapter as approaches that are reconstructions, but also to a lesser extent those that forefront the human-only embodied practices (that in attempting to break down structural oppositions actually reinforce them). However, if our interest is more in the processual character of landscape in keeping the concept of landscape alive and kicking, rather than seeing them as completed articles, let us use them just as a *bricoleur* does, to retain the lived-in and dynamic nature of the past in all of its messiness *and* order. To hold onto landscape's living quality we need to allow motion as much as we possibly can both in terms of what we do in practice and the way in which we think about landscape; allowing it be, in a word, *fluent*.

Landscapes are fluent in all of its definitions (*Oxford English Dictionary* [OED] 1989). Landscapes are an *excess* of objects and events, processes and structures, people and things; it is affluent, copious, and abundant. But importantly, landscape is also in a perpetual state of *readiness*; to both transform and age, to be both practical and meaningful in multiple ways, and is often flowing and smooth (OED 1989). To develop an archaeology of landscape, it is necessary to take a path that weaves not by drawing distinctions that separate past and present, or in bifurcating the sets of relations between the material and body, or between object and subject, but by arguing that people and things are thoroughly entangled along relational paths of signification. While one can separate landscape into categories we have to remember that these categories are productive terms derived from the relations between things. Understanding these relations in archaeological terms are connected with processes relating to residuality and *bricolage* which maintain and influence subsequent landscape configurations. Furthermore, processes of residuality and *bricolage* are intertwined with the "palimpsest" metaphor which is often used to explain the character of landscape (Maitland 1897: 15, Crawford 1953: 51–2, Hoskins 1984: 59, Muir 2000: 5–6, Bowden 2001: 29–45, Johnson 2006: 58ff.).

For instance, Crawford discusses the time-depth of England's landscape by using the "palimpsest" metaphor: "The surface of England is a palimpsest, a document that has been written on and erased over and over again; and it is the business of the field archaeologists to decipher it" (1953: 51). Which is to say, that landscapes have the qualities of a parchment or other writing surface, on which the original text has been effaced or partially erased and then overwritten by another (OED 1989). The palimpsest metaphor communicates the temporal and spatial complexity of landscape but at the same time suggests something about the conceptual thinking relating to its formation and material organisation. For instance, the palimpsest takes a particular view on the material accumulation of events, viewing these in terms of sequences as if a linear temporality; one of accumulation of one layer and then another, in which previous layers are shadows of their former self. As older surfaces are erased and removed in the production of a new surface which by virtue lies on top. In a palimpsest this surface is the only one that is active; previous surfaces are put towards the background.

The issue of what remains after erasure and removal is related to residuality. What may be present in a palimpsest are accumulated features (Bailey 2007: 203–10, Sullivan 2008). However, in many ways the palimpsest metaphor misrepresents the processes of landscape accumulation; these accumulations are not neutral to the new writing on the surface. In fact, they are both negatively and positively associated with the new "text": negatively, in the way that the new text permits their erasure and ceases to exist except as faint traces, becoming as it were a fossilisation of a former surface. However, their influence on new landscape inscriptions occurs not so much by structuring them, but rather in giving the impression that they lie below the new texts and are shadows of their former selves; in short a palimpsest.

The palimpsest metaphor views the landscape in a particular state of accumulation, but it does this by giving an impression of all the compressed layers over time, by assigning them a continued residuality. However, the actual processes involved are more complex and the way in which accumulation takes place is not in terms of layers but a complex mix of use and reuse, making and building. In this way the landscape is in a constant state of flux. In a structural view of landscape, the palimpsest surfaces are passive to subsequent surfaces; previous traces no longer influence the formation of the next inscription. But there is an influence. This is derived in part from the residuality of material organisation, as well as the mobility and fluency composed of real movements, that continue to structure and influence subsequent formation processes. In this way what is produced in terms of simultaneity and duration is a *montage*; different temporalities and residual properties intermingling that overlap and overlay each other where the directionality of time is overshadowed by the use-value that a thing has to the current project at hand. In this way previous inscriptions continue to have presence through their residualities. In this sense, landscapes are never *finished* products because of the way in which they conjoin the old and new together through processes such as *bricolage* and because all of these processes are in a state of constant flux.

Vatnsfjörður's Fluent Landscape

The landscape around Vatnsfjörður, located in the north-west of Iceland, is a good example of the elements that have so far defined this chapter. The premise for the research is based on a landscape archaeology project conducted over several seasons of investigation. It therefore has a current practice-orientated focus but is theoretical informed with a mind to conduct an archaeology of movement. And like most landscapes where human inhabitation has taken place there is strong material culture presence, therefore any discussion on the landscape involves an immediate connection with material organisation and issues connected with usage and *bricolage*, as well as residuality.

The landscape around the farm of Vatnsfjörður is composed of valleys, fjords and uplands. It has a strong coastal relationship which is suggested by the distribution of settlements usually no more than 200m from the coastal edge. Historically, Vatnsfjörður was the local power base, situated in a landscape over which it exerted its influence. However, it was in the medieval period that it had its greatest influence (Tulinius 2005). This historicity is currently being investigated archaeologically through excavation at the farm of Vatnsfjörður (linked to the Viking period as well as the Modern period) (cf. Milek 2009), and a landscape survey of the entire peninsula (e.g. Aldred 2009). The landscape survey that I want to discuss in this chapter are associated with those areas that lie beyond the farm (defined by the infield boundary). Within this landscape there are many different kinds of sites, and in particular stone-built markers or cairns (Icelandic: *varða*): about six hundred have been surveyed from about thousand recorded sites. This are associated with different types of activities including movement, acting as way-markers. Variations in the way in which cairns were built and placed in the landscape, open them up to different means of investigation. Such as an archaeology associated with reconstructing landscapes, linked to typologies and differentiating spatial and temporal attributes, or an archaeology associated with an embodied practice, linked to the experience and documenting landscape through movement, from one cairn to the next, or one sensual field to the next. However, the relational approach that I want to apply to this study of landscape is not distinct from either of these approaches, but rather joins them together.

Typologies are a standard way for archaeologists to categorise complex material organisations, for example we consider sites in terms of things such as form, construction, materials, dimensions, placement and location, visibility, and possible dating. However, these approaches create a certain distance between the object of study and those studying them. Nonetheless, examining the typology of cairns is rather like looking at the residuality of past entanglements which are focused in microcosm into one site. In this way, from an extended resolution perspective, the whole of the landscape is a material matrix of past residual elements which are defined through the associative or relational properties that one site has with itself and with others.

However, the relationships that a site has with others are often interpreted ambiguously. Cairns for example are not exclusively markers of/for movement, but also function as markers for boundaries, burial, folklore and time. But these various states are determined in part by their relationship with other sites; to an extent how connected one site is with another. However, cairns are inevitably more complex than they first appear. Like most other archaeological sites, cairns are imbued with particular material practices and meanings, most of which need to be re-negotiated, while others have been irrevocably removed or lost. Therefore, there is a need to look elsewhere to resolve the levels of ambiguity. The archaeology that is derived from a cairn is therefore also concerned with foregrounding the types of material entanglements and the relations that these they have in connection with archaeologists, alongside other sites and the landscape itself.

In terms of movement there is simultaneity between the project of moving and gathering data, as there is with the movements that took place in the past along the same route. One of the issues that is common to both reconstruction and embodiment is understanding the part that cairns as anchors of movement had in past movements and to what extent they continue to influence and structure subsequent movements; namely to explore the relationship of iterative practices that are re-negotiated and are present or residual in the site itself. In order to retain the qualities of landscape being argued in this chapter, the past and present need to be compressed by looking at the material organisation of the cairns and their fluid residuality through the field practices themselves.

All field archaeology begins literally with getting ones hands or feet dirty. The documentation of movement in Vatnsfjörður was carried out through a field survey with an assortment of people; myself, colleagues and students. Also brought to the ensemble were a number of essential things for recording: camera, GPS, notepad and paper, a resemblance of a pro-forma sheet for recording, and a map. The archaeological survey around Vatnsfjörður followed "paths of observation" which aptly describes the methodology used, which was both an act of discovery through observation but also a tracing from one site to another in such a way that the experiences of movement and the interpretation of sites and landscape were embedded into the field practice of survey. Many of these paths were walked several times, or at the very least, the sites along them observed from multiple view points. Once the these paths were walked and the sites were surveyed, they were packaged in several ways: as an archive of the field experience, through notes, reflections, as well as images, GPS points, and assigned data values. In this way, even though the sites receive an ordering through their categorisation and have lost their material properties and incumbent material organisation as it was in the field, they are able to be recalled either to a particular site or experience after field survey.

As I have suggested earlier in this chapter, the tendency is to see the landscape in terms of several degrees of separation: in creating distance from the field or the human-centred experience, as well as separating the fundamental components of landscape – space and time – into two distinct ontologies. In this way, the sites and the landscape become transformed through a dual process of abstraction which reduces landscape which is arguably not an authentic landscape representation. Part of the problem is in the translation. Distances, as well as spatial and temporal representations of landscape, tend to be fixed which in field experiences are variable and fluid. It is not simply that the representations are always going to be inadequate at portraying the "field". There is always going to be a loss in authenticity, but also a gain in being able to communicate particular aspects associated with "data" in a more communicable form (albeit less complex). But what is often lacking are the indexical connections between the field experience that involve the material practices and the processes of interpretation in the field which have a profound bearing on what is produced.

In one example, along a route that crosses the southern upland area of Vatnsfjörður, the spatial relations between individual cairns are primarily related to the field of vision. While the horizontal distances continue to extend in a field experience these are rarely captured through their translation. In a similar way, the visible links between cairns are represented as lines from fixed points of observation rather than being presented from multiple view points, whereby distances and perceptions are continually being altered. While this visual and perceptual experience is of fundamental importance during the field survey in terms of finding sites and interpreting sets of relations, in translation they become too abstracted so that no longer have much bearing on the reader's interaction with the material.

Often a map is used to show a measured and abstracted version of the field experience by illustrating clusters and distribution of sites from which relations between other sites are made in terms of spatial distances rather than perceived visibility. The variations in topography that affect and influence a view of one site to another in the field are often represented by a further abstraction of the landscape in terms of height, slope and aspect. In addition, the representation is presented as a bird's eye view, in which the horizontal experience of the field is translated into a vertical representation looking down. As such the field experience becomes crystallised as an inadequate representation of landscape in the map. A similar layer of abstraction is also created when temporality is considered, represented by the absolute or relative dating of the sites, reproduced as a graph or a symbolically differentiated map. Both of these are fossilising the landscape by separating the landscape into two distinct spatial and temporal representations, which removes not only the mobility that took place in field experiences, but also the dynamic character of the landscape itself.

There has already been a movement that creates distance between the site, the landscape and the field experience, through the archive, and arguably one wonders if there should there be another? Of course the demands of our work require us to present the research that we conduct and the money that we spend in the process, but there is definitely a need to extend the traditional form of dissemination. What is needed is to join the field experience and observations of the material organisation of the landscape with the representation of the spatial and temporal within the same ontology. As a result, the approach of embodiment and reconstruction become attentive to the archaeology as a "narrated sequence of embodied actions" (Lorimer and Lund 2003: 138) that are unfolded through the field of those forces and relations through the "active and sensuous" engagements of the practitioner and the material that is being worked (Ingold 1997: 112); in other words a relational approach.

For instance, the material presence of the cairns in both the field and the analysis away from it, is creating a mimetic process which has bearing on the narratives that are produced. Keeping the impression that archaeology is still in the landscape contexts does not allow the alterations and transformations to become fully crystallised; as much as the landscape, the report is still in flux. While this creates an illusion of the field through a certain amount of compression and retained fluidity, the landscape also lies open as if a body, subject to its archaeological autopsy (Lucas pers. comm.): *things* and the material world become involved in the operation, though they do not have symmetry with the "body", though the tendency is treat the body as if it is thoroughly anaesthetised and passive.

Embodiment gives an impression of fluidity in the translation of experiences from the field to the report, because they are not able to retain "real" movement as a *moving continuity* (Bergson 2004 [1912]: 260). Bergson divided movement into three types: absolute, which is a change of place; relative, which is movement relative to other changes; and real, which is having real cause to move in a force of motion (Bergson 2004 [1912]: 254–9). What these all imply is that change of one kind or another is a movement which is a transition and transformation in a change of state or of quality (Bergson 2004 [1912]: 258). While the way in which landscape archaeology is practiced often involves a continual change in the state or quality of landscape, such as in the observations and experiences of the world around, as well as the material things being worked on, what one needs to ask is whether at the end of these transformations can landscape still be called landscape? This is to my mind connected intimately to movement; how much of the mobility of the field practices, the material landscape itself is carried with the translation. In a moving continuity what changes and what remains the same, has a bearing on what constitutes landscape.

Returning to Vatnsfjörður, a landscape that is excessive and in a state of readiness is to attend to the spatial and temporal through movement. For landscape archaeology, movement is several things. It is an ethnography of the survey process, that aligns not the motion and rest associated with recording cairns, other sites and landscape, but also in the way the *passage* and the affect of our presence and entanglement has on the material and interpretative outcomes in generating our experience of the archaeology as landscape. This might be illustrated in terms of a time geography of the movement as part of a routine archaeological movement which resides in the recording and documentation of the archaeology and our embodied experiences in terms of the practical, sensual and meaningful relations. Or in terms of an archaeology in which the material organisation of cairns reflects the inherent usages in the movements that occur along the landscape. In particular, attending to the way in which markers continue to act as anchors for movements in the past, suggested by material reorganisations as well as residuality, but also in both iterative and re-negotiated practices which establish further cairns along a particular route, each with their own typology and idiosyncrasies, that continue to have interest for archaeologists.

A practice of landscape archaeology that weaves a path through both ethnographic and archaeological concerns, provides opportunities for the interpretation of the material organisation of landscape to become entirely entangled with the experiential nature of archaeology as a material practice. So much so perhaps that the landscape retains enough of its mobility for it to still be called landscape, after a change of state from the experience of the field to the page. While this is not often practiced, and there are few theoretical tools to help, but thinking differently about time and temporality have currency (Lucas 2005, 2008, Bailey 2007, but also Tilley 1991, Ingold 1993, Thomas 1993, 2001, Olivier 2001, 2008, Olsen 2003, Witmore 2006, 2007b,). Arguably, in this way, the landscape retains its integrity and its coherence through maintaining its material and archaeological rhythm (cf. Lefebvre 2004, Massey 2006: 41). And in doing so, one retains a resemblance of landscape which is in a constant state of readiness or in a state of becoming, not by closing it off or removing it entirely from its context but in keeping it open.

Is Landscape still *Landscape*?

In asking the question does landscape deserve to be called landscape? I have pathed a way which asks us to move and feel as if we ourselves are part of the landscape rather than creating abstractions and by giving symmetry to things other than just ourselves; implying one of the first chapter's more-than-human motif. This is to gravitate towards another underlying concept that informs this chapter, connected with contemporaneity: "The contemporary is a moving ratio of modernity, moving through the recent past and near future in a (nonlinear) space that gauges modernity as an ethos already becoming historical" (Rabinow 2008: 2). In suggesting that the landscape's that archaeologists look at should be contemporary, I am not suggesting the Modern sense of the contemporary as in the present period, but in terms of the *con-temporary* (with-time) or rather belonging to time. Belonging to time involves making connections to the things around us, so that our experiences and identities through a moving and feeling body are entangled with the material organisation of landscape. Rather than seeing these two as distinct from one another, the subjective and objective, I have argued that the two work hand in hand as if tied together in a three-legged-race. To do this, I have suggested that both landscape's experiences and entities can be traced in terms of their relationalities both in terms of residuality and *bricolage* in which duration and use are two fundamental processes. In such a way, the relations that wrap people and things together *remain* entangled from the reflexivity during field work to the fluidity on the page, so that the landscapes that are worked on, communicated with and presented are thoroughly in-the-making.

References

Aldred, O. 2009. Vatnsfjörður Landscape Survey 2008, in *Vatnsfjörður 2008* [Framvinduskýrsla FS426-03098], edited by K. Milek. Reykjavík: Fornleifastofnun Íslands, 11–22.
Aldred, O. and Lucas, G. forthcoming. Events, Temporalities and Landscapes in Iceland, in *Conference Proceedings: Toward an Eventful Archaeology: Approaches to Structural Change in the Archaeological Record*. Buffalo: University at Buffalo.
Bailey, G. 2007. Time Perspectives, Palimpsests and the Archaeology of Time. *Journal of Anthropological Archaeology*, 26, 198–223.
Bender, B. 2001. Landscapes-on-the-Move. *Journal of Social Archaeology*, 1(1), 75–89.
Bender, B. 2002. Time and Landscape. *Current Anthropology*, 43, S103–S112.
Bender, B. Hamilton, S. and Tilley, C. 2007. *Stone Worlds. Narrative and Reflexivity in Landscape Archaeology*. Walnut Creek: Left Coast Press.
Bergson, H. 2004 [1912]. *Matter and Memory*, translated by N.M. Paul and W.S. Palmer. New York: Dover Publications.
Bergson, H. 2007 [1946]. *The Creative Mind. An Introduction to Metaphysics*, translated by M. L. Andison. New York: Dover publications.
Bowden, M. 2001. Mapping the Past: O.G.S. Crawford and the Development of Landscape Studies. *Landscapes*, 2(2), 29–45.
Callon, M. and Law, J. 1997. After the Individual in Society: Lessons on Collectivity from Science Technology and Society. *Canadian Journal of Sociology*, 22(2), 165–82.
Casey, E.S. 1996. How to Get from Space to Place in a Fairly Short Stretch of Time, in *Senses of Place*, edited by S. Feld and K.H. Basso. Santa Fe: School of American Research Press, 13–51.
Casey, E. 2001. Body, Self and Landscape: a Geophilosophical Inquiry into the Place-World, in *Textures of Place: Exploring Humanist Geographies*, edited by P.C. Adams, S. Hoelscher and K.E. Till. Minneapolis: University of Minnesota Press, 403–25.
Crawford, O.G.S. 1953. *Archaeology in the Field*. London: Dent and Sons.
David, B. and Thomas, J. (eds) 2008. *Handbook of Landscape Archaeology*. Walnut Creek: Left Coast Press.
Deleuze, G. 1995. *Negotiations*. New York: Columbia University Press.
Hägerstrand, T. 1970. What about People in Regional Science? *Papers of the Regional Science Association*, 24, 7–21.
Hägerstrand, T. 1976. Geography and the Study of Interaction between Nature and Society. *Geoforum*, 7, 329–34.

Hoskins, W.G. 1984. *Local History in England*. 3rd Edition. London: Longman.
Ingold, T. 1993. The Temporality of the Landscape. *World Archaeology*, 25, 57–80.
Ingold, T. 1997. Eight Themes in the Anthropology of Technology. *Social Analysis: Journal of Cultural and Social Practices*, 41(1), 106–38.
Ingold, T. 2007. Materials against Materiality. *Archaeological Dialogues*, 14(1), 1–16, 31–8.
Ingold, T. and Vergunst, J.L. (eds) 2008. *Ways of Walking: Ethnography and Practice on Foot*. Aldershot: Ashgate.
Johnson, M. 2006. *Ideas of Landscape*. Oxford: Blackwell.
Jones, A. 2002. *Archaeological Theory and Scientific Practice*. Cambridge: Cambridge University Press.
Latour, B. 1999. *Pandora's Hope. Essays on the Reality of Science Studies*. Cambridge, MA: Harvard University Press.
Lefebvre, H. 2004. *Rhythmanalysis: Space, Time and Everyday Life*, translated by S. Elden and G. Moore. London: Continuum.
Lenntorp, B. 1976. Paths in Space-Time Environments: A Time-Geographic Study of Movement Possibilities of Individuals. *Lund Studies in Geography*, Series B 44. Lund: University of Lund.
Lévi-Strauss, C. 1966. *The Savage Mind*. Chicago: University of Chicago Press.
Lorimer, H. and Lund, K. 2003. Performing Facts: Finding a Way over Scotland's Mountains, in *Nature Performed: Environment, Culture and Performance*, edited by B. Szerszynski, W. Heim and C. Waterton. Oxford: Blackwell, 130–44.
Lucas, G. 2001. *Critical Approaches to Fieldwork: Contemporary and Historical Archaeological Practice*. London: Routledge.
Lucas, G. 2005. *An Archaeology of Time*. London: Routledge.
Lucas, G. 2008. Time and Archaeological Event. *Cambridge Archaeological Journal*, 18(1), 59–65.
Maitland, F.W. 1897. *Domesday Book and Beyond: Three Essays in the Early History of England*. Cambridge: Cambridge University Press.
Massey, D. 2006. Landscape as a Provocation – Reflections on Moving Mountains. *Journal of Material Culture*, 11(1–2), 33–48.
Massumi, B. 2002. *Parables for the Virtual*. Durham: Duke University Press.
Milek, K. (ed.) 2009. *Vatnsfjörður 2008* [Framvinduskýrsla. FS426-03098]. Reykjavík: Fornleifastofnun Íslands.
Muir, R. 2000. Conceptualising Landscape. *Landscapes* 1(1), 4–21.
Olivier, L.C. 2001. Duration, Memory and the Nature of the Archaeological Record, in *It's About Time,* edited by H. Karlsson. Göteborg: Bricoleur Press, 61–70.
Olivier, L.C. 2008. *Le Sombre Abîme du Temps. Mémoire et archéologie*. Paris: Seuil.
Olsen, B. 2003. Material Culture after Text: Re-membering Things. *Norwegian Archaeological Review*, 36(2), 87–104.

Olsen, B. 2007. Keeping Things at Arm's Length: a Genealogy of Asymmetry. *World Archaeology*, 39(4), 579–88.

Oxford English Dictionary. 1989. 2nd Edition. Oxford: Clarendon Press.

Pred, A. 1977. The Choreography of Existence: Comments on Hägerstrand's Time-Geography and its Usefulness. *Economic Geography*, 53, 207–21.

Pred, A. 1985. The Social Becomes the Spatial, the Spatial Becomes the Social: Enclosures, Social Change and the Becoming of Places in Skane, in *Social Relations and Spatial Structures*, edited by D. Gregory and J. Urry. London: Macmillan, 337–65.

Rabinow, P. 2008. *Marking Time. On the Anthropology of the Contemporary.* Princeton: Princeton University Press.

Sullivan, A.P. 2008. Time Perspectivism and the Interpretative Potential of Palimpsests: Theoretical and Methodological Considerations of Assemblage Formation History and Contemporaneity, in *Time in Archaeology: Time Perspectivism Revisited*, edited by S. Holdaway and L. Wandsnider. Salt Lake City: The University of Utah Press, 31–45.

Thomas, J. 1993. The Politics of Vision and the Archaeologies of Landscape, in *Landscape: Politics and Perspectives,* edited by B. Bender. Oxford: Berg, 19–48.

Thomas, J. 2001. Archaeologies of Place and Landscape, in *Archaeological Theory Today*, edited by I. Hodder. Cambridge: Polity, 165–86.

Tilley, C. 1989. Excavation as Theatre. *Antiquity* 63, 275–80.

Tilley, C. 1991. *Material Culture and Text: The Art of Ambiguity*. London: Routledge.

Tilley, C. 1994. *A Phenomenology of Landscape. Places, Paths and Monuments*. Oxford: Berg.

Tilley, C. 2004. *The Materiality of Stone*. Oxford: Berg.

Tilley, C. 2007. Materiality in materials. *Archaeological Dialogues*, 14(1), 16–20.

Tilley, C. 2008. *Body and Image.* Walnut Creek: Left Coast Press.

Tulinius, T.H. 2005. The Westfjords. *Archaeologia Islandica*, 4, 9–15.

Witmore, C.L. 2006. Vision, Media, Noise and the Percolation of Time: Symmetrical Approaches to the Mediation of the Material World. *Journal of Material Culture*, 11(3), 267–92.

Witmore, C.L. 2007a. Symmetrical Archaeology. *World Archaeology*, 39(4), 546–62.

Witmore, C.L. 2007b. Landscape, Time, Topology: an Archaeological Account of the Southern Argolid, Greece, in *Envisioning Landscapes. Situations and Standpoints in Archaeology and Heritage*, edited by D. Hicks., L. McAtackney and G. Fairclough. Walnut Creek: Left Coast Press, 194–225.

Chapter 6
Grief Paves the Way

Arnar Árnason

Introduction

> At first she did not think of stones. Grief made her insubstantial to herself; she felt herself flitting lightly from room to room, in the twilit apartment, like a moth (Byatt 2003: 129).

Thus begins A.S. Byatt's not-so-short story *Stone Woman*. It tells of Ines, who upon the death of her mother finds herself gradually turning to stone. Looking for a place where she could stand when completely solid, Ines encounters a stone cutter at work in the "hidden wildernesses" of a nineteenth-century graveyard (Byatt 2003: 148). Showing her his work the stone cutter asks Ines if she likes it. "Like is the wrong word" she says. "They are alive". "He laughed. "Stones are alive where I come from." "Where?" she breathed. "I'm an Icelander"" is his reply (Byatt 2003:154). Later on the stone cutter adds:

> Iceland is a country where we are matter-of-fact about strange things. We know we live in a world of invisible beings ... as well as living things without solid substance we know that rocks and stones have their own energies. Iceland is ... a restless country. ... We live like lichens, clinging to standing stones and rolling stones and heaving stones and rattling stones and flying stones. Our tales are full of striding stone women. We have mostly not given up the expectation of seeing them. But I did not expect to meet one here, in this dead place (Byatt 2003: 158).

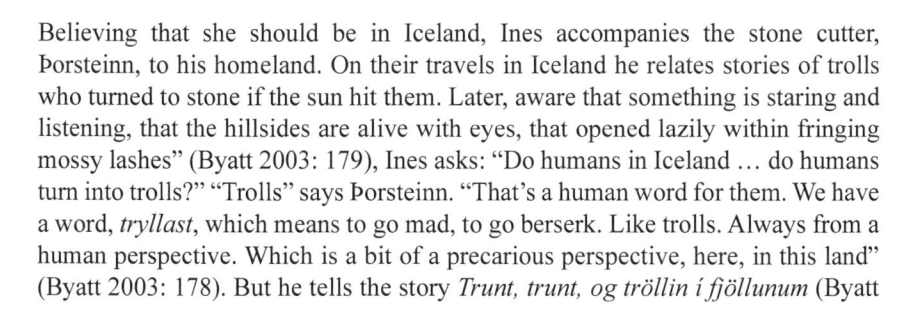

Believing that she should be in Iceland, Ines accompanies the stone cutter, Þorsteinn, to his homeland. On their travels in Iceland he relates stories of trolls who turned to stone if the sun hit them. Later, aware that something is staring and listening, that the hillsides are alive with eyes, that opened lazily within fringing mossy lashes" (Byatt 2003: 179), Ines asks: "Do humans in Iceland ... do humans turn into trolls?" "Trolls" says Þorsteinn. "That's a human word for them. We have a word, *tryllast*, which means to go mad, to go berserk. Like trolls. Always from a human perspective. Which is a bit of a precarious perspective, here, in this land" (Byatt 2003: 178). But he tells the story *Trunt, trunt, og tröllin í fjöllunum* (Byatt

2003: 180–1), a story of a man charmed by a troll woman, who in three years metamorphosed into a troll himself.[1]

In this chapter I am concerned with the issues raised in Byatt's story. I investigate how emotions, grief in particular, are implicated in people's conversations and relationships with landscape. I take as my substantive focus practices around and concern over fatalities on roads as these are currently played out in Iceland. I shall look at how the path of death is traced in landscape, already densely populated with stories, in official investigations of fatal accidents: investigations that in part amount to conversations with, even interrogation of, landscapes. I describe how death is placed and grief focused in private road side memorials that invite further conversations with landscape. I look at how highway travel at speed works to change people's relationships with the landscape and the stories it contains. Furthermore, I will describe how grief works to pave the way of further road construction and speedier travel while warning signs and roadside memorials work as landmarks, as anchors and as reminders of the losses speed demands (Virilio 1998). I set these stories within larger narratives that point to the importance of loss in the conversation with landscape through which the nation-form (Berlant 1998) asserts itself in Iceland.

Through these discussions I address issues to do with the phenomenology of movement, speed and perception, on one hand, and with the politics of the efficient movement of people and goods on the other. In the background is the question of the importance of loss in the process of conversation through which landscapes emerge. I will start there.

Landscape[2]

With some, indeed savage, simplification it can be suggested that theoretical writing on landscape in anthropology and allied disciplines has fallen largely in one of two camps. We have first what we might term loosely phenomenological approaches that seek to understand people's direct experiences of the environment. Second there are what we might term structural approaches that seek to unearth how landscape and the environment have been shaped by political, social, economic and historical forces (see Tilley 1994: 7–8 for a similar formulation, here in terms of spatial science and humanised space). The distinction is of course a grossly simplified snapshot of complex debates but it is worth spending a moment to establish these positions more clearly.

In the structural approaches that seek to unearth how landscape and the environment have been shaped by political, social, cultural, economic and historical forces, the work of Denis Cosgrove and Stephen Daniels (Cosgrove

---

1   I am grateful to Brian White for drawing my attention to Byatt's story.

2   I draw here on discussions with colleagues Jo Vergunst, Andrew Whitehouse and Nicolas Ellison.

1984, 1993, Cosgrove and Daniels 1998, Daniels and Cosgrove 1988) stands out as primary example. Thus they introduce their hugely influential *The Iconography of Landscape* by stating: "A landscape is a cultural image, a pictorial way of representing, structuring or symbolising surroundings" (Daniels and Cosgrove 1988: 1). Clearly, the key terms here are "image", "pictorial", "representing", "structuring" and "symbolising". Furthermore, according to Cosgrove (1993: 9) "the concept of landscape and the words for it in both Romance and Germanic languages emerged around the turn of the sixteenth century to denote a painting whose primary subject matter was natural scenery." Cosgrove (1984: 9) has further traced how "the idea of landscape came to denote the artistic and literary representation of the visible world, the scenery ... which is viewed by a spectator." Cosgrove (2006: 51–2) finds "the roots of the landscape idea" in another structure, "the changing landed property relations in the mercantile urban regions of early modern Europe." This history, or perhaps Cosgrove's work, has been so influential that Tim Cresswell (2004: 11) can state without any hesitation: "We do not live in landscapes – we look at them." While Cosgrove came to place less emphasis on the importance of landscape as view, he still insists that "the English world *landscape* ... retains an unshakeable pictorial association" (Cosgrove 2006: 51).

In contrast to this are what we might term phenomenological approaches to landscape (see Lorimer 2005, Wylie 2009). Here the argument is that in order to understand landscape we need to start from perception, people's direct experiences of and engagement with the environment. Tim Ingold's hugely influential paper on the temporality of landscape is a case in point here. Starting out with an explicit critique of Cosgrove and Daniels's approach, referring to their introduction cited above, Ingold (2000: 193) argues that "landscape is the world as it is known to those who dwell therein, who inhabit its places and journey along the paths connecting them." The contrast with Cosgrove and Daniels is fundamental. The influential work of Chris Tilley (1994) is another case in point here. Thus Tilley (forthcoming) has recently promoted the walk as a research method for studying landscape, arguing that it forces us to study landscape on a human scale, from the inside of direct experience. In contrast, according to Tilley, studying representations of landscape forces us to adopt others' perspective and reproduce their framed and deeply ideological understanding of landscape. Again, the emphasis here is on the direct knowledge and engagement of those who "dwell" in landscapes.

I want to linger over this a little bit longer to highlight the strength and weaknesses of the two approaches. Thus structural approaches have proved fruitful in explaining how political, social, cultural and economic forces shape landscapes and environments. Through that they help us to understand how particular experiences become possible. They help us to understand, for example, physical transformation of the material landscape, and how and why landscape may have emerged as a category of experience in Western Europe. The problem that structural approaches face is to explain how these broader and long-term changes, these larger forces, shape the daily and direct experience of and in landscapes and environments. Moreover, structural approaches fail to address how long-term changes are themselves rooted in experiences. In contrast, phenomenological approaches help us to understand how people experience and understand landscape and their environment. But the problem and the challenge for such a "phenomenological egology" (Bourdieu 2003, see also Bourdieu 1977) is to explain the processes that have made the particular experiences of these particular landscapes possible.

These dichotomies are of course only too familiar to social science more generally, their argument having been played out in terms of structure and agency, society and individual, objectivism and subjectivism and so on for well over a century now (Bourdieu 1977, Strathern 1988). It is not my aim, or indeed my hope, here to resolve these dichotomies. That task is well beyond my ambition let alone my ability. Some would argue that task has anyway already been completed (Strathern 1988). I seek here something more of a sideway glance. I am helped in taking that position by John Wylie's (2009) recent writings on landscape. He notes how much of the recent writings on landscape has been informed by phenomenology and seduced by the tropes of embodiment and performance. It "has sought to define landscape in terms of *presence* in various forms" (Wylie 2009: 9). What is emphasised in these writings is how "self and world come close together, and touch each other, and then go beyond even that, and become part of each other" (Wylie 2009: 9). Furthermore, "phenomenological accounts of landscape in terms of human dwelling and being-in-the-world commonly emphasise, and ground their arguments through, the evolving co-presence of self and landscape, with this self-landscape nexus being understood in terms of ramifying bodily engagements, encounters and inhabitations" (Wylie 2009: 10).

Wylie notes the influence of Ingold's (2000) paper on the temporality of landscape here but also how much of this work is influenced by the phenomenology of Merleau-Ponty (1968). The key element of Merleau-Ponty's philosophy that Wylie seeks to emphasise is that it assumes the "*possible-in-principle coincidence* of self with itself, and self with world" (Wylie 2009: 22). Evoking Jacques Derrida's reading of Merleau-Ponty, Wylie (2009: 22–3) notes how Merleau-Ponty's "accounts of self–other and self–world relations" assumes the primacy of the integrated and perceiving subject; a subject that is aware of its own presence through hearing its own voice and touching itself for example. The problem is that "Merleau-Ponty attempts to address the issue of my relationships with others, and with the "outside" world by analogising these relationships with my relation to myself" (Wylie 2009: 22). Thus Merleau-Ponty argues "for the indubitable existence of a shared, common world of seeing and touching, an intersubjective world of intertwining bodies and gazes" (Wylie 2009: 22). At the same time "this shared world can only be posited, in existential phenomenology, from the basis of a primary presencing of me to myself – a givenness of the ... perceiving subject" (Wylie 2009: 22–3).

Wylie (2009: 23) notes that for "Derrida ... it is precisely this assumption regarding ... this "metaphysics of presence", that is the problem. How could I ever coincide with myself, be myself, in any fulsome way?" (Wylie 2009: 23). Derrida (2005: 180, quoted in Wylie 2009: 23) suggests that "the constitution of the body...already presupposes a passage outside and through the other, as well as through absence, death and mourning". We are all hunted from without, as Wylie adds.

The concern Derrida raises, and Wylie echoes, is in some ways familiar to the social sciences, anthropology in particular. The foundational work of both Emile Durkheim and Franz Boas argues very strongly that meaningful experience is only possible if it is filtered through categories of thought provided to the individual by their culture or society prior to the experience. Presence or direct engagement with the environment is, according to this, not possible (see Hatch 1973). There are problems with this formulation of course (Ingold 1993) and in a way we are back here with the distinction between structural and phenomenological approaches in landscape research. But in questioning presence Wylie has hinted at the importance of absence and loss in the constitution of landscape. And this is the line that I will follow; there are still a few steps left.

Wylie's article starts out as a meditation on memorial benches by an English coastline. His conclusion, that we are all hunted from without, recalls no less an authority than Sigmund Freud. Continuing his musing on mourning and melancholia, begun in a paper of that name, in *The Ego and the Id* Freud eventually concludes that "the ego is constituted through the remains of abandoned object-cathexes" (Eng and Kazanjian 2003: 4). Freud argues that as "a psychic entity, the ego is composed of the residues of its accumulated losses" (Eng and Kazanjian 2003: 4). What this points to, furthermore, is the importance of the other, if oft the times through loss, in the constitution of self. And here, insights from theoretical work on conversations are important. In a celebrated and often quoted assertion, Mikhail Bakhtin (1986: 93) claims that anything we say contains "half-concealed or completely concealed words of others". Certainly the stories we tell each other often contain "reported" or even "quoted speech" (see Holt 1996, Tannen 1989) Reported or quoted speech is an example of what Deborah Tannen (1989: 28) calls "involvement strategies" that "work to communicate meaning and to persuade by creating involvement". Tannen places emphasis here on the "interactive nature" of conversations in which "both speaking and listening include elements and traces of the other. Listening ... is an active not a passive enterprise, requiring interpretation comparable to that required in speaking, and speaking entails simultaneously projecting the act of listening" (Tannen 1989: 12). The listener is active in the creation of the story, but the speaker themselves is simultaneously actively involved in the act of listening. "Not only is the audience co-author", Tannen (1989: 12) observes, "but the speaker is also a co-listener." Yet, as Marilyn Strathern (1988, 2005) has observed the bringing together that relationships, involvement, achieves simultaneously serves to separate, distinguish the parties of the relating.

Together Wylie, Tannen and Strathern are helpful in articulating how landscape emerges through narratives, conversations, of loss, where self and other are simultaneously brought together and pulled apart in a process that fuses the personal and the political. It is a process through which identities, individual and national, are constructed through conversation with landscape, not least landscape as a constant register and reminder of loss.

Speed and the Nation-Form in Iceland

Loss has been an important theme in the construction of Icelandic national identity at least from the early nineteenth Century onwards. The loss of self-determination and with that national dignity following the initial settlement period is a recurrent theme as is the loss of the original vegetation of the island. From that time accounts weave together personal and political losses. The poetry of the most important romantic nationalist, Jónas Hallgrímsson, speaks equally of the love he lost and left behind in Iceland as he settled in Denmark, and of the losses that Icelanders had suffered as a nation. His accounts of these losses were fundamentally important in the very constitution of the nation-form in Iceland.

This prevalence of narratives of loss can be put in the context of the importance of progress in Icelandic nationalism not least because that progress is often seen as undermining of national identity and uniqueness. That is, to quote Marilyn Ivy's (1999: 9) writing on Japan, Iceland's "national successes have produced ... a certain crucial nexus of unease about culture itself and its transmission and stability." These successes, furthermore, are understood to have been achieved and be dependent upon political sovereignty the acquisition of which was justified through references to national identity and uniqueness.

Here I am concerned with how this paradox has been played out in conversations with landscape specifically as regards deaths on roads. It is important to note here that as Iceland's transformation from a poor agricultural society to a prosperous post-industrial society during the twentieth century (see Hálfdanarson and Kristjánsson 1993) happened not least through enhancing the "dromocratic condition" (Virilio 1998) of the nation. Building a road network to facilitate speedier travel of both people and goods became and remains an important project in Iceland. But this project has not remained without ambiguity. *Möl*, gravel, the material from which roads were built, serves as reference to urban areas in Iceland. Living on the *möl*, or growing up on the *möl*, being used to refer to those growing up or living in Rekjavík and other towns, as opposed to those living on or growing up on a farmstead. Here *möl* has frequently, but of course not always, carried connotations of moral and spiritual degradation and poverty, seen to be caused by a lack of contact with the centre around which Icelandic identity is built, the independent farmer and his (the gender is deliberate) farmstead (Hastrup 1990). Deaths on roads are also a significant concern, often understood as the consequence of too much speed. The response has in recent years frequently been to ask for road improvements. These improvements in turn invite even speedier travel. Here again lies the paradox around which conversations with landscape take place. To move there I want to start with a ghost story.

The Girl in Kúagerði

It is said that sometimes, especially if the weather is bad, a young girl can be seen standing by the side of the road in Kúagerði. Her hair and her clothes drenched from the rain, she stands there rather forlornly trying to hitch a lift to town. Asked where she is going, the girl gives an address in the town. She does not say anything else but sits quietly in the back of the car. When driving past the cemetery at the edge of town, the girl disappears suddenly. Drivers, who have given her a lift, are of course shaken by this turn of events, and many have stopped their car and looked for her. Some have gone to the address she gave them. There they are greeted by a middle-aged couple who, on hearing the story, explain that the girl is their daughter and add that many drivers have come to their house in recent years having offered her a lift. You see, they say, the girl died in a car accident in Kúagerði a few years ago and is buried in the cemetery at the edge of town. She is always on her way home to her parents but can never quite make it all the way. Before she gets there she disappears into her grave in the cemetery.

The story of the girl in Kúagerði is well known in Iceland. A number of other similar stories do exist where the theme is ghostly presences on routes of travel. In this the stories are a contiuation of older Icelandic folktales while at the same time they echo widespread stories of the "vanishing hitchhiker" (Brunvald 1981). Together these stories speak of the dangers of the road, the losses suffered there and indeed further dangers resulting from those losses. This is not an unusual theme. Anthropological work emphasises the danger that roads embody and symbolise for many. Thus Mark Auslander (1993: 170), writing on modern Ngoni witch finding as a response to encroaching modernisation, notes:

> Senior men claimed that economically independent market women were bringing AIDS into the village, from "roads" originating in South African gold mines and rural slums. Women, in turn — in ritual and oratory — decried men who travelled "aimlessly" on the region's roadways. Female dominated *vivanda* clubs of affliction sought to restore biological and agricultural fertility by fabricating complex spiritual provinces in which all traces of motor vehicles and roadways were excluded.

Reykjanesbraut, the road that links Reykjavík to Iceland's only international airport in Keflavík, now passes by Kúagerði, which has been the scene of more fatal and near-fatal car accidents than any other place in Iceland. Over the last fifteen years it has also become a public shrine, a monument to those who have perished there. More recently still it has, by extension, become a memorial to all victims of car crashes in Iceland. The shrine in turn has become a focal point for a campaign for road safety, better "traffic culture", better roads; a campaign that involves car enthusiasts, insurance companies, government agencies and private individuals, often bereaved, and sometimes in search of a career, or at least influence, in politics.

But Kúagerði and the road do not simply represent danger, as the road that Auslander speaks of does. Rather, its place is somewhat more ambiguous. Kúagerði lies on what in Iceland is called *þjóðbraut*, a national road. It was for centuries a place of rest for slow moving travellers and their horses on their way between the seasonal fishing settlements on Reykjanes and the farms inland. Grazing is apparently good there and water plentiful. In the summer 1990 a "Group for the Improvement of Traffic Culture" instigated the building of a monument there in honour of those who had died or been seriously injured in traffic accidents on Reykjanesbraut. The monument is a cairn, *varða* in Icelandic (Figure 6.1). Having connotations both of guiding and guarding, *vörður* (the plural) are a reasonably and in fact increasingly common feature of the Icelandic landscape. Their current frequency can apparently be attributed to enthusiastic hikers wishing to leave their signature, a mark of their feat, on the landscape. In this form cairns are by many considered little better than gratuitous debasement of the land, transformation of nature for simple self-aggrandisement. Older cairns, seen as an important cultural

Figure 6.1 The cairn in Kúagerði (*Photograph*: Sigurjón Baldur Hafsteinsson, with permission)

heritage and a natural part of the landscape, served either, and sometimes both, as signs guiding travellers on their way, and as memorials to the dead. These dead would more likely than not have perished on the way (*orðið úti* is the Icelandic phrase), somewhere between inhabited places when roads were non-existent, travel was slower and slowness could be danger.

Kúagerði was chosen as the location for the cairn because of the number of accidents that had happened on that particular stretch of the road. It was a "black spot". The cairn was built explicitly both as a monument to those who had perished on the road, *and* as a reminder, a warning to other travellers to drive carefully (Áhugafólk um Suðurnesin n.d.). It was intended to provoke thought and thus enforce the slowdown of travel that had become too fast. The monument draws travellers' attention to this particular part of the environment. It may remind them of the story of the girl, and hence work as monuments and sometimes landscape features often do and anchor the story in the landscape. For those who know its origin and purpose it may call to mind the lives and deaths of those who have perished on the road, the sacrifices of fast travel. Its impact is reminiscent, then, of Basso's (1996) description of how "wisdom sits in places" or indeed the interplay of landscape and story more generally as discussed by Cruikshank (1998). The sacrifices demanded by the road, by traffic, evoke the place of loss in the construction of the Icelandic nation and its history. This takes a number of different forms. On one hand is the loss of independence and following what is portrayed as the golden age following the island's initial settlement (Hastrup 1998). On the other is the loss of habitat, in particular woodland, understood to have followed settlement. And then there is the loss of individual lives through the struggle to survive in a majestic but harsh land. Here the sacrifices of seamen whose exploits are understood to have fuelled the economic development of a once impoverished country, stand out. If the cairn affects a slowing down through instigating, as it were, a pause for thought, then it is an invitation to passersby to contemplate the sacrifices of modern travel.

In addition to its capacity as a site of remembrance and a reminder of the dangers of the road, the cairn has become of focal point for campaigns for greater road safety and road improvements. In the year 2000 key members of "The Group for the Improvement of Traffic Culture" had become part of a campaign to make Reykjanesbraut safer by making it a dual carriageway. At a public meeting with the Minister of Transport on February the 25th that year relatives of people lost on the road and others who themselves had suffered significant injuries there were present and related their experiences. According to one newspaper in Iceland, the minister – a Member of Parliament for the region – walked out saying that this issue was too serious to be ruled by emotions. After public demands but against the advice and wishes of the Icelandic Highway Agency, the government decided that the Reykjanesbraut would initially be lined with street lights. But it now turns out that the lights themselves are dangerous and one fatality on the road can be attributed to a clash with an unbending street light. It is possible that the lights will now be removed (Ríkisútvarpið 2010).[3]

Reykjanesbraut is now dual carriageway, the first such road outside urban areas in Iceland. Since that time, as campaigners keep reminding the government and the nation, no fatal accident has happened on the road.

Here I want to pause for a moment to note that the expanding of Reykjanessbraut does not seem to have occasioned any protests to speak of. On one level this is not surprising. Road building only rarely meets with direct human protest; such is the demand for improved transport in the country (see Árnason et al. 2007). On another level, though, it is surprising in that transformations of the landscape, such as those affected by road building, are often seen as problematic. Thus driving off the road and leaving your mark in pristine and always fragile landscape, is tantamount to sacrilege in Iceland. And the damming of rivers for hydroelectric projects has of course also occasioned huge protests (see Benediktsson 2007). Maybe grief, the possibility of saving lives, paved the way here, a point I want to pursue a little longer in the following section.

Road Safety

While road safety and traffic accidents have been a concern in Iceland for some time, autumn of 2006 and onwards saw the outbreak of unprecedented panic. The context here was twelve deaths on the roads since the beginning of July that year; eight of them in six accidents in what was dubbed the "black August". In the middle of September 2006 the Traffic Bureau and the Ministry of Transport, in association with a host of other organisations, staged seven more or less identical and simultaneous public meetings in Reykjavík and six of the main towns around Iceland. The meetings were announced with an advertisement in the Icelandic newspapers (Figure 6.2).

Listed are those who have died in road accidents in Iceland during the year with day of death, place of accident, name and age provided. The text reads (in my lamentably stilted translation):

> Now we say stop! This year (12th of September 2006) nineteen individuals have died in traffic accidents in Iceland. This is a terrible sacrifice and we must all ask ourselves if the life of any of them might have been spared with better traffic culture. We encourage all Icelanders to say stop. You can do your bit by going to www.stopp.is and sign a declaration about better traffic behaviour. We extend our condolences to the relatives of the deceased and thank them for helping us in this important mission.

---

3   I'm indebted to Karl Benediktsson for the information on this.

Grief Paves the Way 89

Figure 6.2 Advertisement for road safety
(*Source*: Umferðarstofa, with permission)

The website in question, www.stopp.is, now closed, carried a banner with the photographs of the nineteen lined up, the inscription "nineteen dead this year 28.08.2006", and the following pledge:

> Now we say stop! We challenge all Icelanders to say stop to fatal traffic accidents. You can do your bit by signing a declaration about better traffic behaviour.
>
> I intend to obey the traffic law. I will do what I can not to injure myself or others in the traffic. I will make it as easy as possible for all travellers to reach their destination as safely as possible. I will encourage my loved ones to do the same.

People could then enter their national identification number through which their name should appear on the screen, and then submit. When the campaign ended on the 14th of October, some 37,597 people had signed the pledge. The information officer of the Traffic Bureau explained the thinking behind the pledge in a newspaper interview:

> We are trying to make people aware of the responsibility they have in the traffic. You sign a pledge and you could say that those who feel that they cannot sign the pledge are unfit to participate in the traffic (*Morgunblaðið*, 13.9.2006).

The seven meetings all had the same format. At the beginning at the meeting in Reykjavík, the Minister for Transport said: "They have perished in traffic accidents this year ... " going on to read out the names and the age of the nineteen. He added later "it is because of them that we are here", as reported by the Icelandic National Television and Radio. The meetings involved relatives of people who have died in accidents relating their experiences, and paramedics, police and other rescue workers describing their experiences. The emotionality previously deemed unsuitable is now clearly in.

Paving the Way

A number of ideas are evident in how the problem of road safety is framed. Considerable attention is paid to people's attitudes, their beliefs, their behaviour, both individually and collectively. The pledge, mentioned before, is clearly intended to improve traffic culture. While drink-driving and not using seat belts are acknowledged as problems, the recent crisis has seen an intense attention paid to speeding and the question of why people speed. Some talked in terms of playfulness, particularly associated with younger drivers who to boot may lack experience. Six fatalites in 2006 were very explicitly and publically attributed to this. Others talked in terms of the thrill of driving fast, of people even having the need to speed. Talk in terms of violence, criminal behaviour and terrorism was prominent. The then minister for justice talked about sick individuals on the road. More generally there was talk of the violence on the roads, a state of war even, and of people being terrified of going out in their cars because who knows they might be next.

Attention was drawn to a particular disjuncture between the state of the roads, the capacities of the cars and the abilities of drivers. Not often was it noted that there is a limit to the speed at which people can apprehend their surroundings. More often it was noted that young drivers may lack the experience, rather than the swiftness of reaction, to know how to respond if things start to go wrong and they lose control of their cars. Foreign drivers not used to Icelandic conditions are sometimes placed in the same category. Mostly, though, people point out just how much cars have changed and "improved" in the last few years, just how much more powerful they have become. And they point out how much traffic in Iceland has increased over the last two decades. Here, considerable attention has been paid to the state of Iceland's roads. They are 30–40 years "behind" what is deemed acceptable in other countries in Europe, people are repeatedly told. "The government has to do more, don't you agree?" the Minister for Transport was asked. He agreed that the government had to do more, adding rather mysteriously: "And we already are" (Ríkisútvarpið 2006).

The personal marking of the site of road deaths increasingly found in Iceland, sometimes in the form of a cross whose intent may be simply as personal memorialisation. In some other cases still crosses are erected in memory of people perished but with a political message that demands road improvements. The crosses here, erected in 2006 along the Suðurlandsvegur from Reykjavík at the instigation of a private individual, represent the number of people killed on the road from 1954. When they were unveiled it was announced that they would stand there until the Suðurlandsvegur had been made a dual carriageway. Plans were swiftly made at the government level to turn Suðurlandsvegur into a dual carriageway. An insurance company already heavily implicated in road safety campaigns floated the idea that the project could be carried out with private finance. Again no objections to speak of were raised regarding these plans for a major upheaval of the environment, a transformation of the landscape. All these plans were well developed when the economic crisis hit Iceland in 2008, which put all public spending in question and lead to the virtual collapse of the insurance company.

Tracing the Path of Death

I have discussed how death and grief, the stories they tell and the sacrifices they memorialise are located in the landscape in the form of monuments, official or personal. But the landscape is drawn into conversations, interrogated even, more specifically with reference to road deaths. The Road Accident Analysis Group of Iceland investigates and reports publically on all fatal road traffic accidents. Formal reports are now produced on all fatal accidents. Following is excerpts from one such report:

Figure 6.3 Crosses at Suðurlandsvegur (*Photograph*: Tinna Grétarsdóttir, with permission)

1. The driver lost control over the vehicle in a s-turn. The car went off the road on the left hand side in the direction of driving and landed on a boulder by a side road. The car was thrown against a fence and ended on its side in a field. The driver died in the accident and front seat passenger was seriously injured. Both had worn seat belts.

An expert calculates that the car was travelling at a speed of 116 km/h. The speed limit on the road is 50 km/h. On the road are skid marks made by the car from a sharp left turn where the driver lost control off the vehicle and went off the road with aforementioned consequences. The road is tarmacked. The road was dry when the accident happened, weather good and driving conditions fine. The road follows hilly landscape here, is winding. The road has no surface markings where the accident happened.

The car was a Ford Fiesta. Expert's analysis revealed that both back tyres were worn from having too little air in them for a considerable time ...

Examination revealed that the driver was not under the influence of alcohol or drugs ...

Speeding was the main cause of the accident. The driver went much too fast into a bend ...

> Speeding is the most common cause of serious traffic accidents. It is important that the government continues to work to reduce speeding ...

The reports all have the following three part basic structure: narrative description of accident; causal analysis of accident; recommendations for improving road safety. Attention is paid to the driver, their speed, the vehicle itself, the road, the surroundings of the road, the weather, driving conditions and potential combinations of these as the path of the accident is traced from the marks left in the land. This is the spot that in some cases is then further marked by a road side memorial. Here the final moments of individual lives, the final marks they leave materially in the landscape recall the travels of trolls whose journey's end are still marked by the spot where they were caught in the rising sun and turned to stone. Trolls turn to stone, they petrify, but Icelandic folktales also tell of people who turn to trolls, gradually being covered in lichen and moss, a theme played upon in A.S. Byatt's short story. There is a sense of a return to the land here, of people turning back to provide the very material from which the land is made. Or maybe rather it is a reminder again of the sacrifices necessary to make a land that the remains harsh, inhabitable.

Conclusion

Byatt's story *Stone Woman* evokes the transformative power of grief. A woman turns into stone, a stone that is alive. She turns into a troll and merges with the land. It is a very bodily, corporeal, example of the drawing together that conversations, here with landscape, involves. Self and other, speaker and listener are drawn together so that the speaker is simultaneously a listener and the listener a speaker, as Tannen (1989) has it. Yet that involvement also engenders a distinction as Strathern (2005) reminds us. Relations separate at the same time as they bring together. This, furthermore, is the observation that Wylie makes. Absence and loss are important elements in the constitution of identity. There is a powerful argument to suggest that landscape emerges through conversations (see the introduction to this volume). And if so then absence, loss and distantiation are important elements of that process.

I have attempted to support that suggestion by looking at the conversations with landscape in Iceland in particular as these centre around deaths on the roads and concern with road safety. It is already well established that a conversation with landscape is a fundamental feature of the constitution of the nation-form in Iceland, in the formation of Icelandic identities. What I hope to have added here is a hint towards the importance of loss in that constitution and hence more generally in the process whereby landscape emerges through conversation.

Acknowledgements

Thanks are due to everyone in Iceland who has given of their time to talk to us. The research was made possible by financial assistance from the National Research Council of Iceland, the College of Arts and Social Sciences, and the School of Social Science University of Aberdeen. This chapter comes out of my longstanding collaboration with Sigurjón Baldur Hafsteinsson and Tinna Grétarsdóttir. Kristinn Schram and Katla Kjartansdóttir have at times worked on this with us too. My thanks to all of them. I'm indebted to the editors for their very helpful comments and their patience.

References

Áhugafólk um Suðurnesin n.d. *Ferlir*. Available at: www.ferlir.is [accessed 14 September 2006].
Árnason, A., Hafsteinsson, S.B. and Grétarsdóttir, T. 2007. Acceleration Nation: Speed, Death and Technologies of Patriotism. *Culture, Theory & Critique*, 48(2), 199–217.
Auslander, M. 1993. "Open the Wombs!" The Symbolic Politics of Modern Ngoni Witchfinding, in *Modernity and its malcontents: ritual and power in postcolonial Africa*, edited by J. Comaroff and J.L. Comaroff. London: University of Chicago Press, 167–92.
Bakhtin, M.M. 1986. *Speech Genres and Other Late Essays*, edited by C. Emerson and M. Holquist. Austin: University of Texas Press.
Basso, K.H. 1996. *Wisdom Sits in Places: Landscape and Language Among the Western Apache*. Alburquerque: University of New Mexico Press.
Benediktsson, K. 2007. "Scenophobia" and the Aesthetic Politics of Landscape. *Geografiska Annaler*, 89B(3), 203–17.
Berlant, L. 1998. Live Sex Acts [parental advisory: explicit material], in *In Near Ruins: Cultural Theory at the End of the Century*, edited by N.B. Dirks. London: University of Minnesota Press, 173–97.
Bourdieu, P. 1977. *Outline of a Theory of Practice*. Cambridge: Cambridge University Press.
Bourdieu, P. 2003. Participant Objectivation. *Journal of the Royal Anthropological Institute*, 9(2), 281–94.
Brunvand, J. 1981. *The Vanishing Hitchiker: American Urban Legends and their Meanings*. New York: Norton.
Byatt, A.S. 2003. *Little Black Book of Stories*. London: Chatto & Windus.
Cosgrove, D. 1984. *Social Formation and Symbolic Landscape*. London: Croom Helm.
Cosgrove, D. 1993. *The Palladian Landscape: Geographical Change and its Cultural Representations in Sixteenth Century Italy*. Leicester: Leicester University Press.

Cosgrove, D. 2006. Modernity, community and the landscape idea. *Journal of Material Culture*, 11(1/2), 49–66.
Cosgrove, D. and Daniels, S. (eds). 1988. *The Iconography of Landscape*. Cambridge: Cambridge University Press.
Cresswell, T. 2004. *Place: A Short Introduction*. Oxford: Blackwell.
Cruikshank, J. 1998. *The Social Life of Stories: Narrative and Knowledge in the Yukon Territory*. Lincoln: University of Nebraska Press.
Daniels, S. and Cosgrove, D. 1988. Introduction, in *The Iconography of Landscape*, edited by D. Cosgrove and S. Daniels. Cambridge: Cambridge University Press, 1–10.
Derrida, J. 2005. *On Touching: Jean-Luc Nancy*. Stanford: Stanford University Press.
Eng, D.L. and Kazanjian, D. 2003. Introduction: mourning remains, in *Loss: The Politics of Mourning*, edited by D.L. Eng and D. Kazanjian. Berkeley: University of California Press, 1–28.
Hálfdanarson, G. and Kristjánsson, S. (eds) 1993. *Íslensk þjóðfélagsþróun 1880–1990*. Reykjavík: Félagsvísindastofnun Háskóla Íslands & Sagnfræðistofnun Háskóla Íslands.
Hastrup, K. 1990. *Nature and Policy in Iceland 1400–1800: An Anthropological Analysis of History and Mentality*. Oxford: Clarendon Press.
Hastrup, K. 1998. *A Place Apart. An Anthropological Study of the Icelandic World*. Oxford: Clarendon Press.
Hatch, E. 1973. *Theories of Man and Culture*. New York: Columbia University Press.
Holt, E. 1996. Reporting on Talk: The Use of Direct Reported Speech in Conversation. *Research on Language and Social Interaction*, 29, 219–45.
Ingold, T. 1993. The Art of Translation in a Continuous World, in *Beyond Boundaries*, edited by G. Pálsson. Oxford: Berg, 210–30.
Ingold, T. 2000. *The Perception of the Environment*. London: Routledge.
Ivy, M. 1995. *Discourses of the Vanishing: Modernity, Phantasm, Japan*. London: Chicago University Press.
Lorimer, H. 2005. Cultural Geography: The Busyness of Being "More-than-Rrepresentational." *Progress in Human Geography*, 29(1), 83–94.
Merleau-Ponty, M. 1968. *The Visible and the Invisible*, edited by C. Lefort, translated by A. Lingis. Evanston: Northwestern University Press.
Ríkisútvarpið 2006. *Kastljós* [Current affairs television programme], 14 September.
Ríkisútvarpið 2010. *Ljósastaurar valda lífshættu* [Online, 14 January]. Available at: http://www.ruv.is/frett/ljosastaurar-valda-lifshaettu [accessed 11 March 2010].
Strathern, M. 1988. *The Gender of the Gift: Problems with Women and Problems with Society in Melanesia*. Berkeley: University of California Press.
Strathern, M. 2005. *Kinship, Law and the Unexpected. Relatives Are Always a Surprise*. Cambridge: Cambridge University Press.

Tannen, D. 1989. *Talking Voices: Repetition, Dialogue, and Imagery in Conversational Discourse*. Cambridge: Cambridge University Press.

Tilley, C. 1994. *A Phenomenology of Landscape*. Oxford: Berg.

Tilley, C. forthcoming. Walking in the past and in the present, in *Landscapes Beyond Land*, edited by A. Árnason, J. Vergunst, A. Whitehouse and N. Ellison. Oxford: Berghahn.

Virilio, P. 1998. *Speed and Politics*, translated by M. Polizzotti. New York: Semiotext(e).

Wylie, J. 2009. Landscape, absence and the geographies of love. *Transactions of the Institute of British Geographers*, 34(3), 275–89.

Chapter 7
Slipping into Landscape

Katrín Anna Lund and Margaret Willson

Introduction

> Walking, ideally, is a state in which the mind, the body, and the world are aligned, as though they were three characters finally in conversation together, three notes suddenly making a chord. (Solnit 2000: 5)[1]

> Life itself is as much a long walk as it is a long conversation, and the ways along which we walk are those along which we live. (Ingold and Vergunst 2008: 1)

How the act of walking weaves together lives and landscapes through the paths and routes which the body follows in the course of life has been an emerging topic in social studies during the passing decade. Increasing focus on the body and embodiment has brought scholars to consider the most mundane everyday bodily activities as significant in how the body is "the ground for perceptual processes" (Csordas 1994:7) that ties together that which surrounds. Walking brings human beings into the world and life into motion, temporally and spatially – "it sets the rhythm" (Lund 2005: 34) – and the ideal walk that Rebecca Solnit refers to above gives a sense of rhythm where the walker and the landscape are somehow in alliance with each other. It can nevertheless be expected that this state of alliance will not last for long because the "body's actions and engagements are never wholly determinate, since they must ceaselessly adjust themselves to a world and a terrain that is itself continually shifting" (Abram 1996: 49). In his analysis of rhythms, Lefebvre writes: "Alliance supposes harmony between different rhythms; arrythmia: a divergence in time, in space, in the use of energies" (2004: 68). Although the contrasts are great as spelled out here, Lefebvre's thoughts call forth questions regarding changing rhythms and how they change and also how people may fall in and out of rhythm. As Lund has argued in previous writings (2005), walking is a continuous bodily motion that combines different directions and different speeds including breaks and pauses which make up the ever-changing but ceaseless rhythm of walking. Thus, it is the ground which one's footsteps follow that is the point of ongoing sensual dialogue – the touching point which generates

---

1 "Tracing a Headland", from Solnit, R. (2000) *Wanderlust: A History of Walking.* © Rebecca Solnit. Used by permission of Viking Penguin, a division of Penguin Group (USA) Inc.

the rhythms which, as we will illustrate, engenders conversations with landscapes. But what kind of conversations take place when a walking is interupted by a sudden change of rhythm, caused by a sense of incommensurability between the body and the ground over which the walking body struggles to continue? How does a trip or even a slip alter the rhythms and the conversations? As Vergunst (2008: 120) points out, mishaps that take place during walking journeys often serve as the highlight of the journey in their narration and thus "become part of the rhythm of walking itself." He ends his phenomenological analysis about slipping, tripping and getting lost by bringing forth a question about how "mishaps are linked to the emotions of a walk and thus how emotions become part of our environment" (Vergunst 2008: 120). The emotions he refers to are those that the walker may bring with him or her into walking, such as excitement, joy or even fear, that have piled up from previous walking experiences. This is a question which we intend to take further by discussing how landscapes that become mapped with emotions may in turn respond by echoing these emotions through their appearances.

In order to explore this, we want to invite the reader to take a walk with us. We want to offer the reader to share with us a walking story which includes a slip into near-death experience. This is a journey through a landscape that both of us have taken although we follow the route in entirely different ways. One of us, Willson, physically walked it, took notes and wrote them into a chronologically narrated text about the journey. Lund on the other hand undertook the journey by reading Willson's written piece, but also in a less chronological order in conversations with Willson in which she expressed herself about the highlights of the journey. Thus, this chapter weaves together the footsteps of Willson as both Lund and Willson follow them in order to explore the landscapes that appear in the course of the journey and how they interconnect, the changing rhythm of the journey.

Lefebvre examines the role of the rhythmanalyst, "who thinks with his body, not in the abstract, but in lived temporality" (2004: 21), but who nevertheless situates her/himself "simultanously inside and outside" (2004: 27) as he suggests that the rhythmanalyst is positioned by the window where she or he can look over the scene rather than being located directly in the traffic of rhythms. Thus the rhythmanalyst is someone who grasps rhythms as she/he lives them (from the inside) without being absorbed by them (being on the outside). We on the other hand want to lessen this simultaneous binary position by converting it, claiming that examining the shifting rhythms through the process of walking demands that the analyst(s) do connect to the ground over which the walker goes and enter directly into the narratives to embody the landscape, following Ingold (2000: 56), who states that storytelling

> is not like weaving a tapestry to *cover up* the world or, as in an overworn anthropological metaphor, to "clothe it with meaning". For the landscape, unclothed, is not the "opaque surface of literalness" that this analogy suggest. Rather, it has both transparency and depth: transparency, because one can see into it; depth, because the more one looks the further one sees.

Moreover, by following the narratives, walking is explored as a forward-looking act, indicating what Ingold has spoken about as *"openness to the world"* (2006: 18, italics original), which he describes as:

> a condition of being alive to the world, characterised by a heightened sensitivity and responsiveness, in perception and action, to an environment that is always in flux, never the same from one moment to the next (Ingold 2006: 10).

To introduce the landscapes Willson encountered we will divide her narratives into what we see as three signifying parts of the hike. We will start by examining how she initially gets in touch with the landscape, connects to it and travels towards it by mapping it out in her mind. In the second part we consider the slip, an event which we claim dramatically shifted the rhythm of the walk and altered the relations that Willson had been building up with the surroundings. The last part considers then how she reconnects to the landscape, how it alters through how it becomes re-mapped with her emotions.

Connecting to Landscape – Paths and Visions

The recent academic turn to walking as a topic of study has emphasised how it is fundamental to humans (e.g. Ingold 2004) and as a result, walking has been tinted it with an air of romanticsm, as a bodily motion which gets one directly in touch with the surroundings (e.g. Adams 2001, Edensor 2001). The type of walking that has been academically practiced has in other words been rather trouble-free walking that "unites the walker and the landscape in a lived dialectic of being and becoming, acting and being acted upon" (Tilley 2008: 268). This is a walking that does not account for *how* the procedure of walking, the lived dialectic, the step by step, occurs and therefore not for how arrythmia may transpire as a result of disconnection (e.g. Vergunst 2008, Wylie 2005). Thus, it does not account for the tension which the fusion of the walker and the landscape entails which, according to Wylie, is a blending that involves "a simultaneous opening-onto and distancing-from" (Wylie 2009: 285). This may appear as a contradiction in terms of how we have spoken about how we regard walking as forward motion indicating openness to the world. On the other hand, as we will demonstrate, the opening-onto and distancing-from is an integrated tension in "the openness to the world". Moreover, coupled with the act of walking, opening-onto and distancing-from is inherent in the bodily techniques of walking which requires constant awareness of what is near and what is far. However, when walking takes place through surroundings that are mapped with emotions what is far and what is near melts in with walking as a sensual and bodily act. What is far can be near and what is near can be at a distance, even absent.

Willson's four days of hiking over the mountains of Tröllaskagi in the north of Iceland is characterised by this type of tension. In short, her emotions shift between excitement, vulnerability, humbleness, astonishment and ecstasy during the course of the walk. Her written narratives about the journey commence when the route of the walk is initially described to her and how a combination of paths and visions come into sight in her imagination. This is also our starting point. Willson had been staying in Iceland for a few weeks during the summer of 2009, making preparations for a future research project. During that time she had joined a local hiking group, Útivist, with which she went regularly with on shorter walking trips in the area around Reykjavík. In her narratives she illustrates how Reynir, the guide, portrays the route as a combination of trails that are familiar to him. He describes to her how they will be going "up some valleys" following "old tracks" through the environs of the farm where he and his sister, Una, who also joins them, grew up. Their father still lives on the farm. Of the four days the last day of the hike will be the longest, about 25 kilometers, while the other days require about 16 kilometers of walking. For Willson, an experienced hiker, this sounds reasonable not the least since that she is also told that at the end of each day they will be near jeep tracks where they will be picked up so they do not have to carry everything with them. Willson enters in her notes:

> This sounded relaxing. My vision of the hike was the West Highland Way in Scotland, on the old roman roads and tracks, rolling hills up long valleys, long tranquil days of moorland that ended in a warm inn or farmhouse and a pint of cider. I grew up in the Pacific Northwest and am an experienced backpacker; I have climbed a few of our highest mountains. I had brought backpacking gear with me. The mountains of Iceland are only three to four thousand feet high, ours are three times that. How hard could it be?

The walking has been set in motion and she is excited. She gets a vision of a landscape as she starts imagining herself following the paths through moorlands and up and down rolling hills. This is where Reynir grew up; this is his home, which adds a further significance to the route for Willson. Her body measures itself to the ground according to previous experiences, and she opens up to a familiar yet a faraway landscape. Lorimer and Lund (2003: 137) write about the experienced hillwalker who examines the map prior to a hike as a "way of looking into the landscape" to see "how the topography rises and falls" and to "speculate about the types of terrain likely to be encountered". Unlike the mountaineer that Lorimer and Lund describe, Willson is not faced with an actual map, rather she situates herself "within the historical context of journeys previously made" (Ingold 2000: 219) and a process of mental mapping occurs as she weaves together landscape she yet has physically to enter. This can be compared with what Van Den Berg (1952) writes about the mountaineer who measures the body to the ground from a distance. What he sees is the body "and the whole landscape with which this body contends is centered in this moving living 'object'" (Van Den Berg 1952: 173). This is a body that is conscious of itself and the perspective is on the body itself in relation to the extended view into the landscape the body is *in*. The body gets full attention as the mountaineer takes into account the shape and the texture of the landscape and measures the body to it as it maps out the terrain of walking. In Willson's case her imagination allows her to visualise what may be ahead and she gets into a synchroised rhythm with the surroundings.

The vision into the imaginary landscape is then followed by a trip to the north of Iceland with her friend, María, where they camp in a field near a small village. Willson, not able fall asleep as her thoughts are directed towards the days ahead, sits and watches as the sun quietly sets "as the colors of twilight crawled across the glacier-ground mountain and shrouded blue moraine", adding an Icelandic atmosphere into the visions of Scotland.

The day after a bus arrives to pick her up and she joins the group of fifteen Icelandic hikers with whom she will be spending the next four days with. The bus journey brings her into further proximity with the surroundings that she will be hiking through, nevertheless a proximity that brings about a sense of distancing-from. According to Ingold (2006), an openness to the world is always accompanied by a sense of vulnerability which is when one becomes aware of being an outsider to the surroundings that suddenly take the shape of the foreign. Feelings of "timidity and weakness" (Ingold 2006: 18) take over. Willson describes an elderly bus driver, about eighty years old, who she does not know whether to trust, even though the people travelling with her tell her that he had been driving buses already as a child. The roads also deteriorate the further they go and sometimes the road winds around hills with nothing on side but a steep drop into the ocean. They drive through a tunnel that "was low, carved from the living stone and not finished in the slightest". The road goes through a town sitting beneath a mountainside "waiting for an avalanche to happen" and the last leg of the bus journey is on a track similar to those she had thought they would be walking on. This is a different landscape from the one she had been visualising. It is not soft and inviting, rather it is raw and in the making as the roads and half-finished tunnels bear witness to, and it is not inviting. The former condition of openness seems to be blocked, as she is confused about where she is heading to. Willson feels vulnerable as her previous visions are disturbed; the rhythm has changed. Merleau-Ponty (1968: 139) points out that "there is a fundamental narcissism of all vision". Willson experiences herself as "in the making", as she realises that she needs to align to landscapes that are foreign and to which she feels emotionally at a distance. According to Jackson (1998), when a person faces a sudden change to her situation in which what has been anticipated is over-turned the response is to transform it in order to manage the situation. This is precisely what she does when the bus stops and the actual walking starts. Being comfortable with the motion of walking she now finds herself in familiar landscapes although she adds a new appearance to what she had previously imagined and the vulnerability appears to have vanished at least for a while.

> The terrain reminded me of Kodiak with fewer trees: lush green moss, delicate daisy-like blooms and yellow grasses, snow-capped peaks above us. In the

marshy valley bottom grew a flower, a woody stalk topped by a tuft of what felt and looked exactly like cotton ... At the head of the valley, we headed up, securing footing on loose stone and mud along fissure-like creek sides, then straight up to what I thought was the pass. I was mistaken.

The dialectic of walking continues to weave together images from former experiences that blend in with the physical landscape she is walking through. She feels at ease as she thinks she knows the direction into which they are heading but is mistaken.

The Slip

Van Den Berg, in his writing about the body and movement, writes about the mountaineer who thoroughly plans his walk prior to his journey and how his aims are destroyed "as soon as he takes his first step on the difficult ground" (1952: 169–170). He explains why and illustrates how the mountaineer

> no longer thinks of his shoes to which an hour ago he still gave such great attention, he "forgets" the stick that supports him while he climbs and with which he tests the reliability of a rock point, he "ignores his body" which he trained for days together beforehand with and eye to this trip, nor does his thoughts dwell on the closely calculated plan that occupied him so intensely the day before. For only by forgetting, in a certain sense, his plans and his body, will he be able to devote himself to the laborious task that has to be performed. What there still *is* psychologically speaking, is only the mountain: he is absorbed in his structure his thoughts are completely given to it. Just because he forgets his body, this body can realize itself as living (Van Den Berg 1952: 170).

Previously we mentioned the mountaineer who plans his journey and measures the body to the ground from the distance. This is not a body that is unaware of itself. When the body, on the other hand, enters the landscape, it is not merely *in* it, as when looked at from a distance, but *with* it, or as Van Den Berg claims, absorbed by it and the "body (just as the plan) is realized as a *landscape*" (1952: 170). Thus when Willson starts her walking she gets absorbed in with landscape that adjusts to her rhythm, a Kodiak-like terrain, but as the group heads along she finds out, although not necessarily consciously, that the routes one walks along do have "distinctively social aspects" and "paths reflect the social relations in which they are produced" (Vergunst 2008: 116). This Willson had not anticipated and when the group reaches the pass the walk continues, not through the pass as she had thought, but "straight up to the towering peaks of talus and snow". She describes how they scramble up the rocks before they make their way up the snowfield. "I kicked into the steps ahead of me, mediated on nothing and made it up before the panic reached my throat". It is at moments like this that the walker becomes aware of the rhythm of walking or "when it is felt to be absent" (Vergunst 2008: 116).

Willson feels insecure as the walking continues. She has realised that the people in the group are used to different types of terrains than she is. She regards snowfields as treacherous, something one attempts with axes, ropes and not only with "mere boots and poles" and after reaching the top they head down again over the steep field of snow that only gets steeper. She follows a hiker called Jobbi whom she knows from previous walks and is not aware that the rest of the group is taking another route at the edge of the snowfield instead of going across it like they are doing. She cannot keep up with his speed and loses a track of him but, instead, tries to follow the marks he leaves but the glare of the sun as it hits the snow prevents her from doing so. Beside this it appears that he had not "made much mark anyway since he seemed to do it in some remarkable boot glissade traverse" she has never seen before. She writes:

> I kicked my boots into the snow and tried to get across, but I wasn't sure where to go. Three quarters of the way across I slipped. I screamed and went careening down the slope. I flipped on my belly and started dragging my toes and clawing with my hands and poles as much as I could, but the snow was too steep. My speed only increased.

Suddenly Reynir appears below her. He has made a run onto the snow to attempt to save her. He motions her by waving his arms to run into him which she does. She hits him and …

> … braced as he was I knocked him flat and we both went sliding down together. He threw himself almost on top of me, braced his pole along his arm in a way that allowed him to use it almost like an ice axe. Then he somehow used his entire body as a brace for the two of us and we stopped – I am still not sure how he did this.

She slides about 100 meters down the slope and Reynir is with her the last quarter of it. They are 15 metres away from the boulder-field when they stop sliding. She stands up and Reynir says "looking completely calm, "You will begin to get the shock soon, so you should get across the rocks fast before it hits."" She does not seem to be aware of herself descending until she hits the grassy slope below, where her fellow walkers are sitting and having a snack whilst her legs give away.

> I went into almost uncontrollable shaking and collapsed on the grass. Jobbi smiled up at me from his perch on the grass below and poured me a nip of liquor from a small bottle he pulled from his pack. "Here," he said, "It's Old Danish, made with fresh herbs. It makes the shaking go away."

Lefebvre (2004: 21) explains how "in suffering, in confusion, a particular rhythm surges up and imposes itself: palpitation, breathlessness, pains in the place of satiety". Willson is not sure if she can continue. Her vulnerability has taken over, but Reynir only laughs and encourages her to continue. She realises that although an experienced mountaineer she still is a stranger to this landscape. "Mishaps are particularly pointed examples of becoming aware of what landscapes are *really* like", states Vergunst (2008: 114), and in her confusion Willson is not sure if she trusts herself to do so in a company of people who appear in a seamless rhythm with their surroundings.

In the evening she describes how she sits alone outside her tent "preparing to eat my old rye crisp and cheese" when one of the hikers, Karl, offers her to share with him his dinner of meat and potatoes which she accepts and brings over her bottle of red wine. Whilst frying the meat he tells her that he is

> ... reading a novel written in 1912, a love story of people living in the 1700s after the gigantic Laki volcanic eruption killed a third of Iceland's population, mostly through famine after poisonous gases from the volcano killed most of the livestock.

Listening to Karl appears to give her a glimpse into what the landscape she is in might be really like, and although she now realises that the meat he offers is a whale meat she lets her "years of anthropological training kick in" and finds it delicious.

Paths of Motion and Emotion

In his accounts of the Apache Indians, Basso (1996) illustrates how the landscape speaks to the people through names and stories. The stories are moral tales that can stalk people, continuously reminding them of who and where they are. Thus they move with people at the same time that they move people. Earlier on we mentioned the narratives of walking but we want to add that walking is a narrating act in itself and not the least so because it follows and interacts with the narratives inherent and expressed by the landscape. From this point of view walking becomes an interactive process of storytelling. Basso states that "participants in verbal encounters put their landscapes to work" (1996: 75). When Karl tells Willson about the story he is reading the landscape starts to work. The story gets it into motion and Willson starts sensing a rhythm, and after a short time of sharing both food and words the landscape looks somehow different. She starts recalling how, during the day, every time they "reached a pass or above certain valleys", Una had stopped to tell a story of it; an act that continues throughout the walk. And in the evenings after dinner the group gathers together to listen to longer stories.

I so wish I could have understood her better. I was told these were stories about the "hidden people" who inhabit so many of the rocks and upper valleys, and about the ghosts, often of a child left in the cold to die by uncaring farmers during one of Iceland's many eras of famine, flood and the aftermath of gigantic volcanic eruptions. She told stories of outlaws who had lived below a pass for years until they were killed, or returned to civilization for those few who survived.

Jackson writes about stories and how they "transport us" (2002: 138) and thus if walking is a narrating act in itself, as we claim, it furthermore, weaves together narratives, the narratives of those who have travelled the same paths as well of those who travel them with us. As illustrated above, Willson's narrative start when Reynir initially describes the route they will be travelling. Then he tells her that they will be travelling on routes he knows very well as these are routes located in vicinity to where he grew up. Willson immediately transforms these routes into her own and ties them into her own memories of previous walking. She already stories the route. This is the landscape she initially meets up with and walks into. Van Den Berg (1952: 166) writes:

Whoever wants to get to know a man should leave him as quickly as possible. He is in the last place to be found there where he stands. All the time he silently moves away from himself by expressing himself in the world of things. So one can learn to know another best by travelling with him through a country ...

Moreover, as you are travelling with the one you are getting to know, you are travelling with the landscape as Willson realises:

I began to understand how these histories and sagas give a context for every large boulder, every hill and so many now deserted farmlands. And they do more. Through these stories every natural feature becomes an included part of society, a rock, a hill, becomes a persona itself, through the beings and histories who inhabit this wild land, it becomes connected to the people who have struggled to survive and often lost.

Thus, when we walk with those we are getting to know, "they appear in the conversation", not in the world of things, and we "take them at their *landscape* value" (Van Den Berg 1952: 166). It is through how the relations emerge how we map emotions onto landscape and it is through their appearance how they communicate them back to us. In this the quality of narcissism is reflected, that is, if we can say that people story landscapes it is so because landscapes story people in turn and "any landscape is a state of a soul" (Van Den Berg 1952: 166).

In the course of the hike stories continue to be told by different people Willson walks with. Sometimes the stories are mythical, sometimes historical and sometimes biographical and personal but what they all do is that they weave together a "meshwork of paths" (Ingold 2008: 1808); paths that wind themselves through time and space and bring the landscape into motion. She is now moving with it. She is delighted to hear that Jobbi, the one she followed when she slipped, also grew up near to the mountains they traverse and had herded sheep there until the age of sixteen. He had grown a passion for the mountains and at the age of fifty he "skied alone in winter across Iceland". He told her that on the farm "where they lived they did not have electricity but Jobbi had read his father's books by paraffin light until he knew all the stories of all the mountains that he had as yet not seen". What emerges is that the stories that are embedded in the landscape are simultaneously embedded in the walking and how her companions walk, connect to the landscape; find the rhythm. Thus where the body meets the ground in walking is not merely about stepping onto a surface as in a mere encounter between the walker and the ground. Rather, as Ingold (2008: 1808) states: "Now embodied we may be, but that body, I contend, is not confined or bounded but rather extends as it grows along the multiple paths of its entanglement in the textured world". Thus the landscape and the walker's body are integrated in each other in a togetherness, not to be separated, although they may be at a physical distance from each other. When Willson looks at the landscapes she thought she was heading to at the beginning of this chapter she goes into a landscape whilst at the same time being with different landscapes. She becomes lost, does not know where or how to put her foot down. In her openness towards a landscape that she has not yet entered, she starts walking her own paths. When she is on the other hand physically with the landscape she tries to map her former experiences onto it and looses her feet. She writes:

> What arrogant ignorance. I clearly did not know Iceland. What we really did was hike up trackless long moraines, up talus-covered mountainsides, and then up steep terrifying snowfields. The tracks were from [the year] 1100, and they only made an archaeological appearance twice.

Until the slip she was distant from the very landscape she was walking in because she had not anticipated that the texture of landscapes is always shaped by the social relations they contain. The slipping on the other hand gets her into close contact with the texture of the landscape, not necessarily through the event itself but rather through how she allows herself to slowly get into rhythm of it as she listens to what it has to say. She gets in touch with it but nevertheless in her own way as her description of the last leg of the hike reveals:

> The four of us set off alone, tripping through sodden tundra and lichen-encrusted talus, sliding through snow that didn't feel dangerous, even glissading together, slipping through impenetrable mist in the complete confidence that Una (the guide) knew exactly where she was. And then, we descended into one of the most remarkable valleys I have ever seen, sweeping green steep sides of the glacier-cut moraine, flowers white, yellow, pink and intense blues, waterfalls

cutting white threads, cascading hundreds of feet. Jobbi appeared, pointing out cliffs where he had gathered sheep. A quiet exhilaration seemed to rise from the valley floor and I decided to walk alone – for the last five or six kilometers we actually walked on the still-visible old track – letting it wash over me, passing the ruins of old farms, maybe from the 1200s or maybe from the 1800s, it seems that here in Iceland you can't tell unless you know the farm. We forded two wide raging glacial-fed rivers, but somehow this seemed to only add to a certain stillness I felt. When I saw the Jeeps far in the distance waiting for us across the valley floor, I didn't want to leave.

The walk has come to an end, but she does not want to leave. The landscape she is now walking in is one she wants to be with on her own "letting it wash over" her and what she feels is stillness. This is a very different landscape to the one she entered at the beginning. This is neither Scotland nor Kodiak as seen from the distance, the landscapes she at the beginning heads *into*. This is a landscape that she is *with*; absorbed by. She is no longer kicking into snowfields and scrambling up talus-faced mountains, emphasising the physical tasks that are ahead. Rather she appears to have forgotten her body, which has melted in with the texture of a landscape that echoes her emotions. She is an integrated part of an ever-moving scene that is combined by mountains, snowfields, rivers, waterfalls, farms and flora. Nevertheless, although now, physically separated from it she still can visit her memories and continue to move with it.

References

Abram, D. 1996. *The Spell of the Sensuous: Perception and Language in a More-Than-Human World*. New York: Vintage Books.
Adams, P.C. 2001. Peripatetic Imagery and Peripatetic Sense of Place, in *Textures of Place: Exploring Humanist Geographies*, edited by P.C. Adams, S.D. Hoelscher and K.E. Till. Minneapolis: University of Minneapolis Press, 186–206.
Basso, K.H. 1996. *Wisdom Sits in Places: Landscape and Language among the Western Apache*. Albuquerque: University of New Mexico Press.
Csordas, T.J. 1994. Introduction: The Body as Representation and Being-in-the-World, in *Embodiment and Experience*, edited by T.J. Csordas. Cambridge: Cambridge University Press, 1–24.
Edensor, T. 2001. Walking in the British countryside: Reflexivity, Embodied Practices and Ways to Escape, in *Bodies of Nature*, edited by P. Macnagthen and J. Urry. London: Sage, 81–106.
Ingold, T. 2000. *The Perception of the Environment: Essays in Livelihood, Dwelling and Skill*. London: Routledge.
Ingold, T. 2004. Culture on the Ground: The World Perceived Through the Feet. *Journal of Material Culture*, 9(3), 315–40.

Ingold, T. 2006. Rethinking the animate, re-animating thought. *Ethnos*, 71(1), 9–20.
Ingold, T. 2008. Bindings against Boundaries: Entanglements of Life in an Open World. *Environment and Planning A*, 40, 1796–1810.
Ingold, T. and Vergunst, J.L. 2008. Introduction, in *Ways of Walking: Ethnography and Practice on Foot*, edited by T. Ingold and J.L. Vergunst. Aldershot: Ashgate, 1–20.
Jackson, M. 1998. *Minima Ethnographica: Intersubjectivity and the Anthropological Project*. Chicago: University of Chigaco Press.
Jackson, M. 2002. *The Politics of Storytelling: Violence, Transgression and Intersubjectivity*. Copenhagen: Museum Tusculanum Press.
Lefebvre, H. 2004. *Rhythmanalysis: Space, Time and Everyday Life*, translated by S. Elden and G. Moore. London: Continuum.
Lorimer, H. and Lund, K. 2003. Performing Facts: Finding a Way over Scotland's Mountains, in *Nature Performed: Environment, Culture and Performance*, edited by B. Szerszynski, W. Heim and C. Waterton. London: Blackwells, 130–44.
Lund, K. 2005. Seeing in Motion and the Touching Eye: Walking over Scotland's Mountains. *Etnofoor*, 18(1), 27–42.
Merleau-Ponty, M. 1968. *The Visible and the Invisible*, edited by C. Lefort, translated by A. Lingis. Evanston: Northwestern University Press.
Solnit, R. 2000. *Wanderlust: A History of Walking*. New York: Penguin Books.
Tilley, C. 2008. *Body and Image*. Walnut Creek: Left Coast Press.
Van Den Berg, J.H. 1952. The Human Body and the Significance of Human Movement: a Phenomenological Study. *Philosophy and Phenomenological Research*, 13, 159–83.
Vergunst, J.L. 2008. Taking a Trip and Taking Care in Everyday Life, in *Ways of Walking: Ethnography and Practice on Foot*, edited by T. Ingold and J. Lee Vergunst. Aldershot: Ashgate, 105–22.
Wylie, J. 2005. A Single Day's Walking: Narrating Self and Landscape on the South West Coast Path. *Transactions of the Institute of British Geographers N.S.*, 30, 234–47.
Wylie, J. 2009. Landscape, Absence and the Geographies of Love. *Transactions of the Institute of British Geographers N.S.*, 34, 275–89.

Chapter 8
Landscape and Aesthetic Values: Not Only in the Eye of the Beholder

Guðbjörg R. Jóhannesdóttir

Introduction

An important part of the work done by those who study landscape and landscape quality assessment is examining the aesthetic qualities of landscape. In fact, both the everyday understanding that people have of the word landscape, and its usage in academia, often emphasizes its scenic and visual aspects (Ritter 1989, Lothian 1999, Brady 2003, Benediktsson 2007, Gobster et al. 2007, Muelder Eaton 2008). Thus, there is a strong conceptual and historical link between the landscape concept and aesthetics. As Andrew Lothian points out, philosophers have dealt with aesthetics for a long time and thus "[t]heir findings can inform contemporary landscape research" (Lothian 1999: 177). The aim of this chapter is to examine some ways in which I think that contemporary philosophy (especially environmental aesthetics and phenomenology) can indeed inform landscape research.

Landscape is and has been a very contested concept. For example, landscape assessment has been approached in two very different ways: in an objective way, where landscape quality is seen as inherent in the physical features of the landscape (Martin 1993, Nicholls and Schlater 1993); and in a subjective way, where the quality of landscape is seen as a product of people's perception (Dakin 2003, Schroeder 2007). This dualism in approaches to landscape has a historical root in the developments in philosophical aesthetics from Plato to Kant and beyond (Lothian 1999). Since the root of this dualism is found in the traditions of philosophy, perhaps the path that leads us beyond it can be found in the same field.

But why is there a need to get beyond a dualistic way of thinking about landscape? One of the reasons is that this dualistic approach has, among other things, contributed to the weak status of landscape in environmental decision-making. How can such a contested concept ever become a solid grounding for decision-making? Both approaches to landscape, the objective and the subjective, have flaws that make it difficult to get people to agree on their usage. The objective approach is lacking because it doesn't take into account the side to landscape that is the main reason why people see it as important to protect landscapes: the relationship between humans and the land. The subjective approach is problematic because the values that emerge from people's perception of landscape are seen as being too subjective and relative and thus not able to provide solid criteria for landscape protection.

How can philosophy help with this dilemma? As pointed out, the subjectivity vs. objectivity debate on landscape has its roots in aesthetics. In the history of aesthetics, there was a shift from objectivity to subjectivity in theorizing about aesthetic value and aesthetic qualities; from Plato to the seventeenth century, aesthetic qualities were seen as being inherent in the object, but from the eighteenth century onwards the idea emerged that beauty lies mainly in the eye of the beholder (Cooper 1992). But what has happened since then? There are two philosophical developments that I think can help with the objectivity-subjectivity dilemma. First, the rethinking of subject and object that has occurred in the field of phenomenology can help deconstruct the idea that landscape quality has to be categorized *either* as subjective *or* objective. The ideas of French phenomenologist Maurice Merleau-Ponty are especially helpful in this context. Second, the field of environmental aesthetics has encouraged new developments in thinking about aesthetic valuing that suggest, as Kant did, that at least some degree of objectivity can be found in subjective, aesthetic judgments of nature.

In the first part of this chapter, I will examine the relation between landscape and aesthetics, go through the objective and subjective approaches to landscape and show through an Icelandic example how these approaches can lead to a weak status of landscape in decision-making. In the second part I will discuss how Merleau-Ponty's rethinking of subject and object through the notion of *flesh* can provide a context for understanding landscape and aesthetic value, which suggests that the meaning and value of landscape is determined by the relationship or conversation that takes place between landscape and the people who dwell in it. This phenomenological approach leads into an examination of the subjectivity or objectivity of aesthetic values, since the concept of flesh also suggests that the traditional separation between subject and object – and hence, subjective and objective valuing – is not as clear-cut as once was held. The meaning and value of landscape cannot be found through categorizing its objective features, nor can it be found only in our social construction of it, i.e. in the meanings we are understood to impose on it. Through gaining understanding of the concept of flesh, this chapter will suggest that there is something to be found in between these options. In the third part I will show with an example from my own research on the aesthetic experience of Icelandic landscapes[1] that such experiences and the values attached to them cannot be traced *either* solely to subjective perception *or*

---

1 This research is a part of my PhD-project on the aesthetic values of Icelandic landscapes. It is a qualitative study based on interviews and participation observations. Participation observations were conducted in group-trips to geothermal areas and glaciers and after each observation 1–3 participants were interviewed to get a deeper understanding of their experiences. Geothermal areas and glaciers are landscape types that are characteristic for Iceland since they are common in Iceland but rare worldwide, and therefore they were chosen as representatives of Icelandic landscapes.

objective physical features. In order to shed light on this I will examine Gernot Böhme's aesthetic theory of nature and show how his idea of *atmosphere* provides an example of how Merleau-Ponty's rethinking of subject and object can change the way we think about the subjectivity or objectivity of the aesthetic values of landscapes.

Landscape: Objective or Subjective?

The landscape concept can surely be seen as a very contested and elusive concept, having been interpreted in quite contrasting ways. The point where the concept becomes contested and interpreted in contrasting ways does not primarily circle around the understanding of landscape in aesthetic terms, but rather it involves contrasting ideas of how to understand or define aesthetic qualities and values. The debate is not about whether landscapes should be defined as having aesthetic qualities but rather about *what is the source* of these aesthetic qualities – is it the object's physical features or the subject's experience?

The different definitions of landscape lead to different methods of doing landscape assessment; on the basis of the objective definition, landscape is treated in a similar way as soils, landforms or vegetation, as a feature that can and should be mapped and classified by specialists. A landscape assessment based on this definition would involve documenting landscape features, such as colors, lines, forms, water coverage, vegetation coverage and so on, and as in other sciences, the aim would be not to involve much personal evaluation.

This method of landscape assessment can be criticized from two directions. On the one hand, it can be criticized for being based on subjective values after all. As Lothian points out, when landscape is classified and mapped in this way, certain assumptions are established beforehand, "e.g. that mountains and rivers have high landscape quality" (Lothian 1999: 177), or that rare or diverse landscapes have high quality, and then the landscape is evaluated according to these assumptions. So despite sharing a method with the "objective" sciences, this approach to landscape assessment has a subjective basis. On the other hand it can be criticized for not taking the subjective aspect of landscape into account and thereby ignoring what is in fact important about landscapes: the human relationship to the land.

The subjective definition of landscape leads to a very different way of landscape assessment, using qualitative and/or quantitative research methods to examine the community preferences for landscape. The assumption here is that landscape quality is determined by people's perceptions and interests and so what needs to be mapped and classified are not the physical features of the landscape but rather people's experiences and preferences. This method has been criticized for being based on something that is too relative and subjective to be measured in any meaningful way. Different individuals have different preferences in different times and there can thus never be a static consensus about what counts as a valuable landscape.

This dualistic way of defining landscape and approaching landscape assessment can contribute to the weak status of landscape in environmental decision-making. In Iceland, this has certainly been the case; landscape has had a weak status in decision-making and it is seen as very difficult to deal with because of the subjective valuing associated with it. According to a report from a committee on landscape evaluation working for the Icelandic government's Master Plan for Hydro and Geothermal Energy Resources (first phase)[2] there was no basis for making such evaluation: "The evaluation was especially difficult when it came to landscape and wilderness. There were few foreign examples to work from, the legal structure was badly defined and no existing tradition of taking such values into account" (Verkefnisstjórn um gerð rammaáætlunar um nýtingu vatnsafls og jarðvarma 2003: 10–11, my translation).

From this time on, the need for taking the value of landscape into account in decision-making in Iceland has become more and more evident, with many controversies about changes in landscape created by the construction of new dams, roads or power-lines. The fact is that when new construction projects are being prepared, the most controversial part of the environmental impact assessment has been the visual and aesthetic value of the landscape (Benediktsson 2007, Thorgeirsdóttir 2007). Landscape thus seems to be very important to the Icelandic public and its value largely based on the aesthetic value of the experience of landscape. But taking the value of landscape into account is not an easy task. There are two basic problems that need to be solved; first, reaching an agreement on how the landscape concept should be defined, and second, finding a way to evaluate landscape in spite of the fact that landscape values are seen by experts and laypersons alike as being subjective and thus also relative, offering no possibility of adjudication between differing viewpoints.

In a chapter on landscape conservation in a report on The Nature Conservation Strategy 2004–2008 from the Environment Agency of Iceland, this is mentioned as one of the reasons for the weak status of landscape conservation:

> The value of landscape is mostly visual and aesthetic, and such subjective values are more relative than the yardsticks that can be used to evaluate other natural

---

2 The Master Plan for Hydro and Geothermal Energy Resources was initiated by the Government of Iceland in 1999. Its aim is to evaluate and categorize proposed power projects "on the basis of efficiency, economic profitability, and how they will benefit the economy as a whole. The implications for employment and regional development will also be considered. Furthermore, the impact on the environment, nature, and wildlife will be evaluated, as well as the impact on the landscape, cultural heritage and ancient monuments, grazing and other traditional land use, outdoor activities fishing, and hunting" (Rammaáætlun n.d.). The first phase was finished in 2003 with a preliminary ranking, but was unable to complete the final evaluation due to lack of scientific research. Work on the second phase started in 2007 and will be finished in the beginning of 2010.

factors. Therefore it is much more difficult to describe and categorize landscape than other natural factors (Umhverfisstofnun 2003: 34, my translation).

A qualitative case study of the preparation for the Icelandic Nature Conservation Strategy 2004–2008, where contributors to the strategy were interviewed, confirms this:

> The subjective aspect of landscape was always linked to aesthetic values. This became the experts' recurring, niggling problem. The dilemma ... is that the aesthetic values of landscape resist being measured and evaluated by means of the presumably objective methods of the natural sciences (Waage and Benediktsson 2010: 18).

It can be seen from the above how the dualistic thinking about landscape contributes to its weak status in conservation.

In the debate on landscape it is often assumed that the objective and subjective definitions of landscape are mutually exclusive. Lothian is one of those whose view is colored by this:

> The paradox in [the subjective and the objective] approaches derives from their contrasting underlying premises. They cannot both be correct. The first approach assumes that landscape quality is inherent in the landscape while the second assumes that landscape quality is in the eyes of the beholder. The paradox is that in common usage, the landscape is taken to be beautiful but in actuality this beauty is literally a figment of the imagination, a product of the viewer's own cultural, social and psychological constitution (Lothian 1999: 178).

The paradox should be taken as a sign of the fact that both approaches are insufficient accounts of the roots of aesthetic qualities of landscape, but it is understandable that the sign goes unnoticed in a culture that has for centuries assumed that the gap between so-called objective and subjective values is unavoidable. This gap has a deep root in the Western mind-set which is based on the dualisms between subjective/objective, emotions/reason, nature/culture, female/male, body/mind, non-cognitive/cognitive. The Western worldview has been characterized by a tendency to divide everything into such dualistic pairs, where one part of the pair is seen as having greater importance than the other. Considering this history of ideas it is not surprising that in debates on nature conservation aesthetic values are often associated with subjectivity and emotions and therefore pushed to the side for scientific values that can be measured objectively.[3]

---

3 This was the case in Iceland. From 2003 onwards, decisions to construct large hydropower dams have been hotly debated and in these debates, aesthetic values have been portrayed as being equivalent to personal emotions and therefore too subjective to provide a basis for conservation (Benediktsson 2007, Thorgeirsdottir 2007).

This division between so-called objective and subjective values and the value hierarchy inherent in it is based on an interpretation of the relationship between subject and object that has been challenged, like I will show here with my discussion of Merleau-Ponty. "Subjective" values are much more than just what lies in the eye of the beholder. The meaning and value of our experiences and perceptions of reality are always the result of an intertwining of subject and object, and this counts for both the meaning and value that result from our scientific viewpoint, and from our aesthetic viewpoint.

Recent developments in landscape studies do suggest that there is a growing interest in trying to somehow combine the two approaches and the different methods (Dakin 2003, Schroeder 2007). It could be said that with the increasing acknowledgement of the need to take the subjective aspect of landscape into account, more attempts have been made to try to combine the two approaches in landscape assessment. Thus, a strong acknowledgement of the interrelationship of objective and subjective landscape qualities is evident in the European Landscape Convention (ELC; Council of Europe 2000). The ELC can be seen as a response to a need for recognizing the important part that landscape plays in the quality of peoples' lives. According to the convention, developments in industries and planning brought about by changes in the world economy have accelerated the transformation of landscapes. These fast changes in landscape have made people realize that it is "a key element of individual and social well-being" (Council of Europe 2000). The ELC is a result of the acknowledgment that the "emotional and subjective" relationships that individuals and societies have to their surroundings are vital to our well-being. What is interesting about the ELC is that it includes both the subjective and objective approaches to landscape, as can be seen in its core definition of landscape: ""Landscape" means an area, as perceived by people, whose character is the result of the action and interaction of natural and/or human factors" (Council of Europe 2000: 3). Although this definition strongly emphasizes the subjective account of landscape, the convention also makes it clear that gaining knowledge of "the action and interaction of natural and/or human factors" is important: "The identification, description and assessment of landscapes constitute the preliminary phase of any landscape policy. This involves an analysis of morphological, archeological, historical, cultural and natural characteristics and their interrelations, as well as an analysis of changes" (Council of Europe 2000: 2). The definition of the ELC acknowledges that the subjective and objective qualities of landscapes cannot be separated; the distinction between culture and nature does not hold. The landscape concept makes it possible to look at nature and culture together and see how these two concepts can dissolve into one.

Landscape is a multi-layered concept: it includes nature in the meaning of earth, water, plant and animal life, biological and geological diversity; it includes human-made objects, buildings, roads, sculptures, the products of culture; it also includes movements and action. But on top of all these visible phenomena, landscape includes the invisible. The invisible relationships which emerge in people's actions, movements, speech, thoughts, imaginations and narratives are intertwined with the visual; they emerge in an interaction with the visual (Ingold 2000). The visible landscape has certain potentials; it calls for ideas and imaginations, stories and events; it calls for action.

If landscape is viewed from this perspective, we can see how it adds to our usage of the concepts of nature and culture. Landscape involves a holistic way of looking at the reality of places and spaces. Instead of dividing reality into different boxes and viewing nature in one box and culture in another, the landscape concept invites us to look at the whole picture: how the meaning of landscape emerges through the intertwining of subject and object, of the human and the land.

Some geographers and anthropologists have emphasized this understanding of landscape and many of them have been inspired by Merleau-Ponty and other phenomenologists (Hirsch and O'Hanlon 1995, Tilley 1997, 2004, 2008, Ingold 2000). These authors encourage a new interpretation of the landscape concept which emphasizes how humans are intertwined with their surroundings through their bodies (as well as the artifacts of their existence such as tools, their dwellings, vehicles etc.), and how the meaning of landscape emerges in the interaction between human bodies and the land. Landscape is thus understood as this interaction. What is lacking in these ideas is that they reduce the role of aesthetics and the aesthetic valuing that has to take place if landscape and the values most commonly attached to them are to serve as criteria for conservation. While providing a good way of describing what landscape is – that it is not nature and not human but rather the interaction between those two – what is lacking is a language that is capable of dealing with the aesthetic aspects of this interaction and the values that are most commonly associated with landscapes: aesthetic values.

Perhaps the interviewees from the Icelandic case study mentioned above can give a clue to what is needed. According to Waage and Benediktsson, many of the interviewees seemed to view landscape in both subjective and objective terms:

> [W]hat is of particular interest here is how "beauty" and "landscape" are equated throughout the interviews and how landscape is therefore seen as a subjective phenomenon. Yet, there is the idea of universal beauty or landscapes that everyone finds beautiful. This represents an attempt to objectify a phenomenon, which nevertheless is considered as being essentially subjective (Waage and Benediktsson 2010: 17).

This might suggest that there is a need for understanding how the presumably subjective landscape can be, and is often objectified. But to understand this it is necessary to let go of the objective-subjective dualism that directs the debate on landscape. Merleau-Ponty's notion of *flesh* is a good starting point for doing this and Gernot Böhme's aesthetics of nature allows us to continue on the path toward understanding that the source of the aesthetic meaning and values we find in our surroundings lies neither in the subject nor the object, but rather in the spaces in-between.

Landscape as Flesh: Merleau-Ponty's Rethinking of Subject and Object

Many authors have been inspired by Merleau-Ponty's ideas and used them as tools to provide a new understanding of both the human-nature relationship and of the landscape concept. Philosophers David Abram and Ted Toadvine have examined Merleau-Ponty's ideas in order to rethink the human-nature relationship and to find a basis for a new philosophy of nature and the place of humans within it (Abram 1996, Toadvine 2009). Anthropologist Tim Ingold and archeologist Christopher Tilley have used Merleau-Ponty's ideas to provide a new understanding of the landscape concept (Tilley 1997, 2004, 2008, Ingold 2000). All these authors provide good insights into how Merleau-Ponty's ideas can change the way we think about humans and nature or other environments that surround us. To simplify a bit: Instead of seeing ourselves only as subjects trapped inside our minds and the environment as separate objects that are outside of us, Merleau-Ponty shows us how perception is inherently an ongoing interchange between the body and the entities that surround it, and thus the barrier between the inside and outside is blurred. Abram describes this interchange as "a sort of silent conversation that I carry on with things, a continous dialogue that unfolds far below my verbal awareness" (Abram 1996: 52). This description hints at how Merleau-Ponty's ideas can provide a language to talk about the *conversation* between humans and the land. But what is lacking in Abram's approach is an examination of how Merleau-Ponty's ideas can influence the way we understand the roots of the meaning and values that emerge from our conversation with the land.[4]

This is also missing from the accounts by the other authors I mentioned above. Ingold and Tilley use Merleau-Ponty's thought to gain understanding of the landscape concept as an interchange that constantly goes on between the human body and the land, but in their approaches to landscape, the aesthetic aspect does not play an important role. This may be due to the relation these authors see between an aesthetic aspect of landscape and a strictly visual understanding of landscape. With their emphasis on how we interact with the landscape as bodies they are attempting to get away from the perspective that is confined to the visual, and this may result in an overall phobia of the aesthetic (Benediktsson 2007).

I want to suggest that Merleau-Ponty's phenomenological understanding of reality provides a new way of thinking about aesthetic qualities and aesthetic value that should affect how we understand the landscape concept. In some of his last

---

4   Abram does talk about values, but in a very different context. His main conclusion is that if we acknowledge that we are having an ongoing conversation with our surroundings which are "experienced as sensate, attentive and watchful" then this will lead to a more ethical behaviour towards nature, and we will value it differently: "then I must take care that my actions are mindful and respectful, even when I am far from other humans, less I offend the watchful land itself" (Abram 1996: 69). Here, Abram uses Merleau-Ponty's thought to attempt to change the way we value nature, but what I want to suggest is that his thought should also be used to gain a new understanding of how values emerge in the first place.

works (Merleau-Ponty 1968, 1993 [1961]), he tries to undermine the scientific, objective approach to reality by rethinking its basic assumption: the division between subject and object. Just like the boundaries between the sea and the land are flowing and elusive, the border between the body and the world is not as clear as the traditional account of subject and object describes. Thus Merleau-Ponty makes an attempt to get beyond the two alternatives that have been controlling the way we think about subject and object: strict scientific determinism on the one hand and idealism (or social constructionism) on the other. According to Merleau-Ponty, perception is neither caused entirely by the object nor caused solely by myself: "Neither perceiver nor the perceived ... is wholly passive in the event of perception" (Abram 1996: 53). In order to take a closer look at how Merleau-Ponty describes this intertwining of subject and object, I will now turn to his notion of *flesh* (fr. *chair*).

Flesh for Merleau-Ponty is the word that captures the in-between or the interaction between body and the world:

> The flesh is not matter ... it is not a fact or a sum of facts "material" or "spiritual." Nor is it a representation for a mind ... The flesh is not matter, it is not mind, is not substance. To designate it, we should need the old term "element", in the sense it was used to speak of water, air, earth, and fire, that is, in the sense of a general thing, midway between the spatio-temporal individual and the idea, a sort of incarnate principle that brings a style of being wherever there is a fragment of being. The flesh is in this sense an "element" of Being (Merleau-Ponty 1968: 139).

The perceiver and the perceived are both active in the event of perception, they both affect the flesh. The body is both perceiver and what is perceived, both object and subject, and this in the end should eradicate the division:

> We say therefore that our body is a being of two leaves, from one side a thing among things and otherwise what sees them and touches them; we say, because it is evident, that it unites these two properties within itself, and its double belongingness to the order of the "object" and to the order of the "subject" reveals to us quite unexpected relations between the two orders. It cannot be by incomprehensible accident that the body has this double reference; it teaches us that each calls for the other (Merleau-Ponty 1968: 137).

In the intertwining of body and world, reality somehow affects our senses. The senses cannot independently work out some subjective and individual picture of reality, rather reality projects itself on to our senses and carves out the vision they perceive. The subject looks at the world, but at the same time the world looks at her and it is when their eyes meet that meaning emerges. Merleau-Ponty uses painting as an example of this. Many painters have said that the world looks at them just as they look at the world:

> As André Marchand says, after Klee: "In a forest, I have felt many times over that it was not I who looked at the forest. Some days I felt that the trees were looking at me, were speaking to me ... I was there, listening ... I think the painter must be penetrated by the universe and not want to penetrate it ... I expect to be inwardly submerged, buried. Perhaps I paint to break out."
>
> We speak of inspiration, and the word should be taken literally. There really is inspiration and expiration of Being ... it becomes impossible to distinguish between what sees and what is seen, what paints and what is painted (Merleau-Ponty 1993 [1961]: 129).

When the painter creates art, he perceives the world around him and changes it into a painting; he changes it into a representation of his perception of reality. If we take the word "inspiration" literally, like Merleau-Ponty recommends, we could say that reality projects itself onto the painter's perception; reality has its role in the outcome, and so does the painter's perception, through his perception he draws up a certain picture of reality which sheds light on one possible side of it. The same occurs when the scientist, philosopher or writer try to explain reality to us, they draw up certain pictures and perspectives that can help us understand and deal with the world around us.

Landscape – Flesh – Atmosphere

As we have seen, Merleau-Ponty's idea of flesh suggests that both perceiver and the perceived are active in the event of perception. What does this tell us about aesthetic qualities and the emergence of aesthetic values? It tells us that neither of the accounts of aesthetic qualities that have shaped the debate on landscape can be accurate. What we perceive is neither created solely by me as a subject, nor solely by the physical features of the object. The German philosopher Gernot Böhme builds his aesthetic theory of nature on this assumption (Böhme 1992, 1993, 1995, 2000). The central concept of his aesthetic theory is *atmosphere*. One of the reasons why he chooses this concept is that it has the advantage of being able to draw on our common daily experiences:

> One talks of a pleasant valley, of the depressive mood before a storm, or the tense atmosphere in a meeting, and it is easy to agree on what these phrases mean. If atmospheres are moods, which one feels in the air, then we are describing a phenomenon which is familiar to everyone (Böhme 2000: 15).

Atmosphere is a perfect term to describe the way that perception is the common reality of the perceiver and the perceived. According to Böhme, atmospheres stand between subjects and objects:

[O]ne can describe them as object-like emotions, which are randomly cast into a space. But one must at the same time describe them as subjective, insofar as they are nothing without a discerning Subject. But their great value lies exactly in this in-betweenness (Böhme 2000: 15).

This description of atmosphere is very similar to Merleau-Ponty's understanding of flesh. Atmosphere, as flesh, is a concept that captures the "in-betweenness" of subject and object; it is what Merleau-Ponty thought of as being "midway between the spatio-temporal individual and the idea" (Merleau-Ponty 1968: 139).

What Böhme's concept of atmosphere and Merleau-Ponty's notion of flesh suggest to our understanding of the aesthetic qualities of landscapes is that these qualities can be seen as being both subjective and objective. They are objective in the sense that they are qualities "via which the object projects itself into space" and "modifies the sphere of its surroundings" (Böhme 2000: 15). And they are subjective in the sense that they are perceived by the subject whose mood or feeling is affected by the atmosphere that the object creates. According to Böhme, atmospheres are most clearly experienced as contrasts: "for example, when one is in atmospheres that contradict one's own mood; or they are experienced via the change which occurs when one enters them from inside another atmosphere. Atmospheres are in these cases experienced as suggestive instances, that is, as a tendency or urge toward a particular mood" (Böhme 2000: 15).

The results of my research of the aesthetic experiences of glacial and geothermal landscapes in Iceland, show how atmospheres can be created by the objective physical features of a landscape and how they are then experienced by the perceiver. Both types of landscapes are characterized by an atmosphere of wonder and awe, which were a common response of almost all of the participants.[5] Furthermore, the instances that created this feeling of wonder were directly connected to the perception of certain physical qualities; colors, forms, textures and sounds. On the glacier what caught the participants' attention the most were huge crevasses and water cauldrons (cf. Figure 8.1), holes filled with bright blue water, glacial moraines and so on; in the geothermal areas it was the bright, unusual colors and delicate forms, the sound and smell, the steam and so on. It was quite surprising how many of the participants responded in the same way to the same physical qualities. The size of the glacier was for example something that affected all the participants, the perception of its enormity made them feel small. When the German interviewee was asked to describe any emotions that he felt on the glacier

---

5 The participants of the study were both members of the Icelandic public and foreign tourists. In the study of geothermal landscapes, one group consisted only of Icelanders, one group was mixed with Icelanders and American tourists, and the third consisted of Polish immigrants who had recently moved to Iceland. In the study of glacial landscapes all the groups consisted of tourists, from France, Belgium, Canada, Germany, America and Austria. In addition to interviewing participants from these groups, one Icelander who had not been in the group trips, but had experienced the glacier several times, was interviewed.

Figure 8.1 On the glacier (*Photograph*: Þorvarður Árnason, with permission)

he said: "feeling a bit small in that surrounding"; the Austrian put it thus: "feeling myself small ... you are a little point on this big ice!"; and the Canadians said that what enchanted them the most was "just the enormity of it...just how small it made you feel".

It was always when the participants confronted the biggest crevasses and the largest moraines that they felt this way. These physical qualities seemed to bring out certain feelings that were common to all the interviewees: feeling small, fear, respect and recognizing the glacier's dangerous power. This is an example of how certain physical qualities can create atmospheres that have "a tendency or urge toward a particular mood".

Another example from the geothermal areas shows how different over-all surroundings can create different responses. All the groups were taken to the same geothermal area which is divided into two quite different spaces. The first space is an open (and therefore often windy) area with a big dark-grey mud pot. The appearance of this area is dark and eerie, the sounds from the mud pot are slow and deep, the smell of sulphur is strong and the colors are very dark. While the groups were in this area people's responses were characterized by a fear that someone might get hurt, curiosity and a tense atmosphere. When the second space is entered, the physical features are quite different. This space is sheltered by hills from all sides, the steam is thick and warm and the ground is filled with brightly colored small mud pots, hot springs and fumaroles which make all kinds of boiling and steaming sounds. The people's responses in this area were characterized by lightness and fun, people commented on how warm and cosy it was there, everyone was very relaxed and joyful.

We cannot understand the meaning and value of landscape by focusing only on its objective side or its subjective side. Rather, we have to acknowledge both, and realize how these two sides really are one; a clear-cut distinction between subject and object cannot be made, and so we cannot say that the meaning of landscape is *only* a social construction, or *only* a matter of describing its objective features. The ELC's definition emphasizes the need to *both* identify and describe the more objective features of landscape, and examine people's perception of these features. Identifying the objective features of landscape is important because it allows us to document the changes that occur and also to explore how these changes affect people's perception of the landscape, and what the relationship is between different objective features and people's perception. If it would only focus on the former, it could not truly capture what landscape is; it would be like claiming to understand the value of a glass of wine by describing only its ingredients and the visual features of it without saying anything about the taste – the perception of it. Both in the case of a glass of wine and in the case of landscape, its value cannot be understood only by looking at it from a distance and classifying its objective features; the meaning and value emerge when these objective features are perceived by the subject. They emerge in the intertwining of subject and object, and included in this intertwining are time and history, different social and cultural developments that shape both the subjects and objects. An interpretation of the landscape concept from the perspective of Merleau-Ponty's and Böhme's ideas shows that its role is first and foremost to capture the atmosphere: the invisible depth of the visible that emerges in our relationship to environment and changes and develops as history and time shape that relationship.

In order to get beyond the dualistic approach to landscape and aesthetic values, we need to acknowledge how the meaning of landscape (which largely depends on aesthetic experience) is created in the conversation between humans and the land where atmosphere is the language. This will allow us to account for our aesthetic experience of landscape, and how it is not unreasonable to expect at least some degree of general agreement; and to think that certain landscape features do indeed have a tendency or urge to affect the mood of the landscape and the people who perceive it in specific ways.

References

Abram, D. 1996. *The Spell of the Sensuous: Perception and Language in a More-Than-Human World.* New York: Pantheon Books.

Benediktsson, K. 2007. "Scenophobia" and the Aesthetic Politics of Landscape. *Geografiska Annaler*, 89B(3), 203–17.

Böhme, G. 1992. An Aesthetic Theory of Nature. *Thesis Eleven*, 32, 90–102.

Böhme, G. 1993. Atmosphere as the Fundamental Concept of a New Aesthetic. *Thesis Eleven*, 36, 113–26.

Böhme, G. 1995. *Atmosphäre. Essays zur neuen Ästhetik*. Frankfurt am Main: Suhrkamp.

Böhme, G. 2000. Acoustic atmospheres: A Contribution to the Study of Ecological Aesthetics. *Soundscape, The Journal of Acoustic Ecology*, 1(1), 14–18.

Brady, E. 2003. *Aesthetics of the Natural Environment*. Edinburgh: Edinburgh University Press.

Cooper, D.E. (ed.) 1992. *A Companion to Aesthetics*. Oxford: Blackwell.

Council of Europe 2000. *European Landscape Convention* [Online]. Available at: http://conventions.coe.int/Treaty/en/Treaties/Html/176.htm [accessed 12 November 2009].

Dakin, S. 2003. There's More to Landscape than Meets the Eye: Towards Inclusive Landscape Assessment in Resource and Environmental Management. *Canadian Geographer*, 47(2), 185–200.

Gobster, P.H., Nassauer, J.I., Daniel, T.C. and Fry, G. 2007. The Shared Landscape: What does Aesthetics have to do with Ecology? *Landscape Ecology*, 22, 959–72.

Hirsch, E. and O'Hanlon, M. (eds) 1995. *The Anthropology of Landscape: Perspectives on Place and Space*. Oxford: Clarendon Press.

Ingold, T. 2000. *The Perception of the Environment: Essays on Livelihood, Dwelling and Skill*. London and New York: Routledge.

Lothian, A. 1999. Landscape and the Philosophy of Aesthetics: Is Landscape Quality Inherent in the Landscape or in the Eye of the Beholder? *Landscape and Urban Planning*, 44, 177–98.

Martin, J. 1993. Assessing the Landscape. *Landscape Design*, 222, 21–3.

Merleau-Ponty, M. 1968. *The Visible and the Invisible*, edited by C. Lefort, translated by A. Lingis. Evanston: Northwestern University Press.

Merleau-Ponty, M. 1993 [1961]. Eye and Mind, in *The Merleau-Ponty Aesthetics Reader, Philosophy and Painting*, edited by G.A. Johnson and M.B. Smith, translated by C. Dallery. Evanston: Northwestern University Press, 121–49.

Muelder Eaton, M. 2008. The Beauty that Requires Health, in *Nature, Aesthetics, and Environmentalism: From Beauty to Duty,* edited by A. Carlson and S. Lintott. New York: Columbia University Press, 339–62.

Nicholls, D.C. and Schlater, A. 1993. Cutting Quality Down to Scale. *Landscape Design*, 222, 39–41.

Rammaáætlun. n.d. *Master Plan for Hydro and Geothermal Energy Resources in Iceland* [Online]. Available at: http://www.rammaaaetlun.is/english [accessed: 7 January 2010].

Ritter, J. 1989. Landschaft. Zur Funktion des Ästhetischen in der modernen Gesellschaft, in *Subjektivität* by J. Ritter. Frankfurt: Suhrkamp, 141–63.

Schroeder, H.W. 2007. Place Experience, Gestalt, and the Human-Nature Relationship. *Journal of Environmental Psychology*, 27(4), 293–309.

Thorgeirsdottir, S. 2007. Nature's Otherness and the Limits of Visual Representations of Nature, in *Art, Ethics and Environment: A Free Inquiry Into the Vulgarly Received Notion of Nature*, edited by Ó.P. Jónsson and Æ. Sigurjónsdóttir. Cambridge: Cambridge Scholars Press, 112–24.
Tilley, C. 1997. *A Phenomenology of Landscape: Places, Paths and Monuments.* Oxford: Berg.
Tilley, C. 2004. *The Materiality of Stone: Explorations in Landscape Phenomenology.* Oxford: Berg.
Tilley, C. 2008. *Body and Image: Explorations in Landscape Phenomenology.* Walnut Creek: Left Coast Press.
Toadvine, T. 2009. *Merleau-Ponty's Philosophy of Nature.* Evanston: Northwestern University Press.
Umhverfisstofnun [Environment Agency of Iceland]. 2003. *Náttúruverndaráætlun 2004–2008 – Aðferðafræði. Tillögur Umhverfisstofnunar um friðlýsingar* [Nature Conservation Strategy 2004-2008 – methodology. The Environment Agency's suggestions for protection.] Reykjavík: Umhverfisstofnun.
Verkefnisstjórn um gerð rammaáætlunar um nýtingu vatnsafls og jarðvarma 2003. Skýrsla verkefnisstjórnar um 1.áfanga. Viðauki b3 [The Project management's report on the first phase. Appendix b3] [Online] Available at: http://www.landvernd.is/natturuafl/skyrsla/skyrsla/vidauki_b3.pdf [accessed: 21 October 2009].
Waage, E.R.H. and Benediktsson, K. 2010. Performing Expertise: Landscape, Governmentality and Conservation Planning in Iceland. *Journal of Environmental Policy and Planning*, 12(1), 1–22.

Chapter 9
The Sublime, Ugliness and "Terrible Beauty" in Icelandic Landscapes

Emily Brady

Introduction

On the whole, debates in natural environmental aesthetics focus on positive aesthetic value and tend to neglect more difficult forms of aesthetic engagement. In contrast to the easy beauty of rural landscapes, woodlands, and gentle valleys, many landscapes – vast plains and deserts, high seas, extreme weather conditions, and so on – evoke a diverse range of feelings and emotions, from anxiety and aversion to awe and fascination, where we are drawn out of our more comfortable ways of being. This chapter considers the sublime and explores its relationship to other aesthetic qualities which, arguably, lie toward the negative end of the scale of aesthetic values: ugliness and "terrible beauty". I provide support for my discussion through specific examples from Iceland's landscapes.

Many kinds of places present experiences falling into a category that I will call "difficult aesthetic appreciation". "Difficult" characterizes aesthetic responses which involve feelings of unease, discomfort, something being unresolved or somehow unfitted to our capacities, as well as experiences which take unusual effort or are challenging in some way. While difficult appreciation extends to art, my discussion will be limited to natural objects, landscapes and phenomena that include the overwhelming, frightening, repulsive, strange, alien and disturbing. These kinds of aesthetic responses may be contrasted with easier ones, which take less effort and involve feelings ranging from mild pleasure to ecstatic delight. My focus will be on natural rather than modified environments or cultural landscapes. I shall argue that more negative forms of aesthetic response expand our aesthetic interactions and enrich our experience of landscape. In particular, difficult aesthetic interactions offer insight into some of our uneasy relationships with nature and reflect ways in which we find meaning and value in extraordinary places.

The Sublime

Philosophical discussion of the sublime reached a pinnacle in the eighteenth century, when it was considered a major category in aesthetic theory. Contemporary debates engage primarily with Edmund Burke's and Immanuel Kant's theories of the sublime, but there is significant work on the topic by many other writers in this period. For Burke, the distinctive feelings and emotions evoked by the sublime are expressed as "delightful horror" (1990 [1757]: 123); for Kant, anxiety, quasi-fear, "negative" satisfaction, and "pleasure that is possible only by means of displeasure" (2000 [1790]: 151, 142). Burke's empirical approach attributes the sublime to objects that are great, powerful, vast, infinite, rugged, dark, gloomy, massive, as well as to loud sounds, bitter smells and stenches. The sublime involves an immediate feeling of delight mixed with terror in response to something distant enough not to be painful in a strong sense. Importantly, Burke and later, Kant, argue that the sublime response may only occur if the spectator experiences the sublime object first-hand, and when situated in a safe position relative to it (otherwise the reaction would just be fear rather than an aesthetic response).

Kant's mature theory of the sublime, as it appears in the *Critique of the Power of Judgment* (1790), was influenced by many earlier theories, but he develops the concept through his distinctive critical philosophy, and his account stands out for its exclusive focus on nature. Kant's position is well known for the distinction between the "mathematically sublime", where the senses and imagination are pushed to the limits of their powers by the seemingly infinite magnitude of nature, and the "dynamically sublime", where the power of nature evokes anxious pleasure and calls forth an awareness of our distinctive capacities as moral beings, namely, freedom and the power of reason. We feel insignificant in comparison to the mightiness of nature, yet ultimately we judge ourselves rather than objects sublime as we discover our own capacity to measure ourselves in relation to the natural world.

Much has also been written about how changes in European and North American landscape tastes made appreciation of the sublime possible in the first place, where fear and hatred of mountains, deserts and other wild places was replaced with admiration and reverence (Nicolson 1997). Theories of the sublime emerged in line with these changes, where many people – typically the elite, but also the middle classes – were in a position to appreciate sublime nature rather than simply fear it (Cosgrove 1984). While the sublime was taken up in Romanticism and in some later philosophical and literary discussions, it has since not featured as a *major* category of aesthetic value.

It could be argued that opportunities to appreciate the natural sublime have declined, making this aesthetic category no longer relevant. Many contemporary cultures and societies are less awed by nature, at least because technology allows for greater control of nature and its sublime effects. One might say that there is still room for neighbouring categories, such as wonder and awe, but not really for the complex experience of the sublime as understood in the past. Against this, I believe that we can find a contemporary place for the sublime, where the same kinds of natural qualities impress and overwhelm us, evoking a mixture of positive and negative feeling. Besides identifying a distinctive, felt aesthetic relationship with a variety of environments, the sublime characterizes a range of natural qualities which demand our attention, from the vast and seemingly infinite to the threatening and great.

The dynamic features of Iceland's environments present strong support for this line of argument. Reflection on its landscapes throws up a range of examples which fit especially well with those featuring in eighteenth century discussions. Many of Iceland's volcanoes are still active, with devastating eruptions occurring in recent times. The results of this activity are calderas, vast lava fields and black sand deserts. The lava fields are uneven, dull-coloured, with many easily accessible from populated regions such as Reykjavík. The calderas and deserts are a more common feature of the highlands in the interior of the country, presenting moonscape-like places which can be both eerie and breath-taking. Below the ground are geothermal areas with hot springs, boiling mud, and extraordinary geysers. In sharp contrast, huge glaciers cover vast areas in the interior, with powerful waterfalls, glacial rivers and plains flowing through the landscape, and dramatic fjords cutting into the edges of the country. Looking upwards, there are sweeping high mountains, and in many places free from light pollution, there is the immense night sky.

In the summer of 1881, John Coles, an explorer based in London, traveled across Iceland writing about its landscapes and people (Coles 1882). Although echoing in particular the language of some eighteenth century aesthetic theorists, there is an almost timeless quality to many of his descriptions, looking forward to contemporary accounts. Encountering the great volcanic landscape of Askja, in the highlands, he wrote:

> An extraordinary sight was this huge amphitheatre, 4 ½ miles long by from 2 to 3 wide, filled with lava-rock, piled up in strange confusion, and contained within a basaltic rampart, on which stood here and there peaks like sentinels, affording an admirable illustration of the geological formation of Iceland. The basaltic cliffs, abraded and weatherworn, represented the pre-glacial period, whilst the igneous rocks of much later date filled the floor of the amphitheatre, combining to produce a scene of desolation never to be surpassed. No living creature stirred. The only objects visible were rocks and snow, and far-away thin clouds of steam rising from the craters to the blue sky (Coles 1882: 92–3).

Today's visitors to Askja will find themselves in a safer situation than Coles, who traveled across the country with only his guides and sure-footed Icelandic horses to rely upon, but their experiences may not be so very different. More or less extreme places in, but also, importantly, *beyond* Iceland continue to offer possibilities of this kind. Consider Nick Entrikin's reflections from his essay, The Unhandselled Globe:

As places on the margin, high places are invested with varied and often contradictory meanings, from landscapes of fear to morally valued "pure" and natural landscapes. They have offered people sites of escape, reverence, physical challenge, discovery and learning, but at the same time have been sources of evil, human failure and death (Entrikin 2009: 222).

Many people today find natural places sublime, whether through actively seeking out extreme sports or other physical challenges in the environment, or finding oneself amidst a natural phenomenon: the wonder of the aurora borealis, or being caught – but still relatively safe – in severe weather.

Entrikin is right to emphasize the negative aspects of extreme nature. Sublimity is distinctive for the mixture of negative and positive feeling associated with it, with experiences lying on a spectrum from the more anxious and fearful to those lying closer to uplifting feelings. The volcanic eruption on Heimaey in 1973, in the southern Icelandic Westman Islands, caused widespread devastation, virtually burying the harbour town in lava and ash. The evacuation of people went smoothly, but homes and businesses were destroyed as a new volcano formed beside the older volcano, Helgafell (Gunnarsson 1973). Whatever sublime experiences were associated with this event, they would certainly have been of the more violent, terrible and frightening kind (see Figure 9.1).

Figure 9.1 **Eruption on Heimaey 1973 (*Photograph*: Ævar Jóhannesson, with permission)**

More recently the eruption of the Eyjafjallajökull volcano, also in Iceland, caused huge disruption to flights in Europe, reminding us of the limits of human technology.

The dynamic, catastrophic possibilities of Iceland's landscapes move from heat, fire and lava to vast glaciers (some with ice as deep as 900 metres). Bringing the sublime even more up-to-date, these melting ice caps become symbols of climate change now and for the future. Models predicting the effects of climate change on a global and atmospheric scale provide a kind of indirect, representational sublime by enabling us to imagine – though not fully take in – a world changed beyond our comprehension.

A further objection to the significance of the sublime today will be its links to elitist notions of aesthetic taste, a legacy of eighteenth century accounts (Hitt 1999). But the concept of the sublime can be decoupled from this aspect of its past. I hope that some of my remarks so far have shown the extent to which we can understand a contemporary experience of the sublime, where we are confronted not with some socially constructed phenomenon but a bodily, material experience of a natural world that "surprises and resists human desires and ambitions" (Entrikin 2009: 222). That is, there is something vital about the sublime that outruns criticisms of its theoretical and cultural underpinnings in eighteenth century discussions of taste. It is also worth remembering that those eighteenth century discussions were not just about identifying appropriate categories of taste for a particular kind of subject. They stand as philosophical investigations of a distinctive experience of the world, expressed as beauty, the sublime, ugliness and so on.

The qualities and aspects of violence and terror associated with natural sublime experiences sometimes overlap with ugliness. Incoherence, disorder, irregularity, and bleakness, for example, are associated with both categories. In some cases, sublimity and ugliness also share a mixture of positive and negative feeling. In the sublime it is astonishment, while ugliness evokes feelings associated with repugnance, sometimes mixed with a degree of curiosity. There is no straightforward attraction with either, as with the pleasure associated with natural beauty. Rather, we are somehow pushed away. Fear is associated with the threatening power of nature and, with ugliness, when something is frightening (even terrifying) in virtue of being horrible or strange, removed from what is comfortable or familiar. Violence in nature will have its sublime expressions but also its ugly ones: a predator chasing and devouring its prey.

There are, however, important differences between sublimity and ugliness, and distinguishing between them helps to expand our understanding of each one. Let me begin with content – the qualities or "subject matter" of the experience. While qualities of disorder or bleakness may be common to both, in the sublime they are combined with overwhelming force or magnitude. Imagine a disordered heap of rocks versus rocks high above on a mountain, or rocks blasted into the sky in a volcanic eruption. Sublime experiences are often, but not always, associated with life-threatening things, where natural phenomena make humans feel insignificant. Storms, raging seas, deserts without oases and so on make sublimity more serious, even profound in its subject matter. Closely connected to this is the boundless and limitless character of many sublime encounters, such as the vast night sky. Both profundity and limitlessness push the boundaries of phenomenal experience to their limits and beyond, such that the content and effects of the sublime are commonly linked to *metaphysical* states of being. This association runs through the conceptual history of the sublime from its very beginnings, where the mind is elevated by the force of poetic language, to Kant's transcendental sublime, Romanticism's transformational sublime and, more recently, Lyotard's sublime as encountering the "inexpressible" and "unpresentable" (Lyotard 1989: 199).

For all of these reasons, sublime objects and their effects are, on the whole, more out of the ordinary. Ugliness does not usually centre on life-threatening or powerful qualities, and it moves more easily between both strange and familiar contexts. It may be more frequent too, occurring at both large and small scales and ranging from dull or plain landscapes to repulsive plants and animals. Vast landscapes can be desolate and ugly, no doubt, but ugliness is not as intimately connected to scales of greatness as the sublime. So, although we can be deeply affected by ugliness, its subject matter, while serious enough, is not associated with metaphysical, transformative states of being.

Given these differences in content, the feelings and emotions associated with each category also diverge. With sublimity, feelings of anxiety and fearfulness are evoked in light of overwhelming qualities, but it is normally classified as a form of positive aesthetic value. Recall that to experience sublimity we must be in a safe place, otherwise it would be pure fear, with no opportunity for aesthetic reflection. While made to feel anxious in some way, uplifting feelings and a sense of our place in relation to nature ultimately come to the fore in this type of aesthetic experience. Ugliness, in contrast, is defined as a form of negative aesthetic value, arising from affective responses ranging from dislike to repulsion and disgust (Moore 1998). So, feelings of dislike, discomfort, aversion and so on run through the experience. However, ugly things engage us through closer attention as opposed to the senses and imagination being overwhelmed. As such, interest, curiosity and even excitement may be part of some responses to ugliness. Odd-looking creatures – for instance, the aye-aye, a lemur living in Madagascar – are good examples of this. Where strong interest turns into fascination, and the overall feeling is more positive than negative, it is not ugliness we find, but something falling into another aesthetic or neighbouring response, such as wonder or enchantment.

Ugliness

We can position beauty, the sublime and ugliness along a scale of positive and negative aesthetic value. On the positive side of the scale are varieties of beauty (including "terrible beauty"), with sublimity somewhere in the middle, and varieties of ugliness lying on the negative side. This scale is intended to show that ugliness is something associated with objective qualities; that it can exist in greater or lesser degrees; and that the concept of ugliness is not simply an empty notion understood as the absence of beauty (Moore 1998). Some have argued that in the middle lies a zero point, which suggests a kind of aesthetic indifference. It could be that this represents some sort of aesthetic neutrality. Sibley suggests that this neutrality is given content in terms of our use of certain aesthetic concepts like "plain", "ordinary" or "undistinguished" (Sibley 2001: 192). These expressions are used in aesthetic judgements of things that are considered unremarkable. I think Sibley's got it wrong here. Such judgements are not really neutral at all, but rather belong to aesthetic disvalue. To call a person plain-looking or ordinary is surely to make a negative judgment. The person is not attractive but plain. It makes more sense to describe unremarkable things as lying on the side of negative aesthetic value, but not synonymous with stronger forms of ugliness, which can pique curiosity and interest.

How might we unpack this negative side of the scale? Ugliness, like beauty, varies with objects, environments or whatever else being more or less ugly. It is associated, certainly, with qualities like deformity, decay, disease, disfigurement, disorder, messiness, distortion, odd proportions, mutilation, grating sounds, being defiled, spoiled, defaced, brutal, wounded, dirty, muddy, slimy, greasy, foul, putrid and so on (Sibley 2001, Eco 2007). Frequently mentioned candidates for ugliness include: eels, spiders, ticks, mosquitoes, mudflats, muddy rivers, burnt forests and various insects and animals. By listing these qualities, I am not putting forward a strongly objective or universal idea of what ugliness consists in. Ugliness is not reducible to one property or another, and it is often relative to certain norms. Also, qualities associated with ugliness may exist alongside attractive ones, just as negative and positive aesthetic values can be associated with the same thing, e.g. an attractive bird with a grating call.

In thinking through ugliness, we ought to embrace a broad understanding as indicated by some of the terms or descriptions above. Because beauty has been connected, historically, with order and harmony, many philosophers have identified ugliness with disorder and disharmony (Lorand 1994). For example, Arnheim describes ugliness as "a clash of uncoordinated orders…when each of its parts has an order of its own, but these orders do not fit together, and thus the whole is fractured" (quoted in Lorand 1994: 102). While this approach captures the ugliness of disorder or incoherence, it is both too formal and too narrow, failing to capture the more disgusting qualities of ugly things such as the viscous textures of eels and other slimy things or bizarre sounds – perhaps the unpleasant, eerie sound of a tree creaking in the wind.

Many theories of ugliness, importantly, distinguish it from the non-aesthetic reaction of *strong* repulsion or disgust (Pole 1983, Korsmeyer 2002). Repulsion or disgust of a strong kind may be so overwhelming that attention to the object is either truncated or never gets a foothold in the first place. Because, as many would argue, the aesthetic response necessarily involves some kind of sustained perceptual attention, disgust must be classed as a more visceral sensory reaction. This is not to say that ugliness cannot include repulsive qualities or that the aesthetic response might have elements of disgust in a weaker sense. My point refers to what lies at an extreme and at what stage the response becomes non-aesthetic.

The dark, dull colours and vast disheveled-looking lava fields characteristic of many landscapes in Iceland can appear barren, bleak and ugly; even some of the deserts have been described in negative terms: "The black wastes of Myrdalssandur are chiefly composed of deposits from Katla glacier bursts" (Guðmundsson, in Guðmundsson and Sigurðsson 1995: 69). Clean, white, icy glaciers are seen as less attractive when earth and stone "soil" their edges or surfaces, for example the glacial fronts of Skeiðarárjökull. The mud found in many geothermal areas – probably because of the unappealing texture and colour – provides another interesting focal point for ugliness. Nawrath (in Nawrath et al. 1959: 31) writes evocatively of Námafjall's mud pools and fumaroles: "The churning black mud... nothing but ugly fissured, crusted mud at the stepped brink of the crater". Coles draws a vivid picture of the mud-springs at Hlíðarnámar:

> We reached the principal crater without accident, and ascended its wall to have a look at the spring, which we had heard roaring and spluttering long before we got to it. On looking down, we saw a basin of liquid black mud, about 6 feet in diameter, in a violent state of ebullition, from the centre of which, ever and anon, columns of mud were projected to the height of about 10 feet, accompanied by such groans, that one could almost imagine they proceeded from some imprisoned demon struggling to get free, and we plainly saw the manner in which the walls of the crater had been built up by the splashes of mud ejected from the spring (Coles 1882: 101–2).

Besides identifying some qualities of ugliness, Coles's description provides an example of the association of ugliness with evil and immorality, a key theme in its cultural history (Eco 2007).

So far I've been referring mainly to ugly qualities. But judgements of ugliness are made by valuers ascribing negative value to things and having certain reactions such as shock, (weak) repulsion, dislike and so on. In this respect, ugliness relates to both material objects and to the emotions, imaginative associations, knowledge and biases of individual valuers across communities and cultures (Saito 1998). Ugliness, like other aesthetic qualities, is response-dependent, depending upon a valuer valuing something (Brady 2003). Undoubtedly, while we will find agreement on ugliness across cultures, ugliness will also vary culturally (and historically), as Umberto Eco has shown so well in his recent book *On Ugliness* (2007). Some writers have also explored an evolutionary basis for our reactions to ugliness, but exploration of these ideas takes us into the realms of environmental psychology and anthropology. Suffice to say that there will be, at least, cultural variability where ugliness is concerned.

Terrible Beauty

Although I have less to say about this aesthetic category, I discuss it to show a more difficult type of beauty and to further clarify the distinctive character of sublimity and ugliness. Korsmeyer (2005: 51) characterizes terrible beauty as beauty "that is bound up with the arousal of discomforting emotions", and she clearly distinguishes it from other aesthetic categories such as tragedy, sublimity and disgust. It involves strenuous emotions and the intensification of experience. Identifying examples is not easy, given that this category lies at the edge of beauty, moving very close to the not-beautiful. From the artworld, consider Francis Bacon's paintings or the depictions of war in Goya's works. In the natural environment, there are landscapes which are dramatic and complex, without being overwhelming. Imagine a sunset made more colourful and dramatic because of pollution – with that knowledge the aesthetic response is likely to be more poignant. Some of the major geysers in Iceland, Strokkur for instance, combine elements of excitement with darker elements. The fantastic ejections of water are dangerous, with boiling temperatures, the "partial escape of steam now and then making the most unearthly noises" (Coles 1882: 25–6). Beyond landscapes, Ned Hettinger (2010) has argued that in some cases predation is a form of terrible beauty. Imagine a cheetah chasing a gazelle at high speed (though the cheetah devouring its kill verges on ugly from the human perspective).

Some philosophers have identified categories like terrible beauty to *include* both sublimity and ugliness. In the early eighteenth century Joseph Addison uses the terms "great" and "grandeur" to describe the kinds of qualities and natural phenomena other writers called sublime (Addison 1996 [1712]). However, he also identifies the category of beauty separately, so it's not clear that he intends to categorize sublimity as closer to some kind of grand beauty. Although writing within the context of art, Bernard Bosanquet (1963 [1914]: 47) makes a distinction between "facile beauty" which brings "straightforward pleasure", and "difficult beauty" which challenges and repels, requiring unusual effort for the appreciator. Sublimity, "disguised ugliness", the terrible, tragic and grotesque are all classified as instances of difficult beauty (Jacquette 1984). But Bosanquet's classification is formal in some sense, motivated not by an attempt to mask differences between these aesthetic categories (even ugliness appears to retain some independence despite his classification). Rather, his view is motivated by a theory of art as spiritual expression, so that artworks expressive in this way possess beauty of some kind.

These cases do not, then, fundamentally challenge the view that sublimity and ugliness are distinct categories, with ugliness standing as a type of negative aesthetic value. Instead of doing away with the distinction, "terrible beauty" highlights the variety of aesthetic experiences, from delightful and grand to heartrending (beauty and terrible beauty), to much more challenging experiences, where the subject matter is overwhelming, terrible or unpleasant (sublimity, ugliness).

Conclusion: Enriching Relationships with Nature

Many philosophical accounts attempting to pin down the nature of aesthetic experience link it to feelings of pleasure and pain, with a tendency to focus on experiences of aesthetic pleasure (e.g. pleasure linked to the positive aesthetic value of beauty). But, as we have seen, our aesthetic responses are more complex than this, involving not just a variety of emotions but also, in many cases, other aspects of human life. Given the range of difficult aesthetic experiences identified here, why do we value them and their subjects, animals, landscapes and natural processes?

My answer to this question is in two parts, one relating to felt experience and the second to human-nature relationships. First, the complex emotions experienced in the face of sublimity and terrible beauty may not always be pleasurable, but they are valued nonetheless for their intensity and depth. The sublime brings with it uplifting feelings, even in ways that elevate the mind. But sublime feeling is not reducible to an anthropocentric aesthetic, for accounts of the sublime have always included the important theme of the insignificance of the self, the individual overwhelmed by nature and the feeling of humility that arises in tandem with the elevation of the human mind (Berleant 1993, Hitt 1999, Brady 2010a).

Developing this, secondly, the sublime presents an aesthetic moment in which we come to some greater awareness of our relationship to the natural world and our *inability* to control its astonishing qualities. In that sense, we begin to see how humans are intimately bound up with nature yet also different from it: the ambivalence of feeling at home yet not at home in the world. Through an aesthetic experience of the sublime, a kind of respect potentially emerges, in large part due to nature's threat to our capacities. As respect, it involves admiring features that have scope beyond human nature. In his meditations on Askja, Páll Skúlason points to the independence of nature and a temporal sublime, showing how overwhelming places determine the limits of humans in relation to environment:

> It is a unique natural system, within which mountains, lakes and sky converge in a volcanic crater. Askja, in short, symbolizes the earth itself; it is the earth as it was, is, and will be, for as long as this planet continues to orbit space, whatever we do and whether or not we are here on this earth. Askja was formed, the earth was formed, long before we were created. And Askja will be here long after we are gone (Skúlason 2005: 21).

Similarly, but less poetically perhaps, explorer Ted Edwards describes his experience standing on the top of Hekla, the great Icelandic volcano: "Awesome it was; awesome beyond imagination. The raw power of the earth. This hole, plugged tenuously by a few feet of newly solidified lava, went straight to the earth's core. The enormity of it seeped into my being and it was impossible not to indulge in formless, pre-adamite, worship" (Edwards 1986: 142).

Where does this leave ugliness, especially given that it is a form of negative aesthetic value? If ugliness involves aversion, in what ways can it matter? As with the sublime, experiencing the full range of emotions can deepen and add meaning to our experience of other humans, other creatures and things unlike ourselves. Overlooking ugliness deprives us of a range of meaningful interactions with nature which lie beyond the realm of easy aesthetic appreciation. Experiences of ugliness can bring with them epistemic, if not, aesthetic value (Brady 2010b). They may increase our "aesthetic intelligence" through extending our aesthetic interactions to all things in nature.

Through the exploration of the negative side of aesthetic value, we discover a different kind of relationship to nature, not friendly – rather – one that strains us through its uneasiness. It may be a relationship of distance rather than intimacy because after all, while there may be some fascination in the mix, ugliness is still something unattractive in the end. In any case, it *is* a form of relationship, and one that we seek out for its complexity and, perhaps, in some ways, for its integrity: where recognition of the variety of nature and its landscapes becomes explicit. In this way, an aesthetic response might underpin an ethical attitude, where the epistemic value arising from ugliness leads to caring for what is otherwise passed over.

References

Addison, J. 1996 [1712]. *The Spectator* No. 412 Monday June 23, in *The Sublime: A Reader in British Eighteenth-Century Theory*, edited by A. Ashfield and P. de Bolla. Cambridge: Cambridge University Press, 62–3.

Berleant, A. 1993. The Aesthetics of Art and Nature, in *Landscape, Natural Beauty and the Arts*, edited by S. Kemal and I. Gaskell. Cambridge: Cambridge University Press, 228–43.

Bosanquet, B. 1963 [1914]. *Three Lectures on Aesthetic*. Indianapolis: Bobbs Merrill.

Brady, E. 2003. *Aesthetics of the Natural Environment*. Edinburgh: Edinburgh University Press.

Brady, E. 2010a. Reassessing Aesthetic Appreciation of Nature in the Kantian Sublime. *Journal of Aesthetic Education*, forthcoming.

Brady, E. 2010b. Ugliness and Nature. *Enrahonar: quaderns de filosofia*, 45.

Burke, E. 1990 [1757]. A *Philosophical Enquiry into the Origin of our Ideas of the Sublime and Beautiful*, edited by A. Philips. Oxford: Oxford University Press.

Coles, J. 1882. *Summer Travelling in Iceland; Being the Narrative of Two Journeys across the Island by Unfrequented Routes*. With a chapter on Askja by E.D. Morgan. London: John Murray.

Cosgrove, D. 1984. *Social Formation and Symbolic Landscape*. London: Croom Helm.

Eco, U. 2007. *On Ugliness*, translated by A. McEwan. London: Harvill Secker.

Edwards. T. 1986. *Fight the Wild Island: A Solo Walk across Iceland.* London: John Murray.

Entrikin, J.N. 2009. Afterword: "The Unhandselled Globe", in *High Places: Cultural Geographies of Mountains, Ice and Science*, edited by D. Cosgrove and V. della Dora. London: I.B. Tauris, 216–26.

Guðmundsson, A.T. and Sigurðsson, R, Th. 1995. *Light on Ice: Glaciers in Iceland.* Seltjarnarnes: Ormstunga.

Gunnarsson, Á. 1973. *Volcano: Ordeal by Fire in Iceland's Westmann Islands*, translated by M. Hallmundson and H. Hallmundson. Reykjavík: Iceland Review Books.

Hettinger, N. 2010. Animal Beauty, Ethics and Environmental Preservation. *Environmental Ethics*, 32, 115–34.

Hitt, C. 1999. Toward an Ecological Sublime. *New Literary History*, 30(3), 603–23.

Jacquette, D. 1984. Bosanquet's Concept of Difficult Beauty. *Journal of Aesthetics and Art Criticism*, 43(1), 79–87.

Kant, I. 2000 [1790]. *Critique of the Power of Judgment*, edited by P. Guyer, translated by P. Guyer and E. Matthews. Cambridge: Cambridge University Press.

Korsmeyer, C. 2002. Delightful, Delicious, Disgusting. *Journal of Aesthetics and Art Criticism*, 60(3), 217–25.

Korsmeyer, C. 2005. Terrible Beauties, in *Contemporary Debates in Aesthetics and the Philosophy of Art*, edited by M. Kieran. Malden: Blackwell, 51–63.

Lorand, R. 1994. Beauty and its Opposites. *Journal of Aesthetics and Art Criticism*, 52(4), 399–406.

Lyotard, J-F. 1989. The Sublime and the Avant-Garde, in *The Lyotard Reader*, edited by A. Benjamin. Oxford: Blackwell, 196–211.

Moore, R. 1998. Ugliness, in *Encyclopedia of Aesthetics*, edited by M. Kelly. New York: Oxford University Press, 417–21.

Nawrath, A., Thorarinsson, S., and Laxness, H. 1959. *Iceland: Impressions of a Heroic Landscape.* Berne: Kümmerly & Frey.

Nicolson, M.H. 1997. *Mountain Gloom and Mountain Glory: The Development of the Aesthetics of the Infinite.* Seattle and London: University of Washington Press.

Pole, D. 1983. *Aesthetics, Form and Emotion*, edited by G. Roberts. London: Duckworth.

Saito, Y. 1998. The Aesthetics of Unscenic Nature. *Journal of Aesthetics and Art Criticism*, 56(2), 101–11.

Sibley, F. 2001. Some Notes on Ugliness, in *Approach to Aesthetics*, edited by J. Benson, J. Roxbee Cox and B. Redfern. Oxford: Clarendon Press, 191–206.

Skúlason, P. 2005. *Meditation at the Edge of Askja.* Reykjavík: University of Iceland Press.

Chapter 10

Transporting Nature: Landscape in Icelandic Urban Culture

Anna Jóhannsdóttir and Ástráður Eysteinsson

Changing Places

Icelandic society underwent substantial changes in a relatively short timespan before and around the middle of the twentieth century. These changes were manifested in a crucial interplay of two key factors: a "belated" but rapid process of modernization in matters of technology and industry and a demographic shift from rural areas to urban centres, especially to the capital of Reykjavík and the surrounding towns. It has sometimes been said that with World War Two, and the occupation of the country by first British and later US military forces, the nation practically jumped out of its age-old rural existence into a modern urban world.

While this is of course an exaggerated description of a process that was in fact gradually under way, it may bring home to the reader the propulsion of development effected by the foreign occupation, with all its accompanying enterprises and its demand for an urban work force. The "development" could arguably be called a watershed in the Icelandic way of life, or at least in people's perception of their way of life and their place in a national framework that itself was being shifted and shuffled. And "bringing home" may be an inappropriate expression in this context, where "home" is precisely the matter of contention.

For several decades, until relatively late in the twentieth century, a substantial portion of the population of the Reykjavík metropolitan area were people who had moved from the less densely populated parts of the island to settle in the city, which at the same time was in the process of becoming, in a number of ways, the unquestioned "centre" of Icelandic national existence. This world was significantly different from the one in which these people had been born and bred, and in which many of them had come into adulthood, living and working at close counters with nature and being more dependent upon the forces of nature than city folks usually are. Was there not inevitably some kind of rift in the world view of these people, comparable even to the hiatus characterizing the lives of emigrants who travel to and settle in a distant country?

"World view" may be a diffuse concept, but it is used here to designate self-perception as shaped by residence (long-term dwelling place), history, memory, ideas about nationality and places of origin – and the values pertinent to such mental-material structures. The migration itself may appear to be mainly a matter of the past now. Generations have come along that are city-born and raised, and more than half the population of the country now resides in the metropolitan area. This "rift", however, still runs right through Icelandic world views. It has lately re-emerged in the collapse of the fishing industry in several coastal towns and villages (which had replaced the farms as the main location of employment outside the Reykjavík area), and this has resulted in a renewed migration to the urban southwest. But the rift has also appeared, albeit differently, in the debate about the creation of reservoirs and power stations in the interior of the country, built to drive big industrial plants (which are meant to salvage the employment problems of the respective coastal areas, along with the economy of the country). This debate is part of a global struggle over environmental issues and the protection of nature. It is sometimes presented as if the battle for environmental conservation were mainly the concern of city folk who are far away from location and have scant understanding of attempts to renew the basis of livelihood of the local population. Conservationists then sometimes reply that nature is a communal entity, to be preserved for future generations and not just used as a resource for those wishing to make local use of it at the present time.

More often than not, this debate revolves around the value of the uninhabited interior and the natural wilderness of the island; natural spaces that are indeed far afield for many urban dwellers. Most of the time they only catch glimpses of this part of the country in the media; it is "transported" to them in the form of news reports, and as narrative or visual representation. This essay focuses on such transportation of the landscape – not, however, as witnessed in the mass media, but in aesthetic media, where information value is not at the forefront. Instead, aesthetic and cultural points of emphasis are salient in the factors already touched on above: self-perception, identity, and memory in relation to place; the value of various landscapes and places; and the ways in which different places interconnect in both individual and "national" spheres.

Most if not all societies are characterized by cultural traits emerging from varying degrees of conversation and tension between "city" and "country", as well as between urban life and the natural world (as conceived by the society in question). These cultural traits, moreover, are woven into the respective historical identities in ways that are significantly and variously embodied in literary and other aesthetic products. The endurance of rural ways of life in Iceland, its late industrialization combined with a weak and vague historical concept of art (other than the art of writing), and the island country's rapid modernization in various sectors, including the aesthetic one, where ideology and iconography may intersect in unsuspected ways; all of this should make Iceland an interesting case in point in examining urban conversations with landscape.

Children of Nature?

Literature is, at least historically speaking, clearly the dominant aesthetic medium in Iceland. Indeed, some of its ancient genres are often judged to be vitally intervowen with the historical identity and fortune of the nation. The fact that Icelanders preserved their old Norse language through several centuries of Danish colonialization is often attributed to the strength and resilience of the literary tradition. The aforementioned modernizing changes in Icelandic habitation had inevitable repercussions in the field of literature (cf. Eysteinsson 2006). This can be seen most clearly in the several texts (especially novels and short stories) that deal directly with the migration from the countryside to urban centres, although echoes can also be detected in such texts (often poetry) that focus primarily on natural vistas, remaining silent about the location, the cultural centre, from which the texts may actually emanate.

Changing places – with the often radical change of *habitus* this involved – proved a painful, even traumatic experience for many, especially those who took their leave of farms that had been the family residence, and the soil they had tilled, the land they had cultivated and with which they often deeply indentified. These individuals were saying goodbye to both a way of life and a plot of land, a part of Iceland, in some sense a miniature version of the rural society which Iceland had been for more than ten centuries. This was a place in the world where nature was constantly close at hand, not only in the soil being tilled and in the notoriously changeable weather, but also in the uncultivated interior, where sheep grazed during the summer and where they were rounded up in autumn.

The finality of the departure and of the move to the city could not but summon up memories of the many Icelanders who had emigrated for North America before and around the turn of the twentieth century. These two waves of migration are to some extent conflated in a trilogy of novels which Jóhannes úr Kötlum (1899–1972) brought out 1949 to 1951. Here he describes the emigration of the farmer Ófeigur and his family to the United States. The trilogy has its historical base in the massive emigration of the late nineteenth century, but the author plays a temporal trick on the reader and moves the family across the ocean and into the heavily industrialized and alienated mass society of twentieth-century Chicago, thus boldly magnifying Iceland's own recent "jump" into a modern, "Americanized" world. Ófeigur's son, Siggi, is at first very much a child of romanticism and the nineteenth-century Icelandic countryside, as we see in the following passage, which may serve as a key to Icelandic rural discourse, even as it emerges in the realist novel:

> The boy closed his eyes and listened. And he heard the murmur of the brook, that clear silvery sound which was like a poem by Jónas Hallgrímsson, and he began to tremble all over as if he were himself flowing through the gravel and clay of the land – no, I'll never go to America. (úr Kötlum 1949, 196, our translation)

But of course he does. The unity of soul and land is broken, and the first novel, from which this quote is taken, is ironically called *Dauðsmannsey* (Dead Man's Island); the second is *Siglingin mikla* (The Great Voyage; 1950) and the third, again not without irony, *Frelsisálfan* (The Continent of Freedom; 1951). In the New World, Siggi outgrows his home land, but in the passage quoted, in the mind and body of the child, the author brings together the land (the Icelandic countryside), a literary text, and a porous consciousness, a subject in-the-making. The wealth ("silver") of the land is heard in the rippling brook, which in turn has the sound of a verse by Jónas Hallgrímsson; the boy himself then responds like a string in an instrument or like a rill trickling through the earth.

This thorough symbiosis is interesting, in part because the author does not present it as only a conversation between the boy and nature. The poetry of Jónas Hallgrímsson (1807–1845), the romantic "national poet", is part of the symphonius experience. The land has received its confirmation, its rightful *place*, in certain literary texts, and now resides in these texts and is mediated through them. It is even, to an extent, created with and through the texts and sounds of certain pieces of language. And so the land *dwells* – to choose a verb prominent in studies of landscape and place – in no small part *in* the images and effigies of language, art and culture. They are cultural constructs, but we may be hard put to identify moments when we are actually free from such constructs, enjoying "direct" communion with nature, for it is very often through such constructs that we learn to appreciate nature and landscape.

The trilogy by Jóhannes úr Kötlum raises the question whether Icelanders are losing their land – or rather their inherited deep-rooted relationship with the land. Over a decade later writer Indriði G. Þorsteinsson asks a similar question in a different way in the novel *Land og synir* (Land and sons; 1963). The farmer's son in this novel, Einar, makes a decision to leave the farm and at the end of the novel he is on a bus that is presumably taking him "south" (to Reykjavík), like so many other mid-century children of Icelandic farmers. His father suffers a fatal heart attack with the rake in his hands and the familiar landscape before his eyes:

> After a long life, the horizon was as familiar to him as the face of an old friend. Nothing had changed, but the people had left. Instead they had been given roads and cars, and sometimes he watched the pattering bus approach ... (Þorsteinsson 1963, 63–4, our translation).

With this vehicle of modernity in sight, probably the same bus that later will carry his son away, the old man's thoughts glide over the surrounding landscape and the memories and history connected to it. The son does not care to continue the battle for the debt-ridden farm. On the one hand he appears to be driven by hard-boiled realism, thus negating the "and" of the title: Land *and* sons, and personifying the rift in world view discussed above. The land is not the inevitable heritage of the sons. On the other hand, one may ask what it means that his girlfriend Margrét, another farmer's daughter, does not show up at the bus stop to join him, as they had planned. Here the author resorts to the traditional parallels of land and womanhood. In his last conversation with Margrét, Einar in fact tells her that for him she embodies this region and its beauty. There is no doubt that in spite of the emptiness the son feels as the bus carries him away, he is literally chock-full of the countryside he is leaving behind.

The fact that it is a long goodbye was confirmed when the Icelandic film industry finally got some wind in its sails, in the early 1980s, for the film adaptation of *Land og synir* (1980; directed by Ágúst Guðmundsson) was warmly received by a large percentage of the nation. People flocked to the cinemas to witness the retelling of the story in a film in which Icelandic nature and landscape vistas play a key role (perhaps to a fault, as some have said of this and several other Icelandic films). It is tempting to hypothesize that the Icelandic tradition of landscape painting is effectively built into this as well as some other films and there are other signs, in more recent films and writings, indicating that Icelanders are either still saying goodbye to – or perhaps still hanging on to – the hinterland of their urban society.

The Landscape in the Living Room

Landscape paintings grace the living rooms of numerous Icelandic homes and they are also widely to be seen on the walls of companies and institutions. They are frequently representations, in varying degrees of realism, of particular places in the Icelandic countryside or Icelandic nature, or of landscape at least seemingly characterized by Icelandic features. These landscape pieces have played and probably still play a significant role in the relationship of Icelanders with country vistas outside their immediate environment – places and panoramas to which these paintings provide a certain access. Landscape paintings thus bear significant witness to ways in which nature and cultural memory are entwined.

When such paintings are given a prominent place in the living room of private homes they acquire an added iconic significance, expressing both the pride taken in the home and the homage paid to the work of art hanging on the wall, or at least to its content: a piece of land to which this home is thus connected in a kind of place-to-place relationship.

The following painting (Figure 10.1), photographed some years ago, was prominently placed in the living room of an elderly lady in Reykjavík. It was painted in the 1950s by her neighbor, a University of Iceland theology professor Magnús Jónsson, who was an active amateur painter. It represents the farm (and the surrounding countryside) where this woman was born and raised, and where she in fact lived until she got married and moved to the capital. It constitutes a kind of window into both the domain of childhood and a different Icelandic world, whose representation thus also becomes a part of the frame and space of the urban home.

Figure 10.1 Magnús Jónsson: Dalbær í Hrunamannahreppi, Miðfell
(*Photograph*: Anna Jóa)

This particular painting thus effects both a spatial and temporal move – and historically it could be said to reach beyond the childhood of the owner, to the romantic period of the previous century, just like the passage in the novel by Jóhannes úr Kötlum. The romantics lent Icelandic landscape new meanings and functions, drawing in part on the medieval literary heritage, especially the Icelandic family sagas (*Íslendingasögur*), as they celebrated their fair country: "Whoever reads the sagas with attention is bound to be set alight with a burning passion for his homeland, or he is not understanding them properly" (Fjölnir 1835, 2). The romantics were instrumental in establishing the family sagas as primary national epics, stories to be reread *into* the landscape with which we are still surrounded. At the same time the romantic poets sought to open the eyes of their compatriots to the beauty and grandeur of Iceland.

One problem in this historical act of mapping the relics of Iceland's "golden age" onto the contemporary scene was the fact that the celebrated medieval sagas mostly render the landscape in practical terms, as a terrain that is farmed or traversed, or as property in dispute. However, in a famous scene, which could be called an exception to this rule, the farmer hero Gunnar in *Njal's Saga* looks back at his farmland as he takes his leave, having been sentenced to three years of outlawry. He makes an exclamation about the "beauty of the slopes" and declares that he will not leave the country, but stay home and defy his sentence. Romantic readers of the sagas have frequently latched on to this scene, celebrating it as a declaration of loyalty to the country and an appreciation of its beauty. Indeed, Jónas Hallgrímsson wrote one of his key poems, "Gunnarshólmi", about precisely this moment and the place where Gunnar looked back and made the decision that would result in his heroic death. Just as the view facing Gunnar in the saga has acquired the gestalt of a pregnant landscape "painting" in the romantic and modern reception of the saga tradition, Hallgrímsson paints his own iconic picture of the holy ground where Gunnar turned around, a spot which becomes quintessentially Icelandic.

The Visual World: Nature Near and Far

Icelanders received important backing in forging a paradigm which conjoins ideas about the countryside, the rural society, the literary heritage and the beauty or grandeur of Icelandic nature. Among the first tourists in Iceland were foreign intellectuals who had read medieval Icelandic literature in translation and were especially eager to visit the saga sites. Since there were scant architectural remains, the landscape of the relevant places had to be put into reciprocal relationship with the medieval texts. These intellectuals – among them such prominent figures as writer, designer and social reformer William Morris and historian and aesthetician W.G. Collingwood – frequently published their travel accounts and thus they transported Icelandic places, and Iceland itself as a place, and in a sense "translated" them into their respective cultural contexts. But these travellers also made an impact on some of the natives, who were still in the early stages of transporting places within their own culture. Some of these foreign travellers felt it was not enough to describe the country in writing; they wanted to take it with them in the form of drawings and paintings. Some of them brought along specialists to take care of the visual representation, but others did their own paintings, for instance Collingwood, who visited Iceland in 1897. Thus a visual world comes into being, one that re-confirms sites of history, sites of memory and meaning.

This happened before Icelandic painting had been properly launched as an aesthetic discipline, although the socio-cultural basis for such a discipline emerged around the turn of the twentieth century. The "pioneers" of Icelandic painting, as they are commonly referred to, began to make their mark during the time of the nation's struggle towards independence from Denmark. The country's continuous history of painting, in the modern sense and as a field of specialized activity, is not a long one – in fact, the exhibition of paintings by Þórarinn B. Þorláksson (1867–1924), opened in Reykjavík in December 1900, was the first of its kind by a professional artist. However, there were others who previously had pursued art education in Copenhagen, among them Sigurður Guðmundsson (1833–1874). According to art historian Björn Th. Björnsson (1964, 7), Guðmundsson painted "the first Icelandic landscape paintings" in the form of stage backdrops for *Útilegumennirnir* (The Outlaws), a play by Matthías Jochumsson, premiered in 1862.[1] Björnsson points

---

1 In her recent book, *Mynd á þili*, art historian Þóra Kristjánsdóttir points out that the oldest preserved landscape pictures by an Icelander do in fact date from the year 1752. Their author is unknown, but according to Kristjánsdóttir they were possibly made by Jón

out that the pictures, painted in an academic style, were shaped by Guðmundsson's eagerness, in the spirit of romanticism, to revive the nation's artistic endeavors and generally to strengthen "our nationality". Furthermore, that the landscape, representing the wilderness, was for Guðmundsson mainly a scene of events of former times (Björnsson 1964, 39). These backdrops were not preserved, but written descriptions of them exist. An idea about their appearance may also be drawn from the six backdrops Guðmundsson painted for The Outlaws in 1873, which are preserved in the National Museum of Iceland. This is an early indication of both a visual and historical "transportation" of landscape into a local, cultural context, here in the symbolic form of a theatre stage, as a kind of *trompe l'oeil*. Guðmundsson does not appear to have painted landscapes in other contexts, and his talent and enthusiasm found little response in an environment that still had little to offer as far as the visual arts were concerned.

During the last quarter of the nineteenth century, interest in the arts gradually began to manifest itself in Iceland. The spirit of independence reached a new level of intensity and urban culture began to take shape (arguably a precondition for the reception of paintings). The Icelandic painters, while breaking new ground in their own medium in Iceland in the early years of the twentieth century, in many ways joined the romantic poets of previous generations in drawing the nation's attention to – in fact making it "remember" – the beauty of the country, as well as the cultural and historical values inherent in it. Again, the leading romantic poet, Jónas Hallgrímsson, is the appropriate spokesman for this sentiment, to quote famous lines from his poem "Ísland" (Iceland): "The land is beautiful and fair, with snow-white glacial peaks", but "where is your ancient fame, freedom and courage best?" (Hallgrímsson 1835, 22 and 21, our translation).

The first professional painters received grants from Parliament to study art in Copenhagen where they were, like painter Sigurður Guðmundsson before them, influenced by romantic currents and styles. In their landscape paintings, they sought to concretize visually the nation's focus on, and attention to, the values inherent in the land itself. Their paintings became icons for the uniqueness and distinct character of a country striving to regain its freedom. In this pursuit they recast both sweet country scenes and familiar mountains, but also the panoramas of the interior wilderness, as well as the close-up experience of rocks, moss and lava.

Icelandic landscape paintings are thus traditionally closely linked to the national identity, and landscape was indeed the most common motif in Icelandic painting

---

Ólafsson jr. from Svefneyjar in Breiðafjörður. Jón illustrated the travel book that his brother, Eggert Ólafsson, and Bjarni Pálsson recorded during their journey around Iceland 1752–1757. Five unsigned watercolours, depicting local landscape scenes, are to be found in the book, the oldest dating from June 19, 1752. The pictures are made in an "enlightening" fashion such as the works made by foreign artists who had participated in explorations in Iceland. The preserved landscapes by Sigurður Guðmundsson are in many ways more "theatrical" (see Þóra Kristjánsdóttir 2005, 118–121).

during the first half of the twentieth century. The pioneers depicted the land in an idealized manner, at first influenced by academic landscape styles, yet some soon experimented with post-impressionistic methods and techniques in their search for an expression of their understanding and experience of the country's nature. Painters of the first generation were shaped by their closeness to nature and the rural way of life, and this was where the "soul of the nation" was to be found, even according to some of the intellectuals who had studied abroad and returned to Iceland to take up jobs in Reykavik, as the growing town assumed its role as the institutional centre of Icelandic culture as well as other social affairs.

It has been argued that the precondition for a new conception of the landscape, a new aesthetic vision of the land – a vision detached from utilitarian views of a rural society – lies in the very distance from nature warranted by urban culture. The Icelandic pioneers experienced the urban point of view during their stay in foreign cities, where they were exposed to aesthetic ideas and currents, shaped by urban culture, and well-worn ideas about the interrelationship of the city and the countryside/the pastoral, of culture and nature. A case in point is the symbolic value of the blue colour (especially in mountain views), as in panoramic landscapes by Þórarinn B. Þorláksson and Ásgrímur Jónsson (1876–1958). Art historian Auður Ólafsdóttir has remarked that the light in such paintings, generated by blue colour hues, is coextensive with the new "distance" from nature – a distance closely linked to the "foreign" viewpoint the painters had acquired abroad and imported as they returned home (Ólafsdóttir 2001, 24–5).

The Land and the Sofa Painting

The "importation" of foreign cultural influence in various fields, including art, was in tune with another "transportation" when the formation of urban culture was underway – and city-dwellers began to lose close contact with nature. Landscape paintings played an important role in the formation of a new urban identity. Rapid modernization and increased economic prosperity marked the post-WWII period, along with the migration from rural areas, discussed above. The land itself was also "transported" in the form of paintings, quite often idealized landscapes, into a modern urban context where it acquired the place (which it still holds) of honour in the bourgeois home (and in art museums, of course). Paintings quickly became a cultural commodity and a status symbol. This brings us back to the prominence of paintings in the living room, and the actual place of the painting in the room is not without significance in this context. The concept *sófamálverk* ("sofa painting") has been used to refer to the bourgeois tradition of placing original paintings by prominent artists on the wall above the living room sofa.[2]

---

2 The concept "sofa painting" has sometimes been used in another and more denigrating meaning, about paintings by amateurs or works by painters who work in an epigonal, naturalistic style.

In 2001, visual artists Anna Jóa and Ólöf Oddgeirsdóttir put together an art exhibition in the Reykjavík Art Museum (Harbour House), focusing on the central cultural role of landscape paintings and their active part in the creation of new values and and the preservation of collective memories.[3] Their aim was to raise questions about cultural identity as reflected in the symbolic role and place of paintings in Icelandic homes and public places. The exhibition consisted of several photographs of "sofa paintings" and their near environment, i.e. the central area in many homes, generally the living room, where people tend to place a sofa and above it a work of art. This arrangement is of course to be seen widely in different countries and regions, but it is particularly common in Icelandic homes. Just as the living room is in a sense the centre of the home, where guests are invited to sit, the sofa and the work of art above it constitute the centre of the living room (cf. Jóa 2001).

Figure 10.2 provides a good example of this tradition. It was taken in a respectable bourgeois home which had remained largely unchanged for decades. In it we visit a place which is in a sense formed by the nation's increasing prosperity and urban development, but through the paintings (especially one of them), this place is connected to, and makes a certain claim to, the world of Icelandic nature. Danish furniture is prominent, but the central painting is by one of Iceland's favorite artists, Ásgrímur Jónsson. Jónsson was educated at the Royal Academy of Art in Copenhagen and travelled to Italy and Germany before returning to Iceland in 1909. He began his career in a romantic academic style with panoramic landscapes, but began experimenting with impressionism in the 1920s. After 1949, the expressive influence of Van Gogh began to show in his work, with the use of bright colours and energetic brushwork for instance in this painting, painted in Húsafell in the Borgarfjörður district.

Jónsson was one of the most important painters who produced works for an emerging Icelandic art market, and at the same time we can see him capturing Icelandic nature in an idealized mode which struck a chord with the nation. Such works became valuable commodities as they helped transport the country's landscape into a modern urban context. Compared with European nations that had centuries to develop their urban culture, Icelanders had to adjust to new ways almost overnight, but they wanted to "hold on" to their mountains, in a manner of speaking – including the glaciers. It is of course possible, from a present-day point of view, to judge such "sofa paintings", or this living room arrangement, as decorous and sedate, and as aesthetically conservative. But we should not be overhasty in our judgement.

---

[3] The painting by Magnús Jónsson, discussed above, was among the paintings photographed. Other photographs included in this chapter also come from this exhibition. Anna Jóa (Jóhannsdóttir) is one of two authors of the present chapter.

Figure 10.2 Ásgrímur Jónsson: Húsafellsskógur, Strútur
(*Photograph*: Anna Jóa)

Settlements: Routes and Roots

In the course of urban development, along with the growth of the economy, Icelandic painters played a role in reinforcing the nation's self-confidence. There was much public interest in the development of painting. Attendance at exhibitions was considerable and the response was often vigorous. The public was witnessing the settlement, or re-settlement, of the land in a new medium. Of course, the strong literary tradition of Iceland ensured that recapturing the land, in poems and stories, was from the start an element of the growing urban culture. This "settlement" of the sparsely populated or uninhabited parts of the country also quickly happened through other channels, for instance, as Marion Lerner has demonstrated in detail, in travel associations that were founded in Reykjavík already in the second quarter of the twentieth century, with the express aim of exploring "wild" terrain, and in some sense "settling" it during times of leisure provided by the new urban society (Lerner 2006, 2010).

The exploration and acts of settlement evinced in Icelandic landscape painting clearly touched the visual and tactile senses and mnemonic faculties of many Icelanders in a particularly strong way. The passionate interest in seeing how these early painters conquered the land through their visual medium brings to mind the making of the old Icelandic *Landnámabók* (Book of Settlement, also called *Landnáma* for short), detailing how the country was originally divided up and settled. The painters were eager to capture the land with their forms and colours, thus also challenging their audiences to delve into new aesthetic categories and inquire into their own perception of Icelandic nature.

In fact, the urban public at the time was in some ways involved in a *double* move of settlement. One the one hand they have to find their place, find their routes, in a town that is turning into a city, with all the trappings of a world apart. At the same time, they are renegotiating their relationship with their roots and with what we referred to earlier as the "hinterland" of urban society. It is interesting to look at this cultural double-bind from the perspective of urban place studies. Dolores Hayden notes how significant "public memories" of city life are lost when when buildings or other monuments, or even whole neighborhoods, are bulldozed. She discusses the fight against "this loss of meaning in places", which is also a fight for "cultural possibilities" and at the end of her book she remarks: "Any historic place, once protected and interpreted, potentially has the power to serve as a lookout for future generations who are trying to plan the future, having come to terms with the past" (Hayden 1997, 5, 42 and 246–47). But the past, for a large percentage of the urban Icelandic population at the time, was non-urban. In some ways this non-urban world had been left behind, but in others it was very much a living part of Icelandic culture and social reality. What public memories did it keep in store, memories that had perhaps not received due attention? What were its cultural possibilities, its power to serve as a lookout, and to fight against the loss of meaning in places? How could this power be transported to the urban centre of national life? These were some of the issues facing Icelandic writers and painters, most of whom had themselves settled in the urban centre, due to the laws of "cultural possibilities".

One of these painters was Jón Stefánsson (1881–1962), who originally studied engineering but turned to painting in Copenhagen. In 1908–1911 he studied at Matisse's school in Paris, where he came into contact with fauvism and other avant-garde currents. Stefánsson eventually found his own mode of expression by working through the influence of Cézanne's structural approach, aiming to recreate the structures of nature by drawing on elemental forms. In such works Stefánsson opened a new way of seeing the beauty of the Icelandic wilderness in his paintings from the highlands – as well as demonstrating new and "monumental" valuables.

Þingvellir in Reykjavík

Another painter who has contributed significantly to both the nation's visions of nature and the nation's self-confidence is Jóhannes Sveinsson Kjarval (1885–1972). Kjarval has acquired an elevated status in Icelandic art and culture, and the reception of his works from early on is worth noting. The interest aroused by this young and promising painter was such that a lottery was held to support him to go abroad to study. On the occasion of his exhibition in 1908, printer Guðbrandur Magnússon, one af his most arduous supporters, wrote that his works manifest "such forces of the Icelandic nation that support its brightest hopes for the future and prove that it has a right to a future, no less than other civilized nations" (cited in Vilhjálmsson 1964, 39). During a stay in London, Kjarval observed and admired the romantic works of Turner and Blake, before going to Copenhagen where he obtained traditional academic training at the Royal Academy of Art. In these years he became acquainted with modern art movements, especially when he visited Italy and Paris. His works are characterized by a mixture of styles, such as realism, cubism and expressionism, as well as traits of symbolism.

At the time of Kjarval's return back home in 1922, Iceland had gained sovereignty (although not full independence) and he was inspired by the patriotic spirit of progress that swept through the country. In his book about Kjarval, writer Thor Vilhjálmsson reports how seriously Kjarval took his role as an artist, considering it a vocation to "lay the foundation of Iceland's future art". Vilhjálmsson notes how Kjarval had, during his training years, worked relentlessly, driven by the "power of a whole nation", to "retrieve Iceland's lost time, the imageless centuries" (Vilhjálmsson 1964, 56–8, our translation). Although the response was initially mixed, due to the "exotic" style of his paintings, many were impressed by his unique approach, the way in which he immersed himself into the subject matter. He eventually received widespread recognition and in his paintings of Þingvellir, often called the "heart of the country", many felt that Kjarval had indeed touched the heart of the nation.

Figure 10.3   Kjarval: Frá Þingvöllum (*Photograph*: Anna Jóa)

The above photo shows one of his landscape paintings depicting the natural beauty of Þingvellir, the place where the Icelandic Althing (Parliament) was established in 930, when Iceland was an independent country. The painting embeds this memory – so important for a nation which had been a colony for many centuries – in a natural scene, in a piece of "pure" landscape, "earthy" in its expression and colour; it seems to seek its meaning in the very ground it depicts. It is often said that Kjarval, with paintings that focus on the earth – on rocks, mosses, and lava formations – opened the nation's eyes to the richness that lay at its feet at every turn in Icelandic nature. In his book, Vilhjálmsson likens Kjarval to a prophet who has "given sight to the blind" (Vilhjálmsson 1964, 88), calling him "the Muhammed of Iceland, devoted to bringing the world a new Islam: Iceland. Its nature and life, its grandness and smallness" (87).[4] This is a convincing explication of how painters like Kjarval managed to give the nation (or the world for that matter) not only a new vision (partly shaped by foreign influence), but also a strong sense that their paintings merged with the land itself.

But in the photo, taken in another Reykjavík living room where the arrangement of sofa and central painting is much the same as in the previous one, this painting takes on another layer of meaning, one that may seem double-edged. It does underline, as do the paintings surrounding it, the significance and value of natural landscape to urban dwellers, and it shows how Þingvellir has become a part of a Reykjavík home; indeed, this is not only an example of an "interplace" connection, but also of a heart-to-heart one (between the heart of the country and heart of the home). At the same time, this painting is a valuable commodity, whose cultural capital and monetary value, in these private circumstances, almost inevitably bespeaks prosperous social standing. The value of the painting is shaped by a cultural capital which in turn cannot escape being shaped by social and economic capital. The painting has its place in a cultural system which is not free of social forces, but neither does it take on a unilateral significance in relation to these forces. In fact, in view of more recent debates about environmental issues, the painting could be seen as signifying a borderline space, a contested terrain, where urban developments face the shapes and forms of Icelandic nature.

A great majority of the artists and writers who settled in Reykjavík and made their living in this new centre of cultural activity, had been born and bred in the countryside, and paid tribute to it in their works as well as to vistas of natural landscape. There were some early signs of critical attitude to the purist view of country and nature, for instance in the work of Þórbergur Þórðarson, who scandalized many of his readers in the work *Bréf til Láru* (Letter to Laura; 1924) – a radical autobiographical text that mixes several genres – for instance when he writes about a walking tour in a beautiful area by Breiðafjörður in the west of

---

4   Vilhjálmsson emphazises that Kjarval gave us closeness, and notes: "How many have not tried to see Iceland as if it were some other country and not Iceland!" (Vilhjálmsson 1964, 88) – possibly referring to the blue colour of distance, so common in landscape paintings.

Iceland. He begins by reciting familiar phrases about the beauty of nature, but then seems to realize that he is rehearsing literary formulas. "Where am I?", he asks. "Is this Italy?" And then, in what was to become a famous line: "I squatted behind a bush and took a crap" (Þórðarson 1974 [1924], 23, our translation). To many this was an atrocious act of taking nature to nature, so to speak, a dirty visit to the holy hinterland. Of course, this was a common practice of people moving through uninhabited parts of nature, but to relay it in a work of literature turned it into a problematic act. It is more than likely that Þórðarson aimed to effect precisely such a clash of nature and culture – and a paradoxical one at that, where nature and the basic needs come along with the urban traveller, who does not behave according to the codes of culture and civilization of "the bush".

Transported Mountains

In 1948, a year before Jóhannes úr Kötlum's *Dead Man's Island* was published, Halldór Laxness brought out his novel *The Atom Station*, which is in some ways a groundbreaking work of urban literature in Iceland. Still, it is also strongly linked to the rural culture, for the narrator is a young country girl from the north who has come to work as a maid in the house of a Reykjavík Member of Parliament. His residence is an extreme example of the new Icelandic settlement – one that is in fact linked to another kind of settlement: the deal this parliament member and others supporting the right wing government strike with the US about a permanent American military base in Iceland – an "atom station". At the same time, the house is decorated with paintings of Icelandic landscape – "sofa paintings". This is how the girl, Ugla, sees them:

> Next day I stood in the middle of the room beside two domestic animals – an electric floor-polisher and a vacuum cleaner – and began to study the pictures in the house. I had often looked at these ten- and twelve-centimetre mountains which seemed to have been made sometimes of porridge, sometimes of bluish sago-pudding, sometimes a mash of curds – sometimes even like an upturned bowl with glacier Eiríksjökull underneath; and I had never been able to understand where I was meant to be placed, because anyone who comes from the north and has lived opposite a mountain cannot understand a mountain in a picture in the south.
>
> In this house there hung, so to speak, mountains and mountains and yet more mountains; mountains with glacier caps, mountains by the sea, ravines in mountains, lava below mountains, birds in front of mountains; and still more mountains; until finally these wastelands had the effect of a total flight from habitation, almost a denial of human life ... Quite apart from how debased Nature becomes in a picture, nothing seems to me to express so much contempt for Nature as a painting of Nature. I touched the waterfall and did not get wet,

and there was no sound of a cascade; over there was a little white cloud, standing still instead of breaking up; and if I sniffed that mountain-slope I bumped my nose against a congealed mass and found only a smell of chemicals, at best a whiff of linseed oil; and where were the birds? And the flies? And the sun, so that one's eyes were dazzled? Or the mist, so that one only saw a faint glimmer of the nearest willow shrub? Yes, certainly this was meant to be a farmhouse, but where, pray, was the smell of the cow dung? (Laxness 2003 [1948], 37–8).

On the one hand Laxness may be seen as driving a critical wedge between the countryside and its monumental pictorial representation. These works of art are *not* nature and the countryside; they are commodities owned by a rich bourgeois family, and they contain cultural capital which is closely linked to symbolic and economic capital. They carry a message about a certain social status and thus they contribute to the make-up and demarcation of this particular *place* within the city of Reykjavík.

However, the transportation of landscape to this place does not serve its setting in an unequivocal manner. Ugla's response to the paintings may seem naive, but it does not subvert the "realistic methods of these works; in fact it enhances and contributes to the creation of landscape as it "appears" to us in the text. While Ugla purports to reject this debasement of nature, the dry waterfall and the motionless cloud, she does in fact add her own "touches" to these works: birds and flies, sun (or mist), a willow shrub, and the smell of cow dung.

Thus the novel does not reject the transportation of nature to the city; in fact it underlines, even as it problematizes, the significance of such mobility. Laxness's novel itself tries to achieve the effect sought after in these mountain paintings, for by foregrounding and telling the story through Ugla, he is of course presenting the reader with a portrait of a country girl in the city, a girl who harbours a sense of authencity which the new urban settlement cannot destroy.

In Svava Jakobsdóttir's short story, *Party Under a Stone Wall* (1967), another critical step has been taken as regards bourgeois settlement and its incorporation of nature. After two decades of post-WWII economic prosperity, more and more families are able to own spacious apartments and houses that they can design with some elaboration. The town house has now replaced the farm as the quintessential "homestead" and symbolic settlement, a fortress of independence. The couple in the story are basically broke by the time they move into their new house, they spent the last money they had on a stone wall, erected in the middle of the living room, using rocks from a mountain in the east of Iceland. The strain of finishing the house has left a dent in the marriage.

> He remained standing by her side without touching her. He contemplated her silently, unable to find words to bridge the gap between them. He could say they couldn't afford to fix the garden or buy a mirror right now; that building the house had been too much for them financially; he could say that he dearly and sincerely wished that they had never invested money in transporting mountain

rocks from the eastern fjords to use in building a stone wall in the sitting-room. But it was pointless. The stone wall stood there, immutable and merciless, a monument to his folly, a misplaced shelter where no wind would ever reach (Jakobsdóttir 2000, 86).

In some sense the mountain has been transported into the home, in a more concrete sense than the mountains in the paintings that Ugla watches and touches in the *Atom Station*. The mountain does not belong here, but neither do the people, the new homeowners, the settlers. But their social mandates are as merciless as the mountain. It is showtime – house warming – tonight they are throwing a party for their friends, displaying their new home. Here the husband, Snorri, is talking to one of the other husbands, Tomas:

> Tomas now stood up and walked to the wall. Snorri went up to him. Tomas rapped the rocks with his knuckles.
>
> "From Mount Drapuhlid?" he asked.
> "Mount Bulandstindur."
> "That must have been quite a haul."
> "Three truck loads."
> "Expensive?"
>
> They looked each other in the eye. Their expressions a tug of war, measuring their power.
>
> "Well," said Snorri – desperately trying to remember if Tomas had a stone wall – "it depends on how you look at it. Everything has its price, of course." (Jakobsdóttir 2000, 89)

Nature comes to us here as rigidified ideology – not because it is an empty sign, but rather because it is saturated to the point of not allowing for any challenges of nature, except to bank accounts. One could also say that at this point, nature has become strange, it has become the other, the unknown hinterland, which urban people only know as a symbol. But that also means that this world "out there" – the rural districts, the interior, the wilderness, including the mountains – become a region to visit, with various places to explore.

Seizing Landscape

While the stone (mountain) wall in Jakobsdóttir's story may stem from a temporary fashion in home design, it seems legitimate to ask what the development has been in the visual arts as regards the representation and "transportation" of landscape.

Is the landscape painting still a city window turned towards the country? Or is the painted picture perhaps an obsolete medium by now?

Conceptual art undermined traditional painting as a dominant form of expression in the Icelandic art world – although the latter has maintained its popular appeal, especially landscape-based painting. In the 1960s and the 1970s a generation of conceptual artists searched for new forms of expression, contesting "bourgeois living-room art" (including the "sofa painting") as well as the recent dominance of abstract art during the 50s and early 60s. In fact, abstract art does comprise a certain "transportation" of (transformed) nature. Lyrical abstract painters related to nature in their works, especially to light, mediated through the use of colour. Even hardcore geometrical painters admitted allusions to natural forms, such as river currents.

The painting by Guðbergur Auðunsson in the following photo (Figure 10.4) is from the 1980s and is a good example of the demystification of tradition – of painting – which occurred in Iceland as elsewhere, involving "contaminating" influence from for instance Photorealism and Pop Art.

This was in fact a fertile period for landscape painting and it persisted in various half-abstract/half-figurative, "gestural" styles. The painting in the photo is shaped by the currents of both Pop Art and Conceptual Art. Its title, *Landnáma* (Book of Settlement), prominently displayed, humorously refers to the literary heritage, and its relation to the beginning of the country's settlement. The work also contains a comment (ambivalent as it may be) on the landscape tradition

Figure 10.4 Guðbergur Auðunsson: Landnáma (*Photograph*: Anna Jóa)

and the "taking" (or "seizing") of "land" that landscape painters and others have practised. The literal meaning of the word *landnám*, settlement, is "land taking". The work, furthermore, especially when used as a sofa painting, becomes an ironic reference, but perhaps also a homage, to the whole tradition of transporting the land in the form of images into not only living-rooms, but art museums, art books and catalogues, newspapers, journals and websites, while also reminding us that this transportation occurs in the spoken and written language, and in the subjective form of memories.

References

Björnsson, B. Th. 1964. *Íslenzk myndlist á 19. og 20. öld. Drög að sögulegu yfirliti*, Vol. 1, Reykjavík: Helgafell.
Eysteinsson, A. 2006. Icelandic Prose Literature, 1940–1980, in *A History of Icelandic Literature*, edited by D. Neijmann. Lincoln og London: University of Nebraska Press, 404–38.
Fjölnir [editorial introduction] 1835. *Fjölnir*, 1, 1–17.
Hallgrímsson, J. 1835. Ísland. *Fjölnir*, 1, 21–2.
Hayden, D. 1997. *The Power of Place: Urban Landscapes as Public History*. Cambridge MA and London: MIT Press.
Jakobsdóttir, S. 2000. Party Under a Stone Wall, in *The Lodger and Other Stories*, translated by J.M. D'Arcy. Reykjavík: University of Iceland Press, 84–9.
Jóa, A. 2001. "Sófamálverkið": Hugleiðing, in *Sófamálverkið* (exhibition catalogue), Reykjavík: Listasafn Reykjavíkur – Hafnarhús.
úr Kötlum, J. 1949. *Dauðsmannsey*. Reykjavík: Heimskringla.
Kristjánsdóttir, Þ. 2005. *Mynd á þili. Íslenskir myndlistarmenn á 16., 17. og 18. öld.* Reykjavík: JPV-útgáfa and The National Museum of Iceland.
Laxness, H. 2003 [1948]. *The Atom Station*, translated by M. Magnusson. London: The Harvill Press [translation originally published in 1961].
Lerner, M. 2006. Nýtt landnám – landnám óbyggðanna. *Landabréfið*, 22(1), 21–35.
Lerner, M. 2010. *Landnahme-Mythos, kulturelles Gedächtnis und nationale Identität. Isländische Reisevereine im frühen 20. Jahrhundert*. Berlin: Berliner Wissenschafts-Verlag.
Ólafsdóttir, A. 2001. Visions of Nature in Icelandic Art, in *Confronting Nature, Icelandic Art of the 20th Century*, edited by Ó. Kvaran and K. Kristjánsdóttir. Catalogue published for an exhibition in Corcoran Gallery of Art, Washington D.C., October 13 – November 26, 2001. Reykjavík: National Gallery of Iceland (Publication No. 32), 23–38.
Vilhjálmsson, Th. 1964. *Kjarval*. Reykjavík: Helgafell.
Þórðarson, Þ. 1974 [1924]. *Bréf til Láru*. Reykjavík: Mál og menning.
Þorsteinsson, I.G. 1963. *Land og synir*. Reykjavík: Iðunn.

Chapter 11
Ways of Addressing Nature in a Northern Context: Romantic Poet and Natural Scientist Jónas Hallgrímsson

Sveinn Yngvi Egilsson

In Romantic studies, poetical responses to nature have often been placed under such rubrics as Pastoral, Sublime and even Scientific, depending on the general views or characteristics of individual poems, poets or literary traditions. Such rubrics can be questioned on philosophical or ecocritical grounds, especially if they are used to divide poetry into separate categories or fields. However, if taken as co-existing and interconnected discourses or literary modulations, instead of being seen as representing fixed categories, they can be useful in defining the nuanced and often contradictory representation of nature in literature (Garrard 2004: 7 ff.). This understanding of the Pastoral, Sublime and Scientific will be put to the test in this chapter by looking at the poetry of Jónas Hallgrímsson (1807–1845), who grew up on a country farm in Iceland and later became a geologist by education and profession. As is the case with many a Nordic poet who enjoyed formal education but had rural roots, Jónas's poetry does not fit easily into any single category, but can be seen to modulate constantly between what we can call Pastoral, Sublime and Scientific, and thus reflects a complicated and creative vision of nature in all its diversity. It bears witness to an ongoing conversation between the poet and nature, and it reveals the constant interplay between an inner and an outer nature, between the subject and material reality.

Rural Roots and Urban Education

Jónas Hallgrímsson was born just over two hundred years ago, on 16th November 1807, at the farm Hraun in Öxnadalur, a valley surrounded by high mountains in the north of Iceland. He lost his father at a young age and was brought up by his widowed mother and relatives up north. Despite these difficulties, Jónas had the opportunity to study at the grammar school of Bessastaðir, close to Reykjavík in the southern part of Iceland. He then went to Copenhagen, where he first studied law at the University but soon turned to natural sciences. Jónas became a natural scientist by education and profession, but he is better remembered now for what he did in his spare time – writing poetry. He is the single most influential poet of modern Icelandic literature. "His work transformed the literary sensibility of his countrymen, reshaped the language of their poetry and prose, opened their eyes to the beauty of their land and its natural features, and accelerated their determination to achieve political independence," to quote Dick Ringler (2002: 3). Along with the other members of the group associated with the periodical *Fjölnir*, Jónas defined Icelandic national Romanticism for decades to come. After his early death in Copenhagen in 1845 – at the age of 37 – he became the poetical icon of Icelandic nationalism. When Iceland gained full independence from Denmark in 1918 and became a republic in 1944, Jónas's poetry gradually lost some of its political and iconic status. But this also made it possible to reevaluate his contribution to Icelandic literature and culture on less nationalistic grounds than before. The last decades have seen renewed interest in his poetry, both public and scholarly. Attention has especially been drawn to the final phase of Jónas's writing, when he moved away from nationalistic and medieval motives towards a more personal kind of poetry. These poems are strikingly modern in tone and elegantly balanced between dark broodings and a Romantic irony, which shows the growing influence of the German poet Heinrich Heine. This shift in Jónas's world view has been seen to be part and parcel of a new trend in Scandinavian and Icelandic literature and sensibility, a turning away from national Romanticism and poetical realism towards pessimistic and nihilistic *Romantisme* (Óskarsson 2006: 271–3).

As a child brought up in rural surroundings, Jónas Hallgrímsson was close to nature and although he was to leave his native valley, Öxnadalur, and later his home country, for educational purposes, the Icelandic nature was never far from his mind. He revisited Iceland and went around the country on various scientific excursions as a natural scientist, when he worked on a geological description of the country. But, according to novelist Halldór Laxness (1929: 94–8), it was not nature but the city which made Jónas a great poet. Leaving his home country and being on his own in Copenhagen, in a new world full of life and influences, proved to be a decisive factor in his development as a poet. He made his name with masterfully crafted panorama poems, which reimagined the glory of the golden age of Iceland and contrasted it to the present lethargy of the Icelandic nation. These were such poems as "Ísland" ("Iceland"; 1835) and "Gunnarshólmi" ("Gunnar's Holm"; 1837), which includes a grand and impressive description of the mountains and the countryside known from *Njal's Saga*. He was to write many poems which include memorable images of Iceland, for instance "Ég bið að heilsa!" ("I Send Greetings!"; 1844) and "Dalvísa" ("Valley Song"; 1844), both written in the Danish village of Sorø in Sjælland. Another poem of his embedded in the Icelandic nature is "Ferðalok" ("Journey's End"; 1844–1845), a love poem which also alludes to the end of Jónas's life journey, as he seems to have been haunted by thoughts of impending doom.

Nature is clearly a prominent motive in Jónas's poetry, especially its pleasing aspects, but also its sublime or overwhelming elements, as in his description of a volcanic eruption in the poem "Fjallið Skjaldbreiður" ("Mount Broadshield"; 1841–1845), as we shall see. "Huldulјóð" ("Lay of Hulda"; 1841–1845) is an ambitious but unfinished nature poem in the tradition of the pastoral elegy (Egilsson 1999: 101–109). Nature, formerly a benign force and presence to the poet and the natural scientist, becomes hostile in Jónas's late poems, written with a Heine-like twist of the traditional loco-descriptive genre. This is especially evident in the poetic cycle "Annes og eyjar" ("Capes and Islands"; 1844–1845). It is as if the earth is sinking under his feet. And this brings me to the question: To what extent does nature define Jónas Hallgrímsson as a poet? And which nature?

What Makes a Nature Poet?

Early attempts were made at defining Jónas first and foremost as a *nature poet*. In the year 1883, Hannes Hafstein, then a student in Copenhagen and later the head of the Icelandic administration, worked on the second edition of Jónas's poems and wrote an introduction to them:

> As a poet Jónas is in essence a nature poet (a *naturalist*). The outer nature, the land with its valleys and mountains, rivers and flowers, is what he writes most frequently about, it is the basis of his comparisons and the frame of his thinking. He loved all beauteous forms – beautiful and natural language and well-sounding alliteration, just like beautiful hillsides and the beautiful sound of rivers, and this is why his language is so free-flowing and easy, because in it he is just as far removed from exaggeration, and untrue and unnatural images, as in his thoughts. He gets his language from the hearts of the people, his poetry from the natural beauty of the country. In his nature poetry, he is probably not under some outer influence, as he knew little or nothing of those poets closest to him in this respect, the so-called Lake School in England, and it resulted from the combination of his poetical genius with another gift of his, that of understanding the spirit of the natural sciences and to love them and all that which they introduced to him and put him into contact with (Hafstein 1883: 40, my translation).

It is notable how broadly Hannes defines nature or the natural. On the one hand, he talks about *outer nature*, the land with its valleys and mountains, rivers and flowers, and on the other hand he talks about natural language, which he claims Jónas gets from the hearts of the people. According to this, it is not only the subject-matter of the poetry which makes Jónas a nature poet, but also his manner of expression. Nature is not only that which is outside of man – that which is to be found in natural phenomena, landscape and other such outward things – but also that which resides within each man, that which is his essence and character. Nature is not only an object, but also a subject. All in all, this is quite an advanced definition of the natural in Jónas's poetry, a definition which does not simply make him a kind of poetical landscape painter, but also an artist of the inner nature of man.

Hannes compares Jónas to the English Lake School, although he doubts if there is some direct influence to speak of, as Jónas did not know much about their work. Hannes Hafstein had read Georg Brandes, who covered the Lake School (or "Søskolen", as he called it) in his *Hovedstrømninger i det 19. Aarhundredes Literatur* or *The Main Streams of Nineteenth Century Literature*. This is a quotation from his chapter from 1875 on Naturalism in England, where Brandes writes about William Wordsworth, the most famous poet of the Lake School:

> Poetry, according to Wordsworth's definition, takes its origin from emotion recollected in tranquillity. It tries to adopt the language of nature, but as it is the poet's task to communicate pleasure, not straight-forward truth, he uses metres which offer the reader pleasant little surprises through rhythm and rhyme (Brandes 1906 [1875]: 332, my translation).

Considerations of this kind may be on Hannes Hafstein's mind when he compares Jónas to the Lake School and says that he gets his language from the hearts of the people, his poetry from the natural beauty of the country. Wordsworth also claimed to have gotten his language from the "hearts of the people" as Hannes knew and Brandes describes in his *Hovedstrømninger*. Wordsworth wanted to use simple language or diction in his poems, the kind of which was spoken by ordinary people living in the countryside. He thought they were closer to nature, and to the language of nature, than the sophisticated people of the higher classes living in modern cities (Brandes 1906 [1875]: 330). It is as if Hannes Hafstein sees something similar in Jónas, even though he doubts whether Jónas was directly influenced by the nature and language philosophy developed by the Lake poets.

Let's now turn for a while from definitions of nature poets to what is meant by the term *nature poem*. This is in fact a rather loose term, but literary scholars during the last decades have tended to focus on the way in which these poems centre on *places* rather than the elusive nature in general (Bate 1991, Rigby 2004). The so-called nature poems of the nineteenth century often take their names from a certain place and at the same time refer to a journey which took place at a certain time. Jónas calls a poem of his "Fjallið Skjaldbreiður (Ferðavísur frá sumrinu 1841)" or "Mount Broadshield (Travel verses from summer 1841)". To mention another example, William Wordsworth called one of his poems "Lines Composed a Few Miles Above Tintern Abbey, on Revisiting the Banks of the Wye during a Tour, July 13, 1798". Such titles often suggest the approach used in the poems: they are reflections about places and phenomena where the poet-speaker is on the move and circling around the subject-matter. They are like leaps towards the matter and the thought is somewhat similar to a movement or a journey to a certain place which is revisited time and again. The time factor is also important and it is as if the speaker is saying directly or indirectly: "I was there, then, and I thought about that which had happened." At the same time, we are witnessing a kind of dialectic: the mind is mirroring itself in some natural phenomena, something which is out there (Pite 2003). But the imagination can easily transform the outer reality into different images, which again can reflect the state of mind. This is what happens in the impressive description of the volcanic eruption in "Fjallið Skjaldbreiður" as we shall see. There we are witnessing a transformed landscape. We will take this poem as an example of the nature or the natures Jónas describes in his poetry as a whole. I am not saying it is typical of his poetry, but it certainly reflects various concerns which continued to occupy him throughout his poetical career.

Lava Formation and Levels of Conversation

"Fjallið Skjaldbreiður" is an unusual poem, centring as it does on a volcanic eruption and a grand-scale re-creation of a whole part of the country. As suggested by the subtitle, this is a travel poem originating in 1841, when Jónas visited Þingvellir and the surrounding area in Southwest Iceland (cf. Figure 11.1). He travelled extensively around Iceland during the years 1839–42, in spite of ill health, working on a scientific description of the geography and the natural history of Iceland. He continued working on this project in Copenhagen 1842–43, at Sorø in Sjælland 1843–44 and again in Copenhagen 1844–45, but did not live to bring it

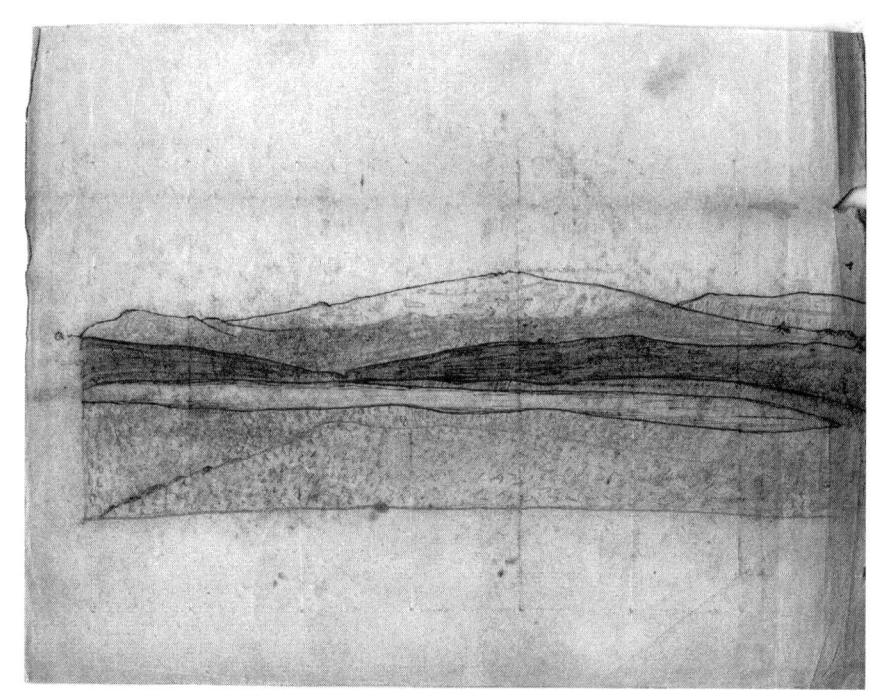

Figure 11.1 A drawing of Skjaldbreiður by Jónas Hallgrímsson
(*Source*: Þjóðminjasafn Íslands)

to a conclusion. But in the summer of 1841 he was still optimistic about his project and went to Þingvellir along with his assistant and researched its geology.

The Þingvellir area is characterised by striking lava formations and deep fissures, surrounded by mountains. In his travel diary, and also in the poem itself, Jónas put forward a thesis or a geological model explaining how the present state of the area came about. He was a bit unlucky in thinking that Skjaldbreiður was the volcano from which the extensive Þingvellir Lava Field was formed, as present-day geologists have come to a different conclusion and pointed out another volcano in the neighbourhood from which all this lava probably flowed in prehistoric times (Sæmundsson 1992). But if Jónas was a bit mistaken in his thesis, it is still interesting to see how he visualised the play of the natural forces in the poem. Dick Ringler describes the geological part of the poem usefully and accurately. He says:

> [A]fter a brief introduction and a description of the lonely, majestic scenery through which he is riding at dawn, Jónas peers far into Iceland's prehuman past. He uses his knowledge as a professional geologist and his enormous powers of imagination to recreate the events that occurred during what he understood to be the second eruption of Skjaldbreiður. In Jónas's view, this eruption had formed the Þingvallahraun (Þingvellir Lava Field), the huge plain of lava stretching south from Skjaldbreiður to the north edge of Þingvallavatn (Lake Þingvellir). Later, when the lava cooled, the local rivers, after flowing through a hollow vault beneath it, emerged from it to form Þingvallavatn. Later still a portion of the lava field collapsed into this underground vault, thus producing the rift valley delimited by Almannagjá (All Men's Gorge) to the west and Hrafnagjá (Raven Gorge) to the east and creating an appropriately impressive setting for the Alþing, or national assembly (Ringler 2002: 197).

I would like to propose that we approach this complex poem like a conversation which is conducted on several levels simultaneously. This, then, would be the first level of conversation, one which we could call *scientific*: we can understand the poem mainly as a short geological thesis written in verse. But we should also keep in mind that Þingvellir is a historical site and Jónas never lets us forget this in his poem. This is where the Icelanders of the medieval Commonwealth period gathered each year and held their assembly. That was obviously a thing of the past in Jónas's days, as the Icelanders had now for centuries been under the rule of the Danish king and did not have a legislative body or an independent government. Jónas and his colleagues in the *Fjölnir* circle had for years tried to convince the Icelanders and the Danish authorities of the need to modernise Iceland and resurrect its Alþingi or Parliament at Þingvellir. The Danish king, Christian the Eighth, proved to be sympathetic to this cause and decreed in 1840 that the Icelandic assembly be resurrected. The king's decree made Jónas and his colleagues jubilant for a while, but then the matter was put into the hands of an Icelandic committee of officials and various representatives, who were to decide whether the assembly should be held at Þingvellir or in the village of Reykjavík. The committee came to the conclusion that it would be more practical and sensible to resurrect the assembly in a coastal village like Reykjavík, rather than in a rural and inland place like Þingvellir. Jónas heard of the committee's decision just before he left Reykjavík for Þingvellir in the summer of 1841, and his bitter resentment of this conclusion is surely one of the main triggers of his poem about Skjaldbreiður. Jónas and the *Fjölnir* circle had claimed that the Icelandic national spirit – *þjóðarandi* or Herderian *Volksgeist* – had originally chosen Þingvellir as the logical site for the assembly, and it should therefore be resurrected there and nowhere else if the nation was to remain consistent with itself (Egilsson 1999: 35 ff.).

This would be the second level of conversation in the poem, one which we could define as *historical or political*. We can see how Jónas interprets the formation of the stone walls and cliffs surrounding the ancient assembly site as predestined or fashioned by God and fire such as to provide the nation with a natural frame around its democratic freedom. These are strophes 8–10, both in the original and in Dick Ringler's English translation:

Svo er treyst með ógn og afli
alþjóð minni helgað bjarg;
Breiður þakinn bláum skafli
bundinn treður foldarvarg.
Grasið þróast grænt í næði
glóðir þar sem runnu fyrr;
styður völlinn bjarta bæði
berg og djúp – hann stendur kyrr.

Hver vann hér svo að með orku?
Aldrei neinn svo vígi hlóð!
Búinn er úr bálastorku
bergkastali frjálsri þjóð.
Drottins hönd þeim vörnum veldur;
vittu, barn! sú hönd er sterk;
gat ei nema guð og eldur
gjört svo dýrðlegt furðuverk.

Hamragirðing há við austur
Hrafna rís úr breiðri gjá;
varnameiri veggur traustur
vestrið slítur bergi frá.
Glöggt ég skil hví Geitskór vildi
geyma svo hið dýra þing.
Enn þá stendur góð í gildi
gjáin kennd við almenning.
(Hallgrímsson 1989a: 131–32)

Thus did fierce resistless forces
fashion Iceland's sacred shrine.
Bound, now, at their burning sources,
Broadshield's restless firewolves pine.
Streams of grass flow down the gracious
glens where lava used to spill;
sited soundly, Iceland's spacious
citadel is standing still.

Who unleashed such lethal power?
Listen! No mere mortal hand
built the battlements that tower
boldly over freedom's land!
God, the prince of force and passion,
planned these bulwarks in his mind:
who but God – and fire – could fashion
fortress walls of such a kind?

Eastward, stony steeps are leaping
stalwartly from Raven Gorge;
westward, walls of rock are keeping
watch above our nation's forge.
Grímur Goatshoe, sage and clever,
grasped the promise of this place:
Almanna Gorge, on guard for ever,
girds the councils of my race.
(Ringler 2002: 193–94)

The Alþing was established at Þingvellir on the recommendation of Grímur geitskór or Goatshoe, who had been commissioned to scour the country in search of an appropriate site, according to medieval sources. We can thus see how Jónas fuses historical arguments with geological arguments, in order to convince his audience that Þingvellir are the only right place for the Alþing. Or, to put it another way, he subverts the argument of the committee regarding Reykjavík as the ideal assembly site. Jónas never mentions Reykjavík in the poem, but it looms large in the background as that *other place* he refrains from talking about directly, a kind of negative presence voiced indirectly through the positive image of Þingvellir, his preferred option in the assembly case. In the poem, he manages to make the inland Þingvellir a cultural and natural centre, whereas Reykjavík becomes an unutterable and marginal place.

Now to the third level of conversation in the poem. I have already mentioned that many of Jónas's poems centre on the more pleasing aspects of nature. They show a general tendency toward the pastoral rather than the sublime, although the pastoral is never simple in Jónas's poems but often ambiguous and even elegiac, which may not come as a surprise, as many critics have noted that a kind of elegy or melancholy often seems to be inscribed into pastoral literature (Gifford 1999: 49 ff.; Garrard 2004: 37 ff.). "Fjallið Skjaldbreiður" and some of Jónas's late poems are yet more complicated in this respect. Sublime elements find their way into them, and nature does not prove to be quite the kindly force and presence of the earlier poems. "Fjallið Skjaldbreiður" is perhaps the most sublime of all of Jónas's poems, describing as it does the terrible and life-threatening forces at play in volcanic eruptions, earthquakes and other natural disasters. The pastoral emblems of flowers, shrubbery and brooks are scorched and scattered by the sublime forces of the burning lava in strophes 5 and 6:

Belja rauðar blossa móður,	Fiery surges snarl and thunder,
blágrár reykur yfir sveif,	smoke is roiling, bluish grey;
undir hverfur runni, rjóður,	birch and rowan both go under,
reynistóð í hárri kleif.	bush and shrub are seared away;
Blómin ei þá blöskrun þoldu,	valley flowers, scorched to vapor,
blikna hvert í sínum reit,	vanish with a fragrant hiss;
höfði drepa hrygg við moldu –	grasses glow like burning paper –
himnadrottinn einn það leit.	God alone beheld all this.
Vötnin öll, er áður féllu	Playful brooks that once went plashing
undan hárri fjallaþröng,	past the hillsides all around
skelfast, dimmri hulin hellu,	flee in dismal panic, dashing
hrekjast fram um undirgöng;	down a channel underground.
öll þau hverfa að einu lóni,	When their waters reassemble
elda þar sem flóði sleit.	where the lava ends, they break
Djúpið mæta, mest á Fróni,	forth in freedom, dance and tremble,
myndast á í breiðri sveit.	forming Iceland's greatest lake.
(Hallgrímsson 1989a: 130–31)	(Ringler 2002: 192–93)

The poem can be read as a part of the *discourse of the sublime* which gathered momentum in the eighteenth century and became an established way of looking at landscape in the nineteenth century (de Bolla 1989, Nicolson 1997 [1959]). Let's not forget that Iceland was – and still is – one of the preferred places of travellers searching for an alternative beauty of nature, a beauty which has been defined as sublime. Many Icelandic poets were to follow in the footsteps of Jónas and write poems on the terrifying beauty of such natural phenomena as gigantic waterfalls, horrifying gorges, chilling glaciers, boundless oceans, endless deserts and other sublime images, providing the traveller and the reader with aesthetic thrills. In Romantic poetry, images of nature often reflect or mirror certain concerns or even show self-images of the poet. One way of looking at this is to see Jónas's sublime descriptions of the volcanic eruption, and the grand play of the natural forces, as reflecting his own creative outburst and the play of his own sublime imagination. In this sense, he is projecting his own self and the forces of his mind and feelings onto the images of nature or landscape.

We have seen how many-sided nature is in a single poem by Jónas Hallgrímsson and on how many different levels it is conducted as a poetical conversation. "Fjallið Skjaldbreiður" can be read as a scientific analysis of the formation of a certain area in Iceland, it can be read as a reflection on history and politics, and the images of nature or landscape can also be seen to reflect the horrors envisioned by the human mind – horrors that are not only evoked by some outer, natural forces, but horrors which are also subjective and self-reflective. We are witnessing the frightening forces of the imagination.

And this brings me to the fourth and final level of conversation I would like to suggest, one which we could call *existential and environmental*. The final strophe is as follows:

Heiðabúar! glöðum gesti	Highland powers, approve my lonely
greiðið för um eyðifjöll.	passage through your vast domain!
Einn ég treð með hundi og hesti	Horse and hound are now my only
hraun – og týnd er lestin öll.	helpers, parted from my train.
Mjög þarf nú að mörgu hyggja,	Curious sights in countless numbers
mikið er um dýrðir hér!	crowd upon my hungry eye!
Enda skal ég úti liggja,	Ghosts will not assault my slumbers,
engin vættur grandar mér.	sleeping out beneath the sky!
(Hallgrímsson 1989a: 132)	(Ringler 2002: 194)

As becomes evident when reading Jónas's travel diary (originally written in Danish, but published in an Icelandic translation in Hallgrímsson 1989b; see especially pp. 409–11), he became lost in the extensive lava field while researching it. Lost in the sense that his fellow-travellers – that is his assistant along with another young man from the neighbourhood who decided to keep them company – accidentally parted with Jónas. This left Jónas alone with his horse and dog (the horse was called Baldur as one can gather from the third strophe), and without any provisions, outer clothing or camping equipment. Now this was in inland Iceland, close to the Highlands, where you could expect any kind of weather, even during the summer. Jónas searched in vain for his train and late in the day decided to sleep in the grass throughout the night. The following day he found his train which had by mistake taken another route than planned.

It is quite obvious that this experience made a strong impression on Jónas and reminded him of his vulnerability towards the environment out in the open and rural landscape. In the last strophe he refers to the powers residing in nature. In Icelandic folklore there are a number of ghosts and other supernatural forces thought to be present in such a place as Þingvellir and its surrounding area (Ringler 2002: 198 cites an interesting example of this in recorded Icelandic folklore). Even if Jónas does not believe in such a superstition as ghosts and local spirits, or rather believes them to be a superstition, he nevertheless gives them a thought in the poem and decides that they will not harm him. But it is still more remarkable that a geologist, aware of the real dangers of the natural forces, having just described the destruction brought about by a volcanic eruption, should choose to end his poem in this way. A literal translation of the last two lines would be "accordingly, I will have to lie outside; / no supernatural being will destroy me". This may be taken as a kind of credo or confirmation of belief. Despite having to sleep without a cover out in the open, far away from human abodes, the speaker of the poem is confident.

One could say that Jónas makes a pact with nature and all its possible forces, whether visible or invisible. As a poet and a Romantic, he certainly identifies with nature and sees flowers and animals as his fellow-beings, as is evident in many other poems by him. In "Hulduljóð", for instance, he has the speaker address individual flowers in an intimate manner, not through formal or rhetorical apostrophes, but like somebody would informally address a bosom-companion. The same goes for the waterfall in "Dalvísa", which is personified and addressed endearingly as an old chum by the speaker of the poem. This closeness to nature and ready responses to the immediate surroundings surely stem from Jónas's rural roots and they are more reminiscent of a poet like, say, John Clare (1793–1864), rather than William Wordsworth, although Jónas and Wordsworth may also share some attributes and approaches in their poetry, as Hannes Hafstein suggested by pointing to the Lake School parallels. Like Jónas, Clare was brought up on a country farm and remained close to nature for the rest of his life, as is evident in the natural knowingness and sympathy which suffuses his poems on all things great and small. This has prompted ecocritics such as Greg Garrard to declare that, compared to Wordsworth, Clare "has a much better claim to be a true poet of nature" (Garrard 2004: 44, see also Bate 2000: 153–75). A similar claim could be made for Jónas in comparison with almost any other Icelandic poet.

On the other hand, as a geologist and scientist, Jónas is only too well aware of the destructive powers of the natural forces. Yet in the conclusion of "Fjallið Skjaldbreiður", he has the speaker put his trust in the powers residing in nature. To quote the German philosopher Martin Heidegger, we could say that the conclusion of the poem is that man should remain open to nature and the world, and respectful of the powers beyond his control (Heidegger 1971 [1946], see also Bate 2000: 243–83). It is a heightened state of awareness, an environmental way of being if you like. Throughout the poem, Jónas shows a strong feeling for the landscape and the place, as is evident in his insightful descriptions of the environment and also in the many place-names he uses to position himself with (Skjaldbreiður, Lambahlíðar, Hlöðufell, Hrafnagjá, Almannagjá). And in the end he does find himself a temporary resting place in a fascinating environment: "Mjög þarf nú að mörgu hyggja, / mikið er um dýrðir hér!" ("Curious sights in countless numbers / crowd upon my hungry eye!") He celebrates his sudden loneliness, because he feels he is not alone after all. He acknowledges that other we call nature or landscape, and he delights in its company.

Inner and Outer Nature in Jónas's Later Poetry

It would be pleasant to end the chapter on this happy note. But in order to realize how Jónas's views of nature, and at the same time his views of himself, developed, we have to look at some other poems he wrote during the next years. And they tend to be rather gloomy.

The poetic cycle "Annes og eyjar" centres on Iceland and describes its various parts, real and imaginary. These poems were written in Copenhagen during the last year of Jónas's life. It is as if he is finally realizing that he may be more of a poet than a natural scientist. His work on the scientific description of Iceland proved to be much harder than he had thought, and maybe he wasn't the right man for this difficult job. Despite all his capabilities as a scientist, he perhaps lacked the stamina to carry such an enormous project through, even if he had lived longer. But instead of the scientific description of Iceland he produced something else – a poetical description of Iceland. And it must be added that it was only a matter of time until another natural scientist would come along and describe the country in scientific terms. But as a poet, Jónas was irreplaceable and his few but brilliant poetical descriptions of the country are quite an achievement in their own right.

At around the same time he was writing "Annes og eyjar", Jónas wrote a couple of poems which are also of great importance in this respect. One is a sonnet and it goes like this:

| **Svo rís um aldir árið hvurt um sig** | **On New Year's Day (1845)** |

Svo rís um aldir árið hvurt um sig,	Thus the years open, each of them in turn,
eilífðar lítið blóm í skini hreinu.	endlessly blooming flowers of transiency.
Mér er það svo sem ekki neitt í neinu,	Their ceaseless passing is of no concern,
því tíminn vill ei tengja sig við mig.	for time no longer means a thing to me.

Eitt á eg samt, og annast vil eg þig,	I have a treasure of eternal worth:
hugur mín sjálfs í hjarta þoli vörðu,	a guardian heart that, girded against harm,
er himin sér, og unir lágri jörðu,	gazes on heaven but is content with earth
og þykir ekki þokan voðalig.	and views the threatening fog without alarm.

Ég man þeir segja: hart á móti hörðu,	"Always be tough!" they tell me. "Hold your own!"
en heldur vil ég kenna til og lifa,	But I would rather live and feel and see –
og þótt að nokkurt andstreymi ég bíði,	even when this earns me men's antipathy –

en liggja eins og leggur upp í vörðu,	than be a hollow half-decayed sheephone,
sem lestastrákar taka þar og skrifa	hidden by pack train boys in stacks of stone,
og fylla, svo hann finnur ei – af níði.	stuffed full of slander and obscenity.
(Hallgrímsson 1989a: 225–26)	(Ringler 2002: 300)

It goes without saying that this is a quite different tone from the one voiced in "Fjallið Skjaldbreiður". Although this poem certainly includes arresting images of nature or landscape, it is highly subjective. Unlike "Fjallið Skjaldbreiður", there is no mention of a particular place or place-name. It is as if the poet-speaker is writing himself into the landscape or the natural phenomena, transferring himself onto images of stacks of stone or cairns like the ones Jónas knew from back home in Iceland. The speaker has somehow lost contact with the passing of the years; "tíminn vill ei tengja sig við mig", he says, and yet there is something he still owns, and that is his own mind in a heart which is guided by perseverance. Even if he cannot connect to time, even if the years somehow leave him by, he still loves the low earth and looks to the sky. And despite everything, he is ready to live a full life and not lie passively and let himself be filled with obscenities like an empty bone. *Beinakerling* is an old Icelandic custom, where passers-by would leave pornographic and erotic rhymes in a sheep bone in a cairn, for the next travellers to read and even continue (Ringler 2002: 303). But another way of understanding this grotesque image in the poem is to see it as a kind of foreboding of death, for it is also a well-known custom to bury corpses under a heap of stones. Yet another way is to see it as a death-in-life, a passive way of living, which obviously is being avoided by the poet-speaker. He wants to live a full life and take his chances, even if it means he will have to suffer at the same time.

The last poem I would like to discuss in this context is the one called "Einbúinn" ("The Solitary", 1845). It is as follows:

Einbúinn	**The Solitary**
Yfir dal, yfir sund,	Over scarp, over fen,
yfir gil, yfir grund	over gully and glen
hef eg gengið á vindléttum fótum;	I have gone on the feet of the breeze,
eg hef leitað mér að	always meaning to find
hvar eg ætti mér stað,	an abode for my mind
út um öldur og fjöll og í gjótum.	in the mountains and valleys and seas.
En eg fann ekki neinn,	But I found not a one,
eg er orðinn of seinn,	all the places were gone,
það er alsett af lifandi' og dauðum.	they were packed with the living and dead.
Ég er einbúi nú,	Now I dwell all alone
og á mér nú bú	in a home of my own
í eldinum logandi rauðum.	where the howling inferno is red.
(Hallgrímsson 1989a: 245)	(Ringler 2002: 350)

This is yet another example of the fusion of inner and outer nature, as Hannes Hafstein would see it. The poet is in Copenhagen but Iceland is on his mind. Again, he is not alluding to certain places or place-names, but using images of natural phenomena in a more general sense. One way of looking at this poem is to see it as a reflection of Jónas's scientific description of Iceland. He has been going around the country in his mind, writing about certain places in terms of geology, but now he feels he has somehow been searching for a place of his own. The poet-speaker is like a spirit, a kind of Ariel moving "on the feet of the breeze", but, as in the sonnet we were just looking at, he is lost in a sense and cannot connect. In the sonnet, the lack of connection was temporal, but in this case it is spatial. It is as if the earth is overfilled "with the living and dead" and the final image is that of red fire. This particular image can be understood in various ways. Some have seen it as a kind of Hell, the everlasting fire which sinful men have been threatened with, or simply as a kind of burning up in life (Ringler 2002: 350–51).

I would, however, want to emphasise that the fire is an imaginary dwelling place, such as the French phenomenologist Gaston Bachelard has described in his book, *La Psychanalyse du Feu*, where he analyzes the fiery images of literature, which he considers to be part and parcel of what he calls "the imagination of matter" (Bachelard 1987 [1938]: 111). In "Fjallið Skjaldbreiður", Jónas had envisioned an eruption and laid out all the fiery details. But he had made his bed out in the open, on the field where molten lava used to run in prehistoric times but which was now overgrown with vegetation. In "Einbúinn", he makes his bed in the fire – a fire by which he may simply mean his own imagination. It may be just another way of saying: "I have searched but have not been able to find my place in the world. The only place now available to me is the fire-place of my own imagination. My being will henceforth be imaginary – I will be living in the furnace of my imagination." Which may be just another way of saying: "Goodbye, world – the rest is poetry." Whichever way we want to interpret this fiery image, it is in any case a glowing reminder of the poetical powers that resided with Jónas Hallgrímsson until the very end.

References

Bachelard, G. 1987 [1938]. *The Psychoanalysis of Fire*, translated by Alan C.M. Ross. London and New York: Quartet Books.
Bate, J. 1991. *Romantic Ecology. Wordsworth and the Environmental Tradition.* London and New York: Routledge.
Bate, J. 2000. *The Song of the Earth.* Cambridge MA: Picador.
de Bolla, P. 1989. The *Discourse of the Sublime. Readings in History, Aesthetics and the Subject.* Oxford and New York: Blackwell.
Brandes, G. 1906 [1875]. Naturalismen i England (1875). *Hovedstrømninger i det 19. Aarhundredes Literatur.* Copenhagen and Christiania: Gyldendalske Boghandel/Nordisk Forlag, Vol. II, 269–586.
Egilsson, S.Y. 1999. *Arfur og umbylting. Rannsókn á íslenskri rómantík.* Reykjavík: Hið íslenska bókmenntafélag and ReykjavíkurAkademían.
Garrard, G. 2004. *Ecocriticism.* London and New York: Routledge.
Gifford, T. 1999. *Pastoral.* London and New York: Routledge.
Hafstein, H. 1883. Um Jónas Hallgrímsson, in *Ljóðmæli og önnur rit* by J. Hallgrímsson. Kaupmannahöfn: Hið íslenska bókmenntafélag, 7–46.
Hallgrímsson, J. 1989a. Ljóð og lausamál [Poetry and prose], in *Ritverk Jónasar Hallgrímssonar, Vol. I,* edited by H. Hannesson, P. Valsson and S.Y. Egilsson. Reykjavík: Svart á hvítu.
Hallgrímsson, J. 1989b. Bréf og dagbækur. [Letters and diaries.], in *Ritverk Jónasar Hallgrímssonar, Vol. II.* edited by H. Hannesson, P. Valsson and S.Y. Egilsson. Reykjavík: Svart á hvítu.
Heidegger, M. 1971 [1946]. What Are Poets For? in *Poetry, Language, Thought,* translated by A. Hofstadter. New York: Harper & Row, 91–142.
Laxness, H. 1929. Um Jónas Hallgrímsson, in *Alþýðubókin.* Reykjavík: Jafnaðarmannafélag Íslands, 75–98.
Nicolson, M.H. 1997 [1959]. *Mountain Gloom and Mountain Glory. The Development of the Aesthetics of the Infinite.* Seattle and London: The University of Washington Press.
Óskarsson, Þ. 2006. From Romanticism to Realism. A History of Icelandic Literature, in *Histories of Scandinavian Literatures, Vol. 5,* edited by D. Neijmann. Lincoln and London: The University of Nebraska Press in cooperation with The American–Scandinavian Foundation, 251–307.
Pite, R. 2003. Wordsworth and the Natural World, in *The Cambridge Companion to Wordsworth,* edited by S. Gill. Cambridge: Cambridge University Press, 180–95.

Rigby, K. 2004. *Topographies of the Sacred. The Poetics of Place in European Romanticism*. Charlottesville and London: University of Virginia Press.
Ringler, D. 2002. *Bard of Iceland. Jónas Hallgrímsson, Poet and Scientist*. Madison: University of Wisconsin Press.
Sæmundsson, K. 1992. Geology of the Thingvallavatn area. Ecology of oligotrophic, subarctic Thingvallavatn. *Oikos*, 64(1/2), 40–68.

Chapter 12
A Stroll through Landscapes of Sheep and Humans

Karl Benediktsson

Introduction

In general, landscape studies have not had much to say regarding non-human animals. For the most part animals[1] have populated the territories of certain natural sciences only, such as biology and ecology, and then as objects to be scrutinised from a safe ontological distance. Landscape scholars have either ignored their existence or taken it for granted, which is curious, given the ubiquitous presence of animals in most landscapes. Indeed, they have long been included as necessary parts in the classical and convenient typologies of landscape (cf. Buller 2004). For instance, the uninhabited "wilderness" is by definition the realm of "wildlife", to be either feared or admired – often both. Happy, contented "livestock" are on the other hand part and parcel of the bucolic farming landscape, complete with its associated ideas of the rural idyll, verdant and virtuous. That both these ideal types may be somewhat removed from the harsh realities of industrial modernity is another story.

With the recent turn to analysing landscapes as sites of inhabitation and dwelling (Ingold 1993, Cloke and Jones 2001), the dearth of studies that centre on the presence of animals is even more peculiar: if anyone or anything could be said to "dwell" in landscape, it is the animal. But the attention of landscape scholars is not often directed to the animals as such. The presence of animals tends to be either very limited or simply assumed without many questions asked. Sure, they may be found there somewhere, munching away quietly or sneaking between the rocks perhaps, but are not really included in the stories as active co-constituents of the landscape.

Recent research has put the non-human squarely on the agenda of the social sciences and humanities. The boundaries between the human and the non-human have been destabilised and the impossibility of rigidly maintaining such boundaries has become all too obvious in an age where biology and technology are together refashioning bodies of all kinds (cf. Whatmore 2002, Haraway 2008). As far as landscape studies are concerned, the task is

---

1 From now on, I will for brevity's sake use the term "animals" for non-human animals and "humans" for the rest of the animal world.

to re-animate the missing "matter" of landscape, focusing attention on bodily involvements in the world in which landscapes are co-fabricated between more-than-human bodies and a lively earth (Whatmore 2006: 603).

This chapter will explore whether the metaphor of conversation can assist in this endeavour, by providing a channel for animal voices into landscape studies. Indeed, animals are in a very literal, or rather, audible sense, through their often resonant vocalisations (cf. Lulka 2006), integral partners to almost any landscape conversation. I will first look at some of the interesting ways in which animals have been brought into academic attention lately. Then an attempt is made to situate animals within the broad phenomenological approach to landscape which the conversation metaphor entails. Jakob von Uexküll's concept of *Umwelt* (von Uexküll 1957 [1934]) receives particular attention here. I argue that, when coupled with the semiotics of Charles S. Peirce, this concept can indeed be useful for landscape research that purports to be more than human, because it extends the acknowledgement of phenomenal worlds beyond humans and radically remaps the categories of nature and environment in relational terms. The remainder of the paper is – to paraphrase von Uexküll himself – a kind of a stroll through past and present landscapes of sheep and humans in Iceland and their conversations via the medium of the landscape.

Animals, Spaces, Places – and Landscapes

In the 1990s, a remarkable number of journal articles and books appeared that heralded a new kind of animal studies where space and place were often foregrounded (e.g. Manning and Serpell 1994, Anderson 1995, Philo 1995, Wolch et al. 1995, Wolch and Emel 1998, Philo and Wilbert 2000). The reasons for this can be found in a number of interrelated developments (see Wolch et al. 2003), among them increased worries about the decimation of "nature" in general; a growing realisation of the problematic situation of animals within the logic of the capitalist economic system; and last but not least, a questioning of the human-animal ontological divide and an increasing interest in the concept of hybridity (cf. Whatmore 2002). This "animal turn" brought with it the tools of social theory and cultural critique for understanding animal-human relations, which has yielded rich and diverse returns.

What about *landscape* and animals, then? While the geographical concepts of space and place lie at the heart of many of the aforementioned studies, few of them have attempted to link the discussion to the equally vibrant field of landscape studies, which has also enjoyed something of a renaissance recently. In a recently published textbook (Wylie 2007), a great many themes and theoretical avenues of recent landscape studies are discussed; yet animals are hardly mentioned. Most of those landscape writers who do consider animals remain centred on the human aspects of the relation. Animals are for instance sometimes brought into social and cultural analysis as symbols in contests about the "moral landscape" (e.g. Proctor 1998), where the humans are those who are calling the shots. Often literally.

There are honest exceptions for sure. Tim Ingold, who brought the concept of dwelling to the attention of landscape researchers through his contemplations on temporality and landscape (Ingold 1993), did in fact discuss the centrality of animate beings of all sorts to the "taskscape", which in his formulation is revealed in a congealed form as landscape. Perhaps the most absorbing recent discussion of animals, humans and landscape, however, is Hayden Lorimer's story of a reindeer herd in the Scottish Highlands and the complex biographies of the persons who brought the animals there and herded them (Lorimer 2006). In the author's evocative narration, where he includes the senses, sensibilities and agencies of both herder and herd, the Cairngorm mountain landscape itself comes alive.

Animal, *Umwelt* and Landscape

But can animal worlds at all be subjectively understood by humans? This is a question with which several scholars have grappled. In a paper that has generated much discussion, the philosopher Thomas Nagel (1974) put it beguilingly simply: "What is it like to be a bat?" His own conclusion was that the world of the bat, sensed through echolocation, was too far removed from any human reality for this question to be answered. But some others are not convinced by this reasoning. Philosopher Raimond Gaita (2003), while sharing Nagel's concern about the limitations of the physicalist approach privileged by the natural sciences when it comes to understanding the animal's being, does not concur with him about the impossibilities for discovering the meaning ascribed by the animal to its world. Gaita reasons that the world of another species can in fact be accessed through a close and emphatic description. It is all there, in the open (cf. Agamben 2004). Gaita elaborates on this by telling stories of companion animals he has shared his own life with, and generally stresses the importance of describing animal worlds through other and more diverse means than those deemed appropriate in traditional natural science.

But not all natural science is reductionist in the sense that both Nagel and Gaita are so justly worried about. On the fringes, alternative approaches have been developed. One of the most intriguing of these approaches centres on the concept of *Umwelt*, developed by Jakob Johann von Uexküll in the early twentieth century (von Uexküll 1957 [1934], 2001a [1936], 2001b [1937]). Many scholars from the social sciences and humanities interested in human-animal relations have found themselves drawn to the writings of this Baltic-German biologist, who indeed in his day attempted to do what Nagel later deemed impossible: to access the phenomenal world of non-human animals. He proposed a new field of study, *Umweltforschung*, consisting of a close examination of the semiotic processes which link any living being with the environment and give meaning to it – meaning which is part and parcel of the animal's *Umwelt*. It is in other words assumed that

> ... organisms are communicative structures. What organisms can distinguish is dependent on the design of their structure and on the work of their functional cycles. The latter, which consist of perception and operation, are responsible for creating the Umwelt (Kull 2001: 7).

Recognition of this, von Uexküll argued, would allow a holistic understanding of the animal's being – even that of animals very much different from the human, such as the sea anemone and the amoeba – without having to resort to a dualist splitting of that being into matter and mind:

> We cannot grasp the sense of a strange subject directly, but we can approach his[sic] body by taking a detour to investigate into his meaning carrier. This is certainly the safest method. When I look from the position of a subject, be it man or animal, I can say that these things in his environment, but not the others, are the meaning-carrier for him. Therefore, I have defined his being in a more accurate and better way by not getting involved with the discussion of his soul (von Uexküll 1935, quoted in Chien 2006: 58).

An ongoing exchange of meaningful signs – in other words, a conversation – is what links the animate organism and the environment, or *Umgebung*. Every animal is equipped with certain organs for sensing the environment (*Merkorgan*) and acting upon it (*Wirkorgan*). Carriers of meaning in the environment differ for the various species, as do the actions by which they are able to affect the world around them. Animals are here not simply conceptualised as passively responding to their environment, but active agents who interpret those signals which they are equipped to sense, and act on them. Each animal thus creates its own subjective world – in his colourful language, von Uexküll (1957 [1934]) uses the metaphor of a "soap bubble" – into which the researcher is supposed to be able to step with the help of her or his imaginative capacities and knowledge of the animal's physiological characteristics. Access to the animal's being is gained when its *Merkwelt* and *Wirkwelt* are considered together as a functioning semiotic whole, as the animal's *Umwelt*, instead of reducing the processes of sensing and acting to their constituent parts.

There is, as Tønnesen (2009) has discussed in detail, a certain static quality to von Uexküll's conceptualisation[2]. His is a world where organisms and their *Umwelten* are a perfect match; with no consideration being given to temporal change, gradual or sudden, that might upset this harmonious whole. In a world where global environmental change is being discussed with ever more urgency, this seems more than a little quaint. Tønnesen (2009) proposes the concept of *Umwelt transition* to accommodate the notion of change with this set of thinking.

---

2 Although it is out of the scope of this chapter, the aristocrat von Uexküll was also a political conservative, deeply critical of ideas of democracy (Harrington 1996).

Above all, what the Uexküllian phenomenal world offers to landscape researchers who are interested in animals is attentiveness to the more-than-human agency that certainly is manifested in every landscape. Seen in these terms, landscape is a part of a continuing conversation between animals and their environment, and between different species of animals. From an ecological point of view, Farina (2008) has indeed suggested that landscape be conceptualised as a "semiotic interface" between organisms and environment. Using terminology from semiotics developed by pragmatist philosopher C.S. Peirce, he places landscape as the *representamen* (or sign vehicle) in a triadic relationship with *objects* (resources) and *interpretants* (functions of organisms). This is a useful conceptualisation which can, I argue, be broadened beyond ecological relations to include social and cultural ones, which are especially important and complex in the case of human interaction with livestock.

In Peircean semiotics, the concept of the sign refers to not only a signifier and that which is signified, as in de Saussure's structuralist and linguistic semiology (cf. Vehkavaara 2008). Neither does it refer to language as such. Instead, the sign is a more complex whole, which crucially includes the category of the *interpretant*.[3] The relations between the three aspects of the sign are described by Vehkavaara (2008: 260–261, original italics) as follows:

> [W]hen a (*first*) thing or event is cognized as a *representamen* of some sign, it is recognized as referring to *another* (*second*) thing or event, the *object* of that sign. This act of recognition is manifested by the production of a *third* thing or event in the mind of the recognizer, the *interpretant* of the sign.

Thus, the interpretant is not to be confused with an interpreting actor as such, but is conceptualised as the effect of the sensing of the object by the actor in question. In turn, the interpretant itself becomes a sign which leads to further semiotic processing or *semeiosis* as Peirce terms it. The representamen is the mediator in this triadic process, between objects and interpretants. The semiotic process continues in a chain of such translations, as interpretants again become the sign objects for further interpretation. It ends in the formation of a "final logical interpretant" (Määttänen 2006: 12): habitual action, which operates from an embodied conception of the object that has been informed by the previous rounds of semiosis (cf. Vehkavaara 2008).

Peircean semiotics is therefore not only about language, but about bodies in the world, multisensory perception and engagement, and non-cognitive as well as cognitive interpretation and response. Putting landscape into this complex and ongoing process of semiosis is an interesting mental exercise which, I argue, can

---

3   The concept of "sign" is sometimes used in Peircean terminology for what is elsewhere covered by his neologism "representamen", but at other times it refers to the whole process of perception, meaning production and action in the phenomenal world of the subject.

enrich landscape studies considerably. In the rest of the chapter, I will offer some stories about landscape as a means of conversation not only between animals and their physical surroundings, but between animals of different species. My example of such relational exchange is the complex interchanges between sheep and humans in the landscapes of Iceland.

Iceland: A Grazed Landscape

> Bleating resounds through all of Icelandic cultural history; the sheep is intertwined in the fate of the Icelanders at all times (Hreinsson 2007).

In terms of human and animal agency, the present landscapes of Iceland are the product of a lengthy and ongoing conversation in which both sheep and people have participated intensely. The country was settled by both species more than eleven centuries ago, an event which instigated momentous changes to its ecology. In fact the environmental history of Iceland is often portrayed as a story of The Fall. With no herbivorous mammals present, the landscape was covered in vegetation which was comparatively lush, given the northerly location: "wooded from mountain to shore", as the scholar Ari the Wise put it in his *Book of Settlement*, written in the twelfth century. This pithy and evocative sentence has provided the benchmark to which later ecological states have been (unfavourably) compared. While its exactness has been questioned, environmental researchers have concluded that some 25% of the country was wooded at the time of settlement, mostly with birch (*Betula pubescens*), whose fragrance adds a layer of olfactory exquisiteness to those landscapes where it is found. The settlers must have rejoiced.

The first ships brought a variety of farm animals with them; breeds of livestock that are still found in the country, including sheep. *Ovis aries* is an old companion of humans, having been "domesticated" aeons ago and transmuted into a tremendous variety of breeds. Those who arrived at Iceland's shores were of a breed that, in the language of agricultural science, is of the Northern European Short-tailed variety (Eythorsdottir et al. 2001). Running the risk of rather simplistic anthropomorphising, these animals must also have rejoiced upon entering this landscape of abundance. While most sheep breeds have definite preference for grasses and herbs, the Northern European Short-tail breeds are true opportunists. They are very adaptable to rough pasture and, importantly for the interaction with landscape in Iceland, they are not only grazers in the conventional sense, but also quite keen browsers. The birch, other woody species such as willows (*Salix* sp.) and dwarf birch (*Betula nana*), as well as various forbs, afforded a virtual smorgasbord for the sheep.

In fact, from this moment the sheep and humans worked together in a remodelling of the Icelandic landscape into what it is today. Although cattle were also important, it is not an exaggeration to say that throughout Iceland's human history the sheep were the cornerstone of the subsistence economy, furnishing meat, milk and wool. A form of extensive livestock farming developed. Throughout most of the summer, the sheep roamed freely through both lowlands and the mountain commons, to be rounded up in autumn by a collective effort by the people in each district, in the cultural event known as *göngur* (or *leitir*). In winter, the flocks browsed on scrubs, kelp or whatever other vegetative material that was accessible, depending on location.

The subsequent story is well known: the vegetative character of the landscape changed drastically in the centuries following settlement (Arnalds 1987). The wood cover shrunk considerably, due to direct clearing and burning by humans as well as animal browsing pressure. Over time the unsustainability of the land use system became evident. Especially in the eighteenth and nineteenth centuries, and coupled with particularly harsh climatic conditions as well as large volcanic eruptions, soil erosion reached catastrophic proportions. An *Umwelt* transition was taking place. Gradually, the conversation between animals and humans via landscape became less and less amicable.

And then "modernity" arrived, manifested in radical changes to Iceland's economy and ecology alike. Finally in the late nineteenth century and the first decades of the twentieth, the subsistence farming economy gave way to a more market-oriented one. New environmental conditions were created through increased cultivation for the purposes of haymaking. The old practice of *útigangur* – letting the sheep fend for themselves outdoors during winter – was made illegal. Industrial fencing materials, notably the barbed wire, made the partition of the land possible; a process that became even more visibly striking in the landscape with the advent of mechanised draining of wetlands, which also had their own wide-ranging ecological consequences. In tandem with these changes in rural spaces, urbanisation finally took hold. Instead of the largely autarkic farms, a networked national economy came into being with all the appropriate paraphernalia, including a system of roads that eventually spanned most of the country. All things considered, the *Umwelten* of both sheep and humans changed considerably in the twentieth century.

This social and environmental change gave rise to new forms of conversation between the species. As for the sheep, the new ecologies afforded new opportunities and constraints to which they had to adjust. In some respects they seemed to be doing well: productivist agricultural policy resulted in a substantial increase in the sheep population until the late 1970s (Benediktsson 2001). For the humans, concerns about the ecological impacts and economic wisdom of sheep farming were intermixed with renegotiation of the cultural placement of the sheep, resulting in a complex and often polarised discourse.

The iconic sheep-in-*rofabarð* is an example of this emotionally charged conversation. The *rofabarð* (erosion escarpment) is a ubiquitous landscape feature in Iceland that has come to exemplify to many humans the evil deeds perpetrated by the sheep. A weakening of the vegetative cover has left the unstable volcanic soils vulnerable to erosional forces of water and wind. An erosion front can open up, with the soil particles removed during storms acting as effective abrasive for remaining vegetation and soil. Often the end product is very graphical: a small and pitiful patch of vegetation, sitting on top of a thick bed of soil, but surrounded by an aggressive-looking *rofabarð*. Great efforts have been expended for halting erosion (Runólfsson 1987, Arnalds 2005), and in fact it is much less of a problem nowadays than in the nineteenth and early twentieth centuries, even if soils are still being eroded (Arnalds 2000). But if the *rofabarð* speaks starkly to humans of environmental mismanagement and loss, it speaks to the sheep in a different manner. They find it a convenient place to lie and bask in the sun, find shelter from winds and rain, and to rub their backs against the escarpment, leaving telltale traces of wool behind. They also appreciate the fresh yet fragile plants that show up in the denuded areas, even preferring such areas to more lush and healthy pastures. This is adding insult to injury as far as the humans are concerned, and has resulted in what literature scholar Viðar Hreinsson – alluding to the sheep's deep religious significance – terms the "crucifixion" of the sheep:

> In Iceland, the sheep is among the most common symbols of farming and the countryside, an enemy that must be eliminated. The sheep carries the sins of the world on its shoulders: soil erosion, high taxes and mountains of unmarketable meat (Hreinsson 2007).

Landscape, humans and sheep are thus elements in an intricate exchange of signs, which involve cultural symbolism, physical processes, and environmental affordances in the differing *Umwelten*. We will next look at how sheep and humans negotiate their passages through two sorts of landscapes in contemporary Iceland.

The Mountain in the Lamb

The first story to be told here centres on a literal stroll in the mountains, which after all are the natural habitat of *Ovis aries* and its relatives. In addition, the "mountain lamb" has come to signify certain important issues for human Icelanders. What follows is a blatantly personal tale, interspersed with some Uexküll-inspired ruminations about the mountain *Umwelt*.

On a beautiful late-September day in 2009 I was in Southeast Iceland, and decided to take to the mountains. A certain crispness was in the air and the vegetation taking on the hues of autumn; a perfect day for being in a contemplative mood alone in the mountains. I parked the car on the banks of a proglacial lake and was astonished to see how far back the terminus of Heinabergsjökull had retreated since I last visited this place. There were occasional rumbles when the ice cracked. Now these mountains and outlet glaciers have been included in the large Vatnajökull National Park (cf. Benediktsson and Þorvarðardóttir, 2005), but the park concept is a mere human construct of course: nature conservation does

Figure 12.1 Sheep in rofabarð (*Photograph*: Andrés Arnalds, with permission)

not prevent glaciers from melting. Global warming speaks loud and clear in these parts of the world.

I slowly ascended the rocky ridge separating the glacier from the valley, enjoying the dramatic views on both sides and feasting on the ripe crowberries (*Empetrum nigrum*) en route. (Some people do not like crowberries – they think that they are too watery. That is their problem – crowberries are a well-appreciated part of my own *Umwelt*.) I recalled the name of this mountain ridge, *Geitakinn*; a reminder of a hirsute past. Then suddenly I heard the unmistakable sounds of *göngur* – the autumn roundup of sheep. A sharp, piercing sound echoed through the valley, coming from somewhere in the mountainside opposite me. After a while I saw the farmer, his dark clothes making him almost invisible from this distance. Well ahead of him a small flock of sheep was running towards the mouth of the valley, bleating intermittently. I continued my ascent. They were definitely not talking to me anyway. The farmer was making his whereabouts known to some other people I did not see, and the sheep were possibly discussing how to outwit these intruders on their territory.

At the farm where I grew up, located down there on the flat coastal plain some 15 km away, many sheep seemed to be perfectly happy sticking to lowland pastures, whereas some others headed for the hills as soon as they were out of the farm gate in early summer. The same ewes will be found in the same spots in the mountains year after year, albeit with new offspring each summer. Narrow tracks that mark a long history of trampling by innumerable hooved feet are found in the most remote valleys. These dedicated mountain sheep are often very wary of humans and have a will of their own when it comes to rounding them up; semi-feral animals that do not come down from the mountains by their own accord even when winter sets in. But why this devotion to the mountain landscapes, which seem in many instances rather barren and uninviting to a domesticated grazing animal? Are the sheep there for the views or what?

This is not really known. But sheep are socially interesting animals. Icelandic agricultural researchers have shown that their choice of vegetative species to graze is highly individualistic, and that much of the grazing behaviour is learned (Thórhallsdóttir and Thorsteinsson 1993). The young learn from the older what kind of vegetation is most desirable, and where it is to be found. The propensity to take to the mountains in summer runs in families, if we can put it that way. There are also some inaccessible spots in the steep, glacially-sculpted basalt mountains of Southeast Iceland where the knowledgeable and intrepid ones can find plants that most sheep find irresistible, for instance narrow ledges fertilised by the droppings of birds. Such ledges often contain plants such as the aromatic *hvönn* (*Angelica archangelica*), *burnirót* (*Rhodiola rosea*) and others well appreciated by sheep. Even if they are supremely agile and capable mountaineers, it is not uncommon in these parts for sheep to end up trapped on ledges they cannot get out of, to end up in *svelti* (lit.: starvation) as it is called.

I recalled my own participation in the *göngur* ritual when I was young. I was about ten when my father first introduced me to its intricacies, assigning me to an area where the roundup was rather easy. As the years passed, I graduated to more tortuous terrain. I still wince in embarrassment when recalling a blunder I made once: having grossly underestimated the speed and wilfulness of some ewes, I managed to allow them to escape from the roundup into the hilly landscape at the back of the drive, where they disappeared completely. There was no time to go back to fetch them; that would have upset the whole operation. A farmer who was much higher up had a perfect view of my miscalculation through his binoculars, but was too far away to do anything. The resulting semantic interchange was not very subtle at all: he scolded me profusely when he caught up with me. After this I was not so keen on the *göngur* anymore. I thought I would never be able to read the terrain – and read the intentions of the sheep – as the farmers did. Mustering sheep in the mountains requires a certain skill of translation, between the intentions of the sheep and shepherd. Any lack of understanding on part of the shepherd, and the sheep are gone.

But let us turn back to the story of that solitary hike. Having followed the ridge for a couple of hours, I finally turned back. When I had passed the crest of the ridge I suddenly saw a man and a dog in front of me. And then another man appeared just below me on the valley side: the farmer. He looked tired. In sturdy hiking boots and with a sizable pole in his hand, he had obviously prepared for a tough day. A few meters of rope lay curled around his shoulder. I offered a greeting. He grunted something. He asked whether I had seen any sheep. I had not; I thought that the valley had been cleared already. He said that a small flock had suddenly crossed the river and headed across the ridge, apparently just under my nose, seeking shelter on ledges somewhere in the mountain's precipitous glacial side. I offered to come with him to look for them. He ogled me for a moment and presumably did not think that this was such a bright idea. "Well, you can follow *him* down", he said, and pointed to the other man. And off he went.

I caught up with the other man and his dog. He told me that he was a fisherman, and not used to dealing with sheep. I guessed that those sheep that the farmer was now searching for had taken advantage of this fact and thus managed to get away. We continued down slowly. My companion seemed to be more interested in taking pictures on his digital camera than keeping a watchful eye on the sheep. When we were almost down, the farmer suddenly turned up behind us, with the missing ewes and their lambs. He had understood and interpreted their intentions correctly and managed to get them quickly back in line. We retreated to the side to let the flock pass.

Finally we were down at the river. The sheep appeared determined not to cross. "Do not get too close to them", the farmer sternly warned me and the fisherman; "these bloody ewes will scatter and we will lose them again up the mountain. We will wait for the quad bike". He tried his mobile phone, but there was no signal. He also had a walkie-talkie and managed after a few crackling attempts to contact the guy on the quad bike and tell him of the situation. We sat down and waited at the river in silence, three humans, one exhausted dog and eleven sheep, the groups keeping a watchful eye on each other. The lambs lay down beside their vigilant mothers. The crystal-clear water continued on its noisy trajectory between the gravelly banks, glistening in the low beams of the autumn afternoon sun, which added a touch of serenity to the scene.

Some three quarters of an hour later, that serenity was rudely shattered. We heard the first growls of the quad bike and before long it came roaring over the hill on the other side of the river. The camouflage-clad and black-helmeted driver and his military-green vehicle looked like a hybrid alien in the landscape. The alien checked the banks in a couple of places in order to find a place to cross. The sheep seemed to sense what was coming. Then suddenly the driver found a ford and hesitated no more. On our side of the river, he went full throttle straight into the small flock. The sheep ran off in all directions – except to the river. One bewildered lamb was too late in deciding what to do. Suddenly the alien split in two: the driver jumped off the bike, grabbed the lamb and threw it into the river. The lamb crossed gingerly, moving away from the menacing creature on the bank. The driver then jumped on the vehicle again and sped off to hinder the other sheep in getting away, making a few sharp turns that left deep marks in the delicate moss. Only moments later the ewes and the other lambs were back at the river. This time they did not put up any resistance but entered the cold, clear water to join their fellow lamb on the other side. Who can argue with a petrol engine?

My portrayal of the "mountain lamb" has been couched in somewhat romantic terms, I know, and intentionally so. This creature has taken on certain significance in the imagining of Icelanders of their landscapes and their lambs as noble and unspoilt. While consumption of sheep meat per capita is still very high in comparative terms in Iceland (Dýrmundsson 2006), sheep farmers have faced increasing competition from industrial white meat producers. In their marketing attempts, they have invoked the *fjallalamb* (mountain lamb) as a symbol for all that which is healthy, organic, wild – and national. Upon eating its flesh, one is supposed to be able to taste the mountain in the lamb, making the meal a kind of communion with the land. In reality, many of the lambs ending up on the dinner table spend their days roaming the roadside, rather than the mountainside. The road is an *Umwelt* that begs attention.

The *Umwelt* of the Road

Iceland has been perceptively characterised by anthropologists as an "acceleration nation" (Árnason et al. 2007). Much of nation's energies have in the past century or so been devoted to what they describe, with reference to Paul Virilio, as "enhancing the "dromocratic condition"" (Árnason et al. 2007: 203). Roadbuilding has been the central plank in these efforts. Roads have a tremendous impact on the landscapes through which they are routed. Icelandic roads are by and large rather humble two-lane affairs, with many minor roads very narrow and surfaced with gravel. But the horizontal humbleness is to some extent made up for by a vertical extravagance which, when coupled with the lack of tree cover, makes the roads quite visible in the landscape. In order to prevent the accumulation of drifting snow, the road is, wherever terrain permits, raised well above the surface of the land.

This again means that the road verge – a liminal space in many respects – is a new and prominent element in the landscape. In the past, the roads were often simply made by bulldozing existing materials into their elevated new position, leaving large swathes of ground on both sides where vegetation had been removed. Increased environmental sensibilities led to efforts of revegetation. For a long time the solution seemed simple: the verges were sown over with a mixture of grass seed and fertiliser. The result was a sloping field of vigorous grassland, which looked much more like a farmer's cultivated hayfield than a zone of reconciliation between the uncompromising space of the road and a "natural" landscape beyond. The Roads Authority has increasingly attempted to coax local vegetation to colonise the verges, in order to minimise the visual and ecological impact of roads (cf. Guðmundsson 2005).

The road stands for new possibilities – and hazards – for sheep and humans alike. It has brought into being a new "breed" of sheep: the *vegarolla*[4] (road ewe, cf. Figure 12.2). For these animals, the roadscape is an irresistible semiotic

---

4   The term *rolla* is a derogatory term for a ewe, which is more properly called *ær*.

interface to an environment which affords both a satisfaction of biological needs and certain "creature comforts". Quite often, the road verge provides by far the most succulent vegetation that a sheep can come across in a given area. Sheep are thus drawn to the roadsides, frequently crossing the asphalt (or gravel) itself in order to get at a nice-looking tuft of grass on the other side. The very surface of gravelled roads, they have also discovered, often contains material which they relish greatly. This is common salt, which is often spread over such roads in early summer in order to minimise the generation of dust (Vegagerðin 2008), which is an "externality" of the acceleration economy that is highly irritating to all those having to bear with it. The salting of roads provides the sheep with a necessary mineral which their bodies crave. Finally, the dark surface of asphalt roads warms up considerably on sunny days, a phenomenon well-appreciated by the sheep who have appropriated the road. It is therefore common for ewes and lambs to lie on the road in evening and at night on such days. All things considered, the phenomenal world of the *vegarolla* thus very much centres on the road and it is perhaps no wonder that preference for this landscape seems to be carried over from the ewe to her offspring.

But roads were built by humans and they do not take the presence of others in this space lightly. Increased speeds with an improved road system have thrown the problem of spatial incompatibility into sharp relief. Each year several hundred accidents occur which involve livestock on the roads, mostly sheep, the number of

Figure 12.2   Sheep licking salt on the road
(*Photograph*: Guðjón Magnússon, with permission)

such incidents having risen in recent years (Vignisson 2005). Usually such clashes of automobility and "animobility" (a term borrowed from Michael 2004) result in the death of the sheep, turning it into the undignified yet complex category of roadkill (cf. Michael 2004, Lulka 2008). Often the vehicle is damaged considerably and its human inhabitants are sometimes physically injured. On occasions human deaths have resulted from collisions between cars and sheep.

Let us now step into the *Umwelt* of the driver, or perhaps we should say the driver-car assemblage (cf. Dant 2004). Here the sense of sight is the primary device by which the driver perceives the phenomena which make up his dromocratic world. Speeding through the landscape, the driver observes a dot in the distance, on the right side of the road. It could be a boulder, or a piece of plastic silage wrapping. As the dot draws closer, it takes on the woolly shape of a ewe. And it moves: it is going to cross the road. Taking into account the distance and the speed, the driver determines that it will complete the crossing before his assemblage reaches the spot, and continues without hesitation. Closer still, he notices two smaller dots, moving rapidly to the left: two lambs following their mother. A swift semiotic processing takes place. The driver's experience in this case ensures the translation of the sensed danger into several actions performed at once: a finger presses the horn button on the steering wheel; the wheel is turned to the right slightly; and the right foot is moved from accelerator to brake pedal. Alarmed by the aggressive sound of the horn, the lambs dash across, following the mother, now safely checking out a vigorous patch of *Festuca rubra* that grows on the opposite verge. Accident prevented, and the driver-car gathers speed again.

Part of the reason why collisions between cars and sheep have become more common is the simple fact that drivers are increasingly unfamiliar with the *Umwelt* of the rural road. The majority of the population is now urban and many people do not all that often venture out of town. When they do, they find themselves ill-equipped to do with the presence of sheep on roads. This has led to a more and more acrimonious exchange between the urban and the rural. Irate bloggers on occasion state their opinion that the *vegarolla* is a *bestia-non-grata*; an animal which is, if not directly criminal, then at least criminally stupid. For such an animal, no sympathy is expendable and no conversation can be had with it. Most opinions are a little more measured, advocating that roads be fenced off, which would in fact be a somewhat radical change. Farmers are not legally obliged to keep their stock within fenced areas: in Iceland the purpose of fences is generally the opposite – to keep stock *out* of hayfields and crops. In most cases, drivers who end up in the unhappy situation of killing a sheep are liable to pay damages to the farmer, which has led to a tendency to not report such incidents. There are increasing demands on the Roads Authority to put up fences alongside all major roads, but it has been deemed prohibitively expensive. The conversation between sheep and humans thus includes both sides of the *oikos* – economy and ecology.

Conclusion: Inter-Species Conversations and Landscape Politics

> We do no longer ask the animal "How does the outer world push you around?", we now ask it "What do you perceive of the outer world, and what is your response?" (von Uexküll 2001b [1937]: 117)

As the quote above underscores, von Uexküll wanted to shift our understanding of the relation between the environment and the animal – from one of mechanistic influence of the former on the latter towards a more active view of the animal as a lively agent that dwells in a subjective world. This chapter has drawn on his ideas and attempted to describe human-animal relations as conversations via the medium of landscape. I argue that this is one way in which landscape scholars can rise to the challenge of mending the rupture between the human and the non-human that occurred a long while ago, and which has not only afflicted theorising about landscape and nature, but also environmental politics and practices.

As far as theory is concerned, the human/non-human rupture has been all too obvious. Speaking specifically about the field of cultural geography, Whatmore (2006: 603) identifies as a major shortcoming the tendency in many previous works to "cast the making of landscapes (whether worked or represented) as an exclusively human achievement in which the stuff of the world is so much putty in our hands". The conversation metaphor may offer a better possibility to avoid this anthropocentric conceit than the metaphor of text, which has until now been the main direct connection between landscape studies and semiotics (cf. Wylie 2007). In the landscape-as-text school, writers and readers alike are almost always human. Other influential avenues in landscape theory have also strongly privileged the human, whether they have emphasised the pictorial aspect of landscape as a "way of seeing" or the allegedly primordial meaning of the landscape concept as human territorial polity.

In political and practical terms, there is also an increasing recognition of the need to find more engaged and ethical ways to relate to non-human nature. The active presence of animals in certain landscapes continues to be a source of conflict, as witnessed for example by the ongoing "carnivore controversies" in many countries (cf. Buller 2008, Sjölander-Lindqvist 2008) or tensions involving feral animals (cf. Peace 2009). Addressing such issues requires, at the very least, an acknowledgement of the fact that landscapes feature in the semiotic processes of animal as well as human subjects: that the phenomenal world of the animal be taken into account.

While I would be the first to admit my own limited capacity to "think like a sheep" (cf. Grandin and Johnson 2006), I would like to think that the stories told in this chapter are of some value for adding a more-than-human dimension to studies of landscape. The metaphor of conversation serves such a purpose well. Sheep and humans are conversing with each other incessantly – via the medium of Iceland's landscapes. Their semiotic exchanges are complex, and sometimes problematic; an intersection of different *Umwelten* that creates a distinct "semiosphere" (cf.

Lotman 2005[1984]. This semiosphere is crowded with objects that are perceived, interpreted and acted upon in different ways: tufts of grass; barbed wire; a sheep track in a valley; white woolly dots in the distance; barking of a shepherd's dog; asphalted surfaces; a ledge in a precipitous mountainside; the beep of a car's horn. Intermixed with these sign-objects are ideas and ideals held by humans about landscape, nature, rurality and national identity. Studying the resulting conversational cacophony is a compelling exercise indeed.

References

Agamben, G. 2004. *The Open: Man and Animal*. Palo Alto: Stanford University Press.
Anderson, K. 1995. Culture and Nature at the Adelaide Zoo – at the Frontiers of Human Geography. *Transactions of the Institute of British Geographers* 20(3), 275–94.
Arnalds, A. 1987. Ecosystem Disturbance in Iceland. *Arctic and Alpine Research* 19(4), 508–13.
Arnalds, A. 2005. Approaches to Landcare – a Century of Soil Conservation in Iceland. *Land Degradation and Development* 16(2): 113–25.
Arnalds, Ó. 2000. The Icelandic "Rofabard" Soil Erosion Features. *Earth Surface Processes and Landforms* 25(1), 17–28.
Árnason, A., Hafsteinsson, S.B. and Grétarsdóttir, T. 2007. Acceleration Nation: An Investigation into the Violence of Speed and the Uses of Accidents in Iceland. *Culture, Theory and Critique* 48(2), 199–217.
Benediktsson, K. 2001. Beyond Productivism: Regulatory Changes and their Outcomes in Icelandic Farming, in *Developing Sustainable Rural Systems*, edited by K.-H. Kim, I. Bowler and C. Bryant. Pusan: Pusan National University Press, 75–87.
Benediktsson, K. and Þorvarðardóttir, G. 2005. Frozen Opportunities? Local Communities and the Establishment of Vatnajökull National Park, in *The Mountains of Northern Europe: Conservation, Management, People and Nature*, edited by D.B.A. Thompson, M.F. Price and C.A. Galbraith. Edinburgh: Scottish Natural Heritage, 335–47.
Buller, H. 2004. Where the Wild Things Are: The Evolving Iconography of Rural Fauna. *Journal of Rural Studies* 20(2), 131–41.
Buller, H. 2008. Safe from the Wolf: Biosecurity, Biodiversity, and Competing Philosophies of Nature. *Environment and Planning A* 40(7), 1583–97.
Chien, J-P. 2006. Of Animals and Men: A Study of *Umwelt* in Uexküll, Cassirer and Heidegger. *Concentric: Literary and Cultural Studies* 32(1), 57–79.
Cloke, P. and Jones, O. 2001. Dwelling, Place, and Landscape: An Orchard in Somerset. *Environment and Planning A* 33(4), 649–66.
Dant, T. 2004. The Driver–Car. *Theory Culture & Society* 21(4–5), 61–69.

Dýrmundsson, Ó.R. 2006. Sustainability of Sheep and Goat Production in North European Countries – From the Arctic to the Alps. S*mall Ruminant Research* 62(3) 151–57.

Eythorsdottir, E., I. Olsaker, M. Tapio,, I. Miceikiene, L-E. Holm, S. Jeppson, and E. Fimland. 2001. *Origin and Genetic Diversity of North European Sheep Breeds.* Book of Abstracts, 52nd Annual Meeting of EAAP Budapest, 26-29 Aug., 262. Available at: http://www.rala.is/beta/Posterabstr01.htm [accessed: 7 November 2009].

Farina, A. 2008. The Landscape as a Semiotic Interface between Organisms and Resources. *Biosemiotics* 1(1), 75–83.

Gaita, R. 2003. *The Philosopher's Dog*. London: Routledge.

Grandin, T. and Johnson, C. 2006. *Animals in Translation: The Woman Who Thinks Like a Cow*. London: Bloomsbury.

Guðmundsson, J. 2005. *Uppgræðsla vegflá med innlendum úthagategundum.* Hvanneyri: Landbúnaðarháskóli Íslands.

Haraway, D.J. 2008. *When Species Meet.* Minneapolis: University of Minnesota Press.

Harrington, A. 1996. *Reenchanted Science: Holism in German Culture from Wilhelm II to Hitler*. Princeton: Princeton University Press.

Hreinsson, V. 2007. The Crucifixion and Resurrection of the Sheep. *The Provincialists* Available at: http://www.provincialists.com/essay.php?e=18&f=1 [accessed: 7 November 2009].

Ingold, T. 1993. The Temporality of the Landscape. *World Archaeology* 25(2), 152–74.

Ingold, T. 2000. *The Perception of the Environment: Essays on Livelihood, Dwelling and Skill*. London: Routledge.

Kull, K. 2001. Jakob von Uexküll: An Introduction. *Semiotica* 134(1–4), 1–59.

Lorimer, H. 2006. Herding Memories of Humans and Animals. *Environment and Planning D: Society and Space* 24(4), 497–518.

Lotman, J. 2005[1984]. On the Semiosphere. *Sign Systems Studies* 33(1), 205–29.

Lulka, D. 2006. Grass or Grain? Assessing the Nature of the US Bison Industry. *Sociologia Ruralis* 46(3), 173–91.

Lulka, D. 2008. The Intimate Hybridity of Roadkill: A Beckettian View of Dismay and Persistence. *Emotion, Space and Society* 1(1) (2008) 38–47.

Määtänen, P. 2006. Space, Time, and Interpretation, in *Koht ja paik / Place and Location: Studies in Environmental Aesthetics and Semiotics V*, edited by E. Näripea, V. Sarapik and J. Tomberg. Tallinn: Eesti Keele Instituut, 11–20.

Manning, A., and Serpell, J. eds. 1994. *Animals and Human Society: Changing Perspectives*. London: Routledge.

Michael, M. 2004. Roadkill: Between Humans, Nonhuman Animals, and Technologies. *Society & Animals* 12(4), 277–98.

Nagel, T. 1974. What is it Like to Be a Bat? *Philosophical Review* 83(4), 435–50.

Peace, A. 2009. Ponies out of Place? Wild Animals, Wilderness and Environmental Governance. *Anthropological Forum* 19(1), 53–72.

Philo, C. 1995. Animals, Geography, and the City: Notes on Inclusions and Exclusions. *Environment and Planning D: Society and Space* 13(6), 655–81.

Philo, C., and Wilbert, C. eds. 2000. *Animal Spaces, Beastly Places: New Geographies of Human–Animal Relations*. London: Routledge.

Proctor, J.D. 1998. The Spotted Owl and the Contested Moral Landscape of the Pacific Northwest. In *Animal Geographies: Place, Politics and Identity in the Nature–Culture Borderlands*, edited by J. Wolch and J. Emel. London: Verso, 191–217.

Runólfsson, S. 1987. Land Reclamation in Iceland. *Arctic and Alpine Research* 19(4), 514–17.

Sjölander-Lindqvist, A. 2008. Local Identity, Science and Politics Indivisible: The Swedish Wolf Controversy Deconstructed. *Journal of Environmental Policy and Planning* 10(1), 71–94.

Thórhallsdóttir, A.G. and I. Thorsteinsson. 1993. Behaviour and Plant Selection. *Búvísindi* 7, 59–77.

Tønnesen, M. 2009. Umwelt Transitions: Uexküll and Environmental Change. *Biosemiotics* 2(1), 47–64.

von Uexküll, J. 1957 [1934]. A Stroll through the Worlds of Animals and Men: A Picture Book of Invisible Worlds, in *Instinctive Behavior: The Development of a Modern Concept*, edited by C.H. Schiller. New York: International Universities Press, 5–80.

von Uexküll, J. 2001a [1936]. An Introduction to Umwelt. *Semiotica*, 134(1–4), 107–10. Translated by G. Brunow.

von Uexküll, J. 2001b [1937]. The New Concept of Umwelt: A Link between Science and the Humanities. *Semiotica* 134(1–4), 111–23. Translated by G. Brunow.

Vegagerðin n.d. *Umhverfisskýrsla* 2008. Available at: http://vegagerdin.is/ [accessed: 7 November 2009].

Vehkavaara. T. 2008. From the Logic of Science to the Logic of the Living: the Relevance of Charles Peirce to Biosemiotics, in *Introduction to Biosemiotics: the Nnew Biological Synthesis*, edited by M. Barbieri. Dordrecht: Springer, 257–82.

Vignisson, Ó.P. 2005. *Vegarollur og umferðaröryggi: Aukið umferðaröryggi með lagasetningu með það að markmiði að koma í veg fyrir tjón af völdum lausagöngu búfjár*. Available at: http://www.samgonguraduneyti.is/media/Skyrsla/Vegarollur.pdf [accessed: 7 November 2009].

Whatmore, S. 2002. *Hybrid Geographies: Natures, Cultures, Spaces*. London: Routledge.

Whatmore, S. 2006. Materialist Returns: Practising Cultural Geography in and for a More-than-Human World. *Cultural Geographies* 13(4), 600–609.

Wolch, J., and Emel, J. 1998. *Animal Geographies: Place, Politics and Identity in the Nature–Culture Borderlands*. London: Verso.

Wolch J., Emel, J. and Wilbert, C. 2003. Reanimating Cultural Geography, in *Handbook of Cultural Geography*, edited by K. Anderson, M. Domosh, S. Pile, and N. Thrift. London: Sage, 184–206.

Wolch, J.R., West, K. and Gaines, T.E. 1995. Transspecies Urban Theory. Environment and Planning D: Society and Space 13(6), 735–60.

Wylie, J. 2007. *Landscape*. London: Routledge.

Chapter 13
Sentience

Anne Brydon

In this chapter, I focus on a seeming contradiction around the (im)possibility of nonhuman sentience that has arisen in the two major environmental debates to occur in Iceland in the last 25 years: over whale hunting and over hydroelectric development in support of heavy industry. During the 1980s and early 1990s when the international protests against Icelandic whale hunting were at their height, many Icelanders perceived foreign activists (and by extension, any Icelander sympathetic to their views) as holding irrational and sentimental beliefs about the intelligence and feelings of whales. Yet a few years later, an Icelandic environmental movement with widespread public credibility arose to protest against state plans to push forward hydroelectric and heavy industry development. In public debate, the highland rivers and moors and their nonhuman inhabitants under threat from hydroelectric reservoirs were talked about in terms suggestive of agency and, in some cases, consciousness.

The question this divergence immediately raises is, what would make geese, rocks and waterfalls more easily perceivable as sentient when compared to whales, a mammalian species arguably closer to humans than, say, minerals? A brief answer would be to argue that people don't ordinarily think or experience according to the hierarchical categories of biological science. While the objective likelihood of nonhuman sentience could be gradated along an evolutionary scale or determined by DNA, the actual perception of nonhuman sentient being by real people in the course of their everyday lives is more shaped by contextual, experiential and ideational factors. As Ingold (2000) notes, even in science-based societies individual lives are nonetheless informed by intuitive understandings of moral connection with human and nonhuman others, despite the hegemonic dismissal of intuition as a legitimate way of knowing.

In the 1990s and 2000s, artists of all sorts – poets, writers, actors, musicians and visual artists – played a central role in the creation and perpetuation of a movement opposing large-scale hydroelectric projects. Collectively the artists raised questions about the long-term economic and environmental costs of dependency on foreign industry, volatility of global aluminium prices and the irreversibility of damage to delicate Arctic ecologies. Further, they spoke of the inherent value of nature and need for limits to the growth driven by neoliberal policies of privatization and large-scale modernist development schemes. This opposition was not only expressed rhetorically: artistic activism also involved poetic invocations, songs, nationalistic appeals to preserve the land's soul, treks and performances in threatened landscapes, and visual imagery revealing the landscape's beauty.

When opposing dams and smelters, Icelandic critics invoked an aestheticized sensibility consistent with the transnational environmental discourse of foreign anti-whaling activists – namely, a nostalgic or solastalgic[1] mourning of nature's transformation once regarded as irrational, over-emotional and foreign. Their ethical–aesthetic representations challenged assumptions about nature as economic resource as well as the managerial and sovereignist rhetoric that dominated state discourse from the late 1970s up to the present day.

Yet during the mid-1980s whaling debate, artists did not have an environmentalist public profile. Instead, scientists formed part of a small movement opposing the government's policy. Whaling was never economically or symbolically central to the nation but became for most Icelanders an example of supposed rational usage of natural resources. Some scientists challenged the constraints of this definition of "rational", raising concerns about the independence of science from capitalist enterprise. Further, they expressed interest in ecologically-oriented research which takes a more holistic approach to the organism-environment continuum (cf. Ingold 2000) than typical management science models. By the late 1980s, members of this movement felt silenced by a nationalist backlash making it impossible to speak critically yet remain acknowledged as reasonable. In contrast, the anti-heavy industry movement gained momentum across society and had some success with re-framing the highland as a beautiful, meaningful natural space, thereby disrupting the government's rhetoric that it was a barren waste.

The metaphor of conversation in this volume's title opens into current explorations of alternative epistemologies and ontologies by raising the possibility of exchange between the human and nonhuman. However, the term "conversation" also suggests an impossible idealism, a frictionless exchange across difference which rarely occurs when landscapes, nonhuman animals or other natures are under discussion. Instead, interactions are more frequently arguments and struggles on the human side of things, in what Bruno Latour (2002, 2004a) calls pedagogical wars, where each side attempts to correct its opponent rather than pay heed to what their differences imply. Notably, Latour argues, Westerners have not perceived themselves as waging war with other ways of being and perceiving, but rather as correcting irrational people's misperceptions of the natural world.

In pedagogical wars, the goal is to eliminate alternative understandings and practices by means of an epistemology of dualisms. These wars, caught as they are in "the transcendent power attributed to abstract discursive reasoning" (Stengers 2003: 14), create false dilemmas of binary choice. Environmental debates such as this chapter addresses are typically cast in binaries separating nature from culture, object from subject, knowledge from belief, reason from folly, fact

---

1 "The pain experienced when there is recognition that the place where one resides and that one loves is under immediate assault ... a form of homesickness one gets when one is still at "home."" (Albers 2004, quoted in Smith 2010: 36).

from construction and so on. In such struggles science is invoked not to ask *how* or by what means are matters of concern addressed and facts constructed, but rather to demonstrate the failure of opponents of state and capitalist interests to fulfil the standards of modernist technoscientific thought. Big-N Nature, the guarantor of truth in modernist thought, is reaffirmed as a singular entity fully knowable through Western science. Culture, in this way of thinking, is where conversations, discussions and debates – namely, the stuff of politics – occur. In an epistemology affirming the scientist as the apolitical spokesperson for a non-actant Nature, alternative knowledges are cast as contradictory to scientific truth – and contradiction, as Stengers so pointedly remarks, is an effective tool for capitalism's domination.

But what if contradiction is thought of instead as divergence? "The difference between a contradiction and a divergence", writes Stengers (2003: 14), "is not a matter of fact, of empirical or logical definition, but a matter of struggle: it is something that must be produced and maintained against the idealist oblivion of practice". To diverge is to ask, what issue is in dispute? If disagreements are ontological, as Latour claims, then how do we think about disputes over the attribution of sentience to nonhuman entities that has arisen in some forms of transnational environmental political discourse? The existence of divergent alternatives to technoscientific knowledge are now increasingly (but belatedly, in my view) explored in social and cultural theory. What remains to be seen, however, is whether these theoretical discussions remain gestures of redemption for Western modernist ways of knowing (that is, only maintain the status quo when it comes to the power to name and unname what is of value) or whether they can lead to a true decolonization of human dwelling in the world.

In this chapter I will not argue for, or review the evidence in support of, the existence of nonhuman sentience nor for human cognitive capacities to apprehend it. These are questions which are addressed empirically by means of multidisciplinary studies of human–animal relations (including in my own field of anthropology) as well as by philosophers, psychologists and others concerned with environmental ethics. The weight of evidence for nonhuman sentience is great enough to allow exploration of ancillary questions as well. Given the environmental politics of Iceland's last thirty years, the more pertinent matter concerns the social, political and ideational forces which have led to the whole or partial denial of nonhuman sentience. What interests me, in a book proposing conversations with landscapes, are the cultural processes bringing forward sentience as a matter of scholarly and popular concern. What does the denial of, or longing for, a conversation with nonhuman being tell us about this moment of late modernity?

In the account of the whaling and power dam controversies which follows, I draw attention to how visual artists evoke or represent nature as it constellates in the modernist imaginary. The fact that artists in various media (written, theatrical, visual and so on) have engaged with environmental issues involving the land points toward culturally pervasive associations of aesthetics, sensual experience and human–non-human exchange that are emergent in everyday life: associations which at times are pressed into political service. The art work, regardless of media, can be considered as the location through which the continuity of self and environment has the potential to be acknowledged and experienced.

Considering Sentience

Sentience, the capacity for sensation and consciousness, is a key concept in environmental philosophy because it raises possible moral entailments in human relations with nonhuman beings. Environmentalists wishing to instil an ethos of care and respect into relations with the nonhuman have transformed in/sentience from, to use Latour's (2004b) phrasing, a matter of fact to a matter of concern. If the nonhuman can experience pain and suffering, or is capable of having experiences, then humans are obliged to recognize their mutual relations.

Discussions of sentience and animacy appear in the anthropological literature concerning the worldviews of small-scale, foraging societies. To my knowledge, it hasn't been discussed in the context I write of here, linking the acknowledgement of nonhuman sentience to the aestheticization of politics in a Western ethnographic context. I'm interested in how artistic agency uses aesthetic means to make the art work the location for drawing the viewer into a more sensual and open regard of their position in what Ingold (2005) refers to as organism-environment relations. If "art is a way of acting in the world" (Morphy 2009: 14), and if "one needs to focus on individual agency in the context of systems of knowledge and in relation to historical and contextual factors" (Morphy 2009: 21), then an anthropological widening of aesthetics's referent would allow for an amodern perspective on Western cultural sensibilities. Welsch's preferred meaning of aesthetics as a sensual and ethical sensitivity to the "heterogeneity of the material with which it works" (Simons 2009: 2) provides a useful starting point for considering how aesthetic agency isn't the means for removal of people from reality, but rather a technology with which paths of being are negotiated and traced.

As an anthropologist researching in a white, Western, middle-class society, I am critical of how some of my colleagues (in particular, in the context of the whaling issue) characterize the West in monolithic terms, claiming its embrace of technoscientific rationality has alienated it from nature. In so doing, they have unintentionally lent credibility to right-wing deniers of ecological damage, and bred scepticism toward diverse voices within the West seeking alternative ways of knowing and living and moving toward what Varela et al. (1991), following Heidegger, term planetary thinking. Both scholars and activists in Iceland have struggled against a predominant instrumental rationality, striving to find a language to make alternative voices and experiences heard (for example, Árnason 2005, Benediktsson 2007, Huijbens and Benediktsson 2007). My concern is for these voices, to be in dialogue with them, and to bring my own discipline to a place where they can be heard.

I recognize that a robust binary between the West and the Rest has been an important rhetorical strategy for underscoring the legitimacy of non-Western ways of knowing. There is also just cause to be critical of Western environmentalists who appropriate indigenous thought yet fail to acknowledge or support the political and social goals of indigenous peoples themselves. Nonetheless, labelling all such uses of indigenous thought as neocolonialist appropriation fails to recognize a larger conversation taking place that strives to bridge cultural differences and find ways of conceptualizing connection with nonhuman sentience. If the capacity for perception of sentience is transcultural and not simply a social construction, then we need to pay greater attention to contexts, intentions and conversational dynamics. An anthropology that measures and essentializes difference in terms of closeness or alienation from nature begins from assumptions no longer tenable in a posthumanist, postnature episteme.

Movement away from objectification and toward ethical engagement with nature (no longer configured as culture's Other) is movement toward recognition of the foundational relation between human and non-human sentient being. Scepticism toward the aestheticization of landscapes and nonhuman sentient being has denigrated the role that aesthetics plays in opening the perceiver of art and visual culture onto a larger moral and politically-democratic sphere of engagement. Nonhuman sentience exists; aesthetics can provide a technology (admittedly a fraught and easily misused one) for acknowledgement of it to occur in a relational field otherwise denied by rational thought.

Sentience and the Whaling Issue

Icelandic whaling was a twentieth-century phenomenon linked to the industrialization and capitalization of the fisheries that made possible the 1944 declaration of the independent republic. Before whale hunting ceased in 1989, and after its sporadic resumption in 2003, whale meat was primarily destined for Japanese markets, consistent with the globalization of the entire fisheries (Einarsson 1987, Lindquist 1997, Pétursdóttir 1997).

Until 1995 when touristic whale watching began in Icelandic waters, photos of whales did not appear on postcards as they now do, nor could one find whale identification guide books or whale souvenirs. In point of fact, the touristic gaze was (and continues to be) directed landward toward the countryside or city. During the 1980s and early 1990s, visual representations of whales and whaling mostly appeared in domestic television news reports about the politics of whaling. Prior to the 1980s, when whale hunting was not under public scrutiny, it was even less visible to the general public. During the summer hunt season, a viewing deck at the old whaling platform an hour's drive north of Reykjavík allowed passersby to watch carcasses being flensed (these visitors were as likely to be Icelanders as foreigners since the rise in international tourism happened in the 1990s, after the platform's closure); a museum display representing that region's pre-WW II whaling stations could be found in the country's east at Eskifjörður; and Hvalur hf.'s four whaling boats were berthed in Reykjavík's old harbour. The politicization of whaling thus made whales and those who hunted them publicly visible for the first time and in the process, whale hunting changed from being a "matter of fact" to a "matter of concern" for the whole nation.

The government's control of information and mobilization of culturally-meaningful narratives and symbols partly shaped the nationalist reaction to antiwhaling campaigns directed at Iceland, Norway and Japan. These linked whaling to notions of independence and the anxieties that the new catch quota system raised about the social and economic future of the fisheries (cf. Pálsson 1994). (At the time, Iceland derived about 75–80 per cent of its foreign export earnings from fish and fish products and only 1.3 per cent from sale of whale meat.) Further, populist understandings of the Cod Wars with Great Britain over Iceland's expansion of its territorial waters, in the 1950s and again between 1972 and 1976, provided a nationalistic template for interpreting any foreign challenge to sovereign control of property rights (Brydon 1996). The government, effectively assisted by the near lack of independent investigative media, represented debates within the International Whaling Commission (IWC) as a clash between Icelandic rationality, honour and pragmatism on one hand and foreign environmentalists's emotionalism, hypocrisy and failure to recognize the necessity of killing animals for food on the other hand.

Missing from media coverage (although some private citizens wrote critical editorials) and public discussion was any suggestion that IWC debates were dealing with divergent yet legitimate strategies for managing natural resources. Icelandic discourse focussed on extremist rhetoric as if it constituted the range of foreign attitudes and the basis of governmental and nongovernmental actions against whaling. Ironically, some foreign activists's shock techniques which were intended to confront Icelanders with the supposed immorality of their whaling industry instead helped entrench local understandings of international environmental movements as unthinking, ethnocentric and violent. Greenpeace's attempts in 1978 and 1979 to interfere with whale hunts, Sea Shepherd Conservation Society's 1986 sinking of two Icelandic whale boats while at berth and the March 1989 broadcast of Magnús Guðmundsson's documentary *Survival in the High North* (*Lífsbjörg í norðurhöfum*) about the whaling practices of Iceland, Greenland and the Faeroe Islands, were significant flashpoints in a decade of increased demonization of whales and antiwhaling environmentalists.

The impact on national attitudes of Guðmundsson's polemical anti-environmentalist documentary cannot be exaggerated. It galvanized public opinion during a period of foreign boycotts against Icelandic fish products by its moral narrative of a threatened nation rather than, more accurately, a threatened commercial industry. *Survival*'s simplistic rendering of a complex issue, its caricaturing of environmentalists as fast-food chomping urbanites and religious zealots and its portrayal of Iceland as an endangered culture of reasonable people making rational use of the sea captured a populist image that has proven persistent as well as amenable for enframing other environmental debates. The documentary went on to some international success among anti-environmentalist groups, as well as among business associations from such diverse fields as fisheries and nuclear energy. The bluntness of its attacks on values seen as anathema to property rights and business interests made it an inspiring polemic for anyone wanting to discredit environmentalists. While something of a polemic itself, Rowell's (1996) debunking of Guðmundsson and his documentary reveals significant details in support of what I have heard repeatedly, namely that the Icelandic government provided backroom funding for the film's making. Certainly, by galvanizing national will, it served the government's capitalist aims of defending the commercial interests of the one whaling company Hvalur hf. and transforming the fishing quota system along neoliberal lines. The claims that antiwhaling activists would destroy Iceland's economy now sound hollow given current knowledge of greater financial risks then brewing. As critics at the time asserted to no avail (e.g. Pálsson and Helgason 1996), the new quota system would ultimately concentrate wealth in the hands of a few. The government was thus laying the groundwork for the financial debacle to come while it portrayed itself as the champion of the fisherfolk.

Guðmundsson's documentary posits nature as an extension of human self-identification. The opening scenes juxtapose images of stormy oceans, steaming hot springs and northern landscapes barren of humanity and vegetation, while the narrator describes the "dramatic", "harsh", "magical natural beauty" of the North Atlantic and the small, vulnerable population dependent on it for survival. Variously termed the "Kingdom of Nature" and "Mother Nature", nature is said to punish or reward, to be "strict yet caring to her human offspring". Nature is perceived as rule-governed, and the video clearly indicates it is whalers and fishers who *know* the rules and obey them. Foreign urban dwellers break the rules, but the peoples of the North Atlantic form "intimate bonds" with each other and with nature. Scientists are framed as authoritative experts imparting knowledge about these rules which, in Guðmundsson's representation, seamlessly connect to "traditional" culture and "centuries-old heritages". Technoscience, business and their rationalizing powers are visually diminished: the viewer sees tiny fishing boats (and never larger freezing trawlers) bobbing precariously in immense stormy seas. The viewer does *not* see the freezing plants, transport ships, warehouses and supermarkets through which processed fish passes before arriving on the dinner plates of the Icelandic fishing industries's foreign customers.

How does sentience figure in this documentary? Guðmundsson, in an interview with an American veterinarian and whale researcher, asks about the purported intelligence of whales. Whales, comes the response, are as intelligent as cows. Claims for cetacean intelligence, he continues (inaccurately), are based on a mistaken supposition that a large brain equals great intelligence. Not so, the documentary tells us: the ratio of brain to body size confirms that whales are not intelligent. At this point as elsewhere, the documentary's goal to debunk all environmentalism relies on a one-sided and poorly-researched representation of the range of environmentalists's arguments. While intelligence and sentience are not the same phenomenon, they are blurred in Guðmundsson's narrative. If whales are not intelligent, we are to assume, they can be killed. Tellingly, intelligence is debunked by the invocation of scientific authority while neither sentience nor intelligence are considered as morally relevant. The more complex and morally-fraught question actually underpinning divergent views of whale hunting is not addressed, namely about determining responsible relations between all living beings. Elsewhere (Brydon 2006) I have shown how the introduction of whale watching in 1995 and the 1998 arrival of Keiko the killer whale from the United States for reintroduction into Icelandic waters weakened but did not defeat the persuasiveness of this distancing denial of nonhuman sentience.

While not directly concerned with whales, Friðrik Þór Friðriksson's film *Skytturnar* (1987; literally "The Marksmen" but distributed in English as *White Whales*) provides a counterpoint to both pro- and anti-whaling stances with its tale of two misfit whalers. The opening sequence set onboard one of Hvalur hf.'s whaling boats contrasts with Guðmundsson's romantic trope of man's [sic] heroic struggle with nature by underscoring the boat's factory-like sounds and sights and workaday rhythms inside the machine. While waiting to arrive at the hunting grounds, one of the men reads pornography; his inability to relate to living women emerges in the course of the film's narrative. Footage of the whale kill itself is quick and distanced, the animal barely noticeable when the harpoonist points and fires. Their shift over, the two anti-heroes head to the city clutching bags of evermore reeking whalemeat and try, but fail, to find compliant company amidst the city's bright lights. They are, figuratively speaking, fish out of water, portraits of working class alienation in a consumerist, middleclass society in denial of its social hierarchies.

Sentience and Hydroelectric Development

In part due to scapegoating of environmentalists, the debate over whaling delayed the development of an overtly Icelandic environmental movement seeking to renegotiate relations with nonhuman nature. Nonetheless, over the intervening years global environmental discourses have been incorporated into specific practices not at the centre of media attention, exemplifying the selective and complex ways globalization is contested and negotiated. For example, scientists working in marine and freshwater biology, geology, soil sciences and agriculture have been developing conservationist strategies for resource management; a nongovernmental environmental collective has raised awareness about how local concerns link to such transnational issues as global warming. As well, increased urbanization and influence of globalized media images have shaped emerging attitudes toward nature and animals as revealed in the increased ownership of pets, treatment of nature as a location for recreation and aesthetic enjoyment and criticism of farmers's killing feral sheep and those polar bears which occasionally drift ashore. Tourism's rapid growth is also altering how Icelanders perceive, represent and interact with nature, in ways increasingly divergent from industrial uses, fragmenting nationalist perceptions of nature along regional and class lines.

While the whaling issue in Iceland continues to be perceived largely as foreign environmentalism turned sentimental and awry, the fight against large-scale hydroelectric development and aluminium smelters has established an active indigenous environmental movement since the late 1990s. While several such projects are now underway or planned, the flashpoint of protest has centred on Kárahnjúkar as well as nearby Eyjabakkar, where a smaller dam project had been halted in 1999.

The Kárahnjúkar Hydropower Project, completed in 2009, is a hydroelectric facility in eastern Iceland supplying power for the Alcoa-owned Fjarðaál aluminium smelter in Reyðarfjörður, itself completed in 2008. Kárahnjúkar is the name of a mountain nearby the largest of several dams. The project entailed blocking two rivers, Jökulsá á Dal and Jökulsá í Fljótsdal, in five locations to create three reservoirs, flooding 50 km^2. Water from the reservoirs is now diverted through tunnels toward an underground power station between 30 and 40 km away. The idea of producing electricity to supply foreign-owned heavy industry had been around for about three decades before 1997 when the government pressured Landsvirkjun, the National Power Company, to begin developing a master plan that ranked about 100 potential hydroelectric and geothermal projects as to their environmental impact and cost effectiveness. Given that domestic energy needs were already well met, this master plan is directly tied to attracting foreign-owned, energy-intensive industries such as smelting.

Kárahnjúkar and other projects now being pushed forward awakened considerable criticism and division within the country. Those opposed to large-scale industrial development represent diverse sections of the society unlike the smaller, narrower demographic opposed to whaling. Opponents raised questions about technical risks, economic costs, financial dealings, working conditions, corruption, destruction of species diversity and wilderness landscapes, social impacts and the sidelining of smaller-scale, possibly more socially- and environmentally-sustainable approaches to economic growth.

In the course of the whaling debate, the dominant view that international anti-whaling values were a Hollywood-spawned sentimentality mixed with an over-aestheticization of animals revealed a potent distrust of mediated imagery. Yet this iconophobia wavered in the anti-heavy industry debates when activists discovered the persuasiveness of photography. Images carried on television and the internet, in documentaries and in art exhibits, of reindeer and pink-footed geese, rivers, waterfalls, rocks and mountains – in short, of landscapes – made hauntingly visible what the government and Landsvirkjun called barren wasteland. Most Icelanders had little or no direct experience of highland travel, thus the art works proved revelatory. Realist or representational photographic and video imagery by Ragnar Axelsson and Guðmundur Páll Ólafsson are noteworthy for conveying the beauty, strength and vulnerability of the highland landscapes. In contrast, photos of the Kárahnjúkar construction site by Pétur Thomsen offer restrained documentation of the landscape's devastation. The title of his collection, *Imported landscape*, suggests that such massive construction, unprecedented in the country, has arrived like an invading power. Not only built with foreign capital and foreign workers for a foreign aluminium company, the landscape itself is rendered strange and otherworldly. Yet unlike foreign capital, workers and industries, all of which are mobile, landscape destruction is not exportable. Thomsen's understated title suggests that a new landscape has been imported just like the infamous Range Rovers brought in by Iceland's nouveau riche.

Combining photography with sound, mixed media and metaphor, Rúrí's conceptual installation *Archive – endangered waters* was Iceland's contribution to the 2003 Venice Biennale. The work consists of transparencies of 52 different waterfalls threatened with extinction as Landsvirkjun strives to harness every possible energy source. Each transparency is held vertically in a steel frame; the viewer pulls on a handle to slide the drawer open, triggering the sound of each individual waterfall's "voice." The photographs, each labelled with a waterfall's name, project these landscapes into the future like a ruin, evoking the irreversible passage of time. Named and given voice, their deaths prefigured, the falls are personified and martyred at once. Audience response in Iceland and abroad demonstrates how successfully Rúrí has used the art object to elicit emotions of loss and mourning.

In 1998–99, a yearlong series of symbolic actions were intended to rouse the public's notice of highland landscapes facing immediate destruction. The challenges of using visual imagery became manifest as activists negotiated the fraught zone between aesthetics and politics, where nationalism, sentimentality and partisanship can eclipse their successful balance. In 1998, Guðmundur Páll Ólafsson planted 273 tiny Icelandic flags in a geothermal area he named Fögruhverir ("the beautiful hot spring"), before it was flooded to make the Hágöngulón reservoir for the Vatnsfell generator west of Vatnajökull. The imagery of drowning flags resonated emotionally for some people yet others expressed distaste for its appeal to nationalism, highlighting activists's challenge to find an imagery of nature distinct from nationalist associations. Other actions such as weekly poetry readings in front of the Alþingi, a hunger strike and a poet's petition to the Norwegian king also received similar ambivalent responses. At a public meeting, the nature filmmaker Páll Steingrímsson screened evocative footage of landscapes and wildlife (footage later incorporated into the documentary *Öræfakyrrð* (*World of Solitude*, 2004)) whose beauty struck home with its audience.

Nationalist love for the land is an effective political tool in Iceland, but to separate its experience from the interests of those in power or to avoid overt sentimentalism required the new environmentalists to tread a fine line. Finding experiential ways to connect people to the land provided one strategy. I participated in two events intended to connect people to the highland by walking across it, thus linking physical, emotional and moral registers. In 1999, along with 130 others, I responded to a flyer soliciting volunteers to go to Eyjabakkar to participate in an artist-led protest performance against an earlier plan to locate there a hydroelectric facility. Without foreknowledge, we became initiates in the metamorphosis of the little-known highland moor into a specific locale of inalienable nature and national redemption. The performance involved laying 68 stones, each engraved with a word from the national anthem, across a staked 3 km line toward the threatened river Jökulsá á Fljótsdal. The invocation "Með gjörningi þessum helgum við þetta land hugsjón verndunar" ("With this performance we consecrate (sanctify) this land to the ideal of protection") ritually transformed the unmarked moor into a specific place where the bond between people and nature could be sanctified. The performance momentarily subverted the hegemonic link between nationalism and state-planned economic development. Soon after, Norsk Hydro withdrew from the consortium investigating this project, prompting Landsvirkjun to reconsider the project.

In July 2006 I accompanied the Icelandic–Canadian video artist Erika MacPherson on an eight-day group trek across land about to be flooded two months later for the Kárahnjúkar project. The trek was one of many led by visual artist Ósk Vilhjálmsdóttir and actor and yoga teacher Ásta Arnardóttir, well-known anti-dam activists. About thirty Icelanders of diverse ages and social positions participated in the trek. Significantly, these treks were promoted only in Icelandic since they were in part to acquaint citizens with this little-visited region; we were the first foreigners among about 800 people who walked with them. The treks's aim was not to solidify national identity but rather to foster and embody a social relation with the land itself, moving it from a passive object to a sentient partner in social relations. As Ásta explained during an interview in 2005, walking was a means for people to give back to and nurture the land, bearing witness to its death and transfiguration and receive from it the energy and strength to continue walking. In this way, the trek leaders were countering the state's imagining of this uninhabited land as a universal smooth space of engineered nature and object of global emission quota exchanges. Instead, Ásta and Ósk guided us to re-imagine our relationship with nature by walking – a motion through which knowing becomes being – and to acknowledge the landscape as sentient.

Recognizing myself in nature as I did through both highland walks came to me as a revelation. I experienced directly how walking can de-essentialize nature, how it is a technology of self, a means to promote attention and comprehension, and to alter perception and experience of time. Walking brings attention to the moment in ways that Loy (1996) refers to in his book's title as a "healing deconstruction." In this sense, it fulfils Welsch's definition of aesthetics I stated earlier: it is a sensual and ethical sensitivity to the "heterogeneity of the material with which it works" (Simons 2009: 2). The trick for activists, and it's a significant trick, is to link such experience to political action that does not re-inscribe neocolonial relations with the West's Others, including that which is othered through the concept of nature itself.

Ocean and Land

Several factors have shaped the whaling and highland cases as to whether acknowledgement of nonhuman sentient being is nurtured or sublimated. These include different historical contexts and understandings of environmental thinking, impacts of the internet, tourism, socioeconomic trends and the location of origin (foreign or domestic) of protests. All are worth further consideration, but the co-occurrence of aesthetic appreciation and the recognition of nonhuman sentient being is, I believe, most relevant to discussing conversations with landscapes. The vehemence with which aestheticizing moves were met in Iceland suggests that something symbolically, dangerously potent is at work. Is there a more fundamental breach at stake, one which operates beyond discourse in realms of embodied cultural knowledge? Is the absence of the ocean in Icelandic visual art a clue to a deeply-held divide between ocean and land? Case in point: this volume's title and introductory chapter speak specifically of the land, and the ocean is not mentioned. Going back to the seeming contradiction with which I began this chapter, the willingness to acknowledge rocks, waterfalls and so forth as sentient yet not whales follows a consistent pattern in Icelandic visual culture that constructs land and ocean as binary opposites. The aestheticization which is, in late modernity, a crucial aspect to the experience of sentience, is not directed at the ocean. In point of fact, as was seen in the whaling issue, *not* aestheticizing oceanic nature is a moral virtue.

One would think that living on an island would lead visual artists to derive inspiration and/or subject matter from the forbidding, storm-tossed, romantically-bleak surrounds of the North Atlantic. Particularly in Iceland, it would seem reasonable to expect that spatial practices of ocean resource extraction and transportation would have been accompanied by a spatializing practice of creative representation. Yet while the exploits of sailors and fishers figure in popular music and broadcast media, and while poets explore "island" and "ocean" as natural metaphors of home, self, loneliness, isolation, the road, a beacon, the centre, the margin, death, paradise or a utopian shimmer on the horizon, none of these possible watery figurations has caught hold with visual artists. Instead, in both modernist and postmodernist genres, it is the land – and not the sea – that engages artists.

In the opening chapter of his novel *Svanurinn* (*The Swan*, 1997 [1991]) Guðbergur Bergsson evokes the difference between sea and land in the quality of the air and the sound and movement of birds; in a child's perception that rivers can be crossed but not the sea; in the realization that "no one can own the sea any more than human love" (4). He evokes the sea as an animal, "a cross between a monster and faithful domestic animal", that is, tellingly, more easily sensed than seen. Land is where home is marked by the dog greeting the farmer, but "no one welcomes anyone who walks down to the sea ... Anyone who does that feels only the sense of welcome in his own breast ..." (5). The author, a perceptive observer of his country, reveals how sea and land call forth differing experiences of self in relation to its environment. The dominant enframing of the sea by rational management seems not to have infringed upon this experience of self in such a way as to call forth aestheticized public critiques of the transferable quotas. However, the moves to engineer the highland wilderness have been experienced as a traumatic violation of a social bond and as doing harm to the national soul.

Given that natural places are created by the extension of a presence, it comes as no surprise that the ocean when encountered in Icelandic art is manifested primarily through the signs of masculine labour. Occasionally in the mid-twentieth century, painters such as Jón Þorleifsson depicted fishing boats in harbour, while others represented land-based fish processing. Only Gunnlaugur Scheving painted life at sea, portraying shark hunters on boat decks in a characteristic flat, stylized manner that de-emphasized oceanic space, giving it a skewed horizon and dramatizing the heroism of the hunters against the blankness of the oceanic backdrop.

For maritime powers such as Great Britain and the Netherlands, nineteenth century seascape painting interconnected with naval warfare, imperialism, the globalizing extension of trade and colonial conquest. These spatializing practices intensified the meaning of the ocean's horizon, as a point toward which the imagination extended. But for Icelanders, the ocean was not a location of sustained human action until the twentieth century. The Danish trade monopoly and conservatism of the landowning class ensured that those promoting independence and nationbuilding focused on the ocean, creating the shipping company Eimskip and an Icelandic-owned fishing fleet. The ocean horizon thus had less to do with looking outward to the rest of the world as it had with turning the gaze inward and defining the limits of experience. In pre-modern fishing, an extension of the farm household, fishers worked from open rowboats and looked landward to navigate by coastal features. Although the nineteenth-century struggle for independence mythified the land, its economic foundation relied on industrialization of ocean fishing and fish processing. Issues of social class, economic development and foreign relations drove twentieth century politics, with gender strongly emergent during the 1970s. While certainly responsive to and interlinked with foreign movements and ideals, differences were nonetheless contested *within* the bounds of a nationalist political economy protected by tariffs and foreign ownership laws, and isolated by geography and language and by the limited international interest in its population.

The ocean has been the location for stabilizing the organization of knowledge through science, technology and rationalized resource management. The whaling issue provided a symbolic resource for the state when consolidating its power over ocean governance by means of the quota system. While whale watching has enframed the sea in more aesthetic terms, it has done little to alter the sense that oceans are locations for profitmaking. Although nothing seems certain following the October 2008 economic collapse, the state and various technical and administrative structures continue to control territorial waters, and foreign investment in the fisheries remains prohibited. However, the post-collapse revelation that catch quotas were collateral in over-leveraged debt may yet have consequences.

Despite remaining sovereign controls, the ocean's protective wrap has become more porous and abstracted. Lucy Lippard (1997 [1972]) identified the "dematerialization of the art object" as characteristic of conceptual art movements of the 1960s. When Gísli Pálsson and Agnar Helgason (1996) asserted that wealth consolidation has shifted economic focus from the sea back to the land, they signalled a conceptual cultural shift wherein the ocean dematerialized for Icelanders. Neoliberal reforms rapidly globalized the economy over the last twenty years, dissolving the ocean's protectiveness as capital flowed in and out of the country. People do not have the same sense of investment with the fisheries's wellbeing. During the economic boom, immigrant workers outnumbered Icelanders in rural freezing plants while the quota system undercut economies of fishing villages. The recklessness of the economic expansion is now well-known if not yet fully analyzed. The economy had been kept afloat on rising debt and had needed to attract considerable foreign capital which dam construction projects accomplished for awhile. Whether triggered by over-extended investments, cronyism and corruption or foreign hedge-fund traders, the bankruptcy of the country is, in the starkest terms, the final dematerialization of the ocean's protection, leaving its citizenry fully exposed to the neocolonial debt regimes of global capitalism.

Analysis and Conclusions

In Indo-European languages, loss is a concept associated with possession, property and commerce. Within systems of exchange, loss exists as the counterpart of gain, such that loss is the sacrifice through which a future abounding in profit is anticipated and imagined. Seen in the abstract form of classical economics, the circulation of losses and gains seems frictionless and unencumbered by the weight of existence. One can imagine a never-ending economy of booms and busts, bear markets and bull markets, where winners offset losers in the seemingly endless cycle of production and consumption. In this realm, the apprehension of nonhuman sentience unsettles the calculation of economic loss and gain and risk and benefit since it calls forth confounding moral entailments of care.

However, in another conceptual realm of the same language group, loss has no opposite, in the sense that that which is lost, is gone forever; it is irretrievable. The experience of loss is a state of being swathed in sorrow in which grief's burden possesses the person and not the other way around: it cannot be given away. While loss takes away the other, grief is the thief which diminishes the self and the future.

Loss of natural spaces is most often weighed against gains in wealth and wellbeing. But in the case of the eastern highland, Icelandic critics managed to enframe the landscape within the moral community, thus removing its loss from the cycle of economic exchange and placing it instead in the experiential realm of life's loss and its mourning. Artists addressing loss of highland wilderness attempted to make this loss-as-finality a palpable presence for audiences everywhere. They made the art object a possible site for the mediated experience of sentience, yet to experience it as such remained contingent upon the recognition of mutual concerns within transnational ecological thought.

The case of the highland demonstrates how anticipated loss carries with it moral entailments, and how imagining loss is an event which creates a future. Environmentalism inverts the experiential notion of past as behind and future in front: instead, the past is the result of what we do in the present, the future is the time for grieving the loss yet to happen. While losses are projected into the future they demand an emotional as well as political response in the present. Such losses are nostalgic futures, countering the modernist trope of monetary gain through progress and development. Environmentalist narratives exemplify how pasts and futures can fold into the experience of the present: as loss or gain, but also as contingency or necessity, rupture or continuity, chaos or order. The future may not bring utopian promises fulfilled; the future can change abruptly, we are told, if decisions taken now turn out to be wrong.

As a final note, I have neglected mention of the enormously important book by Andri Snær Magnason, *Draumalandið* (2006, *Dreamland*) and his 2009 documentary of the same name. I see embodied in this work and the creative ethos for which he and others now struggle, a hopeful gesture. Having recognized early in the anti-dam movement the dangerous power of images, Magnason and others made of beauty a deliberate and effective weapon with which to counter the state's attempts to render the highland insentient. As I write, the documentary is appearing in film festivals in Europe and North America, including my hometown, tracing a much different transnational path than *Survival in the High North* before it. The film and its stunning cinematography of soon-to-be-transfigured mountains and valleys – that is to say, the work of art – is the place where the filmmakers made manifest their own dialogue with the land. They had looked for its "face", looking for the land to return their gaze.[2]

Acknowledgements

In myriad ways, conversations with Anne-Marie Colpron, Brian Tanguay, Erika MacPherson, Hjörleifur Jónsson, Karl Benediktsson, Kristjana Gunnars, Magda Kazubowski-Houston, Tanya Richardson and Úlfhildur Dagsdóttir have enriched the writing, if not the content, of this chapter. My deepest gratitude to those involved with Eyjabakkagjörningur and Augnablik: thank you for showing the way. This research was funded by the Social Science and Humanities Research Council of Canada (SSHRCC).

---

[2] I am borrowing here from John Berger's (2001) discussion of Cézanne's more southern landscapes.

References

Árnason, Þ. 2005. *Views of Nature and Environmental Concern in Iceland*. Linköping: Linköpings Universitet [PhD dissertation].
Benediktsson, K. 2007. "Scenophobia" and the Aesthetic Politics of Landscape. *Geografiska Annaler*, 89B(3), 203–17.
Berger, J. 2001. *Shape of a Pocket*. London: Bloomsbury.
Bergsson, G. 1997 [1991]. *The Swan (Svanurinn)*, translated by B. Scudder. London: Mare's Nest.
Brydon, A. 1996. Whale-siting: Spatiality in Icelandic Nationalism, in *Images of Contemporary Iceland: Everyday Lives and Global Contexts*, edited by G. Pálsson and P. Durrenberger. Iowa City: University of Iowa Press, 25–45.
Brydon, A. 2006. The Predicament of Nature: Keiko the Whale and the Cultural Politics of Whaling in Iceland. *Anthropological Quarterly*, 79(2), 225–60.
Einarsson, T. 1987. *Hvalveiðar við Ísland 1600–1939*. Reykjavík: Bókaútgáfa Menningarsjóðs.
Huijbens, E.H. and Benediktsson, K. 2007. Practising Highland Heterotopias: Automobility in the Interior of Iceland. *Mobilities*, 2(1), 143–65.
Ingold, T. 2000. *The Perception of the Environment: Essays on Livelihood, Dwelling and Skill*. London: Routledge.
Latour, B. 2002. *War of the Worlds: What about Peace?*, translated by C. Bigg. Chicago: Prickly Paradigm.
Latour, B. 2004a. Whose Cosmos, which Cosmopolitics?: Comments on the Peace Terms of Ulrich Beck. *Common Knowledge*, 10(3), 450–62.
Latour, B. 2004b. *Politics of Nature: How to Bring the Sciences into Democracy*, translated by C. Porter. Boston: Harvard University Press.
Lindquist, O. 1997. *Peasant Fisherman Whaling in the NE Atlantic Area*. Akureyri: Háskólinn á Akureyri.
Lippard, L. 1997 [1972]. *Six Years: Dematerialization of the Art Object from 1966 to 1972*. Berkeley: University of California Press.
Loy, D. (ed.) 1996. *Healing Deconstruction: Postmodern Thought in Buddhism and Christianity*. Atlanta: Scholars Press.
Magnason, A.S. 2006. *Draumalandið: sjálfshjálparbók handa hræddri þjóð*. Reykjavík: Mál og menning. (Published 2008 as *Dreamland: A Self-help manual for a frightened nation*, translated by N. Jones. London: Citizen Press.)
Morphy, H. 2009. Art as a Mode of Action: Some Problems with Gell's *Art and Agency*. *Journal of Material Culture*, 14(1), 5–27.
Pálsson, G. 1994. *Coastal Economies, Cultural Accounts: Human Ecology and Icelandic Discourse*. Manchester: Manchester University Press.
Pálsson, G. and Helgason, A. 1996. The Politics of Production: Enclosure, Equity, and Efficiency, in *Images of Contemporary Iceland: Everyday Lives and Global Contexts*, edited by G. Pálsson and P. Durrenberger. Iowa City: University of Iowa Press, 60–84.

Pétursdóttir, G. (ed.) 1997. *Whaling in the North Atlantic*. Reykjavík: University of Iceland, Fisheries Research Institute.

Rowell, A. 1996. *Green Backlash: Global Subversion of the Environmental Movement*. London: Routledge.

Simons, J. 2009. Democratic Aesthetics. *Culture, Theory and Critique*, 50(1), 1–5.

Smith, D.B. 2010. Is there an Ecological Unconscious? *New York Times Magazine*, 27 January, 36.

Stengers, I. 2003. A "Cosmo-politics": Risk, Hope, Change, in *Hope: New Philosophies for Change*, edited by M. Zournazi. New York: Routledge, 244–72.

Varela, F.J., Thompson, E. and Rosch, E. 1991. *The Embodied Mind: Cognitive Science and Human Experience*. Cambridge, MA: MIT Press.

Chapter 14

The Empty Wilderness: Seals and Animal Representation

Bryndís Snæbjörnsdóttir and Mark Wilson

Introduction: The Eclipsed Animal

In the discipline of Fine Art upon which this chapter draws, landscape has traditionally been seen as an aesthetic subject in which natural scenery is represented in order to reflect, literally or metaphorically, a range of human needs. As a concept, nature is thought to encapsulate the elements of the natural world, sometimes including non-human animals but excluding human animals. Landscape on the other hand is something that is cultivated by man but occupied by all living beings including human and non-human animals. Simon Schama (1995) has proposed wilderness, which is often understood as an area of uncultivated land devoid of humans but occupied by other natural elements including some non-human animals, to be a construction of the human mind. In a post-humanist discourse, animals, being part of our environment, constructed and non-constructed, shape and occupy our physical and psychological landscapes. An understanding of this "functionality of landscape" and its instrumentalization is a key to the inclusion in this text of references to non-human animals and our historical and contemporary interaction with them. All are embodiments of the continuous and non-objectified landscape – that is, the landscape from which we have hitherto and traditionally detached ourselves in order to support and sustain a steadfastly anthropocentric view.

In certain locations on the coastline, boulders become seals, grunting and groaning before sliding into the sea. It is not only the shape of the seal that references its environment so closely, but also the colour of its skin. Historically, for seafaring nations, the seal provided a valuable subsistence for human beings. Tellingly, as with many human-animal relations, this relationship is made visible through traces of the actual animal's "death" which heralds the beginning of a "cultured" relationship evidenced in its role as food, clothing or as some representation in anthropocentric form. "Death" refers in this case both to an actual physical death and also the death that occurs through obfuscation, where the living animal is overlaid by whatever metaphorical or symbolic purpose is ascribed to it. When investigating human and animal relations, one of the most significant factors of the research on which this paper relies has been the revelation of the cultural obliteration and cancellation of the "death" of the animal. Our observations have revealed how subsequent reconstructions become [mis]representative not only of entire species but implicitly of a notional, continuous and endless life. Akira Lippit (2000) has written an extensive account of how animal death is reflected within metaphysics, in the history of philosophy and literature. His exploration reveals not only how the animal disappears through representation, but also how humans as beings monopolize the act of dying. According to Lippit, animals don't die; they "disappear", thus removing for us humans the ethical problem of colonizing and consuming their bodies.

In addition to the above, this paper draws on the results of extensive research, which underpins a cluster of art projects conducted by the authors (as the collaborative art practice of Snæbjörnsdóttir/Wilson) between 2002 and 2009. The main emphasis is on the work entitled *between you and me* (2009), the research focus of which is seal–human relations around the coasts of Iceland. In our practice we engage in long-term relational and socially engaged projects. By "relational" we are referring not only to the form but also to the objective in the work: that of reaching across species with a view to encouraging in the audience a cognitive awareness of "parallel lives" or what Donna Haraway refers to as "concatenated worlds" (Gane 2006: 145). We seek to approach and attempt temporarily to occupy or invoke the space of the "other" – in this instance the animal or animals we are working with – in order in turn to enable what may be a revelatory view of our human selves as "other". Using a variety of media, our work takes the form of installations through which the process of the work's making is made visible. This is achieved by means of presenting objects and/or documents that in the context of an exhibition lead the audience to the experience of alternative perspectives, allowing a temporary disruption and shift in their thinking. In this and in other recent projects, one of the mechanisms enabling us as artists to address this issue has been to single out "individual" animals as opposed to a notional, idealized animal and to make these individuals (and our cultural relationship with them and others like them), the specific subject of our scrutiny. In order to conduct our enquiry, we propose through our artwork to identify different spaces of encounter in which an animal "eradication" can be seen to occur and either directly or by implication suggest an alternative, non-eradicative approach.

The Context of the Research

Amongst the numerous reasons for us choosing Iceland in order to explore human-seal relationships, the cyclical change in the commodity value of the seal was central. We talked to people who, within their lifetimes, have regarded and experienced the seal in many different guises: as a valuable catch for subsistence; as government-declared vermin; as a source of bounty because of its alleged role in the lifecycle of a worm that infects cod; and as an object of tourist attention and as a living being with intrinsic value. In contemporary Iceland there are still people who engage in the killing of seal pups for their meat and skin, although these are fewer now due to the failing commercial sealskin and seal meat markets.

There are also people who would happily hunt seals only for the sake of a kill, or on the grounds that it has been designated a pest. This notion of the seal as pest was in fact, reinforced by government policy in the 1970s and 80s, when a bounty was put on its head (Snæbjörnsdóttir/Wilson 2009). Although this law no longer stands, those engaged in salmon fishing still see the seal as a competitor and will thus expediently, endeavour to sustain the myth. In contrast, there are also those who want to protect the seal, as they detect through annual increases in tourism, its potential, in respect of livelihood and income from the animal's role as a large, living, charismatic mammal visible within its own natural habitat.

During the period of our research we were particularly interested in those people who on a daily basis, are engaged in the life and death of seals – both in the stewardship and the killing of the animals. Consequently, we travelled to a number of locations and interviewed several individuals on camera. The farm Húsey in Northeast Iceland, one of the key places that we visited, is notable for its historical association with seals, which for a long time have been the main resource for subsistence of the people living there. Breeding in the estuary of a large river, the seal cows give birth to the pups on the sand flats where the river divides. When we first visited the place in 2007, numerous seal pups had just been killed inadvertently when large volumes of water were released from the dam at Kárahnjúkar, a new and environmentally controversial hydro-electric power project, thereby causing the river to flood. In the ensuing deluge the young pups were separated from their mothers and drowned. The water had been released without prior warning or consultation with those whose livelihood has for centuries depended on working and living with the natural resources in this area (Snæbjörnsdóttir/Wilson 2009).

On our arrival at Húsey for the filming of the preparation for the 2008 seal hunt, we were introduced to Silli, a young seal pup that had been found abandoned on the seashore. The farmer, Örn Þorleifsson had been informed of its presence by tourists staying at the youth hostel at Húsey. He told us that abandoned pups in the wild are subject to a cruel fate; skuas and gulls will attack, typically unravelling and pecking their umbilical cord and plucking out their eyes. The care these pups need to survive without their mothers is substantial, as they must be fed every four hours with a specially made mixture to match the mother's milk. The feeding was done either by Örn Þorleifsson or his wife. The procedure was that approximately 20 cm of soft plastic tube attached to a plastic bottle was pushed down Silli's throat and the milk mixture pumped into his stomach. Afterwards he would be patted and cuddled to help him burp. During the day Silli would be around the place, often in close proximity to humans, but in the evening he would be lifted into the back of an old Land Rover where he had a bed made out of newspapers. At the time of our visit, Silli was approximately five weeks old and it was expected he would stay at the farm until 12–15 weeks old, or until mid-to-late August, when he would be taken to the seashore close to where he was found and allowed to go free. In the interim between our visit and him being released, there would still be a lot of care involved in looking after him. There is a transitional process necessary to take him from fluids to solid food (herring and/or capelin) and involving his learning to catch fish by himself. All these tasks were overseen by Örn Þorleifsson, who even puts on his waders to accompany the seal when he is first introduced to swimming in the local pond.

Silli happened to be male, and once free, should he survive the winter, would be likely to come back to this area year after year. Had the pup been female, she would return to give birth to pups that might well be caught in the nets laid by the farmer at Húsey the following year. This shift from caring to killing calls to mind a statement made by Donna Haraway. She proposes the concept of "killing well", in an attempt to find a model of harmony, responsibility and coherence within omnivore culture and in human/non human animal relations:

> Human beings must learn to kill responsibly. And to be killed responsibly, yearning for the capacity to respond and to recognize response, always with reasons but knowing there will never be sufficient reason ... I do not think we can nurture living until we get better at facing killing (Haraway 2008: 81).

Another pivotal interview was with Knútur Óskarsson at the farm Ósar, in Northwest Iceland. Óskarsson, the youngest in his family and the only family member (apart from his mother) to remain on the farm, runs a small non-profitable business which includes farming a small number of cows and running a youth hostel situated in the old farmhouse. The tourist attraction for the youth hostel is mainly connected to wild life and an old seal colony, which is on sand flats in the estuary and partly belonging to Ósar. The work and words of this young farmer brought theory and practice together substantiating to some extent Haraway's comments above. Amongst other things he told us:

> I think there is a demand for really interesting places with nature. I think people are really actually quickly discovering something that is a unique – unique nature and in this consuming world we live in, what do people do? They come and consume nature. It is just if you buy yourself a trip to Iceland it is like consuming something ...

> I am farming this place and what happens is that from time to time we have sick animals that wash up and then again this is not my land on the other side. I own the land on this side but not on the other side but what happens is that baby seals sometimes wash up on my side and if they are sick or dying then I sometimes have to put them out of their misery or kill them if you can say so. If you have a sick animal dying you don't let it die there because we have seagulls that come and pluck their eyes out while the seal is still alive so I go and put it out of its misery – that is what I do but then again I have to be careful because not to go too close if they want to protect themselves they are quick, much quicker than a human and quick to bite (Snæbjörnsdóttir/Wilson, 2009).

The interview provided us with the audio content for a video work, which is one component of the exhibition *between you and me*. A slow motion sequence filmed from land, showing a seal swimming up and down an estuary, is overlaid with the voice of Knútur. As she swims, the seal occasionally looks towards the camera, the focus of which oscillates between her head and a low boundary of wild heather bushes, privileging alternately the distinct territories of land and water.

The Art and Resonance

Over two years we observed and recorded a variety of "seal encounters". For the most part these were more or less candid – some became documentary in nature, many were anecdotal, but a key component in the project became the organization and filming of the mounting of a seal's skin by a Reykjavík taxidermist. The result, entitled *the naming of things*, was exhibited as a large-screen video projection as part of the exhibition and installation *between you and me* (2009). Our intention for this work was to place the proposed audience as much as possible in the space in which the real seal's skin is being collapsed into a representation of "complete sealness". The idea behind the making of the work was to extend the period of this transformation and have the audience linger amongst the remains and the "act of reconstruction" – between the ruins of the real and the empty promise of the surrogate.

The process began with us having to locate a dead seal. Because we do not sanction the killing of animals for our art, this was not easy. Initially we had

Figure 14.1 Film still from interview with Knútur Óskarsson

contacted a farmer in the North-West of Iceland, where much of the research was conducted, whom we'd heard had three dead seals awaiting taxidermy in his freezer. A seal colony is located on his land and his plan is to create a small tourist information centre with stuffed seal specimens as an attraction, supplementary to the possibility of observing live seals there in their natural environment. In the end, with the schedules of the farmer and the taxidermist being at odds, it proved too difficult for us to co-ordinate our trip to the north of Iceland for the purpose of filming. So after various attempts to locate a dead seal in three different countries, namely Sweden, Britain and Iceland, a call finally came from Húsey, notifying us of a seal that had drowned in the farm's fishing nets.

Örn Þorleifsson, the farmer in Húsey, agreed to freeze the seal for us and keep it until a taxidermist was identified who could do the job. When we did find someone willing to work with us, the frozen seal was sent as frozen meat cargo to Reykjavík. We then travelled to Reykjavík to receive the seal and to bring it to the taxidermist. The first process of the job was to defrost the seal and a couple of days later it was skinned – something we were present for, but chose not to film. We did however take some photographs for the purposes of documentation. The decision not to film the process of skinning was made on the basis that we did not want to sensationalize the dead body through visceral depictions of meat and blood. What we wished to instigate was a challenge to representation itself, by rooting its construction within the familiar and by reapplying methodologies that were, in accordance with contemporary taste – on the face of it at least, "palatable" and non-confrontational. In order to begin to unravel the phenomenon with which most urban dwellers in Western culture are familiar – the sanitized, clinical, human death, a death normally neither seen nor imagined – we focused on the process of transformation where a sanitized, dead body is moulded into a representation of itself. The process of stuffing the seal took just over three hours, although a polystyrene mould had been prepared prior to this. This form was a very basic shape, using measurements taken from the dead seal body. The skin, having already been treated, was wrapped and then stitched up around the polystyrene "body". The claws on the flippers remained when the skin was removed, but metal wire rods were pushed into the front and back flippers to enable positional adjustments of these to be made. Clay was put into the flippers and face for further shaping. Glass eyes were inserted, but the whiskers and nose were those of the seal. Before the seal was skinned we'd produced a rough indication of what kind of posture we required. We had studied the footage of seals taken during our research and we wanted our seal to be on its stomach and slightly to one side looking both confident and alert. For the filming we had two cameras and studio lighting, which brought stark lucidity to the setting of the taxidermist's workshop. In accordance with our approach generally, we did not otherwise attempt to change or manipulate the environment. The filming was in close up, focusing tightly on the "animal" and the hands of the taxidermist.

In the editing suite it became evident that the complete film itself, despite the tight framing, was too close to being simply an exhaustive documentation of the activity of taxidermy. So we decided instead to focus on selected sequences in which the meeting between the human skin (the hands of the taxidermist) and the animal skin was fore-grounded and where any sense of a beginning and an ending was suppressed. When slowing this footage down, the emphasis in the work changed, from showing the purposeful, methodical act of a craftsman, to a kind of protracted dance or a "wrestling" between the two. What the work begins to suggest is an "animation" in the direct sense of "instilling life", although significantly in the film this remains strategically and problematically an unfulfilled ambition. Through the process of slowing the film, the sound was drawn out and lowered in pitch, an effect which further enhanced this sense of struggle. In this contest between human and animal skin, the dead seal is made subject to an expression of power and control and becomes subordinate to the act of its own re-creation.

An associative way of thinking about a lens-based document that tracks the transformation from the "real" to the "unreal" is to consider the linear process of "death" and subsequent resurrection, which is central to the Christian narrative. Amongst the different orders of Christianity, perspectives differ regarding the body and its representation in relation to the sacrifice and resurrection, with Catholics for example, believing the wine and the bread to "be" the blood and the body of Christ where Lutherans/Protestants consider it only to be "symbolic" of the same. However, according to historical, sacred depictions, the "dead body" has a quality of agency that through a form of transcendence in which light often plays a crucial role, allows for its occasional re-emergence as an image. This effect is encountered most remarkably in the shroud of Turin, a Christian "relic", the authenticity of which has been exhaustively contested but which from any perspective (whether it be of miraculous transmission or photographic prototype) constitutes a phenomenon of image-transferral (Picknett and Prince 2007).

This association is compounded when considering the materiality of the tools applied in the process of making *the naming of things*, i.e. light, glass, body. And although a photograph is arguably an object in itself, in the process of its making through light, a presence is recorded, the nature of which still considered by most official institutions to be a reliable, authentic representation, for example in passport photographs, driving licences, police records and CCTV, Judith Halberstam has pointed out that in the contemporary films *Over the Hedge*, *Finding Nemo* and *Bee Story*, the human and non-human characters are featured as "animated and unanimated rather than real and constructed or subjects and objects" (Halberstam, 2007) and by switching the "norm" around so that humans are read as "constructed" and the animals read as "real", our relationship to animals is reworked. So by seeing ourselves as being "human" in a way that is truly novel to us, new possibilities of reappraisal and change in our relations with others are elicited.

In an earlier art project, again involving taxidermy (*nanoq: flat out and bluesome*, Snæbjörnsdóttir/Wilson 2006), which used stuffed polar bears to explore issues of animal representation, we came to realize that the more obvious imperfections in some of the "older" polar bear specimens revealed something uniquely aberrant and yet oddly eloquent, a subtext to the main theme of species-representation and perhaps most acutely, the possibility for the beholder of imagining a life-having-been-lived. In contrast, the newer and more "perfectly" reproduced taxidermy specimens seem to be poorer in this subtle but telling respect. The artist Peter Friedl (2007) orchestrated this phenomenon to striking effect in his appropriation and exhibition of a stuffed giraffe exhibited in Documenta 2007.

> ... Until 2002, Brownie was a favorite among visitors to Kalkilya zoo in the West Bank. She died when the small town became the center of a military offensive and Israeli troops attacked a Hamas camp. Brownie panicked, ran into an iron rod, then fell to the floor and died of heart failure ... (DW-WORLD.DE 2007)

After the accident, her body was stuffed by a local veterinarian, with no training in taxidermy. The result gives her the appearance of an enormous and much abused soft toy rather than that of a giraffe. At the same time, by a strange inversion triggered perhaps by a manifest indignity we are made more aware of the individual animal that has lived and died than of some other function that taxidermied animals are normally supposed to perform. Such observations led us to take seriously problems inherent in the act of representation itself, those qualities that representation must disallow and the lies therefore that representation must tell – the more polished and "believable" the representation, the better and more deceptive, the lie ...

Empathy and Notions of Weakness

It is all too tempting to find prime causality for our conscious separation from nature in the thinking of the Enlightenment. Whilst Christianity must also accept its role in the laying of foundations and subsequent cementing of a relationship summed up in terms of human dominion over animals, the practices of scientists from the mid-seventeenth Century onwards illustrate starkly and disturbingly how such dominion came to be exercised in the spirit of this thinking.

In the seventeenth century, the scientist Robert Boyle carried out an experiment on a skylark using a vacuum chamber or air pump, a glass chamber from which air was removed through a brass tube using a valve to control the flow (Boyle 1660). The idea was to observe and interpret the movements of the creature in its final struggle for breath before the collapse of its lungs. These experiments by Boyle and his contemporaries and successors in the field of natural science were deemed necessary to prove the crucial importance of breath to life. In the experiment mentioned above, Boyle described in detail the last moments of the bird's life, how

> she began manifestly to droop and appear sick, and very soon after was taken with ... violent and irregular convulsions ... the bird threw herself over and over two or three times, and died with her breast upward, her head downwards, and her neck awry (Donald 2007: 6).

The human detachment implicit in the execution of such experiments is clear. In the science of the Enlightenment we even expect it, but in another of our interviews we have detected parallels of detachment and dispassionate clarity within a more contemporary, rural account. In this interview, the farmer and seal hunter Jóhannes Gíslason from Skáleyjar, one of many islands in the bay of Breiðafjörður in West Iceland, describes the hunting of seals in the 1950s and 60s. In his contemplation of animal death, presented as a component of the work *between you and me*, he proposes quite seriously that a seal "doesn't mind drowning". He says:

> Nets were used to catch the seal pups and it was considered good if you caught a pup alive; it was then cut and made to bleed. Most was already bloody meat as most of the pups drown in the nets; this is considered terrible by environmentalists as people don't like the idea of drowning but the seal doesn't mind drowning. If you shoot a seal the seal colony will flee, but no seal cow will run away when her own seal pup is drowned, even by her side. It doesn't upset nature to catch seal pups in nets, as is the custom. It's just humans that think they deserve better than to be drowned but the seal is not afraid, he lives and dies in the sea; for him this is a natural way of dying (Snæbjörnsdóttir/Wilson, 2009).

One hundred years after Boyle's air pump experiments, the English landscape and portrait painter Joseph Wright painted *Experiment on a Bird in the Air Pump* (1768), an image documenting different registers of empathy and detachment in the depiction of the faces of those present during the death of what has been identified as a cockatoo. Diana Donald (2007) draws attention to the respective hierarchical status of animals when she proposes that by choosing to depict as the subject of this experiment an animal identified as a pet rather than for example, "a sparrow or a rat" an attempt was made to highlight moral dilemmas by simultaneously framing a milestone in the process of scientific experimentation and a milestone in consciousness awareness of human nature – that is of sympathy and/or empathy (Donald 2007: 6). James Ferguson FRS, a Scottish astronomer who is thought to have been an associate of Wright, recorded that for the purposes of many such demonstrations, an animal substitute in the form of a "lungs-glass" with a small air-filled bladder came to be used, because otherwise the experiment was " ... too shocking to every spectator who has the least degree of humanity" (Rupke 1987: 30).

The seal and its ways have long exercised the human imagination. The history of human relationships with the species is documented in folklore and songs, often recounting a mythic transformation (by the shedding of skin) from non-human animal to human. It is a conceit that uses the relationship between land and sea creatures as a means of reconciling these two worlds. Hayden Lorimer (2010) draws attention to certain ethologists (Fraser Darling, Lockley, Lorenz) who considered human empathy with large mammals to be rooted in facial expressions and the ability to identify with these and use them to interpret changing moods in the respective animals. For Lorenz, seals were especially significant in this regard

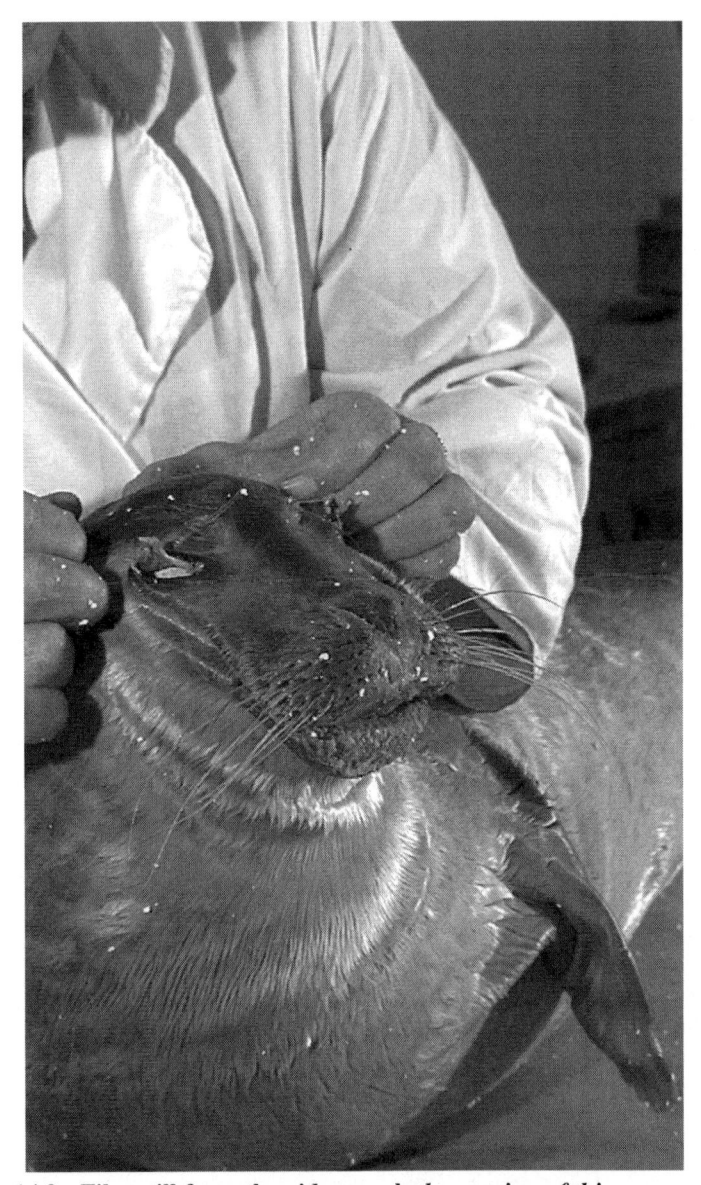

Figure 14.2 Film still from the video work *the naming of things*

for their facial expression and ability to "shed tears", whilst others considered the darkness in the large circular eyes of seals as suggestive of emotional depth and that it was this that fostered human affinity. The role of eyes and mouth, have long been recognized as important factors in representations of the memory of human faces.

In our interview with Jóhannes Gíslason (Snæbjörnsdóttir/Wilson 2009), we were keen to find out how a hunter of seal pups regarded these facial affinities. Although he was aware of the "cuteness" of the prey, it seemed not to interfere with his desire to capture and kill it. We had already observed how the farmer at Húsey was able to nurture and care for the same "wild" animal species that he later killed and ate. Gíslason was brought up with seal meat being the staple in a subsistence diet and local farm families depended on it. From an early age he had been given seal flippers and faces to chew on. Indeed it was the favourite food of children on these islands. The flippers and the face were first singed, the face cut in half lengthwise, then the parts were boiled and stored in whey, resulting in the bones and cartilage becoming soft and easy to bite into.

The face has been given much significance in animal discourse. It is after all the face and the name assigned to an individual that affords him/her/it an identity and in relation to animals, it is mostly those pets and/or animals that have become assimilated within popular culture that are assigned the status of an individual through the process of naming. Traditionally, farm animals in Iceland are also given names though it must be said this form of individuation is not solely dependent on face recognition. In 2001, the organisation PETA (People for the Ethical Treatment of Animals) published an image on one of their posters with the heading "Did your food have a face?" The image, not of a face but of the carcass of a face, symbolizes the "missing" face of the animal in the meat industry. Although the campaign is several years old and promotes vegetarianism, it still strikes a chord today. The artist Damien Hirst's work, *A Thousand Years* (1990), involves a cow head carcass similar to the one depicted in the PETA campaign. A rotting cow's head is placed on the floor in one side of a partitioned glass vitrine, the other side containing live maggots. The flies hatch and fly through a small hole in the partition to feed on the carcass. The section that has the carcass head also has an ultraviolet device that kills many of the flies. The work draws attention to the cycle of life and death, simplifying the many indeterminable factors involved in this equation. This work could be said to animalize human attitudes to life and death, whereas the image on the PETA poster attempts to humanize the animal as a call for the humane treatment of animals. Una Chaudhuri (2007) argues that Damien Hirst's work belongs to a posthumanist programme of re-substantialization, or what the philosopher John Gray calls "removing the mask from our animal faces" (Chaudhuri 2007: 15).

In popular culture, celebrity chefs have been busy putting the face back on the animal in an attempt to reconnect us with the simple idea that the neatly packaged, disembodied meat on the shelves of the supermarkets is in fact from a living being with the right to a decent life before ending up on our plates. The philosopher Levinas (1906–1995) declared that non-human animals were faceless and could therefore not demand or expect an ethical response (Wolfe 2003). Although this may seem to be borne out in the example of the seal face-as-food above, one wonders if Levinas' position is perhaps only relevant when viewed in the context of specific cultures or circumstances and that such a position requires a kind of emotional and rational blinding in order to be genuinely sustainable. Levinas' study on the ethical face of the animal was based on the dog Bobby, whom he and his fellow prisoners befriended in a German concentration camp. In respect of the Holocaust in particular, it should be noted that the question is often asked as to whether the ethics of animal rights can be taken seriously at all in the context of extreme human rights abuses of this nature. The eating of animal faces as food is only acceptable by most meat eaters in the West, as a part of other cultures or traditions. Christianity defines humanity by acknowledging the unique presence of a soul. In the writings of Descartes and central to ideas of the Enlightenment, the difference between men and animals was considered to be absolute – where animals were likened to machines and a boundary was drawn signifying the soul's perceived respective presence and absence (Lippit 2000). With advances in the sciences (in addition to philosophy and animal studies), this boundary is contested. It had hinged on what was known about biological and behavioural characteristics, including intentionality and language. It was Darwin, however, who developed these Western criteria, when the difference in evolutionary progress became the taxonomic tool for measuring and placing species on a hierarchical scale (Darwin 1859). Different human "races" were similarly placed on the scale creating a human taxonomy, where people of exotic appearance from distant (non-Western) lands were often placed at the bottom of this hierarchy and thereby along with the animals, denied possession of a soul (Elder et al. 1998).

Whilst visiting natural history collections around the UK, Europe and the USA, we have noticed that they are peppered with individual animal specimens with a "popular history" – that is, animals that have been local or national favourites in zoo collections for many years, prior to dying and being stuffed and deposited in their local museum. Chi Chi the panda from London Zoo, Guy the gorilla, Jumbo the elephant, and many more – all public and media favourites in their time – occupy a strange but distinctive niche which contradicts the "animal-as-representative-of-species" model, paradoxically and somewhat uncomfortably allowing the animal to retain the celebrity status befitting the former star of an emporium of popular culture, specifically the zoo. Here, where the normal course of events gives an ex-zoo animal a new and more serious currency as it passes into "the museum", these individuals undergo a transformation. Coloured and even tainted by their unwitting colonisation of the affections and imagination of countless human admirers, they are destined to remain forever in a kind of limbo – neither assuming the "serious", representative role of a natural history exhibit, nor sustaining their capacity to delight or command affection. Because we have registered the individual in these cases, the indignity of their having been stuffed and put on public display is made palpable (Marvin 2006: 160).

Certain species have been historically singled out as lending themselves to anthropomorphism. Daston and Mitman (2005) refer to Stephen Gould – an evolutionary biologist who suggests that phylogeny and domestication are important components in addition to neotenic features in determining which non-human animals appeal to human animals. This anthropomorphic exercise has a dual edge to it. On the one hand it allows humans to demonstrate kindness towards the animal but, on the other, it also shows practical disregard in that, through anthropomorphic projection, the needs of the animal in question become secondary to our knowledge of humans, thereby undoubtedly distorting what we consider these needs to be. Despite our desire for closeness to seals and other sea mammals, the very nature of their water habitat limits not only our understanding but also our opportunities for observation and our attempts at fostering intimacy. In Icelandic culture (and others like it), the sea was, and to some extent still is seen as a source for food and nourishment upon which communities have depended through the ages for their survival. Furthermore, the ocean is considered by many to embody a history of the successful dominion of man over this natural resource, albeit an environment that continues to command respect in acknowledgment of its unpredictability and danger. Contemporary ecological concerns and the disappearance of certain species from territorial waters have enforced a re-thinking of established values, highlighting more intrinsic evaluations of nature.

A Proposed Meeting of Human and Animal

Three Attempts (Snæbjörnsdóttir/Wilson 2009) is a performative video work that was initially made for an exhibition in the Seal Centre in Iceland in June 2007 but subsequently reworked as a crucial component of the installation *between you and me*. Having been made aware of the curiosity of seals and their apparent preference for bright colors, the artist (Bryndís Snæbjörnsdóttir) is seen kneeling down at the seashore overlooking an estuary with her back to the camera. Our preliminary research had revealed that it was common for hunters to imitate seal sounds when trying to entice the seal pups away from the cow, suggesting that seals were sensitive to certain types of sound or sound frequencies at least. In the initial video performance, a variety of vocal sounds was used, from singing to the imitation of mobile phone ringtones. Initial attempts prompted little in the way of "reciprocation" on the part of the seals and nothing very much altered at all in their behaviour. The technical reasons why the work came to be remade are not in themselves important for this text, but rather the fact that they necessitated another visit, which resulted in giving us more than the remake we planned, to the extent that it became a completely new work. We are very much aware of the difficulties in attempting to remake works and it is something we generally try to avoid. Nevertheless the location was the same, as was the time of year – the same clothing was worn and we even began at the same time of day. Even the weather was similar. The only thing that seemed beyond our control that day was the behaviour of the non-human animals in the water – and sure enough, their response confounded our expectations. From the moment we arrived on the shore to set up the equipment, the seals made an appearance, popping up from the water, looking, playing, diving and reappearing. The "control" had shifted from us to them – it was their game now.

Figure 14.3 Film still from the video work *Three Attempts*

Our initial reaction was a sense of despair but slowly and convincingly it dawned on us that the only appropriate response was to be "with" the seals in this moment. The performer soon relaxed into the role of the one being looked at, whilst visualizing the image being recorded in the rolling video camera behind – the back of a seated human being on black sand at the shore, the rippling, bright water revealing numerous dark heads popping in and out of view, against a backdrop of distant snow-topped mountains. The process of making this work is described here in order to draw attention to the requisite states of vulnerability and surrender necessary for its execution. This vulnerability is manifest in an image taken in a natural environment, of a lone figure with his/her back to "the watching world". A sense of apprehension experienced by the artist is conveyed in the tentative approach of her performance. The unpredictable behaviour of the participant animals required an acceptance of the relinquishment of human control in this instance, and indeed its desirability.

Three Attempts is the embodiment of a number of principles underpinning our work and its functionality. From one perspective the work seems a novelty – its charm we've observed to be infectious and disarming. From another it touches on the absurd – it echoes with pathos and even melancholy. It's difficult to see the work without acknowledging a degree of sentimentality but in common with absurdity and vulnerability our rejection of sentiment is a cultured, negative response based on the desirability of strength through the application of intellect. At this juncture, we ask what if intellect alone is not enough for us to understand our new and challenged position in the world? Indeed, what if the rationality of our approach obscures or limits the possibilities of wider understanding? All the readings mentioned above are indeed embedded in the work and yet just as crucially, they serve to cohere, fuel and extend another more fundamental reading – that "landscape", if it is to mean anything in the future, must cease to be an objectifying term, which denotes something to be looked at or used whilst simultaneously functioning as a register of our detachment from it. Just as we increasingly understand that other animals are specifically such in relation to the constitution of their dwelling, so we must recognize our own interdependence with habitat and the danger that by sustaining our unfettered and exploitative use of "resources", including land and "animal others", we resolutely keep our backs turned against the illuminating and rewarding conversation we might otherwise have.

What is clear is that the cultural deployment of animal representations in general seeks or manages to frame and delimit our understanding of the animal whereas art of the kind proposed in the above examples may test these preconceptions and force them open for reappraisal. Because most representations are constructed to perform some agenda of our own – in the case of animals, to entertain; to inform; to provide food; to remember; to stand for all others of its species; to symbolize human behavioural characteristics, etc. – in this process, the animal itself is occluded. It is eclipsed by its avatar or likeness, which is always a simplification and therefore must accordingly signify a loss. The work *the naming of things* scrutinizes and we believe reveals the flawed nature of the presumption and pitfalls in our attempts to close up and enforce a reductive approach in our world-view. In juxtaposition to the other works (the interviews, *Three Attempts* etc.) in the exhibition *between you and me*, it allows us the space to think through and thus challenge what we have come to believe it is to be "animal", what it is to be "human", and what indeed is "landscape", and to consider the consequences of the abbreviated forms with which we populate our intellect and our experience. Since it is upon these accepted but polarising constructions that we human animals base our behaviour towards other species and to our environment, at this time it seems appropriate to dig deep and deploy necessarily unconventional methods in order to reappraise their contemporary validity.

References

Boyle, R. 1660. *Spring and Weight of the Air*. Oxford: H. Hall.
Chaudhuri, U. 2007. (De)Facing the Animals: Zooësis and Performance. *TDR: The Drama Review*, 51(1), 8–20.
Darwin, C. 1859. *The Origin of Species*. London: Johan Murray.
Daston, L. and Mitman, G. 2005. *Thinking with Animals, New Perspectives on Anthropomorphism*. New York: Columbia University Press.
Donald, D. 2007. *Picturing Animals in Britain*. Singapore: Yale University.
DW-WORLD.DE. 2007. Stuffed Giraffe Could Become Star of Documenta Show [Online]. Available at: http://www.dw-world.de/dw/article/0,2144,2616936,00.html [accessed 19 October 2009].

Elder, G., Wolch, J. and Emel, J. 1998. Le Pratique Sauvage: Race, Place and the Human-Animal Divide, in *Animal Geographies, Place, Politics, and Identity in the Nature-Culture Borderlands*, edited by J. Wolch and J. Emel. London: Verso, 72–89.

Friedl, P. (Artist). 2007. *Brownie*.

Gane, N. 2006. We Have Never Been Human, What Is To Be Done? : interview with Donna Haraway. *Theory, Culture & Society*, 23(7/8), 135–58.

Halberstam, J. 2007. Pixarvolt – Animation and Revolt [Online]. Available at: http://flowtv.org/?p=739 [accessed 19 October 2009].

Haraway, D. 2008. *When Species Meet*. Minneapolis: University of Minnesota Press.

Hirst, D. (Artist). 1990. *A Thousand Years*.

Lippit, A.M. 2000. *Electric Animal*. Minneapolis: University of Minnesota Press.

Lorimer, H. 2010. Forces of Nature, Forms of Life: Re-Calibrating Ethology and Phenomenology, in *Taking Place: Non-Representational Theories and Human Geography*, edited by B. Anderson and P. Harrison. Farnham: Ashgate, forthcoming.

Marvin, G. 2006. Perpetuating Polar Bears: The Cultural Life of Dead Animals, in *nanoq: flat out and bluesome, A Cultural Life of Polar Bears*, by Snæbjörnsdóttir/Wilson. London: Black Dog Publishing.

Picknett, L. and Prince, C. 2007. *The Turin Shroud*. New York: Touchstone.

Rupke, N. A. 1987. *Vivisection in Historical Perspective*. London: Routledge.

Schama, S. 1995. *Landscape and Memory*. London: Fontana Press.

Snæbjörnsdóttir/Wilson. 2006. nanoq: flat out and bluesome, *A Cultural Life of Polar Bears*. London: Black Dog.

Snæbjörnsdóttir/Wilson (Artists). 2009. *between you and me* [Installation].

Wolfe, C. 2003. *Zoontologies: The Question of the Animal*. Minneapolis: University of Minnesota Press.

Wright, J. (Artist). 1768. *Experiment on a Bird in the Air Pump* [Painting].

Chapter 15
Aurora Landscapes: Affective Atmospheres of Light and Dark

Tim Edensor

Introduction

This chapter focuses upon tourism that is organised around the natural spectacle of the Aurora Borealis in Iceland. I investigate the experience of these Northern Lights as a means to interrogate recent theoretical conceptions of landscape. The aurora are a diverse array of shards, veils, ribbons, curtains, cascades, flashes, beams and numerous other effusions that constitute an ever-shifting panoply of light in the Northern skies of the world. A widespread desire to witness them has given rise to an expanding tourist sector where visitors travel to an increasing number of destinations within or near to the Arctic Circle. Iceland is one of the most popular destinations, where aurora tourists either reside in urban centres and venture into rural settings at night on organised trips or stay in rural settings where the lights may be witnessed in situ. Sightings, however, cannot be guaranteed even if the ideal wintry conditions of clear skies prevail. The aurora have become an integral part of Iceland's tourist branding and they intersect with broader notions about the experience of its landscape, as we will see.

In tourism, depictions of the aurora borealis commonly revolve around rather prosaic scientific explanations. The lights are caused by great streams of electrically charged particles blown from the sun by the solar wind at enormous speed that are attracted to the earth's magnetic poles. These potentially devastating electrons are shielded from the earth by its magnetic field but glow when they collide with the gases in the ionosphere (that part of the earth's atmosphere that roughly extends from 60 to 600 kilometres above the surface). The dancing lights are instigated by the magnetic field buckling as it is hit by high-velocity gusts of these particles.

However, technical depictions of the aurora are usually regarded as insufficient by those who experience them, and this is acknowledged by the *Iceland on the Web* website: "By all means don't let any scientific explanation spoil your appreciation of the beauty of the Northern Lights. They are a truly impressive spectacle, whatever their cause" (*Iceland on the Web* n.d.). Savage (2001: 129) similarly remarks that "(T)he aurora is not just a puzzle to solve; it is a mystery to experience". Indeed, the magical qualities of the aurora typically shape appeals to those who might be tempted to come to the North to witness them:

Mystery and wonder shroud the northern lights, otherwise known as the aurora borealis. Mesmerizing, stunning, other-worldly are just a few words used to describe the experience of watching this spectacular phenomenon. When conditions are favourable this fantastical display lights up the Arctic and sub-Arctic regions, leaving all who catch a glimpse of this magical wonder, memories that will last forever (*Discover the World* n.d.)

In what follows, I firstly explore the ways in which representations of sites and recommended strategies in tourist literature highlight particular approaches to the experience of landscape. I recognise the representational production and practical engagement with aurora landscapes though I subsequently explore how these conventions merely frame expectations, narrative and performance. After this, by way of contextualisation, I investigate how a consideration of the much neglected relationship of light to space, and specifically the aurora, can expand an understanding of the landscape. This is followed by an examination of the sensual, embodied apprehension of the aurora to consider how this extraordinary spectacle is also apprehended in more-than-visual ways, thus critiquing the notion of landscape as visually-perceived entity. Here I will draw attention to the qualities of stillness that typify the aurora experience. I then explore how vitalist notions of landscape can be enhanced but also confounded by considering the Lights. Next, I discuss how these experiences might inform an appreciation of the relationship between landscape and affect, analysing how the relationalities that inhere in the aurora landscape produce a powerful affective atmosphere which fosters embodied involvement and sociality. I conclude with a discussion of the excessive qualities of landscape and the limits of representation as exemplified by responses to the aurora, that reintroduces the notion of the sublime.

Tourist Doxa and Sensual Experience

Entry into any form of space or landscape is surrounded by a host of conventions about what that realm is *for*, what modes of comportment, communication and other forms of bodily practice are appropriate. For instance, it is frequently imagined that to walk in rural settings is to cast off the cloak of self-consciousness and expressive identity that may accompany urban pedestrianism (Edensor 2000). These conventions of practice and performance also resound throughout tourism (Edensor 2001, 2007), which might be conceived as a habitual way of being in the world, accompanied by a common-sense understanding that it is a cultural right and a normative leisure practice to go to other places in order to witness different cultures, historical sights, food, natural histories and landscapes. This doxa, with its focus on belonging (to the world) and becoming – with a high value placed on forms of self-development – is replete with unreflexive, practical, embedded codes of performance, and when collectively enacted, particular place ballets are produced whereby regular routes and stages of experiencing place are consolidated in tourist landscapes (Edensor 1998). The specific practice of sightseeing is a tourist endeavour informed by doxic understandings about what kinds of social and somatic practices should be undertaken in the realm of "nature" in order to consume landscape (Adler 1989). In western tourism, Urry (1990) argues that such confrontations are conditioned by the imperative to enact a solitary, romantic gaze, where the landscape is appraised according to particular aesthetic criteria, sites and scenes are photographed, noise minimised, and a sense of wonder and appreciation is communicated to fellow tourists.

However, the expansion of tourism into ever more spaces and practices has produced numerous ways of experiencing the landscape alongside this distancing visual apprehension. For instance, the rise in adventure sports tourism means that the landscape in destinations such as New Zealand is appraised and experienced as a realm for physically intense escapades, of visceral plunges, immersive engagement and tactile enervation in which the visual senses are relegated to a subsidiary role. More broadly, we might question this over-emphasis on visual consumption by acknowledging the host of other sensations that are produced when tourists interact with space and landscape (Edensor 2006). The graininess of sand and the swelter of sunbathing, the swash of the waves and sound of the seagulls foreground non-visual sensations in beach tourism. Accordingly, it is crucial to acknowledge the different forms of landscape that proliferate throughout an expanding tourism, recognise the conventions through which they are pleasurably experienced, and take stock of the affordances within which tourists are enmeshed and that inculcate ways of being and sensing. For tourists, like other people, reproduce space through the reiteration of conventional performance but they also sense *with* the landscape. Emphatically then, despite the unreflexive consistencies of tourist doxa, practical embodied conventions do not necessarily restrict phenomenological, sensual, social and imaginative experience, for they are always apt to be confounded by the excessive or ineffable qualities of landscape as I will later discuss. In order to explore these affordances in more depth, I now explore the unregarded energies of light and dark in conceptions of landscape.

Landscape and Light

Light is an integral part of space yet the very word landscape seems to exclude the celestial, focusing upon that which is of the earth, the realm that extends away before us, the landforms, contours and configurations, geomorphologies, natural histories, cultural inscriptions and distinctive features of particular kinds of *terra firma*. This absence becomes even more glaringly evident when we investigate notions of the landscape at night for as Jakle notes, "landscape has been conceptualised primarily in terms of daytime use" (2001: vii). Despite the fact that most forms of familiar space are illuminated for much of the time, depending upon season, theories invariably focus upon that which is perceived during daylight, although the landscape at night, with its illuminated and dark areas, possesses enormously different qualities and is apprehended in very different ways to the daylit landscape. The lighting of modern cities has transformed nocturnal urban experience, widespread artificial illumination producing cityscapes of regulation, hierarchical selectiveness, consumption, fantasy and imagination (McQuire 2005, Edensor and Millington forthcoming), yet thus far, academic writing has focused upon the cityscape by day. Similarly, the luminescent qualities of the non-urban landscape have been wholly neglected although a brief consideration of landscape painting reveals that artists have expended much effort trying to "capture" the effects of the light: for they "know that to paint ... a 'landscape' is to paint both earth and sky, and that earth and sky blend in the perception of a world in continuous formation" (Ingold 2005: 104).

Nevertheless, the relationship of the sun, moon and stars and more evanescent illuminations caused by lightning, rainbows, will o' the wisp, fireflies and a range of atmospheric phenomena are rarely discussed in conceptions of landscape. This is despite the ways in which sunsets and sunrises bathe landscapes in glowing hues, transforming the perception and feel of space, as exemplified in popular depictions of landscape in relation to the effects of the sun, where people talk of a pitiless glare, a rosy glow, or thin shafts of winter sunlight. Moreover, regions and nations acquire associations related to the qualities of the light with which they are suffused. Toxic but spectacular sunsets differentiate Los Angeles from the impassive sun beating down on the dunes of the Sahara or the ever changing panoply of cloud and sun in North-West Scotland's skies.

In conceiving of the intrinsic entanglement of landscape and light we can draw a parallel with Tim Ingold's discussion of forms of weather, elements which equally lack the solidity associated with illumination. Like light, wind, clouds and fog have frequently been ontologically conceived as the immaterial opposite of the concrete earthliness of the land, around and above which they swirl and float. Ingold draws attention to Gibson's notion that the features of the earth – as opposed to more evanescent qualities of the sky – are akin to "furniture", as if the earth is always already equipped, like a stage set, with its fixtures and fittings. However, he argues, this congealed, static understanding of earthly fixity misses entirely the state of flux in which the world is always enmeshed, the "dynamic processes of world-formation in which both perceivers and the phenomena they perceive are necessarily immersed" (Ingold 2007: S29). A refutation of the distinction between material and immaterial qualities foregrounds instead a conception of the landscape as a fluid and becoming entity, an indivisible field. Stars, cloud and sunsets, are not objects but

> rather an incoherent, vaporous tumescence that swells and is carried along in the currents of the medium. To observe the clouds is not to view the furniture of the sky but to catch a fleeting glimpse of a sky-in-formation, never the same from one moment to the next (Ingold 2007: S28).

The land is similarly continuously in formation, despite the illusion of stability. Moreover, the whole landscape is a heterogeneous medium of sensual, affective and emotional experience in which the light, the weather and the ground underfoot are not merely external objects available for inspection and perception, for the perceiver is inextricably entangled with that which is perceived:

> (T)o inhabit the open world, then, is to be immersed in the fluxes of the medium: in sunshine, rain, and wind. This immersion, in turn, underwrites our capacities respectively – to see, hear, and touch. (Ingold 2007: S30)

These media thus condition the limits and possibilities of what can be apprehended and in this realm, light is a medium of perception productive of "the experience of inhabiting the world of the visible, and its qualities – of brilliance and shade, tint and colour, and saturation" (Ingold 2005: 101). Light is thus "immanent in the life and consciousness of the perceiver as it unfolds within the field of relations established by way of his or her presence within a certain environment" (Ingold 2005: 99). Crucially, the land is not "an interface" separating earth and sky but is a "vaguely defined zone of admixture and intermingling" (Ingold 2007: S33). Similar to weather, the light continuously enfolds and is enfolded into the world to produce the ever-shifting qualities of landscape and provide the means through which it is perceived.

However, having discussed light, and insisted that it is an integral part of the landscape and not separate from it, we also need to explore its absence, for to see in and with the dark is to see otherwise, to apprehend space as an entity that lacks the complex configurations sensed by day, to not see certain features of the landscape at all, but to sense others vividly.

The expansion of electric lighting across most spaces in the West has resulted in what is increasingly regarded as an over-illuminated world, where darkness is hard to find. For instance, the *Campaign for Dark Skies* points to an aesthetic loss as well as the environmental, social, health and economic problems produced by poor and excessive electric illumination (*Campaign for Dark Skies* n.d.). In the countries of Northern Europe, with their very short periods of wintry daylight and contrasting summers filled with 24 hours of daylight, light, or its lack, is central to seasonal experience. In winter, across scantily populated tracts of land there is the promise of a kind of darkness that lies beyond the reddish glow of human settlement. This Northern darkness attracts those who wish to move away from over-illuminated landscapes, and to experience a denser darkness against which the Northern Lights may be witnessed. Indeed, as is emphasised in promotional literature and by those who watch the Lights, the ideal conditions for viewing are when the land descends into a black darkness away from the glare of urban centres.

A striking feature of the aurora is the extent to which it dominates space, especially when there is little light cast by the moon. Where this is the case, the land is contrastingly a dark gathering of matter, with few features perceptible save for the marked horizon that seems to enclose this murky mass. The constant play of light above this shadowy earth rarely suffuses the land with a warm glow as with the sun but seems to constitute a separate sphere that confirms the existence of two opposite realms: light and dark. The interpenetration of light and earth is minimal and the apparently quiescent, unilluminated land seems dormant in contrast to the dynamic, shifting panoply in the heavens. It is with this surrounding darkness in mind that we can interrogate Wylie's citation of Merleau-Ponty's point that the seeing subject is always also intertwined with a consciousness that one can be seen as part of the "landscape of visible things" (Wylie 2007: 152), as an observable as well as observing subject. This double consciousness, further emphasising the ways in which people are part of, and not apart from, the landscape is less evident for all that may be visually perceived are perhaps a few vague outlines of the self and others. However, the presence of others is not primarily signalled by visual evidence but by the coos and murmurs which are uttered as the aurora is beheld, the breathing and sighs, and a sense of bodily warmth and tactile presence. Here, underlining the non-visual apprehensions of landscape, we sense the presence and energies of fellow humans and generate noises and tactilities of our own through which others sense us. I will return to the effects of these inter-human sensations shortly but firstly focus further upon the impacts of the lights on spectating bodies.

The Still Sensing of the Landscapes of the Aurora

As Ingold (2005: 97) insists,

> our experience of the weather, when out of doors, is invariably multisensory. It is just as much auditory, haptic and olfactory as it is visual; indeed in most practical circumstances these sensory modalities cooperate so closely that it is impossible to disentangle their respective contributions.

Of course, the tourist conventions of consuming the aurora persist in that it is primarily consumed visually, the eyes fixated on the swirling lights, and this usually occurs as a solitary practice in the presence of other fellow tourists involving little talk, although with non-linguistic verbal communication as I have mentioned. Yet while the visual consumption of the aurora predominates, non-visual apprehension of the lights and the broader landscape of which they are part emerges. For in addition to the non-visual sensations produced by other people, the landscape is surrounded by the effects of weather, the particular temperature, the wind, the sounds of rivers and streams, the levels of moisture in the atmosphere, all of which contribute to a wider sensual apprehension, though largely unreflexive.

Another sensual dimension is produced through the ground upon which one stands. While consuming the cascades of light in the skies, stance is dependent on the textures underfoot but primarily the feet remain rooted: "For the aurora watcher, the experience is mesmerising" (Akasofu 2009: 7). Although the experience of the aurora involves movement from a light to dark place via mechanised transport, once the sights are beheld outside the standing stillness of the observer contrasts with the whirling illuminations overhead. Falck-Ytter (1999: 10) quotes Norwegian polar explorer Fridtjof Nansen: "I went on deck this evening in a rather gloomy frame of mind but was nailed to the spot the moment I got outside (and saw the aurora)". This motionlessness testifies to the immersion of bodies in a landscape in which they are stilled, spellbound by the flows of light. The eye moves, the pulse races. This is a stillness that is not epitomised by fatigue or lethargy (Bissell 2009) but by being transfixed by another (heavenly) body. In contradistinction to the often hyperbolic depictions of travel and tourism as synonymous with mobility and flow, animation and flux, we might consider this stillness to be a touristic "attunement" (Bissell and Fuller 2009) through which the body's ability to sense landscape is enhanced. Peter Adey (2009) contends that the adoption of stillness might be conceived as a sensibility and a technique through which bodies become "finely attuned to their exteriors ... apprehending and anticipating spaces and events in ways that sees the body enveloped within the movement of the environment around it" to produce "a heightened and contemplative sense of the moment". In response to the capacities that inhere in this space of light and dark, a lack of self-consciousness evolves through absorption in the scene, sense-making recedes and onlookers become detached from ordinary rhythms, compulsions and anticipations, as the aurora become a moment in the flow of events. Yet connected to the huge dark land that stretches beyond the immediate spot, there is a further sense of the mass of the earth to which we are tethered by gravity. And these feelings of stillness, of connection to earth and landscape, combined with an awareness of the sounds and touch of other humans, and the shared absorption through which the tour party collectively beholds the aurora can heighten a particularly human shared sense of communitas (Cocker 2009).

Finally, there are numerous accounts, mostly dismissed by scientific research, that the Northern Lights also emit a sound as well as illumination. Whether this sense is identifiable seems dubious although some experienced observers swear that the noise is clear and audible. However, this may be an example of synaesthesia whereby the overwhelming visual impact of the lights, the pulsing and flowing, provokes deceptive sensations of noise, highlighting just how the landscape is experienced in a multi-sensory manner (see Savage 2001). Other forms of agency are also attributed to the lights, notably that they carry a physical potential to threaten, that they might catch you and enfold you into the sky, a sensation particularly remembered by those who experienced the aurora as children. Why, Akasofu (2009: 8) writes, "does it seem at times that the aurora is reaching down?" This is perhaps unsurprising given the force of the uninterrupted energy emitted when the lights are in full flow, as well as their otherworldiness, and these sensations are both informed by and inform the production of myths discussed shortly. It is to the extraordinary and vital energies of the aurora that I now turn in the light of recent vitalist conceptions of landscape.

Vitalist Landscapes

In 2003, in his history of the ways in which landscape has been conceptualised within geography, from the Sauerian interpretations of cultural landscapes, to humanist readings of subjective meanings projected onto landscape, to the understanding of landscape as a power-laden realm that is textually read and a material expression of dominant, but precarious ideological meanings, Tim Cresswell sceptically critiques the notion that landscape retains utility as a concept. Since it is presented as a "text already written" (Cresswell 2003: 270), he contends that landscape "does not have much space for temporality, for movement and flux, and mundane practice" and lacks an appreciation that space is processual (Cresswell 2003: 269). Yet though he rightly laments the ways in which landscape is conceived as being visually apprehended, as "an image ... as fixed form of "framing"" (Cresswell 2003: 275), he subsequently suggests that it might be retrievable through being conceived through a more fluid understanding that also foregrounds how it is subject to multi-sensual apprehension. In the light of this critique, it is notable that landscape has indeed recently been rescued from such immobile, visual framings, with the emergence of vitalist ideas that emphasise the processual, immanent and emergent (Wylie 2007). In these conceptions, landscape is alive with energies, eternally fluid, its rocks, earth, vegetation and climate continually undergoing change as elements from near and far, and from different times, are entangled and folded together in a continual making. This re-vitalisation of landscape thus moves away from sedentarist, static, visually apprehended notions of landscape that suggest being and permanence.

Strikingly, such vitalist conceptions resound in the representation of Iceland's landscape, a brand identified by an appeal to non-human energies that secures a specialist niche in the global tourist supermarket. Accordingly, the lure of the Northern Lights chimes with the special emphasis placed upon the wild landscapes of Iceland, as epitomised by the following claim of the Icelandic Tourist Board (n.d.): "the youthful exuberance of the land boldly greets travellers. The landscape is alive with the restless play of nature's forces". Within this vitalist conception, the aurora further supplement the image of Iceland, the "land of fire and ice", as a site for a more visceral engagement with landscape. With its glaciers, geysers, volcanic eruptions, rocky peaks and geothermal pools available for physical encounter, this is a wildscape that can be traversed by means of canoe and raft, crampons and ice-picks, swimming costume and backpack, a great outdoors in which bodily immersion and exertion are required. This young landscape, seething with geothermal, volcanic and climatic energies at an earthly level, is complemented by the unearthly energies which churn above the earth.

As I have emphasised, as we apprehend landscape we are immersed in the currents and energies of a world-in-formation. Plunged into light, weather and earthliness, bodies are situated in the continuous and generative becoming of the world, and any sense of a discrete embodied condition separate from this realm is deceptive. However, illusory sedentarist and reified apprehensions of landscape are produced through the persistence of dense cultural histories of representation and practical conventions about the proper disposition to adopt towards particular kinds of space. Moreover, besides these social and cultural conventions about how to read and practice landscape, the ontological conditions of human existence also curtail the ability to perceive the vital seething of certain (elements of) landscapes. Many agencies are invisible or overlooked – consider the constant recreation of the soil and the movements of bacteria and fungal spores – and numerous processes of change are too slow for human perception. They can only be apprehended over longer periods than that of the short visit or even the human life span. Because the appearance of nature seems to be constituted by particular *discrete* agencies – the cascading of rivers, the bending of trees in the wind and the flights of birds – the connections through which *all* elements within the landscape are reproduced and transformed is imperceptible. Yet the seething animal, plant, geological, chemical and climatic energies that are in constant occurrence often only become apparent when, for instance, time-lapse photography reveals the dynamic (but slower) processes through which a flower blooms and fades, corpses decay and fungus grows. Such human limitations thus foster representations of landscape as a passive realm available to the gaze, an inert surface upon which human action takes place.

Ben Anderson (2009: 78) points to how certain features such as clouds, winds and rainbows are "associated with the uncertain, disordered, shifting and contingent – that which never quite achieves the stability of form". The same is apparent in the ever-changing configurations of waves and curtains of the Northern Lights. These profoundly visible phenomena echo the less evident energies that suffuse all elements of landscapes. With the aurora therefore, the contrasting darkness and the relative seeming quiescence of the land produce the illusion that the heavens are alive whilst the earth lies dormant. The earthly topologies embedded in the relationalities, flows and networks through which the world is continually (re)produced seem absent. While the aurora emerge out of the relationality between sun, atmosphere and the earth's gravitational pull, these forces all seem far removed from more grounded connections that make space, place and landscape. In other words, it is difficult to conceive of the aurora as being enfolded within earthly networks. This sense of disconnection contributes to the affective power of the aurora, which I now discuss.

Aurora Landscapes and Affect

In the promotional literature that advertises the charms of the aurora to tourists, a series of phrases and words recur: the aurora is "magical", "spectacular" and "mystical". It is striking that such accounts have drawn upon fantastic, supernatural and mythic explanations and these continue to resound through contemporary narratives. The oneiric qualities of the Lights are characterised by mystical tales of how they ethereally reflect the ghosts of virgins or the murdered, constitute human spirits playing with walrus skulls, are the dancing spirits of the deceased, the energies released by celestial and supernatural wars (see Falck-Ytter 1999, Savage, 2001, Akasofu 2009).

These myths contribute to stories of the aurora that are related and consumed prior to a period under their spell. Yet though such ideas feed into the immersive experience of the aurora landscape, they tend to be rather swamped by an immanent *affective field* in which only shreds of representation may interweave with other, stronger intensities and feelings about landscape. Dominant here is "the emergent and fluid dimension of how place is sensed and experienced" (Adey 2009: 5). The notion of affect, prominent in recent thinking about landscape, is useful here because it highlights the transpersonal relations between elements within particular contexts and provides a broader, more-than-human concept of the social. In decentring the individual from analysis, it prompts us to think about how different configurations of objects, technologies, energies, non-human life forms, spaces, forms of knowledge and information combine to form "affective fields" that are distributed across particular geographical settings.

These affective fields can also be depicted as "temporary configurations of energy and feeling" (Conradson and Latham 2007: 238). They are characterised by affective atmospheres, which McCormack (2008: 413) describes as being "something distributed yet palpable, a quality of environmental immersion that registers in and through sensing bodies whilst also remaining diffuse, in the air, ethereal". Such atmospheres, as Böhme (1993: 114) suggests, "seem to fill the space with a certain tone of feeling like a haze". Affect is thus generated by immersion in an atmospheric environment that folds subject and space together, occurring "before and alongside the formation of subjectivity, across human and non-human materialities, and in-between subject/object distinctions" (Anderson 2009: 78). Such notions summon up the effects of the weather and the qualities of light (and dark) as they pervade space and the bodies that perceive them. Clearly, light and weather can be powerful contributory elements within these affective atmospheres. Lam (1977) asserts that electric lighting possess unique power to intentionally and unintentionally produce mood affecting qualities, from feelings of safety to urban liveliness, but the affective power of sun, stars, moon and aurora surely transcends that of these human-produced illuminations.

In the confrontation with the Northern Lights, the affective realm is constituted out of the elements already identified, above all, the swirling aurora, but also the pervasive dark, the black mass of the land, the temperature, the quiet, and the sounds and gestures of human bodies. This affective landscape provides an environment of energies and capacities, a context within which a body feels and acts. As Brennan (2004: 1) notes, the transmission of affect alters the biochemistry of the subject so that the ""atmosphere"" or environment literally gets into the individual". These sensual and biological responses to the landscape are thus further productive of the affective atmosphere. The affects generated by the coalescence of aurora, dark, temperature, silence and closeness to others thus *penetrate* the body, enfolding it into the field.

As I have described, the disposition of most visitors is to assemble and watch the heavenly dancers in stillness, and largely in silence apart from the odd expression or sigh. Such conventional tourist procedures and habits and the immersion in an affective atmosphere generate an attunement to space. The expression of such an engagement further promotes a kind of affective contagion. The gestures of bodies, their postures, and especially their stillness, set the tone for the experience and practice of the landscape, acting upon other bodies to maintain the collective disposition. As Sarah Ahmed (2004: 27) insists, affects and emotions "are also *about* attachments, about what connects us to this or that" and to other people. They also prevent a sense of detachment from others. Bound together with the landscape, the affective sense of communitas mentioned above is engendered through a connectivity to the landscape and to others under the spell of the aurora.

The Ineffable Landscapes of Aurora: A Return to the Sublime

I have highlighted the perceived disconnection between the numerous scientific explanations of the Northern Lights and the experience of them, and the tendency to seek recourse in mythological accounts. The aurora is thus an excellent example of the ways in which the experience of the excessive qualities of landscape confounds attempts to represent it. Encountering the Northern Lights dramatises the ineptitude of words to capture the apprehension of their affective and sensual qualities, although mythical interpretations symbolise their powerful impact upon observers.

One mystery contributing to their ineffability concerns the perceived location of the aurora. Are they part of the world or otherworldly? And how far are they from the earth? The stars are regarded as being unfathomably remote from the earth and part of a borderless immensity, and our own star, the sun, is understood to be a great distance from the earth, though it gives it life. The moon, although now reachable, is conceived as being outside the orbit of the earth, although phenomena of illumination that are enclosed within the earth's atmosphere, such as rainbows and clouds, are apprehended as much closer at hand. Any assessment about the distance of the aurora from the surface is confounded by their seemingly minimal impact on the earth, unlike the weather with which the earth seems inextricably entangled. They neither heat the land nor bestow much light on it like the sun, but seem disconnected from all else, impassively aloof from earthly immediacies. The impression is that the aurora belongs to a space to which we do not belong, and it thus has no relationship to the endless production of the landscape. Similarly, it belongs to a temporality that transcends human history and the formation of the landscape, blurring notions of past, present and future.

This understanding of the aurora seems to disavow the conception of the landscape as a congeries of relationalities, endlessly reproduced through a vitalist, dynamic materiality, as discussed above. The notion of landscape as constituted out of manifold, earthly and non-earthly connections that are intertwined in continuous and dynamic production acknowledges the connective tissue that connects sun and earth, the sun being a part of the landscape whose every feature has depended and continues to depend upon it. With the aurora, such connection seems obscure.

In a different vein, the consumer of landscape frequently imagines the histories and lives of those who have forged the land and continue to dwell within it. Apprehension is intimately related to the attempts of humans to identify evidence of the social and cultural processes that have produced a lived landscape. However, the emergent landscapes of Iceland lack such signs of human agency. Yet despite this, the observer may empathise with other aspects, for the eye might try to recoup what it might be like to feel the texture of rocky land underneath, the visceral force of the raging torrent or the splash of icy water. But the evanescent spectacle of the aurora allow for no such apprehension, since there are no recognisable forms of matter into which the body might imaginatively insert itself. Unlike weather, the aurora suggest no wind, heat or cold, wetness or dryness. Its ever-changing configurations are the embodiment only of distant light, lacking any phenomenological grasp.

Nevertheless, as I have emphasised throughout this chapter, despite these sensations of utter disconnection, the aurora are part of the landscape, which cannot be contained or bordered by what merely lies upon the earth. I have drawn attention to the multisensory apprehension of aurora landscapes and the peculiar qualities of light as a medium for perception. Yet the numinous qualities of the Northern Lights are responsible for the confounding of modes of representation as we enter the landscape of the ineffable. The other-worldly, uncanny effects of the aurora, devoid of tethering landmarks save the horizon of the earth, provokes a conscious struggle for words and an awareness of their limitations. Overwhelmingly, accounts of the aurora discuss being overawed and unable to depict the phenomena. Akasofu (2009: 7) avers that "published accounts, then and now, seem unequal to the subject matter". He cites polar explorer William Hooper from 1853 who reports "language is in vain in the attempt to describe its ever varying and gorgeous phases" (Akasofu 2009: 12), and similarly points to the limitations of pen or pencil. Words can't suffice and it seems as if we have once more entered the realm of the sublime, a seemingly archaic notion. Nevertheless, according to McHugh (2009: 215), this "is an experience that exceeds our imaginative powers to comprehend in sensible form. The sublime is an aesthetic of immensity and excess that disrupts and disturbs". Ben Anderson emphasises these excessive qualities of affective atmospheres, and this particularly seems to apply to those atmospheres generated in the experience of viewing the aurora. There is an inability to contain such immersion in thought or express it through language, since it is always lies beyond as a "kind of indeterminate, affective excess" (Anderson 2009: 80). More broadly though, landscape in general resists such representation and we can see clearly how the conventional representations and performances of tourist doxa are transcended by the plenitude of the aurora landscape. Landscape, is always far more than a cultural construct.

References

Adey, P. 2009. Holding Still: The Private Life of an Air Raid [Online]. *M/C Journal*, 12(1). Available at: http://journal.media-culture.org.au/index.php/mcjournal/article/viewArticle/112 [accessed 24 February 2010].

Adler, J. 1989. Origins of Sightseeing. *Annals of Tourism Research* 16, 7–29.

Ahmed, S. 2004. On Collective Feelings or, the Impressions Left by Others. *Theory, Culture and Society* 21(2), 25–42.

Akasofu, S-I. 2009. *The Northern Lights: Secrets of the Aurora Borealis*. Anchorage: Alaska Northwest Books.

Anderson, B. 2009. Affective Atmospheres. *Emotion, Space and Society* 2, 77–81.

Bissell, D. 2009. Travelling Vulnerabilities: Mobile Timespaces of Quiescence. *Cultural Geographies* 16, 427–45.

Bissell, D. and Fuller, G. 2009. The Revenge of the Still [Online]. *M/C Journal*, 12(1). Available at: http://journal.media-culture.org.au/index.php/mcjournal/article/viewArticle/136 [accessed 24 February 2010].

Böhme, G. 1993. Atmosphere as the Fundamental Concept of a New Aesthetics. *Thesis Eleven*, 36, 113–26.

Brennan, T. 2004. *The Transmission of Affect*. New York: Cornell University Press.

Campaign for Dark Skies n.d. *The British Astronomical Association's Campaign for Dark (starry, natural) Skies* [Website]. Available at: http://www.britastro.org/dark-skies/index.html?7O [accessed 24 February 2010].

Cocker, E. 2009. From Passivity to Potentiality: The *Communitas* of Stillness [Online]. *M/C Journal*, 12(1). Available at: http://journal.media-culture.org.au/index.php/mcjournal/article/viewArticle/119 [accessed 5 March 2010].

Conradson, D. and Latham, A. 2007. The Affective Possibilities of London: Antipodean Transnationals and the Overseas Experience. *Mobilities* 2(2), 231–54.

Cresswell, T. 2003. Landscape and the Obliteration of Practice, in *The Handbook of Cultural Geography*, edited by K. Anderson, M. Domosh, S. Pile and N. Thrift. London: Sage, 269–82.

Discover the World n.d. *Northern Lights* [Website]. Available at: http://www.discover-the-world.co.uk/en/special-interest/northern-lights.html [accessed 5 March 2010].

Edensor, T. 1998. *Tourists at the Taj*. London: Routledge.

Edensor, T. 2000. Walking in the British countryside. *Body and Society* 6(3/4), 81–106.

Edensor, T. 2001. Performing Tourism, Staging Tourism: (Re)Producing Tourist Space and Practice. *Tourist Studies* 1, 59–82.

Edensor, T. 2006. Sensing Tourist Spaces, in *Travels in Paradox: Remapping Tourism*, edited by C. Minca and T. Oakes. London: Rowman and Littlefield, 23–45.

Edensor, T. 2007. Mundane Mobilities, Performances and Spaces of Tourism. *Social and Cultural Geography* 8(2), 199–215.

Edensor, T. and Millington, S. forthcoming. Thinking about Illuminated Geographies. *Progress in Human Geography.*

Falck-Ytter, H. 1999. *Aurora: The Northern Lights in Mythology, History, and Science.* Glasgow: Bath Press Colourbooks.

Iceland on the Web [website] n.d. Available at: http://iceland.vefur.is/iceland_nature/Northern_Lights/ [accessed 5 March 2010].

Icelandic Tourist Board n.d. *Iceland.* Available at: http://www.icelandtouristboard.com [accessed 5 March 2010].

Ingold, T. 2005. The Eye of the Storm: Visual Perception and Weather. *Visual Studies* 20(2), 97–104.

Ingold, T. 2007. Earth, Sky, Wind and Weather. *Journal of the Royal Anthropological Institute* (N.S.) 13, S19–S38.

Jakle, J. 2001. *City Lights: Illuminating the American Night.* Baltimore: Johns Hopkins University Press.

Lam, W. 1977. Perception and Lighting as Formgivers for Architecture. New York: McGraw Hill.

McCormack, D. 2008. Engineering Affective Atmospheres on the Moving Geographies of the 1897 Andrée Expedition. *Cultural Geographies* 15, 413–30.

McHugh, K. 2009. Movement, Memory, Landscape: An Excursion in Non-Representational Thought. *Geojournal* 74(3), 209–18.

McQuire, S. 2005. Immaterial Architectures: Urban Space and Electric Light. *Space and Culture* 8(2), 126–40.

Savage, C. 2001. *Aurora: The Mysterious Northern Lights.* Buffalo, NY: Firefly Books.

Urry, J. 1990. *The Tourist Gaze.* London: Sage.

Wylie, J. 2007. *Landscape.* London: Routledge.

Chapter 16
Epilogue

Tim Ingold

I

A lizard basks upon a stone in the warm sunshine of a summer's day. The stone lies on the ground, beside a path along which a man is strolling. The sight of the lizard brings him up short. Fascinated by the jewel-like precision of the lizard's form, which contrasts so strikingly with the rough-cut stone, and by the lizard's capacity to remain completely motionless while yet fully alert, he begins to reflect on the relationships between the lizard and the stone and between the stone and the ground on which it lies, and on his own relationships with both lizard and stone. This man, you see, is a philosopher, and he considers it his business to reflect on such matters. Later on, his reflections would figure in a course of lectures in which he would try to explain, once and for all, the difference between what it means to be a stone, a lizard and a human. The lectures, delivered in 1929–30 but not published until 1983, were called *The Fundamental Concepts of Metaphysics* and the philosopher's name was Martin Heidegger.

Let us start with the stone. Weighed down by the force of gravity, it touches the ground on which it lies. Yet as Heidegger is quick to point out, what we call "touching" in this instance is quite unlike the sort of relationship that the lizard has with the stone (Heidegger 1995: 195–6). Were we, somewhat unkindly, to remove the lizard from its resting place, and to pick up the stone and throw it, then it will come to lie wherever it falls, on the meadow or at the bottom of a water-filled ditch. The unfortunate lizard, accustomed to basking on that particular stone, will surely notice that something is amiss, but the stone notices nothing. It will not sense the contrast between hard ground, soft grass and cool water. It will not sense, period. The stone, says Heidegger, is *worldless*. This is not to say that it lacks a world, for that would imply that it could in principle have access to a world that has, for some reason, been withdrawn from it. Rather, worldlessness has to be understood affirmatively as a condition of being of which things such as stones partake (Heidegger 1995: 196).

What, then, of the lizard? No more than the stone does the lizard have access to things for what they *are*. It seeks the warmth of the sunlight but knows nothing of the sun; it seeks a hard surface on which to bask in the light but knows nothing of stone. Yet it would not be true to say that, like the stone, it is *indifferent* to these things. The lizard's "touching" the stone is a modality of sensory engagement and not just an exertion of pressure, as with the stone's "touching" the ground. And whereas the stone merely warms up in the sun, the lizard *feels* its warmth. In Heidegger's words, "the lizard has its *own relation* to the rock, to the sun, and to a host of other things" (1995: 197). Yet for the lizard they remain unequivocally "lizard-things" – that is, things which open up pathways for the animal to carry on its own lizardy form of life. In a sense, therefore, the lizard has a world – a lizard-world of lizard-things – but this is not the sense in which the world exists for the philosopher.

For in the world of the human being, argues Heidegger, things are disclosed for what they are. When he chances upon the lizard basking on the stone in the sunlight, lizard, stone and sun are things to be apprehended, things that have their own being distinct from his, that are revealed to him, and towards which he has to take a stance. Unlike the animal that is "captivated" by its world, bounden to it, absorbed in it, and therefore unable to apprehend it as such, the human recognises this world *as* a world, but only because, to an extent, he is set apart from it. This separation, unique to the human condition, is the price we have to pay for the privilege, in one sense, of "having" a world (Heidegger 1995: 117). The lizard does not have a world in this sense, and yet in another sense (and unlike the stone) of course it does. In order to distinguish this latter sense from the former, Heidegger goes on to co-opt the notion of "environment". Thus the animal, he tells us, "*behaves within an environment but never within a world*" (Heidegger 1995: 239).

The environment is literally all-around the animal: Heidegger calls it an "encircling ring". But this encirclement, he insists, is *not* an encapsulation (Heidegger 1995: 255–7). It is not as though all that lies beyond the animal were closing in on every side. For the ring is not drawn around the animal by forces exterior to it; rather it is the animal that draws the ring around itself, in the conduct of its own life, and in so doing, opens up a sphere for its activity. The ring was not there before the animal takes up occupation, nor is it built up around it subsequently. Wherever there is life, the ring is being drawn, and things are being drawn into the ring. The lizard, as it basks in the sun, draws the stone into its ring as a basking place. Other animals might draw it into their respective rings in other ways, such as the insect that shelters beneath it or the bird that uses it as an anvil to smash the shells of snails. But only in the world of the human is the stone disclosed as a stone (Heidegger 1995: 248).

II

Now Heidegger was not the first to take a metaphysical ramble down the path I have just described. His most immediate predecessor was the Estonian-born biologist Jakob von Uexküll, recognised today as a founding figure in the fields of both ethology and semiotics. In his essay, "A Stroll Through the Worlds of Animals and Men", dating from 1934, von Uexküll invites us to join him on a sunny day, as he wanders through a "flower-strewn meadow, humming with insects, fluttering with butterflies" (von Uexküll 1992 [1934]: 319). It seems a familiar world, a pastoral idyll, until we stop to ask what it is like to be one of these lowly dwellers of the meadow: a beetle, a butterfly, a worm or a field-mouse. To enter the world of any such creature is to step into a bubble. Inside this bubble the meadow is transformed. It becomes a strange place. Many of its colourful features disappear; others are reconfigured in new relationships. To be inside the bubble is to perceive the world as the animal does, to be alert to the perceptual cues that it is able to detect and to which, in its movement, it is primed to respond.

To denote this world, as it is constituted within the animal's circuit of perception and action, von Uexküll (1992 [1934]: 320) adopted the term *Umwelt*. As with Heidegger's "encircling ring", the Umwelt comes with the animal. It is not like a niche that is already there before the animal arrives and to which it subsequently accommodates itself. Rather, the animal fits the world to itself by ascribing qualities to the things it encounters and thereby integrating them into a coherent system of its own (von Uexküll 1992 [1934]: 360–1). Indeed, so wrapped up is it in its own particular bubble that no other worlds are accessible to it. Though the perceptual and effector organs of different creatures may be perfectly attuned, neither can access what is real for the other. For example, the threads of the spider's web, as von Uexküll elegantly showed in his *Bedeutungslehre* or "Theory of Meaning" of 1940, are precisely proportioned such that they evade the sensors of the fly, and yet the spider knows absolutely nothing of the fly's world (von Uexküll 1982 [1940]: 42).

How, then, should we understand the relationship between different creatures in their respective Umwelts? To answer this question, von Uexküll adopts a musical analogy. The lives of creatures, he suggests, are like melodies in counterpoint. The life of the spider runs in counterpoint to that of the fly: to the melodic line of the first, the second figures as a refrain. So likewise, bees join in counterpoint with the scent, colour and shape of plant blossoms. Indeed the entirety of living nature, so conceived, might be understood as an immense, polyphonic score. Reading between the lines, the equivalent of harmony in music is meaning in nature. Thus, concludes von Uexküll, "the meaning-score is a description of nature, just as the score written in notes may be equated with description of music" (von Uexküll 1982 [1940]: 64). In the meadow, with its flowers and insects, von Uexküll hears the "orchestra of nature" of which every particular plant and animal is an instrument, each attuned to every other in respect of not only the tones it emits but also the manner of its very construction.

Indeed there is a sense in which any creature must take into itself the characteristics of another if it is to enter into a contrapuntal relation with it. To return to the example of the spider and the fly, in both its bodily structure and the mesh of its web, the spider incorporates certain of the fly's characteristics. It is "fly-like", not because it resembles the fly, but because it *corresponds* to it (von Uexküll 1982 [1940]: 67). There is a similar correspondence between the structure of the flower and that of the bee. But if the counterpoint is to work, the correspondence must be reciprocal:

> If the flower were not bee-like
> And the bee were not flower-like
> The unison could never be successful. (von Uexküll 1982 [1940]: 65)

The inspiration for these lines is drawn from the poetic wisdom of Goethe: "If the eye were not sun-like, it could not see the sun" (Luke 1964: 282). For von Uexküll, however, Goethe's insight is but half-formed. To complete it one should add the corollary: "If the sun were not eye-like, it could not shine in any sky." His point is that the sky, and the sun as a celestial light that illuminates the sky, can only exist in the Umwelt or phenomenal world of creatures with eyes. Perhaps as an astronomical body, the sun could exist even if there were no creatures to see it, or in its light. But the sun we perceive in the sky, and that lights the world of our experience, can exist only through its essential correspondence with the eye. And conversely, as Goethe had observed, the eye can see only by virtue of its correspondence with the sun.

III

For the people of the Trobriand Islands, an archipelago off the eastern tip of New Guinea, the performance of garden magic is critical to the growth of crops and successful harvest. Most performances take place during the early part of the monsoon season. The magician, squatting alone in a corner of the garden, addresses the soil, as well as the tubers – the staple yams or *taytu* – whose abundance he aims to secure. As he launches his words into these things, rumbles of thunder, lightning flashes and gusty winds – phenomena not uncommon in this season – portend that the surrounding world is listening and that the words have been received. In due time, the yams will swell below ground, while above it the luxuriant growth of vines and drooping foliage attest to an abundant crop. In his classic account of Trobriand horticulture, *Coral Gardens and Their Magic*, Bronislaw Malinowski explains that the recitation of a magical formula is neither a snippet of conversation nor a prayer, nor a statement or communication (Malinowski 1935: 214). On the face of it, is seems to be a solitary monologue. How, then, can it possibly be supposed to have an effect?

Consider for example the dolphin spell. The words invoke a dolphin playing in the waves, weaving up and down, in and out, in a swishing, swirling movement. The spell is recited at a moment in the cycle of cultivation when the fields have been strewn with leaves in order to make the vines droop, as they must do at harvest time. Its words transform the garden, with its foliage swaying in the wind, into a seascape. "The richer the foliage", Malinowski writes, "the more the garden will resemble the undulations of following waves" (Malinowski 1935: 310–11).

Indeed, once the harvest is done, the field – festooned in wreathes and garlands – resembles nothing so much as a sea of greenery, especially when whipped up at midday by the strengthening trade winds. At the same time, the spell calls for the yams to grow as big in the soil as the plump body of the dolphin in the sea. We might say, echoing Goethe, that the spell makes the garden sea-like and the yams dolphin-like, thus bringing into unison the regenerative powers of land and ocean. These likenesses, however, are based not on correspondence but on resemblance.

Yet the magician's performance remains enigmatic. The islanders are convinced of its beneficial effects, and so is their ethnographer, but for different reasons. For the former, the plants of the garden, indeed the very soil itself, are aroused by the force of magical words. The latter, however, declines to be bound to a native belief that seems incredible. Plants have no ears, and while the magician may profess to commune with them, he – and everyone else – is deluded to think that they will reciprocate. People, however, do have ears, including the magician himself and all those who work under or alongside him. It is in its effects on everyone within earshot, Malinowski argues, that the real power of the incantation has to be understood. In a wonderfully pithy summation, he concludes that in magic, "words which are meant for things that have no ears fall upon ears they are not meant for" (Malinowski 1935: 241). Taking this conclusion at face value, it would seem that the significant distinction is not between human persons and non-human things but rather between beings with ears and beings without. And it leaves us with the following question: can beings without ears actually listen?

IV

The Northwest Pacific coast, where Alaska, British Columbia and the Yukon Territory meet, is a massively mountainous region threaded with some of the most active glaciers in the world. Periodically, these glaciers have surged, making sudden and rapid advances. Advancing glaciers can block rivers, creating neoglacial lakes which, when the ice thins or retreats again, can empty with catastrophic consequences for human settlements in the valleys below. The oral traditions of the Tlingit people, who already inhabited the region at the time when Europeans began arriving there, are replete with stories of such events. And a theme that runs through all these stories is that glaciers are vital and sentient beings, equipped with senses of smell and hearing, and even sight, alert to the conduct of human beings, and quick to respond to any indiscretion towards them. They can also be extremely noisy, especially when surging, emitting thunderous cracks and explosions of ear-splitting intensity. Aboriginal people know to treat them with the utmost respect. Glaciers are not to be trifled with.

In her fine study of the intersections of Aboriginal storytelling and European exploration in the region, *Do Glaciers Listen?*, Julie Cruikshank (2005) observes that there is one particular way of trifling with glaciers that they find particularly offensive. This is to cook, in their vicinity, with grease. It is said that they object to the smell of frying meat. Thus, when cooking food near glaciers, it should be boiled and never fried. One way of explaining this taboo against cooking with grease would be to note the resemblance between what happens to grease when it is heated and to glaciers when they surge. Refined and stored, grease takes the form of solid white blocks, but when heated it liquefies into a puddle. Surging glaciers, as Cruikshank notes, behave in much the same way: solid at one moment and swept along in the flood at the next. Moreover, frying grease crackles noisily, as does the advancing glacier. To cook with grease near a glacier is thus to taunt it through mimicry. And the response of the glacier may well be to respond in kind, on a vastly greater scale, through surging (Cruikshank 2005: 74).

Unlike the Trobriand magician who calls up the powers of land, wind and ocean to assist in the enterprise of plant growth, the Tlingit are concerned above all to avoid meddling with the powers of glaciers. Indeed to call up a glacier as, in one story, a bored teenage girl nearing the end of her puberty confinement is alleged to have done, is to risk bringing disaster down upon an entire community (Cruikshank 2005: 159–60). In the story, the girl's village was literally swept away by the ensuing surge. Could it be though, following Malinowski's logic, that words or actions deemed offensive to glaciers – which in truth have neither ears nor noses to pick up the taunts of humans, whether uttered as verbal insults or enacted in frying food – are actually avoided because of the offence they could cause to other humans who, of course, *do* have noses to smell with and ears to hear? After all, in the case of the story to which I have just alluded, it is said that the main offence of the girl was to address the glacier directly, in breach of the conventional self-restraint expected of a young woman in her position.

In Tlingit understanding, the life of every being is an ever-unfolding story. People have their stories, as do glaciers. To make one's way in the world, it is important not just to listen to these stories, but listen *for* them (Cruikshank 2005: 76). Impending phenomena are often heard before they are seen, and one must listen out for them to ensure a timely response. Located in one bay, for example, is a cottonwood tree that is known for picking up the reverberations of an approaching storm. If travellers put their ears to the trunk, they can hear it coming. The inhabitants of another bay are said to have heard the sound of an advancing glacier before they saw it, allowing them to escape before it swallowed up their village and covered the harbour (Cruikshank 2005: 229). Glaciers, however, do not have ears. How, then, can they reciprocally listen out for what human beings, or any other creatures, are up to? How can we possibly avoid the conclusion that, whatever native people may say, it is actually on other people, and not on glaciers, that the words and deeds of humans, in speaking of glaciers or mimicking their behaviour, take effect?

Perhaps we could return for an answer to the wisdom of Goethe – "If the eye were not sun-like, it could not see the sun" – and to the response of von Uexküll: "If the sun were not eye-like, it could not shine in any sky". As a geological formation, an unstable mass of ice, the glacier could exist even in the absence of eyes to see or ears to listen. That, typically, is how it is understood by western science. But it is not how the glacier figures in the phenomenal world of the Tlingit. It is not disclosed as an *object* of perception. Rather, just as the thunder, lightning and wind that greet the performance of the Trobriand magician, the glacier manifests itself as an all-enveloping experience of sound, light and feeling – that is, an *atmosphere*. Like thunder, it *is* its explosive sound, not an object that makes a sound. Like lightning, it *is* its blinding white light (often expressed as heat), not an object seen in the light. Like the wind, it *is* its icy feel, not an object touched. In this atmospheric manifestation the glacier is not set over against perceivers but invades and saturates their consciousness, wherein it is generative of their own capacity to perceive: to see, to hear and to touch, even to smell. The glacier, in short, is "ear-like" in the same way that the sun in the sky is "eye-like". That is why it listens.

V

More generally, it is impossible to be sentient in an *in*sentient world – in a world, that is, which has turned its back on its inhabitants, presenting only its already congealed, outer surfaces for inspection. In such a world, light, sound and feeling figure not as qualities of experience but merely as vectors for the projection – respectively visual, auditory or tactile – of the final forms of things from world to mind, or for the conversion of objects into images. To be sentient, to the contrary, is to open up to a world, to yield to its embrace, and to resonate in one's inner being to its illuminations and reverberations. Bathed in light, submerged in sound and rapt in feeling, the sentient body rides the crest of the world's becoming, ever-present and witness to that moment when the world is about to disclose itself for what it is (Ingold 2006: 12). Thus in a sentient world there are no subjects or objects of perception; rather perception inheres in the creative movement of emergence, where "things become things", as the philosopher Maurice Merleau-Ponty put it, and "the world becomes world" (Merleau-Ponty 1964: 181). To perceive things, then, is simultaneously to be perceived *by* them. For Merleau-Ponty this reversibility, most obvious in the exemplary instance of two hands touching, is fundamental to all perception.

In conversation with Georges Charbonnier, the painter André Marchand observed that in a forest, he had often felt that it was not he who was looking at the forest. "On some days", Marchand said, "I felt it was the trees that were looking at me" (Charbonnier 1959: 143, see also Merleau-Ponty 1964: 167). The painter sees the trees; the trees see the painter – not, as Christopher Tilley explains in his work on landscape phenomenology, because trees have eyes, "but because the trees affect, move the painter, become part of the painting that would be impossible without their presence" (Tilley 2004: 18). As an archaeologist, Tilley's particular concern is with monuments of stone. To feel the stone, he reports, is to feel its touch on his hands: "I touch the stone and the stone touches me" (Tilley 2004: 17). Admittedly, the reversibility entailed here is not quite of the same order as in the case of two hands touching. For the stone, in itself, is not sentient. But this does not, in Tilley's view, invalidate his claim that he is indeed touched *by* the stone. Precisely because it affects him bodily and structures his awareness, the stone, he thinks, may be said to possess an agency of its own.

Were Heidegger alive today, and able to respond to Tilley's intervention, he would undoubtedly have objected that the alleged reversibility of touch in this instance rests on a fundamental confusion between the world-forming activity of the human and the worldlessness of the stone. The touch of the former is a modality of perceptual engagement; that of the latter amounts to nothing more than the pressure of physical contiguity. To argue that the stone touches back, Heidegger would have said, is to indulge in anthropomorphic fantasy. But this is not exactly the argument. For according to Tilley, such things as trees and stones "are sensible without being sentient" (Tilley 2004: 19). By this he means that they are as much a part of the phenomenal world as are human bodies and, as such, are already *with* perceivers, just as bodies are, in the very process of perception. Thus the painter does not just observe the tree; he observes with it. And the archaeologist does not just touch the stone but touches with it. The eye that sees the tree is already tree-like; the hand that touches the stone already stone-like. Tree and stone are at once on both the hither side and the far side of sight and touch respectively.

As Merleau-Ponty (1962: 317) put it, the eye that knows moonlight and sunlight, and the hand that knows hardness and softness, roughness and smoothness, bring these qualities of light and feeling into their own ways of perceiving. When I touch, stone touches, because the texture of stone has already invaded my haptic awareness. When I look, the sun and the moon look, since these celestial bodies, in their luminosity, have already invaded my visual awareness. And were I to listen as a Tlingit person would, the glacier would also listen, because the glacier, in its sonority, would have already invaded my auditory awareness. Neither stone, nor sun and moon, nor glacier, are in themselves sentient. But *immersed in sentience*, they can, as it were, double back so as to touch, see and hear themselves. The stone touches through hands that have become stone-like; the sun and moon look through eyes that have become sun-like and moon-like; the glacier listens through ears that have become glacier-like. Every perception of the world, in short, is part and parcel of the world's perceiving itself.

VI

In their introduction to this volume, Katrín Lund and Karl Benediktsson draw our attention to an important debate conducted in the pages of the journal *Environmental Values*. It is about whether it makes sense to understand human relations with the constituents of the natural world as ways of conversing with them. On one side, Stephen Vogel (2006) is adamant that it does not. We may admit that this nature abounds in movement and gesture, and that much of this movement is manifested as sound: think of the clap of thunder and the howling of the wind, the cracking of ice and the roar of the waterfall, the rustling of trees and the calls of birds. We may also admit that at one level, human talk may also be understood as vocal gesture, and that the voice manifests human presence in the world just as the call manifests the presence of the bird and the clap the presence of thunder. On this level, voice, call and thunder are ontologically equivalent: as the voice *is* human being in its sonic manifestation, so the call *is* the bird and the clap *is* thunder.

Yet none of this, Vogel maintains, warrants the conclusion that human beings converse with natural entities, let alone that the latter converse with one another. This is for two principal reasons. Firstly, conversation requires participants to attend and respond, in turn, to one another. Humans do indeed attend and respond to the sounds of nature: they listen out for bird-calls and are moved, even terrified, by thunder. But does nature, Vogel asks, respond to us? "Do the self-speaking entities we attend and respond to in nature ever give us their full attention …, engage us, respond to our claims?" (Vogel 2006: 148). Despite what various philosophers and indigenous people may say, Vogel is convinced that the answer is "no". The sounds of nature, he suggests, are more like the commands of a monarch who is deaf to his subjects but compels their obedience. Secondly, a conversation is necessarily *about* something (Vogel 2006: 151–2). It enables participants to compare each other's perceptions of the world in the common task of figuring out how the world actually is. Human interlocutors do this, but birds, trees, rivers, thunder and the winds do not. It is not that they are irresponsible interlocutors; rather, they are not interlocutors at all (Vogel 2006: 157).

On the other side of the debate, Nicole Klenk (2008) replies that non-humans *can and do* respond to human voice, gesture and presence in ways that are meaningful both to them and to us. For example, Cree people of north-eastern Canada, when hunting geese, notice things that geese do not. But by their own admission, geese also notice things that hunters do not. They are alert to warning signs of human predation, and from past experience are able both to distinguish predatory from non-predatory humans and to adjust their behaviour accordingly. They can also communicate these adjustments to other geese. Thus human hunters attend to the presence of geese "*in the knowledge that geese are attending to them*" (Ingold 2000: 51–2, original emphasis; see Scott 1989). It is true that geese and humans do not compare their respective perceptions of the environment in a collaborative effort to establish the truth of what is actually "out there". But to insist that conversations can only take this form, Klenk argues, is to take such a narrow view of conversation that it would exclude most of what we commonly call conversation in the human world. For most people, most of the time, conversation is a matter of understanding what others are telling us – of "getting the story right" (Klenk 2008: 333), not of verifying the rightness of the story.

Who is correct? Should we side with Vogel (2006: 164), and conclude that anyone who purports to render what nature is saying to us, in a language we can understand, is less a translator than a ventriloquist? Or should we side with Klenk (2008: 333) in claiming that humans are *not* ventriloquists but interpreters of nature's speech, just as non-human beings are interpreters of ours? In this volume, Gabriel Malenfant (Chapter 3) comes out most firmly for the former position.

"Our utmost relationship with nature", he writes, "is and always was *perceptual* and *sensuous*, not dialectical, dialogical and linguistic". Others veer towards the latter, as when Karl Benediktsson (Chapter 12) writes that "sheep and humans are conversing with one another incessantly – via the medium of Iceland's landscapes", and when Guðbjörg R. Jóhannesdóttir (Chapter 8) speaks of "conversations between humans and the land where atmosphere is the language". In the preceding pages I have presented five stories which could be taken to represent points on a spectrum between these two extremes.

For Heidegger, at one end of the spectrum, there is no possibility of conversation with the lizard, or for that matter with the stone. Humans alone can engage in conversation because, thanks to language, only they truly inhabit a world. Yet to inhabit this world they must forsake the ties that hold the animal captivated within its environment. Open to its environment but forever denied access to the world, the animal cannot converse. While von Uexküll would concur that non-humans are unable to converse in *words*, he would allow that they can converse in the way that musicians do, in gestures whose meanings lie in their melodic inflections and contrapuntal relations. Yet the music that each hears is radically different and impenetrable to others. To hear the same music as another, one would have to *become* the other, moving and perceiving as the other does; and this is a matter less of translation than of metamorphosis. Malinowski, for his part, recognises that the practice of magic entails acts of communion, leading to an empathetic merging of self and others, yet it turns out – in his view – that these others are actually human, or at least equipped with ears, rather than the soil and plants of the garden to which the magical incantation is ostensibly addressed.

Could we not argue, however, that in the very act of communion the magician *opens up* to the garden, not as a physical landscape of horticulture but as an oceanic atmosphere of viridescent colour and billowing movement in which yams swim in the soil like dolphins in the sea? Then, as the magician and his entourage listen, so the garden would also listen, for in experience they and the garden have become one and the same. This is how it seems, for the Tlingit, that glaciers listen (though they would rather they did not): with the ears of humans, but of humans whose consciousness – flooded in light, drowned out by sound and carried away by feeling – has been invaded and overwhelmed by the intensity of sensory experience. And finally Tilley, drawing on the phenomenology of Merleau-Ponty, not only touches stone but is touched by it, to the very foundation of his being. He has become the very stone he studies! Now none of these stories is right or wrong. What they reveal, however, is the power of conversation to condense experience at many levels and in many registers, from the sensuous to the linguistic, from the atmospheric to the dialogical, and from the haptic to the optical, into the singularity of landscape.

References

Charbonnier, G. 1959. *Le Monologue du Peintre*. Paris: René Julliard.

Cruikshank, J. 2005. *Do Glaciers Listen? Local Knowledge, Colonial Encounters and Social Imagination.* Vancouver: UBC Press; Seattle: University of Washington Press.

Heidegger, M. 1995. *The Fundamental Concepts of Metaphysics: World, Finitude, Solitude*, translated by W. McNeil and N. Walker. Bloomington, IN: Indiana University Press. [Based on a course presented in 1929–30, originally published in 1983.]

Ingold, T. 2000. *The Perception of the Environment: Essays on Livelihood, Dwelling and Skill*. London: Routledge.

Ingold, T. 2006. Rethinking the Animate, Re-Animating Thought. *Ethnos*, 7(1), 9–20.

Klenk, N. 2008. Listening to the Birds: A Pragmatic Proposal for Forestry. *Environmental Values*, 17(3), 331–51.

Luke, D. 1964. *Goethe*, edited, translated and introduced by David Luke. London: Penguin.

Malinowski, B. 1935. *Coral Gardens and Their Magic: A Study of the Methods of Tilling the Soil and of Agricultural Rites in the Trobriand Islands, Volume 2, The Language and Magic of Gardening*. London: Allen & Unwin.

Merleau-Ponty, M. 1962. *Phenomenology of Perception*, translated by C. Smith. London: Routledge & Kegan Paul.

Merleau-Ponty, M. 1964. Eye and Mind. Translated by C. Dallery. In *The Primacy of Perception, and Other Essays on Phenomenological Psychology, the Philosophy of Art, History and Politics,* edited by J.M. Edie. Evanston, IL: Northwestern University Press,159–90.

Scott, C. 1989. Knowledge Construction among Cree Hunters: Metaphors and Literal Understanding. *Journal de la Société des Américanistes*, 75, 193–208.

Tilley, C. 2004. *The Materiality of Stone*. Oxford: Berg.

von Uexküll, J. 1982 [1940]. The Theory of Meaning. Translated by B. Stone and H. Weiner from *Bedeutungslehre* (ed. T. von Uexküll). *Semiotica*, 42(1), 25–82.

von Uexküll, J. 1992 [1934]. A Stroll Through the Worlds of Animals and Men: A Picture Book of Invisible Worlds. Translated by C.H. Schiller. *Semiotica*, 89(4), 319–91.

Vogel, S. 2006. The Silence of Nature. *Environmental Values*, 15(2), 145–71.

Index

aboriginal people 2, 245
Abram, D. 3, 7, 13, 29, 31, 34, 35, 36, 37, 97, 116, 117
accidents 80, 85–93, 185–186
actor–network theory 4, 48–49, 50, 56
Adams, P.C. 99
Addison, J. 133
Adey, P. 233, 236
Adler, J. 229
aesthetic appreciation 38, 39
    and geothermal areas 119–121, 132
    and glaciers 119–120, 132
    and sentience 204
    negative 130–132, 133
aesthetic judgement 52
aesthetic quality 51, 52, 54, 56, 109, 110, 111, 113, 116, 118, 119, 125, 132
aesthetic value 14, 22, 109–121, 125, 126, 130, 131, 133, 134, 135
aesthetics 9, 31, 41, 194, 195, 196, 197, 202, 204, 205
    and art 4
    and terrible beauty 125, 133, 134
    and the sublime 125, 126–130, 238
    and ugliness 125, 130–132, 135
    cognitive 23
    see also: environmental aesthetics
Afeissa, H–S. 40
affect 2, 7, 18, 52, 55, 65, 130, 227, 228, 231, 235–237, 238
Agamben, G. 175
Ahmed, S. 237
Akasofu, S–I. 233, 236, 238
Aldred, O. 68, 71
Alþing 164
Anderson, B. 235, 236, 238
Anderson, B. 235, 238
Anderson, K. 174
Angeles, P.A. 35

animals 22, 29, 30, 33, 36–37, 38, 173–188, 193–195, 198, 200, 201, 204, 241–244
    and anthropomorphism 222
    and death 211–219
    and face 220–222
    and naming 221
    and representation 211–225
    and stewardship 213
    as commodities 212
    as pests 212, 213
    as subjects of scientific experiments 218–219
    in folklore 219
    rights 222
animism 2, 36
anthropocentrism 30, 31, 33, 39, 40, 41, 42, 187, 211
    moral 38, 39
    see also: non–anthropocentrism
anthropology 9, 40, 80, 83, 132, 195, 197
anthropomorphism 30, 222–223, 248
anti-environmentalism 198
archaeology 59–76
    and embodiment 62, 72, 74
    and fieldwork practices 60, 62, 69, 72–73
    and movement 59, 65, 70, 71–75
    and representation 60, 73
    reconstruction of landscape in 61–63, 65, 69, 72
Arctic Circle 227
Ari the Wise (Ari fróði) 178
Arnalds, A. 179, 180
Arnalds, Ó. 180
Arnardóttir, Á. 203
Árnason, A. 88, 184
Árnason, M. 51
Árnason, Þ. 196
arrythmia 97, 99

art 4, 9, 211, 212, 217–218, 219, 221
   and activism 193, 201
   and agency 196
   conceptual 154, 206
   installation 202, 212, 215, 223
   visual 201–203, 204
   see also: painting; literature; performance art; photography; film and video
Askja (Iceland) 127, 134
atmosphere 9, 11, 101, 111, 118–121, 247, 250
   affective 227, 228, 236–237, 238
aurora borealis 128, 227–239
Auslander, M. 85, 86
Axelsson, R. 201

Bachelard, G. 169
Bærenholdt, J.O. 4
Bailey, G. 70, 75
Bakhtin, M.M. 83
Basso, K.H. 87, 104
Bate, J. 160, 166, 167
being-in-the-world 1, 2, 17, 20, 55, 82, 228
Bender, B. 5, 6, 60, 62, 64
Benediktsson, K. 8, 47, 48, 51, 52, 112, 113, 115, 116, 179, 196
Berger, J. 207
Bergson, H. 65, 67, 74
Bergsson, G. 204
Berlant, L. 80
Berleant, A. 16, 22–23, 134
Bessastaðir (Iceland) 157
Bissell, D. 233
Björnsson, B.Th. 143–144
Blais, F. 37
Boas, F. 83
body 3, 97–99, 100, 107, 237
   and movement 102
   gestures of 236, 237
   practices 228, 233
   techniques of 99, 100, 102, 233, 237
   see also: embodiment
Böhme, G. 18, 111, 115, 118–119, 121, 236
Book of Settlement 147, 154, 178
Bosanquet, B. 133
Bourdieu, P. 82
Bowden, M. 69

Boyle, R. 218–219
Brady, E. 8, 14, 31, 49, 50, 109, 132, 134
Brandes, G. 160
Brennan, T. 236
bricolage 65, 68–69, 70, 71, 75
Brinkmann, R. 29
Brydon, A. 198, 200
Buller, H. 173
Burke, E. 126
Byatt, A.S. 79–80, 93

cairns 71–75, 168
   as memorials 85–87
Callon, M. 64
Carlson, A. 14, 22, 23
Casey, E. 7, 67
Cézanne, P. 207
chair, see flesh
Charbonnier, G. 247
Chaudhuri, U. 221
Cheney, J. 29, 31–32, 34, 35, 36
Chien, J–P. 176
Christianity 217, 218, 222
climate change 36, 200
   and glaciers 19, 24, 129, 180–181
Cloke, P. 2, 4, 187
Cocker, E. 233
Coeterier, J.F. 45
Coetzee, J.M. 38
cognition 18, 20, 21
Coles, J. 127, 132
colour in landscape 51, 55, 127, 132, 133, 145, 147, 150
communitas 233
Conradson, D. 236
conservation 47–48, 51, 55, 112–113, 115, 138, 180–181, 200
Cooper, D.E. 110
Cosgrove, D. 5, 45, 52, 54, 80–81, 126
Crawford, O.G.S. 69
Cresswell, T. 6, 81, 234
Cruikshank, J. 87, 245–246
Csordas, T.J. 97
cubism 149

Dakin, S. 109, 114
dams, *see* hydroelectric dams
Daniels, S. 5, 80–81

Dant, T. 186
Darwin, C. 222
  see also: social Darwinism
Daston, L. 222
David, B. 63
de Bolla, P. 165
de Saussure, F. 177
Deleuze, G. 65
Denmark 55, 84
Derrida, J. 82–83
Descartes, R. 33, 39, 54, 222
determinism 117
Dewsbury, J.D. 2, 46
Donald, D. 218, 219
dualism 14, 18, 31, 49, 121
  epistemology of 194–195
  human-nonhuman 1, 173, 179, 193–196
  mind-matter 176
  nature-society 48
  objective-subjective 30, 109–115
  ocean-land 204
  see also: Descartes, R.
Duncan, J. 5
Duncan, N. 5
Durkheim, E. 83
dwelling 5–6, 81–82, 140, 169, 173, 175, 195
  of animals 187
Dýrmundsson, Ó. 184

Eco, U. 132
ecocriticism 157, 166
Edensor, T. 99, 228, 229, 230
Edwards, T. 134
Egilsson, S.Y. 159, 163
Einarsson, T. 197
Elder, G. 222
embodiment 1–2, 3, 5–7, 15, 19–20, 21, 41, 62, 63, 72, 74, 82, 97–99, 100, 204, 228–229, 233, 234, 238
  see also: body
Emel, J. 174
Emmeche, C. 4
emotion 3, 14, 18, 80, 98, 99, 101, 114, 125, 231, 237
  and aesthetic response 126, 130–135
  and animals 220, 222
  and atmosphere 119
  and environmentalism 194, 198
  of loss 83–84, 87. 202, 207
  when walking 98–100, 104–107
Eng, D.L. 83
English Lake School 159–160, 166
Enlightenment 3, 7, 218, 219, 222
Entrikin, J.N. 127–128, 129
environmental aesthetics 13, 14, 16–17, 23, 109–121, 125–135
  see also: aesthetic appreciation; aesthetics
environmental change 176
  see also: climate change
environmental movement 193, 198
environmental psychology 132
environmental politics 195
environmentalism 3, 194, 196, 197, 198–199, 201, 202, 207
  and emotions 198
  see also: anti–environmentalism
epistemology 5, 18, 29, 32–35, 37, 39, 63–65, 194, 195
ethics 31, 36–42
  environmental 17, 28, 29, 33, 195
  evolutionary 40
  Kantian 30
  of animal rights 222
ethology 219–220, 242
European Landscape Convention 114, 121
expressionism 149
Eyjabakkar (Iceland) 201
Eysteinsson, Á. 139
Eythorsdottir, E. 178

Falck-Ytter, 233, 236
Farina, A. 177
Ferguson, J. 219
Filion, M. 37
film and video 141, 198–200, 202, 207, 220, 223–225
Finland 55
flesh, Merleau-Ponty's notion of 9, 20, 110, 115–119
folklore 22, 166, 219
Freud, S. 83
Friðriksson, F.Þ. 200
Friedl, P. 218

Fuller, G. 233

Gadamer, H-G. 1, 2, 4, 7
Gaita, R. 175
Gallagher, S. 20
Gandy, M. 19
Gane, N. 212
Garrard, G. 157, 164, 166
Gehring, K. 45
geography 4, 5, 9, 45, 46–47, 66–67, 74, 187, 234
geothermal areas 22, 110, 119, 120, 127, 132, 202, 234
geysers 127, 133, 234
    see also: geothermal areas
Gibson, J. 230
Gifford, T. 164
Gíslason, J. 219, 221
glaciers 19, 24, 110, 119–120, 127, 129, 132, 180–181, 234, 245–247, 248, 250
Glacken, C. 3
global warming, see climate change
Gobster, P.H. 109
Goethe, J.W. 244, 245, 246
Gould, S. 222
Granö, J.G. 45
Grazzini, B. 30, 32
Grétarsdóttir, T. 88
Guðmundsson, Á. 141
Guðmundsson, A.T. 132
Guðmundsson, J. 184
Guðmundsson, M. 198–200
Guðmundsson, S. 143–144
Gunnarsson, Á. 128

habitus 139
Hafstein, H. 159–160, 166, 169
Hafsteinsson, S.B. 88
Hägerstrand, T. 66
Halberstam, J. 217
Hálfdanarson, G. 84
Hallgrímsson, J. 84, 139, 140, 142–143, 144, 157–170
Haraway, D. 29, 31, 35, 173, 212, 214
Harrington, A. 176
Hassard, J. 4
Hastrup, K. 84, 87

Hatch, E. 83
Hay, P. 17
Hayden, D. 148
hearing 1, 55, 82, 245
    see also: listening; sense, auditory; sound
Heidegger, M. 6, 13, 17–18, 21, 31, 167, 196, 241–242, 243, 248, 250
Heimaey (Iceland) 128
Helgason, A. 199, 206
Hepburn R.W. 13–17, 23
Hettinger, N. 133
Heyd, T. 36
Hirsch, E. 115
Hirst, D. 221
Hitt, C. 129, 134
Hoffmeyer, J. 4
Holt, E. 83
home 137, 141, 146
Hooper, W. 238
horizon (in phenomenology) 1, 5–8
Hoskins, W.G. 69
Hreinsson, V. 178, 180
Huijbens, E. 8, 196
Hull, D. 29
Húsey (Iceland) 213–214, 216, 221
Husserl, E. 6–7, 17, 36
hybridity 55, 174
hybrids 48, 64
hydroelectric dams 14, 88, 112, 113, 194, 195, 201, 203, 206, 207, 213

idealism 33, 39, 117
illumination 22, 229–230, 231–232, 233, 236, 237
imagination 9, 100, 101, 115, 126, 130, 160–161, 165, 169, 230
    aesthetical 24
    metaphysical 15, 16, 23
Ingold, T. 2, 5–6, 60, 61, 62, 65, 74, 75, 81, 82, 83, 97, 98–99, 100, 101, 106, 115, 116, 173, 175, 193, 194, 196, 230, 231, 232, 247, 249
International Whaling Commission 198
intersubjectivity 50, 82
Ivy, M. 84

Jackson, M. 6, 101, 105

Jacquette, D. 133
Jakle, J. 229
Jakobsdóttir, S. 152–153
Jeangène Vilmer, J-B. 37
Jóa, A. 146
Jóhannesson, G.Þ. 4
Johnson, Mark 2, 28
Johnson, Matthew 69
Jones, A. 64
Jones, O. 4, 47, 173
Judaeo-Christian doctrines 3
   see also: Christianity; religion

Kant, I. 15, 17, 30, 50, 109, 110, 126, 130
Kárahnjúkar (Iceland) 14, 201–203, 213
Kasanjian, D. 83
Kirkman, R. 37, 38
Klenk, N. 4, 249
Kohsaka, R. 45
Korsmeyer, C. 131, 132
Kortelainen, J. 4
Kristjánsdóttir, Þ. 143–144
Kristjánsson, S. 84
Kúagerði (Iceland) 85–87
Kull, K. 176

Lakoff, G. 2, 28
Lam, W. 236
landscape
   aesthetic representations of 194, 197, 201–202
   and aesthetic values 109–121, 229
   and aurora 228, 236, 239
   and dwelling 81
   and embodiment 100–101, 106, 145, 150
   and objectification 225
   and stories 87
   and stories 87, 104–106
   as a way of seeing 52–53, 148, 187
   as narratives 83
   as scenery 81
   as semiotic interface 177
   as text 187
   assessment 109, 111–114
   Icelandic concept of 45, 46–48, 51–56
   imaginary 100–101
   materiality of 1, 81, 93
   moral 175
   Nordic understanding of 8
   perception of 81–82
   temporality of 6
   texture of 106–107
   visual understanding of 116
   vitalist conceptions of 233–234
   volcanic 162–167
landslag, see: landscape, Icelandic concept of
Latham, A. 236
Latour, B. 3, 4, 19, 48, 64, 194, 195, 196
Law, J. 4, 48, 49, 64
Laxness, H. 55, 151–152, 158
Lefebvre, H. 75, 97, 98, 104
Lenntorp, B. 66, 67
Leopold, A. 3
Lerner, M. 147
Levinas, E. 21, 221–222
Lévi–Strauss, C. 68–69
Light, A. 40
Lindquist, O. 197
Lintott, S. 22
Lippard, L. 206
Lippit, A.M. 212, 222
listening 83
   see also: hearing; sense, auditory; sound
literature 9, 139–140, 144, 147, 151–153, 204
   and realism 140
   see also: poetry
livestock 173, 178–179, 185
Lorand, R. 131
Lorimer, H. 8, 74, 81, 100, 175, 219
Lothian, A. 109, 111, 113
Lotman, J. 187–188
Loy, D. 203
Lucas, G. 65, 66, 67, 68, 74, 75
Luke, D. 244
Lulka, D. 174, 186
Lund, K. 7, 8, 74, 97, 100
Lyotard, J-F. 130

Määtänen, P. 177
MacPherson, E. 203
magic 244–245, 250
Magnason, A.S. 207

maieutics 28–35
Maitland, F.W. 69
Malinowski, B. 244–245, 246, 250
Manning, A. 174
mapping 98–99
    mental 100–101
maps in archaeology 73
Marchand, A. 118, 247
Martin, J. 109
Massey, D. 6, 75
Massumi, B. 59, 65
Master Plan for Hydro and Geothermal Resources (Iceland) 112, 201
materiality 1, 51, 61, 217, 238
    semiotics of 49
McCormack, D. 236
McHugh, K. 238
McQuire, S. 230
McShane, K. 39, 40
Mels, T. 8
Merleau–Ponty, M. 3, 5, 7, 20, 31, 49–50, 82, 101, 110, 111, 114, 115, 116–119, 121, 232, 247, 248, 250
metaphor 1–5, 9, 21, 27–30, 37, 41, 46, 56, 69–70, 98, 174, 176, 187, 194, 202, 204
metaphysical experience 13–24
metaphysics 30, 41, 130, 212, 241, 242
    of presence 82–83
Michael, M. 186
Milek, K. 71
Millington, S. 230
Mitchell, D. 45
Mitman, G. 222
modernity 3, 48, 54, 75, 140, 173, 179, 193, 195, 204
    see also: modernization
modernization 85
    in Iceland 137–139, 145
monuments 85, 86–87, 148, 91, 247
Moore, R. 130
Muelder Eaton, M. 14, 16, 24, 109
Muir, R. 69
Murdoch, J. 49
myths 22, 36, 105, 219, 233, 235–236, 237
    see also: folklore

Naess, A. 27

Nagel, T. 175
Nansen, F. 233
narrative 74, 98–99, 100, 105, 114, 138, 198, 228, 235
    Christian 217
    environmentalist 207
    moral 198
    of loss 80, 83–84
    of walking 104
    see also: stories
nationalism 158, 162–163, 194, 198, 201, 202, 203
nationality 84, 87, 137, 139, 144
Nature Conservation Strategy (Iceland) 47, 112–113
Nawrath, A. 132
networks 49, 50, 55
    see also: actor–network theory; hybrids
Nicholls, D.C. 109
Nicolson, M.H. 126, 165
Nietzsche, F. 13, 14
Nolt, J. 37
non-anthropocentrism 29–42
    see also: anthropocentrism
non-human sentience 193–207
northern lights, see *aurora borealis*
Norton, B.G. 39, 40

O'Hanlon, M. 115
Ólafsdóttir, A. 145
Ólafsson, E. 144
Ólafsson, G.P. 201, 202
Ólafsson, J. 143–144
Oldfield, J.D. 45
Olivier, L.C. 60, 75
Olsen, B. 64, 75
Olwig, K.R. 8, 45, 52
ontology 5, 28, 30–35, 37–41, 45, 48, 64–65, 66, 73, 174, 194, 195, 230, 235, 249
Ósar (Iceland) 214
Óskarsson, K. 214, 215
Óskarsson, Þ. 158
Öxnadalur (Iceland) 157, 158

painting 52, 118, 141, 143, 145–146
    and realism 149
    Icelandic 143–144, 147, 205

in bourgeois culture 154
romantic 29
sofa 145–146, 149–151
see also: representation
palimpsest, landscape as 69–70
Pálsson, B. 144
Pálsson, G. 198, 199, 206
pastoral, the 157, 164
Peace, A. 187
Peirce, C.S. 4, 174, 177
perception 2, 3, 7, 8, 16, 18, 24, 28, 31, 39, 41, 45, 47, 48–50, 55, 73, 80, 81, 99, 109, 111, 114, 121, 148, 193, 194, 203, 204, 230–231, 235, 248, 249
    aesthetic 23, 24
    and atmosphere 118–119
    and light 283
    and representation 118
    and the subject 82
    and Umwelt 176, 243
    as embodied experience 62–64, 116–118
    bodily 18, 20
    multisensory 177
    objects of 247
    of sentience 197
    of space 230
    subjective 110
    tactile 5
    visual 7, 56
    see also: senses
performance 48, 82, 228, 229, 239
    artistic 194, 202–203, 223–224
performativity 4, 46, 48, 49, 50, 55, 223
PETA (People for the Ethical Treatment of Animals) 221
Pétursdóttir, G. 197
phenomenology 5–7, 9, 16, 17, 20, 31, 36, 38, 41–42, 80, 81, 82, 83, 98, 109, 110, 115, 116, 169, 174, 229, 238, 247, 250
    eco- 3
    existential 82
    in archaeology 62
    of landscape 63, 82–84
    of movement 80
Philo, C. 174

photography 201, 202, 217, 235
Picknett, L. 217
picturesque, the 16
Pite, R. 160
place 66–67, 87, 137–138, 139, 140, 141, 143, 148, 152, 203, 235, 236
    and animals 174
    and poetry 160, 163, 164, 167
    and the landscape concept 6, 8, 47, 115
    and tourism 228
Plato 14, 28, 29, 30, 33, 34–35, 109, 110
Plumwood, V. 29, 31, 33, 34, 35, 36, 38
poetry 84, 157–170, 204
    and the Pastoral 157, 164
    and the Scientific 157
    and the Sublime 157
    realism in 158
Pole, D. 131
post-humanism 211
pragmatism 4, 40, 177
Pred, A. 66
Preston, C. 29, 31–32, 36, 41
Prince, C. 217
Proctor, J.D. 175

Rabinow, P. 75
rationalism 3, 33, 39, 49–50
reductionism 17, 27, 45, 175
relationality 41, 59, 61, 65, 228, 238
religion 3, 13, 30, 180, 198
    see also: Christianity
representation 60, 73
    in archaeology 63
    painting as 118, 138, 141, 144, 145
    of animals in art 211–225
residuality 65–68, 69, 70, 71, 72, 75
Reyðarfjörður (Iceland) 201
Reykjanesbraut (Iceland) 85, 86, 87–88
Reykjavík (Iceland) 84, 85, 127, 137, 138, 147, 157, 163, 164
rhythm 6, 233
    of walking 97–99, 101, 103–104, 106
rhythmanalysis 98
Ricoeur, P. 2
Rigby, K. 160
Ringler, D. 158, 162, 163, 164, 165, 166, 168, 169
Ritter, J. 13, 109

roadkill 186
roads 80, 84–93
  death on 84–91
  safety on 86, 88, 90–93
  animals on 184–186
Romantic studies 157
romanticism 3, 18, 126, 130, 139, 142, 144, 158, 165, 166, 184
Rose, M. 4
Rowell, A. 199
Runólfsson, S. 180
Rupke, N.A. 219
rural society 137–139, 145, 153
Rúrí (artist) 202

Sæmundsson, K. 162
Sagas of Icelanders 47, 53–54, 55, 142–143
Saito, Y. 24, 132
Sauer, C.O. 5, 45
Savage, C. 227, 233, 236
Schama, S. 211
Schelling, F.W.J. 14
Scheving, G. 205
Schlater, A. 109
Schön, D. 27–28
Schopenhauer, A. 13, 14, 30
Schroeder, B. 15
Schroeder, H.W. 109, 114
science 4, 13, 24, 29, 30, 38, 51, 194–195, 199, 200, 227, 233, 237
  biological 193
  experiments on animals in 218–219
Scott, C. 249
Scott, G.A. 30
Sebeok, T.A. 4
semiology 177
semiosphere 187–188
semiotics 4, 49, 63, 174, 175–177, 187–188, 242
senses 1
  auditory 232, 247, *see also:* sound; hearing; listening
  haptic 232, 248, 251, *see also:* tactility; touch
  olfactory 178, 232, *see also:* smell
  visual 1, 229, *see also:* vision; sight
sentience 193–207, 247, 248

Serpell, J. 174
Setten, G. 6, 8
settlement of Iceland 84, 87, 178–179
Shaw, D.J.B. 45
sheep 178–186, 187
  roundups 179, 181, 182–183
Sibley, F. 131
sight 1–2, 56, 186, 200, 241, 245, 248
  see also: sense, visual; vision
Sigurðsson, R.Th. 132
Singer, P. 38
Sjölander-Lindqvist, A. 187
Skjaldbreiður (Iceland) 158–165, 167, 168
Skúlason, P. 13, 45, 134
smell 55, 119, 120, 126, 152, 245, 246, 247
  see also: sense, olfactory
Smith, D.B. 194
Snæbjörnsdóttir/Wilson 212, 213, 214, 217, 219, 221, 223
social Darwinism 40
Socrates 28, 33, 34–35
  see also: maieutics
soil erosion 39, 179–180
Solnit, R. 2, 7, 45, 97
sound 18, 55, 119, 120, 126, 131, 139, 152, 159, 223, 229, 232, 233, 236, 247, 248, 249, 250
  see also: hearing; listening; sense, auditory
space 59, 64, 73, 75, 80, 97, 106, 115, 120, 194, 206, 228, 231, 233, 235, 237
  and atmosphere 236
  and light 229
  and tourism 229
  as processual 234
  as relational 45, 48–51, 55–56
  in animal studies 174
  liminal 184
  oceanic 205
  representational 60
  rural 179
Spencer, H. 40
spirituality 36, 40
Spirn, A.W. 45
Steingrímsson, P. 202
Stengers, I. 194, 195
stillness 107, 233, 237
stories 79–80, 83, 85–87, 91, 246

of Dreaming 2
of loss 85
of walking 98
see also: narratives; myths
Strathern, M. 82, 83, 93
structuralism 80–82, 83
subjectivity 3, 4, 15, 63, 110–111, 113, 236
sublime, the 15, 17, 20, 165, 228, 238
    discourses of 165
    in poetry 157, 158, 164
    see also: sublimity
sublimity 125, 126–130, 133, 134
    dynamic 126
    mathematical 126
    see also: aesthetics; sublime, the
Sullivan, A.P. 70
sunousia 30, 35, 39
synaesthesis 62

tactility 5, 147, 229, 232, 247
    see also: sense, haptic; touch
tactility 97, 99, 229
Tannen, D. 83, 93
taskscape 175
taxidermy 215–218
temporality 21, 61, 67, 70, 73, 75, 98, 175, 234, 237
    of landscape 60, 69, 81, 82
terrible beauty 125, 133, 134, 165
    see also: aesthetics; sublime, the; ugliness
texture 51, 55, 101, 106, 119, 132, 232, 238, 248
Thomas, J. 60, 62, 63, 75
Thompson, J. 42
Thomsen, P. 201–202
Thorgeirsdottir, S. 14, 20, 112, 113
Thórhallsdóttir, A.G. 182
Thorsteinsson, I. 182
Thrift, N. 46
Tilley, C. 6, 7, 62, 63, 65, 69, 75, 80, 81, 99, 115, 116, 247–248, 250
time-geography 66–67, 74
Tlingit 245–247, 250
Toadvine, T. 116
Tønnesen, M. 176
touch 7, 82, 97, 117, 231, 233, 241–242, 247–248, 250

    see also: sense, haptic; tactility
tourism 228–229
    and visual consumption 229
transcendentalism 3
travel 79–80, 81, 85, 87
Trobriand Islands 244–245, 246, 247
Tulinius, T.H. 71

ugliness 126, 130–132, 135
    see also: aesthetics; sublime, the; terrible beauty
Umwelt 175–176, 180, 181, 184, 186, 187, 243–244
    transition 176, 179
urban culture and society 137–138, 144, 145, 146, 148, 150, 152
urbanisation 146, 147
Urry, J. 6, 229

Van Den Berg, J.H. 100, 102, 105
Varela, F.J. 196
Vatnajökull (Iceland) 19, 202
    National Park 180
Vatnsfjörður (Iceland) 59, 71–75
Vedder, B. 2, 9
Vehkavaara, T. 177
Vergunst, J.L. 60, 97, 98, 99, 102, 103, 104
Vignisson, Ó.P. 186
Vilhjálmsdóttir, Ó. 203
Vilhjálmsson, Th. 149–150
Virilio, P. 80, 84, 184
vision 6, 7, 16, 73, 99–101, 117
    see also: sense, visual; sight
visual culture 204
vitalism 233–234
Vogel, S. 3, 248–249
von Uexküll, J. 174, 175–177, 180, 187, 242–244, 246, 250

Waage, E.R.H. 8, 47, 48, 51, 52, 113, 115
walking 9, 81, 97–107, 203, 228
    and tactility 97, 99
    as a narrating act 104–105
    narratives of 98–100, 104
    rhythm of 97–99, 101, 103–104, 106
    routes 98, 100, 102, 106
Warren, K. 31, 32, 35
whaling 193–196, 197–200, 204

campaign against 198
visual representations of 197
Whatmore, S. 173, 174, 187
Wilbert, C. 174
wilderness 19, 42, 112, 153, 173, 201, 211
experience of 20
in Iceland 138, 144, 148, 153, 205, 206
Witmore, C.L. 64, 75
Wolch, J. 174
Wolfe, C. 221
Wordsworth, W. 160
Wright, J. 219

Wylie, J. 4, 6, 52, 81, 82–83, 93, 99, 174, 187, 232, 234

Zahavi, D. 20
zoos 222

Þingvellir (Iceland) 149, 150, 161–164, 166
Þórðarson, Þ. 150–151
Þorleifsson, J. 205
Þorleifsson, Ö. 213–214, 216
Þorsteinsson, I.G. 140